The Sanctity of Rural Life

THE
SANCTITY
OF RURAL
LIFE

Nobility, Protestantism, and
Nazism in Weimar Prussia

Shelley Baranowski

New York   Oxford
OXFORD UNIVERSITY PRESS
1995

Oxford University Press

Oxford   New York
Athens   Auckland   Bangkok   Bombay
Calcutta   Cape Town   Dar es Salaam   Delhi
Florence   Hong Kong   Istanbul   Karachi
Kuala Lumpur   Madras   Madrid   Melbourne
Mexico City   Nairobi   Paris   Singapore
Taipei   Tokyo   Toronto
and associated companies in
Berlin   Ibadan

Library of Congress Cataloging-in-Publication Data
Baranowski, Shelley.
The sanctity of rural life :
nobility, protestantism, and Nazism in Weimar Prussia /
Shelley Baranowski.
p.   cm.   Includes bibliographical references and index.
ISBN 0-19-506881-5
1. Prussia (Germany)—Politics and government—1918–1933.
2. Agriculture and state—Germany—Prussia.
3. Church and state—Germany—Prussia—History.
4. Prussia (Germany)—Church history.
5. Prussia (Germany)—Social conditions.
6. Conservatism—Germany—Prussia—History.
7. National socialism—Germany—Prussia.
8. Germany—Politics and government—1918–1933.
I. Title.
DD453.B37   1995   943.085—dc20   94-19307

1 3 5 7 9 8 6 4 2

Printed in the United States of America
on acid-free paper

For my parents
Robert R. and Ann S. Osmun

Acknowledgments

Scholarship is a paradoxical enterprise. While it is one of the most solitary undertakings one can imagine, its success depends on the cooperation and encouragement of others. It is thus my pleasure to name those who have aided my project throughout its long incubation.

First, I thank the American Council of Learned Societies, Kenyon College, and the University of Akron for their generous financial support toward my travel to collections. Above all, I convey my gratitude to the National Endowment for the Humanities. The fellowship I received from the Endowment not only enabled a year of continuous research, it also boosted my career at a time when I, like many other independent scholars of the 1980s, struggled for recognition in a profession that values permanent institutional affiliation. This book is modest repayment for the confidence that the NEH demonstrated.

During my frequent research trips, I relied heavily on the personnel of numerous archives and libraries for their expertise and suggestions. I extend my warmest appreciation to the staffs of the Evangelisches Zentralarchiv and Archiv des Diakonischen Werkes der Evangelischen Kirche in Deutschland, both in Berlin, the Bundesarchiv in Potsdam and Geheimes Staatsarchiv Preußischer Kulturbesitz in Merseburg, the archive of the Deutscher Evangelischer Frauenbund in Hannover, the Wojewódskie Archiwum Państwowe of both Szczecin and Koszalin, the Vorpommerscher Landesarchiv in Greifswald, the Archive of the General Conference of the Seventh Day Adventist Church in Washington, and the Historical Department of the Church of Jesus Christ of Latter Day Saints in Salt Lake City. My special thanks go to Anke Dietzler, Bogdan Frankiewicz, Bert Haloviak, Stephen Sorenson, and Michael Wischnath. My regards also to the staffs of the New York Public Library, the Deutsche Bucherei in Leipzig, the library of the city of Szczecin, the Staatsbibliothek in Berlin, the Kenyon College Library, the Library of the University of Akron, and particularly the Ohio State University Library, Columbus.

I am happy to acknowledge as well the support of colleagues and friends, especially those whose thoughtful and constructive comments confirmed my belief in the necessity of refining one's arguments through discussion. Robert Berdahl, Richard Bessel, Jochen-Christoph Kaiser, and Kurt Nowak provided valuable assistance in identifying relevant archival collections, neither a foregone conclusion nor an easy task given that the former eastern Prussian provinces have been underresearched. Geoff Eley and Vernon Lidtke convinced Oxford University Press of the merits of my project, although fortunately not sparing my proposal from their insightful and challenging criticisms. William Sheridan Allen, David Barclay, David Diephouse, Ellen Furlough, Larry Eugene Jones, Robert Moeller, Robert Soucy, and George Vascik raised important questions while responding to the various presentations of my work. Arno Mayer read an earlier draft of the book, forcing me to economize when my newly found, though unpolished, expertise with word processing was leading to murkiness. I hope that this book will at least dimly reflect their contributions.

I further thank the editors of *Social History* and *German History*, as well as Larry Eugene Jones, James N. Retallack, and Berg Publishers for allowing me to try out various aspects of my story as articles. I am especially pleased to recognize the efforts of my editors at Oxford University Press, notably Nancy Lane whose interest carried my proposal to publication. Thanks also to Colby Stong, Anna Taruschio, and Linda Pawelchak for their professionalism and patience. They confirmed the belief of my sister Marion Osmun that my manuscript would be in good hands.

Last, but most of all, I pay tribute to my parents Robert and Ann Osmun, to whom this book is dedicated, my brother David and my sister Marion, my in-laws Mary and Edwin Baranowski, whose contacts facilitated several forays into Poland, and particularly my husband Ed. All worried through my numerous trips to places where communicating with them was difficult. Yet all ended up learning more about interwar Pomerania than they ever thought imaginable.

Gahanna, Ohio   S.B.
July 1994

Contents

The Sanctity of Rural Life

Introduction

EARLY ONE WINTER morning in 1945 as the Soviet armies encircled their eastern Pomeranian estate, the remaining members of the von Krockow family prepared to carry out the suicide pact they had sorrowfully composed to avoid falling victim to Germany's enemies. Although World War II had already claimed the lives of two sons and one son-in-law, the remnant of that distinguished Junker clan reached the unspoken consensus that its self-destruction comprised the only plausible solution. Reports from German refugees of Soviet atrocities farther east, committed especially against the owners of large landed estates, convinced the family of the impossibility of escape. The family's stepfather and patriarch, Baron Jesko von Puttkamer, ever conscious of himself as a symbol of a way of life that was soon to meet its brutal end, dressed in his uniform bedecked with the decorations of service in two world wars.

Suddenly, as the family gathered for the last time in the estate's park, Jesko's stepdaughter, Libussa, halted, refusing to take her own life for the sake of the child she carried. Believing that Libussa was simply afraid, her stoical mother, Jesko's wife, urged her daughter to have faith in "what was written on the cross: Fear not, only trust in the lord." Despite Jesko's helpless protests, Libussa's determination to bring her child into the world, even though it faced a precarious future, undermined the family's agreement.[1]

In the months that followed, Jesko languished in a succession of Soviet prison camps while Pomerania's Russian and Polish occupiers forced Libussa, her mother, and Libussa's newborn daughter to flee westward, sacrificing convention in order to survive. Eventually Jesko escaped thanks to Libussa's resourceful plotting. Yet afterwards her sullen and ungrateful stepfather could only rage at his family's compromised existence. Jesko's new life included not only the demoralizing search for gainful employment paid in increasingly worthless currency, a common enough experience in the early postwar era. It also required coming to terms with the autonomy and resourcefulness that his beloved Libussa acquired in his absence. Jesko was fortunate not to have met the fate of many other estate owners, summary execution, but his role as the family's provider and protector had evaporated. The prewar world of the Krockows and their values had come to an end, leaving its Junker patriarch without moorings in a radically new setting.[2]

The eastern Prussian province of Pomerania, like Prussia itself, no longer exists in its prewar form except in the memories and memoirs of expellees, such as the Krockows, who fled from their homes in the closing days of World War II. In fact, the unification of Germany in 1990, accomplished in the wake of the Soviet empire's stunning disintegration, could not have occurred had the new Federal Republic not formally acknowledged the eastern boundaries that the victors imposed forty-five years earlier—boundaries that ceded the lion's share of Pomeranian territory to the Poles. Yet Pomerania played a central role in the tragic outcome of the first German unification— the rise of National Socialism. Its ruralism, its Protestantism, its susceptibility to the Hitler movement as the Weimar Republic disintegrated, and the pervasive right radicalism of its dominant landowning class to which the Krockows and Puttkamers belonged not only apotheosize many of the distinctive features of Prussia east of the Elbe River, but also render Pomerania's history crucial to recovering the German past.

We can no longer uncritically accept the interpretations that once framed our understanding of German history. The view that Germany's retarded political and social development, that is, the lack of a politically self-confident middle class and a mature parliamentary democracy to complement its rapid economic modernization, distorts both German history as well as that of Western Europe whose own pasts Germany allegedly failed to replicate. Nonetheless, because Germany spawned fascism in its most vicious incarnation, we must still recognize and confront the sources of its "uniqueness."[3] Thus, this book will focus on the role of eastern Prussian estate owners, and particularly those of Pomerania, in the rise of National Socialism. Estate owners not only encouraged the spread of National Socialism by various means, subtle or otherwise, but the regions they spoke for also embodied many of those features that distinguished Germany from its industrialized neighbors.[4]

At the beginning of the Nazi dictatorship, nearly one-third of the German population depended directly or indirectly on agriculture for its livelihood, a remarkably high percentage given that Germany supported one of the world's most advanced economies. Certainly in the decades since unification in 1871, the agricultural sector contracted dramatically in comparison to industry, both as to its share of the gross national product and its place in the

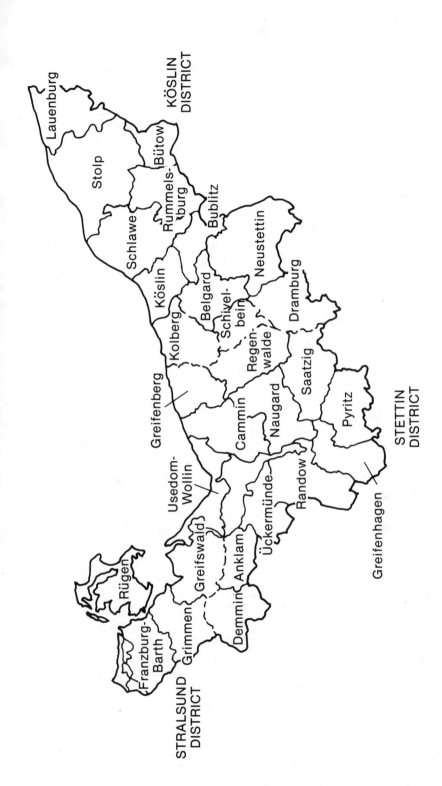

Lauenburg

Stolp

Bütow

Rummels-
burg

Schlawe

Bublitz

Köslin

Neustettin

Belgard

Schivel-
bein

Dramburg

Kolberg

Regen-
walde

Greifenberg

Saatzig

Cammin

Naugard

Pyritz

Usedom-
Wollin

Rügen

Franzburg-
Barth

Grimmen

Greifswald

Anklam

Demmin

Ückermünde

Randow

Greifenhagen

STETTIN
DISTRICT

STRALSUND
DISTRICT

Pomerania: Districts and counties, 1918–1932

—— County Boundaries
---- Boundaries of Districts

work force. The relative "decline" of agriculture gave rise to vociferous demands, particularly from estate owners, that the state institute tariff protection and preserve the rural way of life. Yet without insisting on a "normal" pattern of economic development from which Germany diverged, it is nonetheless clear that German agriculture retained a degree of political influence unmatched by its major industrial rival, Great Britain.[5]

Partially because Germany's experience appears so anomalous, it is tempting to exaggerate the long-term structural deficiencies of the primary sector, the full consequences of which its political strength prevented it from confronting. Nevertheless, there is little question that the predominantly agrarian Prussian east constituted a weakening and industrially underdeveloped rural backwater whose viability grew especially precarious during the Weimar Republic, despite the efforts its farmers expended in modernizing their holdings.[6] Economic hardship, which achieved disastrous proportions in the late 1920s and early 1930s, transformed the Prussian east's ingrained antidemocratic conservatism into a virulent and radical antirepublicanism that estate owners especially articulated. That right radicalism pushed the Nazi party from the fringes of the Weimar political spectrum to center stage.

The extremism of the right frequently invoked a powerful "myth" that reflected the profound clash between the still prominent rural sector and Germany's mushrooming urban-industrial complexes: the myth of the sanctity of rural life. As a rule, myths tell stories that describe the origins and essential character of the communities adhering to them. They defy the establishment of clearly discernible boundaries between history and fiction, precisely because they elevate as sacred not just the "real" or existing status of the communities they serve, but also the dreams, fears, visions, and expectations of those communities.[7] For the Prussian east, the myth sanctified rural culture as a distinctive, genuine, and wholesome way of life that was vital to Germany's future as a great power. Whether vocalized in the strident propaganda of rural elites or embodied in the quietly exercised patterns of everyday behavior, it idealized the countryside, as well as the possession and tilling of the soil, as the source, even the very essence, of social stability, harmony, and peace.

The rural myth allowed for the possibility of social advancement, particularly that arising from the acquisition of land, as long as the land did not become an object of speculation. Yet it also presupposed the maintenance of stable hierarchies as the key to social harmony, the survival of the rural community, and the health of the German nation. The myth asserted without contradiction the common bonds of rural society and the common goals of all agricultural producers at the same time it upheld social stratification as a necessity. Implicitly in fact, sustaining community depended on preserving hierarchy, because accepting one's place reduced the potential for social discord. To mitigate the tensions that unavoidably arose from the juxtaposition of those seeming opposites, the rural myth reified the populist image of the independent peasant who farmed his land as a sacred trust and with whom all rural dwellers identified. More generally it elevated farming as a "vocation" or "calling" (*Beruf*) that sharply distinguished those engaged in agriculture, whatever the size of their holdings, from others more narrowly defined by profit and market production.[8] Most important, the myth depended on the vitality of personal interactions within and between each rank in the hierarchy, for personal connection provided the means by which each rank recognized its obligations to the larger community and submitted to them.

Myths not only reassure their listeners with positive depictions of the cultures that embrace the communities adhering to them. They possess an equal capacity to disturb their audiences, because in order for them to sustain the unity of their communities over time, myths often provide adversaries that threaten community values. For the Prussian east, the rural myth incorporated the countryside's direct antithesis, the cities. For those who subscribed to the myth, indeed especially for the elites who propagandized it, urbanization meant not simply unregulated growth, overcrowding and unhealthy conditions, both material and psychic—conditions presumed to be opposite to those on the land. The myth also conjured up visions of lives spent in isolation from caring neighbors and of individuals without roots, without community, without even an identity that came from knowing one's position in a hierarchy of ranks. The social fluidity of the cities and the class conflict it engendered threatened moral ruin and national fragmentation. The rural myth both reflected and recreated a culture that believed itself on the verge of extinction, one that National Socialism effectively addressed as it captured a critical percentage of the Prussian east's electorate. Despite the conflicts that periodically arose in the countryside that should logically have undermined the rural myth's central premise—the existence of harmony and common objectives among all rural producers—the myth proved remarkably durable as a set of explanations for the uniqueness of rural society and the woes that beset it.

Extolling the blessings of rural life and condemning the ills of urbanism dominated conservative intellectual and academic debate during the Kaiserreich, calling into being such pressure groups as the Farmers League (*Bund der Landwirte*) that in East Elbian Germany united peasants and the lower middle classes under the leadership of large estate owners. In the 1890s, the League successfully exploited the rural myth in its incessant attacks against Chancellor Leo von Caprivi's trade policies, which it deemed destructive of agriculture.[9] Indeed, Germans hardly distinguished themselves among other Europeans or Americans in harboring misgivings toward the consequences of industrialization. The wrenching economic changes that industrial development produced could not help but bring disorientation in their wake.[10] Nevertheless, the sheer size and political weight of the German primary sector, coupled with the Weimar Republic's inability to resolve the conflicts among the major interest groups including agriculture, produced a uniquely portentous and devastating form of radicalism in the countryside that fused elite and popular militance.

Pomerania serves as the subject of this analysis of the political consequences of the rural myth for four reasons. First, one could scarcely
envision a more rural province, given Pomerania's heavy dependence on
agriculture, its slender industrial base, and its low level of urbanization.
Even by the standards of the eastern Prussian region that embraced it,
Pomerania embodied for many of its denizens the wholesome alternative
to the cities that the rural myth depicted. For outsiders, its vast underpopulated expanses interrupted occasionally by a village or small town seemed
curiously disconnected from the dominant cultural trends of the industrialized west. It seemed a wholly "premodern world order," to use the words
of Pomerania's best-known contemporary chronicler, Count Christian von
Krockow, Libussa's only surviving brother.[11] Although, the term "premodern" can be misleading in defining the qualities of Pomeranian rural life, it
remains suggestive here as a means of highlighting the province's distinctiveness when compared to Germany's industrialized and urbanized
regions.

Second, beginning in the fall of 1930, Pomerania consistently yielded one
of the highest Nazi votes in Germany, undermining the long-time preeminence of the conservative German National People's Party (DNVP), the
enlarged offspring of its prewar successor, the German Conservative Party
(DKP). Until then Pomerania was unfavorable terrain for political chal-
lengers (the notable exception being the elections conducted in the heat of
the postwar revolution), except in the cities where the Social Democratic
Party (SPD) performed well.

Recently, upper-middle and working-class support for National Socialism
has drawn considerable attention in the effort to establish the Hitler movement as a genuine populist party (*Volkspartei*), and not merely the sheet
anchor of lower-middle-class disaffection. Furthermore, the Nazi party drew
substantial support from urban areas, even after 1928 when the Hitler
movement's electoral successes in the Protestant countryside seemed so dramatic, not only to contemporary observers, but also to scholars looking
back.[12] Yet there is little doubt not only that the Nazis performed extraordinarily well in rural areas (or more precisely Protestant ones), but also that
they gained principally at the expense of the DNVP. During the presidential
elections of 1932 Hitler's own performance was exceptionally strong in regions that had voted heavily for Hindenburg in 1925.[13] All three
determinants, ruralism, the proclivities of Hindenburg voters, and the eroding position of the DNVP, characterized Pomerania. The DNVP's losses
simultaneously fragmented and radicalized that party, while encouraging
the rural electorate to vote Nazi and pushing the rural elite to the negotiations that culminated in the Hitler chancellorship on January 30, 1933.
Although it is deceiving to label the Nazi party as "conservative," it
nonetheless appealed to conservative Pomeranian voters who feared and re-
sented the demise of their economy and culture. In addition, the Nazi party
became the best vehicle for Pomerania's agrarian leadership to undermine
the republican system it so detested.

Third, with its overwhelmingly Protestant and principally Lutheran population, Pomerania highlights another indisputable characteristic of the Nazi party's mass support. The Nazi movement was born in heavily Catholic Bavaria during the first tumultuous years of the Republic. Nonetheless it owed its phenomenal electoral growth after 1928 to Protestant voters, drawing as a rule less well among Catholics.[14] The unique, albeit declining, ability of the Catholic Center Party to unite diverse social elements under the banner of religion partially accounts for the difference in Protestant and Catholic voting behavior. Yet considerably less attention has been devoted to what might have been distinctive about the Protestant experience itself. Thus, the possible contributions of Protestant *religious* identity to the decision of so many Protestant voters to choose Nazism requires sustained analysis.[15] The Pomeranian case illustrates the salience of Protestantism as a widely dispersed but deeply held system of values that contributed much to the myth of the sanctity of rural life and obviously to the culture that myth celebrated. In a more concrete if conventional way, Pomerania also demonstrates the considerable influence of the Evangelical Church in sustaining the hierarchies and community of rural life. Moreover, the obsession of the church with moral "decadence," particularly in the issues of gender roles and sexual identity *and* behavior, both created and gave expression to the rural fear of the cities.

Finally and most important, Pomerania's reputation as a province where estate agriculture dominated the economy and estate owners sat atop the social structure, presents an opportunity to analyze the relationship between landed elites and the National Socialist party at the very source of large landowner influence, the estate villages of the Prussian east. There is to be sure nothing new in citing the rural foundations of National Socialism or of fascism. Nor is it novel to call attention to the role that the East Elbian agrarian elite and its noble core, most commonly known as the "Junkers," played in Hitler's rise to power, especially through their influence on President Hindenburg. The Junkers, so it appears, have drawn more than their share of scrutiny for sponsoring Nazism, either in a counterrevolutionary partnership with big capital, according to the interpretation that prevailed in the former German Democratic Republic, or as the primary contributors to Germany's authoritarian, and grotesquely misshapen, political development.[16]

Yet the behavior of this elite on its estates, and its attitude toward the rural dwellers with whom it interacted, not to mention the position of rural dwellers toward it, are just beginning to draw the close analysis we should expect given the putative contribution of estate owners to the emergence of National Socialism.[17] The Pomeranian noble caste within the province's mixed bourgeois-noble landed class was the most consistent and articulate exponent of the rural myth while acting most forcefully for agrarian interests in the province. The Pomeranian nobility also demonstrates how the influence of estate owners at the commanding heights of the Weimar state, however tenuous it became, grew from power exercised locally.[18] The success of the Hitler movement in achieving power resulted not simply from the complicated interplay between the Nazi party's mass support and the machinations of conservative elites in the rapidly disintegrating Weimar state. Rather, the Nazis' mass support itself received nourishment from the social hierarchies, "local notables," and associational life then in place as the party sought to become the dominant alternative for a profoundly disenchanted electorate.[19] Indeed Pomerania was a region where the "local notables" possessed a greater than normal prominence, one with direct national implications. Estate owners, and especially the landed nobility, deserve the notoriety they have received, precisely because their behavior exposes the interrelationship between two phenomona that have often proven difficult to connect: the collapse of the Weimar Republic that the disintegration of its party political system occasioned and the rise of Nazism as the successful, if volatile, reaggregation of the dominant interests.[20]

The structure of this book, divided as it is in two parts, means to illustrate the significance of the large landowning class, and especially the nobility, to Pomerania's social, economic, and political life. Part I, "Hierarchy and Community," briefly analyzes Pomerania's economy and landowning patterns as they evolved, particularly after the Napoleonic Wars. Moreover, emphasizing the Weimar period, it examines the conduct of the Pomeranian landed elite and its relationship to the rest of rural society. It discusses how the acceptance of a hierarchy with estate owners at the top coexisted with the shared perception among rural dwellers of a common interest in the vitality of agriculture. That perception prevailed even among those who at first glance appeared to have had little stake in the preservation of that hierarchy. This section also pays heed to the role of Pomeranian Protestantism in enlivening the rural myth and sustaining the power of estate owners, because in addition to the reasons set forth previously for recognizing the salience of religion, Christianity traditionally permeated the mentality of European landed elites, particularly the nobility.[21] Finally, Part I underscores the fundamental continuities in rural relationships that survived World War I and the revolutionary beginnings of the Weimar Republic. Although the rise of National Socialism cannot be attributed to long-term trends alone, the recognition of continuities remains vital to understanding German history.[22]

Building on those foundations, Part II, "A World Collapses," describes the political mobilizations that erupted in early 1928 and ended with the triumph of the Nazis, not only connecting them to the initiatives of the rural associations that Pomerania's estate owners led, but also to the contours of rural life and its institutions, which the hegemony of the landed elite had so thoroughly infused.

Given the debate about the Nazis' volatile and pervasive populism, a sharp note of caution is in order: In Pomerania as elsewhere, the Nazis styled themselves as radical and anti-elitist, true populist alternatives to the politics-as-usual of the best organized interests, be they big labor, big business, or big agriculture. They postured as "revolutionaries" determined to eliminate "reactionaries" root and branch. Yet simultaneously, the party showed little reluctance to cooperate with local elites, principally estate owners in Pomerania's case, recognizing that the social prestige and major organizations of local "establishments" would ultimately prove indispensable to the success of the Hitler movement. Thus, although the party never entirely suppressed its antagonism toward elites, it tempered its agitation at crucial moments when the party's viability depended on the strength of its alliances with elites.

As it began its electoral surge after 1928, the Nazi movement in Pomerania devoted most of its efforts to exploiting the values and fears embedded in the rural myth that Pomeranian rural dwellers shared, although here too the Nazis could not resist firing potshots at what they termed "reactionaries." The party's uncompromising antirepublicanism, which its exclusion from power rendered credible, comprised the most consistent "radical" element of the Nazi platform. The same could not be said for the DNVP, the party that regularly expressed agrarian elite interests in the province. The German Nationals' periodic participation in Weimar cabinets compromised its own radical rhetoric beyond what its vituperatively antirepublican party chairman, Alfred Hugenberg, and his Pomeranian supporters could muster to assure that party's survival.

Yet the very antirepublicanism of Pomeranian estate owners themselves, those who had composed the backbone of the DNVP in the province, not only exposed the fluid boundaries between conservatism and right radicalism as the Weimar Republic crumbled. It also bestowed legitimacy on the Nazis as an acceptable alternative to rural voters who, despite periodically venting their dissatisfaction with Pomerania's elite, were either unable or unwilling to reject the estate owners' hegemony. It is thus an oversimplification, to attribute the Nazi party's electoral achievements to its independence from elites, as is now repeatedly argued. Although we can neither ignore its propagandistic anti-elitism nor fail to take seriously the nonelite sources of its financial support, to cite but two evidences of its populism, the party's partial symbiosis with elites necessarily explains the Nazis' success.[23] Political realignment does not necessarily entail an accompanying shift in social relations, and in fact the political realignment that transpired in Pomerania after 1930 owed much to the rural hierarchies then in place.

The interest that has surfaced lately in the insidious workings of power beyond the visible operations of the state confirm the dangers in instrumentalizing the relationship between eastern Prussia agrarian elites and the social groups below them, be they peasants, artisans, or farm laborers.[24] In past narratives, German elites, notably estate owners, have appeared as having "manipulated" the lower-middle and rural working classes beneath them into following their antidemocratic and authoritarian agendas, often against the best or "rational" interests of those whose virulent antisocialism led them to sacrifice independence for tutelage. Thus, the subordinate classes have seemed merely the faceless and passive objects of initiatives from on high, lacking the capacity to protest, or even to negotiate limits to, their own domination. Much like sheep, they dutifully followed their shepherds, succumbing in the end to the right radicalism of the Nazis.[25]

Yet the influence of Pomeranian estate owners depended on their ability to win the consent of those they dominated, not just through force or by crude manipulation (although we can by no means deny the significance of these), but also by intrusively asserting their "responsibility" for the welfare of rural society as a whole. Their intervention in the countryside, assured the deference, or at least the begrudged compliance, of their social "inferiors." While ruthlessness characterized that intervention, especially in the immediate aftermath of World War I, the landlords' charity, particularly that exercised by the nobility, lent credibility to the rural myth's seemingly odd marriage of community and hierarchy. Estate owners conveyed their obligation to the community, successfully enough to prevent intermittent dissatisfactions from directly challenging the social structure of rural Pomerania.[26] Their ability to substantiate the values of community implicit in the rural myth assured that the sentimental ideal of social harmony amounted to more than wishful thinking or self-deluding propaganda.

How the landed elites of Pomerania and the Prussian east came to play such a critical role, not only in the destruction of the Weimar Republic, but also in the Nazis' accession to power, is the primary question that this book seeks to answer. The Republic presented unusual challenges to a class that, under the Second Empire, had enjoyed extensive political privileges and a relative economic prosperity reinforced by protective tariffs.[27] The removal of the Hohenzollern monarchy, whose aegis had assured the disproportionate influence of the landed elite, the elimination of the three-class franchise in Prussia, and the creation of a fully representative democracy with an effective national parliament created a political system, which of necessity was significantly less responsive to agrarian pressure than its predecessor. Weimar threatened to rupture the connection between power in the state and power in the countryside that historically sustained the eastern Prussian landed class. Moreover, the unprecedented economic hardships of the republican years that affected the primary sector disproportionately convinced large landowners, who did not need much convincing to begin with, of Weimar's irremedial and intrinsic hostility to rural interests.

Over its brief lifetime, the Republic chipped away at the props of estate owner dominion. Continuing one of the major legacies of World War I that brought the Socialists into the management of the economy of total war, Weimar paid heed to the trade unions whose influence promoted the expansion of the welfare state and the taxation that supported it. In unprecedented fashion, the Republic also attended to Germany's industrial exporters, whose demands frequently opposed the interests of agriculture, the centrality of which rural advocates had so fervently asserted. The agrarian elite's noble core, which was especially prominent in Pomerania, felt the negative impact of Weimar priorities most acutely, not merely because noble estates suffered materially, but also because the eastern Prussian nobility had long benefited from its relationship to the Prussian state. It retained a

collective memory of better times before military defeat, before the institu-
tionalization of the power of organized labor, and before the mushrooming
of urbanization.[28]

Yet although the threats to the political influence of estate owners are
central to our story, the Republic failed to institute the extensive land
reform that was essential to dissolving the bedrock of the landed elite's
power, the estate villages of the Prussian east. As a consequence, the hardships of agriculture that grew especially profound after 1927–28 provided
the incentive for large landowners to demagogically assert their command
of the rural myth once again while claiming to speak for the totality of
agrarian interests. They organized peasants, rural laborers, even shopkeepers and artisans into an assault force that grew progressively more
radical in its opposition to the "system." The personal bonds inherent in
rural social relations and the remoteness of serious political alternatives
aided their enterprise. The dangers inherent in the radicalism that estate
owners spawned never deterred them from their mission to destroy Weimar
and replace it with an authoritarian regime. Moreover, agrarian influence in
the state, while increasingly limited, was far from inconsequential. Estate
owners could still pressure the relevant ministries at key moments, not to
mention exert their tragic sway over the President Hindenburg who facilitated the Republic's demise. Thus, although rural elites correctly saw their
political and economic impact eroding at the highest levels, their continuous local power and their strategic placement in Berlin enabled their radical
antirepublicanism to nurture National Socialism.

There is no denying the deep populist resentment against the Weimar
system and the Republic's dominant interests that fueled the growth of the
Nazi electorate. Notwithstanding the importance of German conservative
elites in giving Hitler the chancellorship and granting legitimacy to the Nazi
regime, the elites would never have deemed the Nazis suitable coalition
partners had the party not spoken for a sizeable popular constituency. The
inability of one of the last and most self-consciously elitist of the Weimar
cabinets, that of Franz von Papen, to attract broad-based support gave evidence that authoritarianism without a mass base could not long survive.
Employing repression to dissolve the Socialist-dominated Prussian government, however effective in weakening one of the principal mainstays of the
Republic, could not permanently replace popular consensus.

Nevertheless, the role of the rural elite in fostering the Nazis' electoral
growth in the first place demands that we recognize the crucial contributions of the eastern Prussian landed elite in the Nazi party's accession to
power. Nowhere in interwar Europe did a landed class, particularly one
with a significant hereditary noble contingent, assume such influence, or
more pointedly, produce such consequences, despite the undeniable, if paradoxical, weakening of its position against a state that could not consistently
protect its interests. Not even the British aristocracy, which throughout
most of the nineteenth century bested the eastern Prussian nobility in the
size of its holdings and overall wealth, could match the Prussians even as

the latter saw the parliamentary system erode their power. While the British landed class experienced its precipitous decline from the decades after 1870 into the twentieth century, its counterpart in the eastern Prussian provinces retained enough leverage not only to foreclose nonFascist alternatives to the Republic, but also to enhance considerably the prospects of the Fascist one.[29] Certainly no other German elite was able to combine its voice in the corridors of power, particularly those leading to the office of President Hindenburg, with a significant mass following. And that mass following, although increasingly angry and volatile, represented a degree of popular support at the "disposal" of estate owners that was not available to other major economic factions.[30] That combination yielded the Hitler-led government in January 1933.

The Krockow family's resolute procession to their estate's park (resolute at least until Libussa's dramatic change of heart) reminds us that the final elimination of the Prussian east's landed class came only with Germany's catastrophic military defeat and subsequent dismemberment. To be sure, the urban and industrial priorities of the Weimar Republic weakened the protective bonds that had long existed between eastern Prussian landowners and the state. Moreover, the Nazi regime's policies often threatened the political power and social influence of estate owners in other ways, even if it proved unwilling to eliminate estate agriculture after 1933. Yet until the end of the Third Reich, the Pomeranian nobility's striking combination of militarism, austere sense of duty, religiosity, rootedness, and patriarchalism so evident in the Krockow-Puttkamer family organized and defined the society that surrounded it. Its durability forces us now to look at the structures of local power and the character of the social relations in rural East Elbia.

I

HIERARCHY AND COMMUNITY

1

Foundations of Continuity: Pomeranian Agriculture and Landownership from the Reform Era to World War II

THE HISTORY OF Germany has often entailed the search for continuities to explain that nation's violent course until the collapse of the Third Reich resulted in its occupation and and division. Because of the horrors of National socialism, identifying long-term trends unfavorable to Germany's development as a nation-state has become morally as well as intellectually compelling. Once it was commonplace to expose the roots of Nazism as far back as the Reformation or the rise of Prussian absolutism. More recently, however, the Bismarckian "revolution from above" and the power of the anachronistic "pre-industrial" Junker elite have received greater emphasis.[1] Yet such interpretations, sweeping as they are, risk excluding more recent, more contingent, and more relevant, explanations as they sow the seeds of Nazism in a more distant past.

Indeed Germany's political and social evolution produced alternatives to authoritarianism and to National Socialism that could have prevailed had the circumstances been "right," or different choices pursued. Germany's defeat in World War I and the formation of the Weimar Republic provided the most promising opportunities for democratization and the elimination of the structures that would foster Nazism. Nevertheless, Pomerania's history forcefully attests to major continuities in German history, notably the longevity and impact of the East Elbian landed elite.

Agriculture and Industrial Underdevelopment

We can read this from German sources about Pomerania's past: "History shows us that the land of Pomerania was occupied by a variety of peoples down through the centuries, but never did any one people settle at the cost of the destruction of another. This land was settled and cultivated peacefully. That Pomeranians were brutally driven from their land following Pomerania's over seven hundred-year history as German territory remains a crime against human rights."[2]

A different version of Pomerania's heritage comes from a billboard in Szczecin, the Polish city that before 1945 was called Stettin: "Western Pomerania [the land embracing the entire prewar German province] forever Polish."[3]

Pomerania is a revealing example of how contested the past often is. For many Poles, the Oder-Neisse boundary that divided their country from Germany after World War II is minimally just, for according to their understanding of the past, Slavs inhabited Pomeranian territory well before Germanic peoples migrated there.[4] For Germans who superimpose nationalist claims on the fluidity of medieval Europe, however, Pomerania's history is integral to German history and identity because Germans came to reside there as much by invitation as by invasion. Only the ruthless Soviet penetration westward and the concessions of the western Allies denied them territories, including Pomerania, that were sacrificed to the reconstruction of east central Europe.[5] Yet this much is beyond dispute: Pomerania was once a part of Prussia and then Germany, and that province helped to define traditions understood as "Prussian."

From the twelfth to the fourteenth centuries, Germans migrated eastward across the Elbe and Saale Rivers into the Slavic lands. Consisting of nobles, peasants, monks, and merchants, the German "colonization" established towns along the Baltic coastline as far as the western border of the present-day Russian Republic, settlements that the Hanseatic League later incorporated in its Baltic network.[6] Most of the German newcomers looked to the east as an opportunity to establish farms, the grain from which the towns shipped to expanding markets to the north and west. In Pomerania, the Slavic dukes who governed their territories as far east as the towns of Bütow and Lauenburg, invited Germans to populate their vast expanses and cultivate their land. Over time, the German settlers intermarried with Slavs, in many instances taking Slavic names, while the Pomeranian dukes strove to preserve a measure of independence against a host of claimants and invaders: the Poles and Teutonic knights in the south, the Danes from the north, as well as the Brandenburg margraves and German emperors in the west. In the last quarter of the fifteenth century, Bogusław X achieved the high-water mark of ducal rule when he reunited the Pomeranian duchies after a protracted period of disintegration. He subordinated Pomerania's towns to his authority, strengthened the administration of his lands, and negotiated an end to his dependence on the German Emperor Maximilian I.

In return, he granted the Hohenzollerns of Brandenburg the right to inherit Pomeranian lands if his family's line died out.[7]

In 1637, in fact, the extinction of the ducal line came while Pomerania comprised part of the killing fields of the Thirty Years' War, the scene of pitched battles among Swedish, Imperial, and Polish forces. Thus, by the terms of Bogusław's agreement, Pomerania passed to the Hohenzollerns. Yet the Hohenzollerns' own claim to the totality of Pomerania suffered a setback when the treaties of Münster and Osnabrück gave Sweden all of lower Pomerania (*Vorpommern*) to the west of the Oder, including the ducal capital of Stettin, plus a strip of territory to the east of the river. Brandenburg retained the rest of upper Pomerania (*Hinterpommern*), including the bishopric of Cammin while sacrificing the fiefs of Lauenburg and Bütow to Poland.[8]

By the third decade of the eighteenth century, Poland's and Sweden's decline as major powers provided the Hohenzollerns with the opportunity to regain most of what they had lost when Prussia, Russia, and Austria, emerged to fill the power-political void in Central and Eastern Europe. As early as 1658, the Great Elector exploited his alliance with Sweden to reacquire Bütow and Lauenburg from the Poles. In 1720, however, the defeat of Sweden in the Northern War with Russia allowed the Prussian king Frederick William I to claim over half of Swedish Pomerania. Finally, the defeat of Napoleon in 1815 brought Prussia another reward. At the Congress of Vienna, Sweden ceded the last of its Pomeranian holdings to the Hohenzollerns.[9] Shortly thereafter, the Prussian government reorganized the administration of its newly enlarged province, dividing it into the three major districts (*Regierungsbezirke*) of Stralsund, Stettin, and Köslin, each of them subdivided into counties (*Kreise*). The smallest of the districts, Stralsund, which incorporated the four counties that Sweden held between 1720 and 1815, was absorbed into the neighboring Stettin district in 1932.[10]

Despite the political transformations affecting Pomerania, the legacy of the Thirty Years' War proved difficult to eradicate, because of the devastation it wrought and because it solidified Pomerania's Protestant identity. During the reign of the dukes, the Lutheran Reformation quickly penetrated the larger towns and spread to the countryside thereafter, capitalizing on the widespread resentment against the Catholic Church's powers of taxation. The Reformation even converted many of the Slavic nobles who had intermarried with Germans.[11] Yet Pomerania's effort to preserve its neutrality in the religious wars that followed came to naught, and its suffering produced a lasting folk legacy, a poem that every German child came to learn by heart:

> Maikäfer flieg,
> der Vater ist im Krieg
> die Mutter ist in Pommernland,
> Pommernland ist abgebrannt,
> Maikäfer flieg![12]

The Swedish occupation and the encroachment of Brandenburg-Prussia, notwithstanding the competition between the two powers, prevented a re-catholicizing of the region.

Subsequently, the Calvinist Hohenzollerns observed religious toleration in their lands as a means of preserving order and attracting talented dis-senters. Yet the privileged position of the churches that followed Luther and Calvin soon became evident. After the Napoleonic Wars, the Prussian Evan-gelical churches, including Pomerania's, were merged into a united church under royal supervision, which in the process transformed the Evangelical clergy into a political and cultural elite.[13] Until the end of World War II, Pomerania remained a Lutheran bulwark with a small Reformed minority, a place where the parish church rivaled the landed estate in its prominence in the village landscape. The province was hardly immune to the intrusions of secularization that appeared during the nineteenth and early twentieth centuries, particularly in Germany's cities. Nevertheless, formal religious participation, and a deeply Protestant identity, characterized Pomerania's population, especially in its vast rural expanses. That identity grew more pronounced under the Weimar Republic after the postwar settlement re-constructed Catholic Poland on the province's eastern border, and Catholic settlers from the west assumed civil service positions or attempted to eke out a living in agriculture. Protestantism shaped the outlooks of Pomerani-ans, in much the same way that Catholicism defined the Poles.[14]

Following the Napoleonic Wars, Pomerania's low population density and its urban and industrial "underdevelopment," provided the sort of environ-ment that most often retarded secularization. As the nineteenth century progressed, industrialization did have an impact: The proliferation of rail-road lines and the emergence of Stettin as a major harbor, to give but two examples, comprised evidence of modernization. Still, Pomerania occupied the margins of industrial growth in Prussia before and after the unification of Germany in 1871, even after World War I. The province had few of the necessary natural resources, specifically coal and iron, that could have been profitably extracted.[15] By 1925, only 1.9 million inhabitants occupied a total area of 30,220 square kilometers. Even after the Nazi regime annexed the border province (Grenzmark) to Pomerania the year before World War II broke out, the enlarged entity, now embracing 38,000 square kilometers, sustained a population of only 2.4 million. The province's distribution of fifty to sixty persons per square kilometer not only averaged significantly less than the 130-odd persons per square kilometers in Prussia (minus the Saar region), but also compares to contemporary Greece and Spain in its sparseness.[16]

Given Pomerania's low level of urban concentration, admittedly unremark-able for Prussia east of the Elbe (Silesia being a notable exception), the thinness of settlement should not be surprising. Yet the small population, in-dustrial underdevelopment, and the lack of urbanization reinforced each other: Low population density resulted in a constricted labor pool, and thus even less reason for industries to settle either in Pomerania or in the east

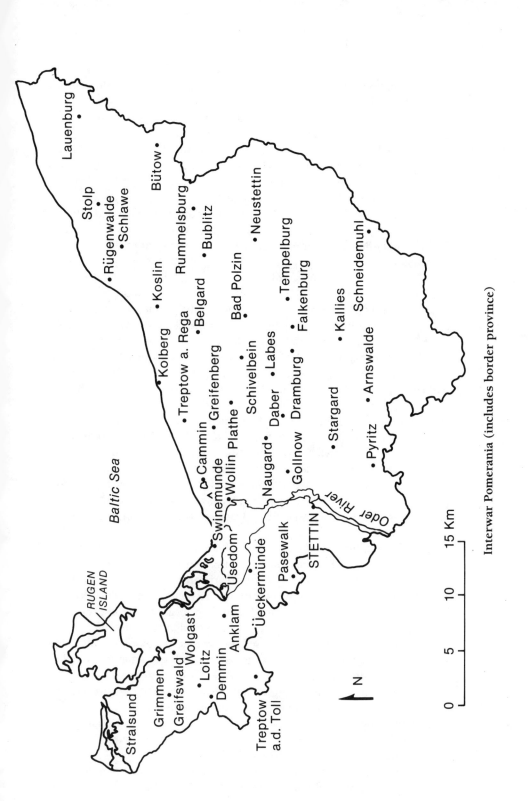

Interwar Pomerania (includes border province)

generally. In turn, underindustrialization meant less urban growth, less migration into Pomerania, and thus smaller population growth overall.[17] As a consequence, only Pomerania's capital city of Stettin, which in 1925 had a population of 270,000, could be categorized as a "metropolis" (*Großstadt*). To compare Stettin's population with that of the province's other "cities" is to recognize Pomerania as a rural backwater. Stolp, the next largest Pomeranian town, led with a population of 44,000 followed by Stralsund (43,000), Kolberg (36,000), Stargard (35,000), Köslin (31,000) and Greifswald (29,000).[18]

Pomerania's long Baltic coastline sustained its existing industry and commerce. Because of that access to the sea, Pomerania was integrated into the northern European trade belt extending from Scandinavia to France, Great Britain, and the low countries, as well as various points to the east. Throughout the nineteenth century Stettin expanded as a seaport to become the third largest in Germany after Hamburg and Bremen. By 1913, its volume of trade exceeded that of Königsberg, Lübeck, and Danzig combined.[19] Stettin's prominence stemmed not merely from its proximity to the Baltic, but also from its strategic location on the Oder River 65 kilometers inland. Its harbor serviced the eastern territories of Prussia and the industrial districts of Saxony and Upper Silesia. Pomerania's other coastal towns, however, particularly those that once belonged to the Hanseatic League, contributed their share as well.[20] Pomerania's international trade reflected its principal means of livelihood, for goods shipped from its harbors consisted primarily of agricultural products such as grain and potatoes, fodder, and fertilizer, in addition to fish, paper, and lumber. Although Pomerania's industry, mainly concentrated in Stettin, consisted of shipbuilding, iron manufacturing, cement-making, and chemicals, its center of gravity lay in agriculture and forestry. Wood products (furniture included), pulp and paper, sugar processing, brick-making, fertilizer manufacturing, breweries and dairy product refineries, evolved from what the surrounding countryside produced.[21]

Aside from industry and trade, urban life in Pomerania took on an additional stereotypically Prussian characteristic, a strong military presence. No fewer than fourteen towns featured army garrisons, Stettin's having been the largest. These outposts not only contributed to the local economies by providing employment and generating income for local businesses, they also guaranteed, in a manner that had become accepted in Prussia, military force if disorder from the lower classes arose. Moreover, the garrisons, although situated in the towns, upheld Pomerania's rural culture and elite, as well as the military traditions long associated with them.[22] Eligible young officers could always count on receiving invitations to estates in the surrounding environs, either to be introduced to the daughters of landowners or to join estate owners on the hunt. Military parades not only displayed smartly uniformed soldiers to attractive young women who lined the routes, but more importantly upheld Germany's veneration of the army.[23]

Despite the appearance of diversity in the province's economy, agriculture comprised Pomerania's lifeblood. In a nation where employment in agriculture and agricultural-related occupations appeared so disproportionate in an advanced economy, Pomerania's engagement with the primary sector was stunning: During the Weimar Republic, over half of its gainfully employed earned their living directly or indirectly in agriculture, a figure that changed little between the censuses of 1925 and 1933. An additional one hundred thousand who resided in towns counted agriculture as the source of a second income. Like other provinces of the Prussian east, as well as such predominantly agrarian regions as Schleswig-Holstein, Pomerania's independently employed were significantly more numerous than such occupations as industrial wage laborer, white collar worker, and civil servant. Taking into account the family members who worked the land, fully three-quarters of the self-employed earned their living in agriculture. At the end of World War I, over 80 percent of Pomerania's total area was devoted to farming, also a figure that changed little during the twenties.[24]

Yet as overwhelming as these statistics may seem, they convey little of the rhythms of everyday life in the countryside, patterned as they were by the demands of farming: planting in the spring and harvesting in the fall year after year, always tending to the animals and to the other chores that needed to be done day in and day out. Interruptions to those rhythms, especially such sophisticated and modern notions as "leisure," scarcely existed in a world that knew no time clock. Newspaper reading, although increasing, mainly occupied the attention of the privileged and politically significant. Even at the end of the 1920s, the use of that rapidly emerging instrument of the mass media, the radio, was relatively slight. Such amusements as pubs, dime novels, and sport, made their presence felt, a special concern and abiding irritation to Pomerania's Evangelical clergymen. Yet church holidays, including the all-important "harvest festival" (*Erntefest*), provided the primary entertainment. Vacations remained largely unheard of until the Nazis created a sensation by introducing their "Strength through Joy" excursions.[25]

South of the Baltic coastal towns, a traveler could (and indeed still can) be impressed by the vast expanses of farm land, punctuated here and there by small villages with their prominent church steeples. Even if one avoided the harsh winters, a visit to the Pomeranian countryside could be a desolate experience for those more inclined to the excitement and diversity of the city. Theodor Fontane's novel *Effi Briest* captures Pomerania's isolation and particularly the attitudes of its provincial nobility, characterizations for which the author is justly famous. Married to Gert von Innstetten, the dull Pomeranian provincial governor with an ingrained military bearing, Effi, the heroine receives a poor reception from the resident gentry despite her family's acceptable pedigree. She feels their disdain not merely because she is an outsider, but also because they see her as an "atheist" whose carriage and dress reflect the imprint of the city: "The influence of Berlin was, indeed, obvious in everything, they seemed to be saying: a taste for externals and a remarkable awkwardness and uncertainty in handling important questions."[26] Effi's subsequent adultery and disgrace arise tragically from the conflict between her effervescent personality and her environment. Appropriately enough she is exiled, if only temporarily, to the "metropolis" Berlin, the only place where she can hide her shame. Nevertheless, she is permanently estranged from her husband and child. Her parents struggle to tolerate her even as she dies in disgrace.

The poignancy of Effi's story aside, the majority of Pomerania's denizens likely saw their lives as "natural" to the core because of their tremendous stake in agriculture. Rural life was stable with its consistent rhythms, and it provided the security of knowing one's assigned role and relations, a wholesome antidote to the flux of urban civilization. Pomerania's ruralism was sufficiently ascendant as to force local historians into assuring their readers that the historic ties of the province's coastal towns to the Hanseatic League complemented rather than subverted the province's culture. According to one writer, the German colonization of the east during the high and late Middle Ages could not have succeeded without the trader and the merchant. In fact, he argued, the Teutonic knightly order solidified an alliance between merchants and crusaders that had previously formed in the Holy Land, and that relationship carried over to the Hansa association. Yet as if to compensate for his unease over this unseemly urban intrusion into Pomerania's history, the author hastened to add: "A good merchant who is rooted in his *Heimat* [such an evocative and ultimately untranslatable term could hardly have been accidental] and looks for his salvation not to the international stock exchange, but in personal risk-taking trade with the foreign merchant, is just as good a pioneer for German nationhood [*Deutschtum*] as the soldier." The language of rootedness so characteristic of agriculture applied even to this aspect of Pomerania's past.[27]

Ironically Pomerania's climate and soil was less than ideal for planting. With colder winters and shorter summers than those in the agricultural belts of central, southern and western Germany, the growing season averaged only 150 days per year, thirty days fewer than elsewhere. East of the Oder River in "Upper" Pomerania (*Hinterpommern*), an even less hospitable climate shortened the growing season still more. The possibility of late killing frosts was always present. Nor were such potential liabilities limited to the spring and summer. The snows and cold of winter damaged seed while producing parasites and disease, the cost of which every landowner, large or small, had to calculate, especially in upper Pomerania where temperatures fell below freezing for over half the winter. Taken together, such conditions required more labor, not only for planting and harvesting, but also for maintaining the machinery which during the republican years grew increasingly prevalent across Pomerania's landscape.[28]

Like the climate, Pomerania's soil, although subject to wide variations, was generally poorer than that of other agricultural regions. The soil most conducive for wheat and sugar beets stretched along the left bank of the Oder in the vicinity of Stettin, or could be found in the lower Pomeranian counties of Randow and Demmin. Average soils, which produced oats, clover, and rye, were geographically less restricted, and scattered throughout the province. The poorest and sandiest soil, however, was concentrated in upper Pomerania, particularly near the Polish border in the counties of Bütow and Rummelsburg. Farms there specialized in the few crops that thrived in such ground, namely rye, oats, and potatoes.[29] Although one most commonly thinks of rye as the primary staple of the Prussian east, the potato assumed greater importance in areas with the appropriate soil and weather conditions. It not only fed the animals belonging to peasants and farm laborers, its surplus earned cash in the marketplace, especially for estate owners who relied less on potatoes for fodder. Upper Pomeranian landowners went so far as to erect monuments in the countryside to it.[30] All told, the lighter soils prevailed in the province, so much so that under the Republic, rye and potatoes comprised Pomerania's principal saleable commodities.[31]

The limits of soil and climate speak compellingly to the issue as to why Pomeranian farmers, particularly the estate owners who owned one hundred hectares or more, favored crops that increasingly lost favor with urban consumers. In no way could Pomeranian or East Elbian farmers be considered "backward," especially not estate owners.[32] Mechanization came slowly before the war, yet they took to tractors and threshing machines in greater numbers afterward, resorting increasingly to artificial fertilizers and new, more productive strains of seed, whatever was necessary to recover prewar production levels. Although more central to peasant holdings, raising livestock with obvious consumer value, such as swine and dairy cattle, was by no means unimportant to the large landlords. Telephones and electricity became commonplace by the early 1920s, while a good many estates possessed distilleries, dairies, mills, and brickworks.[33] Because of their investment in technological and horticultural advances, the more "modern" and mechanized enterprises in Pomerania suffered the skyrocketing indebtedness that became so glaring during the agrarian depression of the late twenties.[34] One need only look at Klaus Graf von Bismarck-Varzin, the grandson of the "Iron Chancellor," to understand the degree to which agrarian improvement influenced even Pomerania's nobility.[35] Bismarck-Varzin's fascination with American farm technology (he loved to work in his overalls on his threshing machine manufactured by Massey-Harris and he played jazz on his saxophone during his off-hours) intensified his desire to modernize and rationalize his six estates. Unlike others who covered their estates on horseback, he surveyed his holdings from behind the wheel of his Ford Model Double T "Tin Lizzy."[36]

Dairy production and such "modern" crops as sugar beets most certainly attracted those farmers whose soil could fully utilize their potential. Agricultural schools for peasants, which the provincial Chamber of Agriculture (*Landwirtschaftskammer*) founded beginning in the 1890s, testified as well to the willingness, even eagerness, of Pomerania's agrarians to improve their holdings.[37] Some such as the bourgeois estate owner Dr. Fritz Tangermann, ran a model estate near Stettin; one engaged in intensive agriculture similar to that practiced in Saxony. He behaved more like a modern manager than a patriarchal landlord.[38] Yet the soil and climatic conditions in Pomerania simply did not compare to the fertile "black earth" region surrounding Magdeburg where during the nineteenth century landowners opted whole-heartedly for a highly capitalized and entrepreneurial sugar beet production. That estate owners often could not utilize the available sophisticated machinery for harvesting potatoes because the rocks in the soil would damage it effectively highlights the province's natural limitations.[39]

All economies lag at one time or another. Thus, it is easy through hindsight to exaggerate Pomerania's deficiencies, given the province's debt to its primary sector. Nevertheless, Pomerania's weaknesses, together with those of the Prussian east as a whole, were obvious in the interwar period, even before the Great Depression. In addition to the low level of industrialization, a sparse population, and the lack of natural resources, the dearth of outside investment and relatively low wages defined the Prussian east as an underdeveloped region. Pomerania thus participated in two interacting "divides" that would carry serious political consequences: the disparities in wealth between the cities and the countryside and the division between east and west evident in Prussia itself.[40]

The postwar settlement that redrew Germany's eastern boundaries in favor of a reconstructed Poland magnified Pomerania's difficulties, a point to which right-wing propagandists throughout the 1920s frequently alluded. Although Pomerania did not suffer the territorial revisions that beset Posen, West Prussia, East Prussia and Silesia, the newly resurrected Poland disrupted Pomerania's commerce and culture sufficiently to inflict genuine hardship. The 200-kilometer border severed sixty-eight railroad lines, 133 highways and 722 other byways. The only major transportation link not disrupted was the rail line extending from Stettin via Stolp to Danzig and East Prussia.[41]

Worse still, the high freight costs across Polish territory and the Polish government's unfavorable tariff and import policies, handicapped trade between the province and points east.[42] Such Pomeranian border towns as Rummelsburg, Lauenberg, and Bütow suffered special hardships because of the interruption or outright loss of their markets in West Prussia and Danzig—markets that in Danzig's case had existed since the settlement of the Teutonic knights. The removal of key industries to the Polish side of the border, and the influx of refugees from West Prussia whose needs could never be fully accommodated, created an insurmountable burden. Throughout the 1920s, high unemployment plagued the economies of those provincial towns and contributed to the anti-Polish bitterness of the Germans living there.[43]

The consequences of the Versailles territorial arrangements were not limited to the border regions, however. The disruption of inland connections with Upper Silesia, Posen, and West Prussia, territories with a population of 4.4 million, undermined the economy of Stettin, that served as the key point of transfer between the eastern territories and overseas markets. Despite subventions from the Prussian government after the war earmarked for rebuilding its merchant fleet, Stettin's harbor could not compete with those either to the east or west.[44] Although by 1932 Stettin had recovered slightly over one-half of its prewar trade, its performance could not approach the recovery rates of 79 percent for Hamburg and 68 percent for Bremen. The port of Gdynia, situated between Danzig and the mouth of the Oder, which the Polish government expanded in the interwar period, capitalized on Stettin's losses. The trade war that erupted between Poland and Germany in the mid-twenties only amplified Gdynia's importance.[45]

As a result of the transformations in the east, Pomerania was forced to look westward for new markets for everything it produced, from salt herring to agricultural commodities. This state of affairs could not help but damage estate owners because they produced most of the surplus for market, especially those from upper Pomerania who traditionally looked to the east as their primary outlet.[46] Yet Polish discrimination was not the only problem. High transportation costs arising from the Reich's privileging of railroads at the expense of shipping by sea or river, undercut the ability of Pomeranian producers to remain competitive. In any case, the water route connecting Stettin to Swinemünde, the logical channel to the west was too shallow to allow Pomerania's largest harbor to compete with Hamburg.[47] Thus, the outcome of Germany's defeat in World War I thrust Pomerania into an environment in which competition would be difficult at best, and it constructed a major obstacle to economic growth during the republican years. Pomerania's experience broadly paralleled that of the Prussian east as a whole. The new hardships that the province confronted and its underdevelopment contributed to the low levels of support the Weimar system enjoyed from the very beginnings of its existence.[48] The myth of rural life so evident in Pomerania owed its tenacity to the belief of Pomeranians that outside forces victimized them, be they industry and the cities west of the Elbe or the Versailles *Diktat*.

Noble Landownership and Marriage Patterns

Although agriculture supported Pomerania's masses, relatively few landowners controlled the province's arable and forested lands, for Pomerania joined with the rest of East Elbia as the home to *Großgrundbesitz* (large landed property). To be sure, it has become simplistic to distinguish East Elbian Germany from the south and west, characterizing it as the preserve of estate owners and the south and west as the domain of peasant proprietors. The divide between *Grundherrschaft* in the west, that is, the system of landownership in which proprietors lived from their rents and payments-in-kind from peasants, and *Gutsherrschaft* in the east, where resident owners extracted labor services from their peasant-serfs, cannot account for important variations.[49] Not only were large estates in Prussia west of the Elbe economically more significant than once supposed, rather, substantial differences in the pattern of property holdings, even in the Prussian east, suggest caution in habitually resorting to stereotypes.[50] Yet all reservations aside, the prominence of estate owners east of the Elbe deserves continued recognition because so few alternatives existed to contest the political and economic power of big agriculture.

In Pomerania, striking local variations in landowning patterns existed: The Stralsund district west of the Oder, comprising most of the territory that once belonged to Sweden, led in the density of large estates there. In the 1890s, properties of 100 or more hectares accounted for 76 percent of the land devoted to agricultural production. That figure dropped only slightly (to 70 percent) by 1933, remarkable given that the agrarian crisis of the late twenties and early thirties should have exerted a more devastating impact.[51] The magnitude of the position of large estates in part reflected that region's past under Swedish occupation. In contrast to their counterparts in old Prussia, the peasantry of lower Pomerania obtained little protection against the nobility's expropriation of their lands, a trend that persisted throughout the eighteenth century.[52]

Still, even if large estates in the province's two other districts did not dominate the landscape to the same extent as in Stralsund, their place was hardly negligible: In 1933, 49 percent of the land devoted to agricultural production in the Stettin district, and 40.7 percent in the Köslin district belonged to estate owners. Although the land linked to estate agriculture declined farther east, the paternalism frequently associated with large landholding grew more pronounced because tenancy was less common than in Stralsund where a significant percentage of the land belonged to the Prussian state.[53] As late as 1938, most of the estates located in the entire eastern half of Pomerania from the Oder to the Polish border possessed from five hundred to one thousand hectares, despite the steady increase in peasant holdings of all sizes.[54] The degree to which estates dominated Pomerania's land appears in an analysis that evaluates the extent of large landed property between 1882 and 1926: Pomerania's estate owners placed a close second in the Reich in terms of their share of the total area of the province, nearly 50 percent.[55] Although the raw number of large estates fell during the Weimar Republic because of sale and resettlement while the number of middling peasant holdings (20 to 50 hectares) increased, over 48 percent of the province's land devoted to agriculture and forestry together stayed in the hands of large landowners well into the 1930s. Villages composed exclusively of independent peasants were rare as estate villages constituted the "norm."[56]

The precise composition of the agrarian elite in the eastern Prussian provinces is only beginning to emerge from the tentative suggestions that have thus far described it.[57] On the one hand, it consisted of middle class estate owners coming primarily from the military, the state bureaucracy, and the management of the royal domains who began purchasing estates in the late eighteenth century, even before the Prussian reforms lifted the prohibition against bourgeois ownership. Notwithstanding prominent exceptions, the captains of industry and finance showed less interest in acquiring landed estates, or otherwise assimilating aristocratic values than once believed. They preferred to assert their own distinctively bourgeois ethos.[58]

Yet the core of the agrarian elite consisted of the heirs of the lesser German nobility, the Junkers, whose origins lay in the colonization period. Originally of mixed Slavic-German composition and diverse social provenance, the Junkers (the term means "young lord"), possessed considerable independent regional power. With the rise of absolutism in Brandenburg-Prussia, they evolved into a bureaucratic and military caste in service to the Hohenzollerns, although not without resistance to royal intrusions against their regional prerogatives. The monarchy frequently added to the Junkers' numbers by ennobling talented bourgeois from the civil service. Whether used out of respect or as a means of denunciation, the label "Junker" came to apply not only the "ancient nobility" (*Uradel*) of the colonization period and those subsequently ennobled, but the entire landed class as well.[59]

Regardless of the nobility's attachment to the Hohenzollerns, the ownership of a landed estate remained the *sine qua non* of its political position. The relationship between the emergence of Prussian absolutism and the reimposition of serfdom on the eastern Prussian peasantry is more complicated than suggested by the claim that the Junkers appropriated unfree labor in return for submitting to Hohenzollern power. Moreover, the assertion that the peasantry capitulated to their lords until the Prussian reforms is also prone to exaggeration. Yet despite the tensions that surfaced periodically between the East Elbian nobility and the monarchy, or between the nobility and their peasants, the nobility's rural dominion anchored its influence in the Prussian state.[60]

That this elite joined nobles of various vintages with commoners attests to the dramatic transformations in estate-owning that began in the late eighteenth and continued into the nineteenth century. Land became a commodity to be bought and sold with ease, especially if its owners placed a priority on profit and speculation. Although the nobility benefited from the reforms passed after Napoleon's victory over Prussia in 1806, wresting land and labor from peasants unable to profit from the abolition of serfdom, the number of noble estate owners fell precipitously in the years immediately following because of plummeting commodity prices.[61] Despite the robust commodity market of the 1850s and 1860s, which favored the nobles who survived the shakedown, bourgeois estate owners significantly exceeded noble landowners by the end of the century.[62]

However impressive the bourgeois invasion may seem, the decline in the nobility's position in the estate-owning class was decidedly limited. The larger the estate, particularly estates of one thousand or more hectares (including arable land and forests), the more likely it belonged to a noble family, a rule that applied throughout the Prussian east.[63] Moreover, during the Wilhelmine period the nobility capitalized on the Prussian government's disposition to strengthen its hereditary landed caste. Nobles entailed their estates to prevent their sale, foreclosure, or even taxation upon the succession of the estate's heir. The entailed estates (*Fideikommisse*) failed to serve their intended purpose of expanding the east's population to preserve that region's German identity against the Slavic "threat." Their propensity to engage in less profitable extensive agriculture and forest economy, as well as the low birthrate among the families who held such estates, unintentionally sabotaged the imperatives of German nationhood (*Deutschtum*).[64] Nevertheless, the rush to entail in the decades prior to World War I reflected the nobility's determination to preserve its position and identity.

Pomerania's landowning patterns correspond to those of the Prussian east as a whole, yet its nobility assumed even greater than normal prominence. The character of serfdom and the outcome of the emancipation era help to explain the nobility's position. The condition of serfdom in the seventeenth and eighteenth centuries had been especially harsh as landlords transferred ostensibly free peasants from one village to another with impunity and imposed the most burdensome labor obligations in the expanding Prussian kingdom.[65] Pomeranian peasants, compared to their counterparts elsewhere in the Prussian east, remained quiescent prior to emancipation. Pomeranian estates were smaller than those in regions where peasant unrest transpired, and as a consequence, their owners managed their estates personally, overseeing them with the sort of attention that effectively curtailed dissatisfaction.[66] Emancipation, the success of which (and for whom) remains a subject of lively debate, yielded some of its poorest results in Pomerania. The majority of Pomeranian peasants belonged to the category with the weakest claims to property and independence.[67] Yet here too, subordination failed to produce disenchantment powerful enough to overturn the outcome of the Prussian reforms.

To be sure, the economic disruptions following the Napoleonic Wars resulted in a turnover of estates, and the bourgeois contingent grew. From the last quarter of the nineteenth century through the first quarter of the twentieth, the amount of land in bourgeois hands grew larger.[68] The frenetic turnover of estates immediately before and during World War I intensified trends begun much earlier. Pomerania's oldest resident noble families complained sharply of the inexperience and rage for speculation of war profiteers who took advantage of the high market value of estates to dabble in an occupation for which they were ill prepared to succeed.[69] Yet in Pomerania too, nobles predominated among owners of estates that exceeded one thousand hectares, while many bourgeois proprietors leased their holdings either from nobles or from corporations.[70] Equal to or greater in significance than elsewhere in the Prussian east, entailed estates comprised 9-percent of the large landed property in 1920, a minimal change from 1895. Moreover, entailed estates did not disappear as rapidly afterward despite the Republic's determination to abolish the practice.[71]

Notwithstanding the complaints about the fluidity in the market for estates, neither the war nor the "November Revolution" disrupted the nobility's pre-eminence, for estate address books of 1914 and 1921 vividly illustrate their durability. They show relatively little change, not only in the size or number of properties that Pomerania's most distinguished families controlled, but also in the taxable income they generated. To be sure, there were signs that a few families found it necessary to retrench: Of twenty-six estates owned by the Borckes in 1914, five had been sold by 1921, four of them to bourgeois and one, an estate of 640 hectares, to a lumber business. Likewise, the Ramins parted with the largest of their three estates, a property of nearly 2,000 hectares, with 70 horses, 164 cows, 775 sheep, and over 200 pigs. They sold it to a bourgeois. One of the Knebel family's fourteen estates, a sizable property of 979 hectares was, by 1921, in the hands of the Pomeranian Land Society for parceling and settlement. But especially because the reasons for sale remain hidden, these examples constitute exceptions to a picture of relative stability.[72]

A table of landowners with at least fifteen hundred hectares of land devoted exclusively to agricultural production or twenty-five hundred hectares overall further underscores the nobility's preeminence during the Republic. The roster contained the names of some of the most distinguished families in Prussian history: The Bismarcks, Bonins, Kleists, Flemmings, Heydens, Knebels, Massows, Maltzahns, von der Ostens, Puttkamers, Schwerins, Wedels, and Zitzewitzes. Together they controlled 10 percent of the total land area devoted to agriculture and forestry or slightly over 9 percent of the land devoted solely to agriculture. As of 1928, 641 noble families held nearly 58 percent of the land contained in the province's 2,644 large estates.[73] Despite the agrarian crisis of the late Weimar period, noble families weathered the storm remarkably well, selling some land when they had to cover their debts, but in the main retaining most of their properties.[74]

Indeed, Pomerania excelled as a province of "land-loyal" (*Bodentreu*) noble families who stuck with their estates through thick and thin. According to a survey of old estates undertaken during the Third Reich to underscore the value of the nobility against the Nazi regime's privileging of the peasantry, Pomerania led Germany in the number of "old noble residences" (*Adelsbesitz*).[75] These consisted of estates identified with the same family more or less continuously since their acquisition. To be sure, of 367 Pomeranian estates included in the survey, 117, or nearly one third had been acquired as late as the eighteenth century. Yet twenty-nine of them originated during the thirteenth century, seventy-eight during the fourteenth, sixty-two in the fifteenth, forty-one in the sixteenth, and finally, forty during the seventeenth century. Only four of the 367 estates comprised fewer than 125 hectares. Another sixteen fell in the range of 125 to 250 hectares. The remainder included eighty one in the 250 to 500 hectare category, fifty three that ranged from 500 to 2,000 hectares, and ninety four with holdings of over 1,000 hectares.

Moreover, the oldest families dominated entire districts, families who acquired their holdings and presumably their noble designations well before 1400: Some of them stemmed from Germanized Slavic nobles, others from Germans who migrated eastward. Even in upper Pomerania where peasant holdings more evenly balanced the estates than across the Oder to the west, Junker clans were highly visible.[76] The counties of Cammin, Greifenberg, Regenwalde, Belgard, Stolp, and Rummelsburg featured the estates of the

Flemmings, Borckes, Kleists, Zitzewitzes, and Puttkamers, all of them an-
cient Pomeranian nobility and true Junkers. In lower Pomerania, the
Veltheim family, princes of Putbus, reigned over the isle of Rügen, while the
Schwerins, Heydens, and Maltzahns dominated the counties of Franzburg,
Anklam, and Demmin.

In their official records, Prussian government officials customarily sub-
sumed bourgeois and noble landlords under the common term "large
landowner" (*Großsgrundbesitzer*), infrequently distinguishing between
them. Yet, marriage and sociability patterns suggest that Pomeranian nobles
preferred the company of their own kind. Not only did they congregate by
themselves for informal business meetings at the local hotels,[77] they also
carefully scrutinized the suitability of marriage partners, taking commoner
spouses only when the gains, either those of passion or practicality, out-
weighed the potential losses. Although genealogies do not reveal the motives
behind the choices of spouses, the patterns that emerge are suggestive.

To be sure, the practice of endogamy found less favor among the eastern
Prussian nobility in the eighteenth and nineteenth centuries, as estate
owning opened up to the bourgeoisie, and nobles won the state's permission to pursue bourgeois occupations.[78] From the end of the eighteenth
century to the defeat of the Third Reich bourgeois marriage partners proved
anything but rare among Pomeranians as their numbers approached,
equaled, or in some cases exceeded marriages with other nobles. The "rule"
applied not merely to such families as the Platens of Rügen Island whose
Swedish and American wings had become thoroughly bourgeoisified, or the
Normanns whose Swedish and Danish branches accounted for most of the
bourgeois marriages in that family. It also included families with extensive
landed properties such as the Zitzewitzes, Belows, or Dewitzes whose offspring chose bourgeois mates as often as noble ones.[79] Yet gender differences
emerged in the selection of spouses. Noble sons chose bourgeois wives
more often than noble daughters opted for bourgeois husbands, mainly because sons could not forfeit their claims to nobility by doing so, and the
acquisition of an acceptable bourgeois bride seemed worth the "risk." Noble
daughters, although rarely in a position to inherit an estate anyway, could
lose their noble standing by marrying bourgeois.[80]

The occupations of the fathers-in-law of noble sons not only converge at
the point of solid respectability, they ironically suggest a substantial interaction between the nobility and the commercial and industrial bourgeoisie,
as well as older urban elites. The fathers-in-law of the male offspring of the
Wedel-Parlow family included factory owners, large-scale industrialists and
merchants, bank officers, officials, and professionals, along with a smatter-
ing of pastors, teachers, and middle class estate owners.[81] Similarly, the
fathers-in-law found among the marriages in the Dewitz family included
officers, merchants, factory owners and industrialists, officials, the owner of
a department store, and a professor.[82] The Puttkamers, both their baronial
and untitled wings, also included their share of merchants and factory
owners, as well as estate owners, officers, and officials.[83]

Yet the numerous bourgeois marriages among the Pomeranian nobility belies its conviction that choosing within one's caste was more desirable, a preference that carried ample supporting evidence. Of forty-eight marriages in the Ramin family, thirty-three were with nobles.[84] The Flemming, Bandemer, and Rohr families revealed an even more striking preference for endogamy. Of twenty-five marriages in the Flemming case, only four involved bourgeois partners, while just two of eighteen marriages in the Bandemer family were to bourgeois. Only one out of fourteen members of the Rohr-Demmin clan chose a bourgeois spouse.[85] More recently ennobled families such as the Enckeworts and the Knebels often followed suit. Marriages to other nobles among the Enckeworts outstripped bourgeois alliances by over two to one, while out of twenty-five marriages in the Knebel family, none was to a bourgeois.[86]

As a result, although Pomeranian noble families often chose spouses from outside the province, they appeared remarkably inbred because of their preferences for marriages appropriate to their station.[87] It was not unusual for nobles, generation after generation, to choose spouses from the small circle of families, and even to limit the number of acceptable first names given to their offspring.[88] Bismarck's grandnephew, Klaus, who gives enormous credit to his bourgeois mother for restoring the health of the family estates after his father died of tuberculosis, acknowledges the unspoken, yet unmistakable disapproval that he sensed during his youth when he disclosed his mother's heritage. Could he have avoided such an admission? Not likely, given his love for his mother and his pride in her accomplishments. Yet the social occasions he attended routinely included the obligatory smalltalk about family pedigrees. Despite his desire to find a wife just like his mother, Bismarck's own marriage was appropriate to his station (*Standsgemäß*). He married a Wedemeyer.[89]

The intense concern with the cohesion of the family through generations, and each member's obligations to the larger unit, constrained the marriage prospects of Pomeranian nobles until the end of the Third Reich. We return to the Krockow-Puttkamer family for an illustration of the degree to which family alliances preserved noble bonding. In June 1944, Libussa von Krockow married Baron Jobst von Oldershausen, scion of lower Saxon *Uradel*, who fathered the couple's child before losing his life in battle as the Soviets pressed toward Berlin.[90] The flag of both families draped the manor house of the bride, until the red and gold in the Oldershausens' banner offended stepfather Jesko: The colors reminded the unreconstructed monarchist of the flag of the Weimar Republic. Military-like precision governed the wedding ceremony itself, not merely because it was wartime and many of the available men, including the groom, were in uniform, but also because by tradition military conduct defined the nobility as a caste.

The marriage may well have resulted from Libussa's and Jobst's mutual attraction, even if Libussa's memoir subtly lets on that her decision to wed resulted more from the couple's familiarity with each other than from passion.[91] Regardless, the union entailed much more than the private choices of two people. At the banquet following the wedding, Jesko lifted his voice to toast the young couple with a treasured family heirloom, a sixteenth century goblet that an ancestor had obtained as a gift from Henry of Navarre. His act came as a surprise because the family looked upon the artifact as a near-sacred object to be used only on the wedding day of the estate's male heir, the firstborn son. Yet the deaths of Libussa's two older brothers in Poland, Jesko explained, demanded that she and her new husband assume this visible part of their inheritance, affirming their identities as members of two distinguished families now joined: "Don't ever forget it! Hold fast to it!" The entire wedding celebration embraced what in pre-industrial times was called "the extended family" (*das ganze Haus*, the entire household). It not only included the couple's immediate and extended families, but also the local peasantry, the employees of the Krockow family estates, and even the village schoolchildren who were called upon to sing.[92]

For those accustomed to equating power with great wealth, the position of the Pomeranian nobility in rural society, not to mention the historical importance of the Junkers in the formation of Prussia, might seem curious. Aside from the landed magnates of Silesia, few eastern Prussian nobles appeared on the list of that state's wealthiest rural families immediately prior to World War I, a period of relative agrarian prosperity.[93] Only two, Franz, Prince of Putbus, and Count August von Behr-Negendank were Pomeranians. The majority of Pomeranian nobles owned property valued between one and five million marks, not a paltry sum to be sure, but not the assets that competed with the landed magnates of Great Britain or the urban-based wealth of Germany's leading industrialists. In fact, the yield in ground taxes per hectare (the ground tax was based on an estate's net profit after the deduction of operating costs) was substantially lower than in Saxony, the Rhineland, Hannover, and Schleswig-Holstein and similar to that of estates elsewhere in East Elbia. Although an admittedly imperfect means of measuring the value of agricultural holdings, such tax receipts reveal that farms in the Prussian east, including Pomerania, required significantly more land to generate fifteen hundred marks in ground taxes than in the Prussian provinces to the west. That underscores the precarious underpinnings of agrarian profitability in the east, which would only become more obvious under the Republic.[94] Nevertheless, the very lack of competition to the Pomeranian nobility at the source of its power lessens the consequence of comparisons based on wealth. Its influence in the Pomeranian countryside proved durable enough to survive numerous challenges, especially World War I and the Revolution of 1918.

2

Continuity Survives Revolution: Pomeranian Conservatism from the Reform Era to Stabilization

POMERANIA COULD NOT help but be predisposed to conservatism because the lack of industry and urban development discouraged the growth of classes prone to supporting alternatives. Moreover, Protestantism saturated the aristocratic underpinnings of that conservatism, providing Pomerania's nobility with a way to legitimate itself by sanctifying their estate villages. Pomerania became one of the leading outposts of the post-Napoleonic religious revival known as the neo-pietist "Awakening," a profoundly conservative movement that in Prussia conceived of the wars of liberation against Napoleon as the triumph over revolution.[1] Strongly influenced by romanticism, neo-pietism rejected the rationalism of the Enlightenment for faith, the primacy of feeling, and the intense personal experience of conversion. As a movement defined by strong lay participation rather than clericalism, neo-pietist laypersons conducted their own services and administered their own sacraments, boycotting the "rationalist" pastors of the official church.

Religious revival erupted elsewhere in Europe during the early nineteenth century, as it did in Great Britain and the United States, and it appealed to diverse constituencies. Junkers, however, played an especially prominent role in the Prussian and Pomeranian Awakening. They looked to neo-pietism for solace against the traumatic consequences of the French

Revolution and the Napoleonic invasions, including the emancipation of the peasantry, the legalized sale of knights estates to bourgeois, the impoverishment of numerous members of their caste, and the encroaching centralization of the Prussian state. To the nobles who participated, many of them bound as much by kinship as by religious zeal, the revival condemned revolution as an abomination, although early on some Junkers sympathized with the French upheaval because it attacked royal absolutism. Noble revivalists emotionally reaffirmed patriarchal authority as consistent with Luther's doctrine of the "two kingdoms."[2]

The Awakening in Pomerania emanated from the Bible-reading and prayer-offering circles that congregated on the estates of the Thaddens and Belows, Junker families of Slavic ancestry. It joined nobles, peasants, and laborers as "sisters and brothers" before God in a common religious-conservative enterprise deeply affecting even the future Chancellor, Otto von Bismarck.[3] Yet as Gustav von Below himself revealed, the movement's most pronounced feature was its fusion of hierarchy and community: "We are estate lords and house fathers, and as such we are concerned, not only with the physical but also spiritual, welfare of our house comrades (*Hausgenossen*). In the future, we will go regularly with our people to Sunday and holiday services in God's house, as well as hold morning and evening prayer meetings in our own houses."[4] Neo-pietism not only paralleled the evolution of emancipation in the landlords' favor, however much the lords had predicted otherwise. It extended the political influence of nobles, allowing them to strengthen their control over local institutions, including the parish churches that the absolutist state had been so determined to subordinate.[5] That in turn helped to foreclose alternatives to the province's conservatism. In fact, despite lively debate in the provincial press, Pomerania remained one of the most quiescent of the Prussian provinces during the revolutions of 1848. Even in Stettin where one might have expected urban unrest to have arisen, little protest took place aside from the brief resistance to employing the city's regiment against revolutionaries in Berlin.[6]

Furthermore, the Awakening laid the groundwork for the nobility's successful exploitation of populist politics after 1848, which united peasants, artisans, and rural laborers against the pernicious encroachment of the cities. It established a pattern that would shape the political behavior of the Pomeranian nobility until the Third Reich, the willingness to risk engaging the political energies of rural people beneath them upon the conviction that such mobilizations sustained the rural community.[7] That the Awakening became a family legacy passed down from generation to generation arises clearly in the example of the Thaddens: One can draw a straight line from Adolf von Thadden, one of neo-pietism's leading vessels, to Reinhold von Thadden-Trieglaff who, during the Nazi period, emerged as one of the lay leaders of the Confessing Church, the Protestant opposition grounded in conservative premises.[8] The Thaddens were not the only case of a continuous Junker presence.

The solidarity to which the bonds of family and religion testified helped to ensure the nobility's domination of the province and its leadership of the landowning elite as a whole. Taking a long view from the end of the Napoleonic Wars to the rise of Hitler, only three of Pomerania's governors (*Oberpräsidenten*), the Prussian officials responsible for overseeing each province's district and county administrations, came from the middle classes. The other fourteen were noblemen, nearly all conservative in their political views. A good many, more so than in Saxony or Brandenburg, arose from families who claimed an aristocratic heritage from both sides extending as far back as their great grandfathers. Few of the governors had any administrative experience in the industrial regions of Germany, and in fact appointment to that senior position was biased toward Pomeranians.[9] During the Second Empire, nearly 87 percent of the Pomeranian county magistrates (*Landräte*), the Prussian government officials most directly in charge of local administration, were nobles, many of them estate owners in the districts they served. Although increasingly expected to undergo formal professional training for their positions, it was a truism nonetheless that birth determined one's entry into the provincial government.[10]

Also during the Kaiserreich, the provincial Landtag, the county assemblies (*Kreistäge*), and the German Conservative Party that prevailed in both heavily favored noble representation. Despite the greater social and political diversity of the towns, the sheer number of manorial districts (*Gutsbezirke*) that the German government accepted as units of public administration undermined any reformist illusions that might have arisen.[11] The influence of the nobility did not confine itself "simply" to the institutions of politics and government: It carried over into the economic interest organizations, such as the Agrarian League and the Chamber of Agriculture that beginning in the 1890s professionalized and politicized the province's primary sector. Founded in 1894, the *Landwirtschaftskammer* naturally gravitated to the sway of the large landlords, although in the spirit of generosity, it invited a few peasants to "honorary and official collaboration."[12]

Away from the countryside, however, the East Elbian elite saw formidable opponents. There were moments in imperial politics when the Bismarckian alliance of "iron and rye," the politically weighty coalition of industrialists and landowners, nearly disintegrated or at least approached irrelevance. Competing wings of industry vied for influence to an extent that questioned the privileges of the estate owners, and all factions that composed Germany's elite confronted populist mobilizations that did not conceal their resentment of the dominant classes. Yet if the combined aspirations and discontent of the lower middle classes and peasantry discomfited those above them,[13] the largely working-class Social Democratic Party (SPD) presented the strongest possibility for democratization.

In fact, in the two decades before World War I, the Social Democratic Party challenged the rural elite by recruiting in the countryside after the expiration of the Anti-Socialist Law, the legislation once passed under

Bismarck's aegis that outlawed the left. The SPD significantly expanded its share of the electorate now that it had less to fear from state repression. It took root not only among urban workers, but it also achieved a measure of success in East Elbia, particularly among laborers on short-term contracts whose numbers grew rapidly in the wake of agrarian modernization.[14] Yet the obstacles facing the SPD's attempts to unionize the agrarian workforce were formidable and forbidding.

In part, the SPD's experiential distance from the agrarian world hindered recruitment. The party's agitators who cruised the countryside on bicycles found it hard to communicate with the rural workers they sought to convert, many of them illiterate. The Marxist concepts of the organizers seemed foreign to the needs of their country audiences; and the distances they had to travel, a notably acute liability in Pomerania, prevented them from reaching all but those hamlets closest to the towns. Moreover, Socialist organizers found it difficult to overcome the entrenched hierarchies that divided farm workers from each other so that they could achieve the minimum of commonality that unionization required. Although few rural working-class testimonies have survived, those that exist depict a near visceral hostility toward outsiders expressed in barely comprehensible dialect, a problem that would remain pronounced in rural Germany as a whole until well into the Nazi period.[15]

Yet Socialist organizers faced other problems as well. Estate owners ruthlessly disrupted, discredited, and undermined Socialist agitation: They commandeered the police, watch dogs, estate overseers, and even pastors of the Evangelical Church to drive intruders off the land. Obtaining the approval of local magistrates to hold SPD meetings required a near herculean effort. Even if an estate laborer flirted with the idea of supporting the SPD with his vote, the manner in which his employer supervised elections discouraged him from doing so, lest he lose his job and suffer blacklisting. The estate owner's administrators simply paraded the lord's "people" to the polls where they received ballots already marked with the approved candidates.[16] (Female farm workers lacked the right to vote until 1919.) Although we ought not to overstate the role of force in reinforcing the hegemony of estate owners, repression did indeed prove intimidating to the most dependent members of rural society, the *Landarbeiter*. Before the collapse of the Kaiserreich, agricultural laborers had few rights, bound as they were to the Servants' Law (*Gesindeordnung*), a statute that forbade strikes and collective bargaining.[17] Further, even had they been receptive to the Socialists' message, they often lacked the energy to defend their interests given their long workdays especially during planting and harvesting. Those most determined to pursue alternatives emigrated to Pomerania's towns, to the cities west of the Elbe where higher paying jobs with shorter workdays permitted more leisure, or failing that, even to the Americas.[18] In the Pomeranian countryside, however, the estates held firm.

A New Beginning?

World War I and its aftermath gravely upset the accepted order of things. Like other rural regions, Pomerania suffered a high proportion of military casualties because it did not possess the industrial base that would have spared young men from conscription. On top of that, farms of all sizes experienced a dramatic reduction in livestock, the result of the military's commandeering of draft animals and the excessive slaughter of livestock.[19] Moreover, the unprecedented government intrusion into civilian lives and such daily privations as the shortage of food elevated social tensions. The black market thrived and food prices escalated. The impact of the British blockade that obviously extended to the Baltic coast, the so-called "hunger blockade," encouraged price gouging and black marketeering. The Controlled Economy (*Zwangswirtschaft*), the imperial government's attempt to limit the cost of food through price controls and requisitions so as to restrain popular disenchantment in the cities, antagonized farmers large and small, but otherwise failed to accomplish its purpose. Although the hardships affected even rural areas despite the greater availability of food, the suspicion between town and countryside grew markedly, as in other parts of Germany. Because the Weimar government did not abandon the Controlled Economy until the summer of 1923, bitterness continued into the postwar period, contributing significantly to urban-rural divisions.[20]

Furthermore, the war brought with it not only the perception, but also the reality of unsettling cultural changes. Although seemingly trivial and in retrospect humorous, they pointed to the instability of established hierarchies and social values against which the Pomeranian right would direct much of its wrath thereafter. The "looser" moral behavior of the young brought about in part by the shortage of schoolteachers irritated many, despite the upsurge in formal religious observance.[21] As one former Pomeranian pastor vividly (and disapprovingly) recalled, drunkenness and promiscuity ran rampant, particularly among returning veterans who wanted to enjoy themselves. Yet even women who had received a strict upbringing were not immune either according to the pastor, an indication that fears regarding the increase in "immorality" centered on the disruption of gendered hierarchies and the accepted definitions of masculinity and femininity.[22] He pointed to one young woman from a "good" family who worked on an estate, became drunk, got pregnant by a married man, killed her child after giving birth, and finally went to jail. Moreover, he rued, because so few prospective brides could convince the clergy that they still retained their purity, the church abandoned its insistence on virginity as a precondition for wearing a veil and carrying a wreath in its weddings. "The erosion of centuries old church customs was especially evident in the case of church marriages," the pastor complained.[23]

Thereafter the military defeat and accompanying political restructuring of Germany raised the possibility that a transformation in Pomeranian social relations might take place, if only as the unintended consequence of the Revolution of 1918. The provisional government that the moderate left, the Majority Socialists, dominated took up with renewed intensity the mobilization of agricultural laborers against the tyranny of the big landlords, while the radicalism of Bolshevik agrarian policies raised the spectre of socialization at home. Major institutions that had once favored estate owners either disappeared like the monarchy or had been gravely weakened. The "enemies of the Reich," the Social Democrats, the Catholics, and left liberal Democrats had come to power, and regardless of their well-known compulsion to restrain the radical left, their very presence meant that Germany's elites faced an environment altogether different than that of the Kaiserreich.[24]

To some degree, provincial politics mirrored the most radical proposals articulated elsewhere as the first German republic came into being. Workers' and soldiers' councils sprang up in the province's urban centers, and their more militant members advocated socialization, both in industry and on the land, as well as the creation of a socialist republic. Until the fall of 1919, leftist strikes were commonplace, and the most extreme of the once united Social Democratic Party, the Spartacists (later the Communists), made their presence felt, especially in Stettin's Vulcan Shipyard. Yet the revolution also galvanized the reconstructed liberal parties that in the past performed poorly in Pomerania: In 1919, the German Democratic Party (DDP), one of the mainstays of the moderate, parliamentary "Weimar Coalition," polled 19.2 percent of the vote for the new Prussian Landtag, compared to 16.1 percent in Prussia as a whole. The Majority Socialists walked away with 41 percent in the same election, roughly 5 percent over the Prussian average. By contrast, Pomerania's conservatives who previously faced little competition, achieved just 26.6 percent through the newly created German National People's Party.[25] Moreover, by 1920 the revolution accomplished the dismissal of one fifth of the province's county magistrates, disturbing the very core of landed aristocratic influence in the civil administration.[26]

For Pomerania's large landowners, the changing political environment proved unsettling at best, even if the parties that dominated the Prussian and Reich governments in 1918–19, including the Majority Socialists, rejected socialization as contrary to enhancing production.[27] Almost immediately after assuming power, the provisional government lifted the Servants' Law, thus granting agricultural laborers freedom of association and the right to strike. Within months, a new legal framework was created governing the negotiation of employment contracts, the length of the workday, and the payment of overtime.[28] Correctly sensing a more supportive political climate than that of the Kaiserreich, estate laborers came to life to advance their interests: Strikes occurred throughout the province in the summer of 1919 at a time when workers were needed for the upcoming harvest, and at a moment when agricultural producers found it difficult to encourage the return of demobilized veterans who had little desire to take up their former occupation.[29] The Socialist German Farm Workers Association (*Deutscher Landarbeiterverein* or DLV), which strove to negotiate higher wages through collective bargaining, found its most successful recruiting in Pomerania, especially west of the Oder where the size of estates, the relative prominence of tenancy, and the historically more contentious social relationships encouraged greater politicization among the workforce. Communist agitators also made inroads, as did organizers from the Christian trade unions.[30]

Everywhere in East Elbia, the agricultural laborer strikes created enormous discomfort among the Majority Socialists, but particularly at the highest levels of state. The SPD intended to equalize agricultural and industrial workers by granting farm laborers the right to bargain collectively, and in fact, that right became enshrined in Article 159 of the Weimar Constitution.[31] Believing that the enhanced economic leverage of the agricultural workers, coupled with a reformed political system would together weaken the estate owners, socialization could then be avoided, particularly when Germany's cities and towns needed food. An explosion of strikes only undermined that immediate goal. The Prussian minister of agriculture, Otto Braun, to give but one prominent example of the Majority Socialist position, accused not only obdurate estate owners, but also the Spartacists, of having provoked rural workers to extremes.[32] Yet such "moderation" failed to impress estate owners who rose to meet this threat to their livelihood and their prerogatives.

Labor conflict was most intense in Pomerania from the first summer after the war into 1921, yet it paralleled the turmoil that persisted nationally, not spending itself fully until the resolution of the Ruhr crisis. The surprising bitterness that surfaced between agrarian employers and their striking employees, as well as the obdurancy of Pomeranian estate owners, rendered Pomerania the most contentious of the eastern Prussian provinces.[33] Even issues that in retrospect appear narrow and modest, and thus most capable of resolution, caused discord because military defeat and the political transformation at the top spawned a more coherent, aggressive, and organized worker opposition than in the past. The militance of estate workers implicitly challenged the traditions of estate owner hegemony. The grievances of estate laborers concerned themselves first with bread-and-butter issues, such as the demand for a shorter workday (ten to eleven hours maximum during planting and harvesting) and in particular, higher wages to compensate for the declining value of their incomes through inflation.[34] From one official discussion that took place in early 1920 in the Reich Interior Ministry came the observation that Mecklenburg-Strelitz remained calmer than Pomerania due to the political moderation of the agricultural labor force and the high incomes the workers received. "Where the wife works along with her husband, the estate worker can earn twenty thousand marks per year and in a few years he is able to buy a small piece of land (property for himself)."[35]

Other demands sought to remedy the immediate postwar exigencies: Workers pressed for desperately needed clothing and shoes from the army's ordinance or additional fodder to increase swine production.[36] Still others fused material and national concerns, especially when estate owners resorted to Russian and Polish labor to meet their need for workers and to avoid hiring the urban unemployed whom they feared political radicalism had infected.[37] One such incident occurred on the lower Pomeranian estates of Count Fritz-Ulrich von Bismarck-Bohlen, when workers protested the firing of three of their compatriots who threatened Russian reapers.[38] By late 1920, the magistrates of Greifswald and Franzburg counties, where strikes were particularly disruptive, cautioned the landlords in their jurisdictions against the excessive use of Polish workers because layoffs of German workers, to which the use of foreign labor apparently encouraged, rendered their areas ripe for radical agitation.[39] Ultimately the authorities restricted the landlords' access to foreign seasonal labor.

Because the DLV met with uneven success in drawing farm laborers to its banner,[40] the union found it difficult to channel dissatisfaction among workers to its own ends. Either workers remained resistant to organization out of fear of, or loyalty to, their employers, or strikes broke out spontaneously without the DLV's sanction.[41] Nevertheless, conflict most consistently arose because of the hard-line attitude of Pomeranian estate owners who had simply presupposed the loyalty of their "people" and recoiled in anger as their assumptions proved incorrect.[42] Thus, strikes erupted when estate owners refused to recognize the arbitration committees that the state composed to achieve agreements between employers and employees, and especially when estate owners refused to conclude agreements that covered entire districts.[43] The workers also reacted when landlords fired workers they suspected of having joined the DLV, or when estate owners engaged Freikorps troops as strike breakers.[44] The strikers frequently and unashamedly resorted to violence against the "scabs" from the Freikorps or against employees otherwise unwilling to join the walkout.[45]

Constructing a detailed profile of the strikers is difficult. What can be ascertained correlates with the evolution of labor relations before and during the war in a way that opposed the vision of a rural community that estate owners would propagandize as the "reality" of the countryside. Strikes occurred over the entire province, not just in lower Pomerania where the leasing of estates generally meant tension between employers and employees. Protracted battles also took place in upper Pomerania where one might have expected the presence of resident owners to curtail unrest. The strikes resulted not only from the expectations that the Revolution raised, but also from the structural changes in the labor force that the estate owners themselves undertook before war broke out.[46] Having increasingly opted for short-term workers, Polish seasonal labor in particular, as well as having decreased the percentage of payment-in-kind (*Deputat*) in the compensation of more permanent workers, estate owners diminished the economic community of interest that customarily governed labor-owner relations.[47]

Official documents often blamed workers' dissatisfactions on outside agitators of the left—"in many instances people who have absolutely no

familiarity with rural relationships."[48] Indeed, young and temporary workers drawn from the generation most politicized by the war catalyzed much
of the unrest, and some of the strikers were urban and industrial workers
reluctantly imported to compensate for the labor shortages prevalent in
1919.[49] It is easy, certainly, to overgeneralize, for even older and more settled workers challenged their employers once the war experience exposed
them to wider influences,[50] and much depended on the way in which each
landowner treated his "people."[51] Klaus von Bismarck recalls the tense
moment when a worker shot his father, injuring but not killing his employer. Despite that obvious display of insubordination and even criminality,
Bismarck's mother answered the plea of the worker's wife that she see to the
man's well-being after he was jailed. The strike on the Bismarck estates
ended soon after.[52] Yet all told, the increased use of short-term workers, the
reduction of payment-in-kind, and the weakened bonds between employers and employees, which the common interest in the success of the harvest
once forged, promised long-term headaches for estate owners, who would
learn from their mistakes. Despite the oft-repeated claim of estate owners
that the goals of the strikers and their agitators equaled "Bolshevism" in the
countryside,[53] striking estate laborers expected neither land reform nor the
elimination of the estate-owning class. Rather they wanted to protect their
livelihoods against erosion by modernization and inflation.

The challenges that the left spawned eventually dissipated, victimized by
the SPD's unwillingness and inability to pursue more radical strategies
beyond the institution of parliamentary democracy. The Majority Socialists,
who dominated the left in Pomerania's towns, could not fully subordinate
the provincial administration to the workers' and soldiers' councils.[54] Their
attempts to purge it not only ran into insurmountable opposition from conservative peasant and farm laborer councils in the countryside, but also
succumbed to their own reluctance to undertake a thorough housecleaning.[55] Their hesitation accorded wholly with the position of their party
leaders in Berlin who influenced the provisional government, and with that
of the first Weimar cabinets who refused to undermine existing property relations. The victorious Entente powers, who wanted to prevent the German
Revolution from evolving into the extremes that occurred in Russia did
nothing to discourage that attitude. Even if the inclination to eliminate
estate agriculture had been stronger, the continuation of the Allied blockade until the summer of 1919 provided sufficient incentive early on to
abandon radical experiments conveying even a whiff of "Bolshevism."[56]

The result of the Reichstag elections of June 1920 and the Prussian Landtag elections of February 1921, both in Pomerania and elsewhere in the
state, revealed the ephemeral nature of the leftward drift during the first
postwar year. The right, namely the DVP and the DNVP, campaigned successfully on the slogan that most captured the sentiments of estate owners
eager to reassert their primacy; "lords of the household" (*Herr im Haus*).
Major losses for the SPD, a near catastrophic decline for the DDP, and a
surge of support for the DNVP ruined the prospects of even moderate re-

formism. Stralsund was the only district where the SPD retained its following among agricultural laborers. The more radical Independent Socialists (USPD) enjoyed but temporary success, polling over 16 percent in the Reichstag elections, declining noticeably in the Prussian Landtag campaign several months later.[57]

Moreover, the province's social hierarchies and civil administration had not deteriorated to the point that the landed elite could no longer assert its control. Pomerania became an outstanding—arguably the most outstanding—example of the ability of German conservative elites to limit the November Revolution. Exploiting their ties to the military in the numerous garrisons, as well as the surly right-wing Freikorps troops returning from the Baltic campaigns, estate owners resisted the left's efforts to unionize rural laborers, while employing strikebreakers as replacements. Workers fired for their union activity found themselves permanently blacklisted. Yet many landowners showed scarcely more concern for their Freikorps men who, once they had outlived their usefulness, roamed the countryside stealing.[58] The provincial administration, which still consisted of many from the landed elite, either openly encouraged the right's unsanctioned stockpiling of weapons, or looked the other way. Even Julius Lippmann, the Democrat who in March 1919 replaced the archconservative Georg Michaelis as provincial governor, succumbed to the landlords' claim that an "emergency" on the land endangered their own security and the Reich's food supply. Although paramilitary units and unregistered weapons continually threatened the public order, the Pomeranian administration acted halfheartedly in curtailing them.[59]

To add to that, the abortive right-wing putsch attempt of Wolfgang Kapp in March 1920 that many Pomeranian estate owners cheered did little to undermine their position despite their endorsement of treason. To be sure, a general strike that brought the putschists to their knees found wide support among Pomeranian workers, including estate laborers who demanded the disarming of estate owners, the removal of the Freikorps, and the dismissal of magistrates hostile to their desire for an improved standard of living.[60] In marked contrast to the prewar period, the position of the nobility in the civil administration declined. Yet less administrative or political housecleaning resulted than the counterrevolutionary insurgency should have demanded, particularly at the county level where nobles maintained an influence vastly disproportionate to their numbers in the population. As late as 1925 officials of noble pedigree comprised 42 percent of the province's county magistrates, although only 30 percent in the Köslin district.[61]

The political leanings of the magistrates lend added significance. In 1930, the DNVP commanded the loyalties of twenty out of twenty-eight county officers with the remainder drawn from the German People's Party (DVP).[62] Although their conservatism did not necessarily prevent them from approaching their constituents with a certain detachment, most magistrates accepted the provincial hierarchies. Similarly, the presidents (*Regierungs-*

präsidenten) of the three administrative districts retained a conservative cast, although with a few prominent exceptions. The Social Democrat Karl Simons served as president of the Stettin district from 1930 until 1932 when the Papen cabinet toppled the Prussian government, while Hermann Haussmann of the DDP presided over the Stralsund district from 1919 until its liquidation.[63] Few appointments at all levels of the provincial administration, however, arose from the ranks of the working class who obtained their experience in party politics. Jurists still predominated.[64]

The revitalization of Pomerania's main agrarian interest associations, the Chamber of Agriculture and the Agrarian League, accompanied the resurgence of the estate owners. By 1921 knight's estate holders chaired nineteen of the twenty-eight county commissions of the Chamber; ten of them were noblemen. Estate owners led over 40 percent of the various other associations under the Chamber's aegis, with peasant proprietors heading another 20 percent. Tenants, teachers, pastors, and communal officials directed the remainder.[65] The Rural League, expanded and reconstituted in 1920 as the National Rural League (*Reichslandbund*), emerged from the coalition of regional Rural Leagues of which Pomerania's was the largest. Ultimately, the Pomeranian league became the most powerful of the regional associations.[66] Like the DNVP that strove to democratize its image, the Rural League, at the initiative of its founders, Baron Ulrich Conrad von Wagenheim, scion of an ancient noble family with over fifteen estates, and the retired army major Johann Georg von Dewitz, placed peasants, agricultural laborers, estate administrators, pastors, and teachers on its provincial and local boards. The League exploited the popular rural resentment against the Controlled Economy's suppression of commodity prices and the high cost of industrial products ranging from machinery to clothing.[67]

Nevertheless, estate owners kept control of the Rural League that in Pomerania remained a highly centralized institution, in marked contrast to the decentralization of the League nationally. Estate owners, especially noblemen, ran the Rural League's county chapters.[68] They not only governed its everyday affairs at the district and provincial levels, they also served as its most prominent and articulate spokesmen. Representatives from Junker families such as the Schwerins, the Flemmings, and the Rohrs served as the League's directors during the Weimar era. The Rural League's propaganda and its repeated intercessions with the provincial administration and the military, particularly the notorious Second Army Command in Stettin, justified "emergency" measures on the grounds of national interest: The employment of regular army and Freikorps troops on estates, as well as the institution of a state of siege in strike-ridden areas, was essential, it argued. If the crops went unharvested and the animals went unfed, the German nation would go without food and the entire economy would suffer.

The triumph of estate owners became abundantly clear as the Rural League beat the DLV at its own game, organizing workers into "economically peaceful" unions under its own roof through which it proposed to "negotiate" wage contracts with the owners. The "Employees' Groups" of the Rural League represented an accommodation to reality in that they permitted bargaining between employees and employers in a way the Servants' Law had expressly forbidden. Yet their very subsumation in an organization that estate owners so completely dominated deprived workers of the leverage that they might otherwise have held. The Pomeranian model of labor relations served as the means by which the province's Rural League fatefully linked itself to the efforts of the former director of Krupp and newspaper magnate Alfred Hugenberg to organize a right-wing assault force against the Republic. Hugenberg looked to Dewitz and especially to the emerging Rural League leader, Hans-Joachim von Rohr-Demmin, to pose an alternative to trade unionism that even the DNVP accepted initially to attract a mass constituency.[69]

Both the DLV and the Ministry of Labor considered the Rural League's unions suspect: How could they represent their membership when estate owners so obviously ruled them, particularly when the laws permitting unionization and collective bargaining stipulated proof of autonomy?[70] Yet even though the republican courts did not recognize the Employees' Groups until 1930,[71] the League's ability to draw increasing numbers of agricultural laborers into the fold forced the Reich and Prussian governments early on to include such groups in contract negotiations, if only in an advisory capacity. "Given the great significance which employers in Pomerania ascribe to the participation of the Employees' Groups in wage agreements," admitted the Labor Ministry, "common sense" (*das Gebot der Klugheit*) demands that we permit such groups to join the negotiations in districts where their members are numerous, even if their illegitimate status in wage negotiations (*Tarifunfähigkeit*) formally stands." The DLV relented, although only on the condition that the representatives of the Rural League-sponsored unions were genuinely workers, not estate administrators or overseers.[72]

Johannes Wolf, a DNVP Reichstag deputy and national leader of the Employees' Groups tried to account for the Rural League's success among agricultural laborers.[73] In a statement that the League circulated in early 1919 to counter the DLV's charge that the Employees' Groups were the pawns of estate owners, Wolf evoked the myth of community on the land. No sharp divisions existed in the countryside between employers and employees as in industry where a worker survived not as a person, but rather as a number. The object of agriculture, Wolf suggested, was not the attainment of wealth but rather a "secure existence." Those who made large fortunes during the war could not be found in agriculture, only in industry. "Our agriculture is somewhat more constant, more stable," he said. "Agricultural holdings pass down from generation to generation. Furthermore, landownership is like a small business when compared to industry. There are no estates in Germany with a thousand workers, a number that in industry does not appear to be unusual." Argued Wolf, agricultural workers in Pomerania worked on the same estates across generations. Families who moved about were rare. Even as children, future employers played with the offspring of laborers. Thus the attempt to extend class consciousness to the countryside, suggested Wolf, could not but fail.[74]

That the Republic's painful beginnings with their devastating implications for Germany's ruling classes, should have galvanized Pomeranian landowners into utilizing repression, is scarcely surprising. Repression was a critical weapon in the arsenal of European landed elites in maintaining their political and social influence.[75] For many, such as the upper Pomeranian Junker, Ewald von Kleist-Schmenzin, the economic and material needs of the strikers upset them less than the political goals of the left that exploited agricultural laborers for their own ends. Though neither the Spartacists nor the USPD ever became very strong in the province, the threat of "Bolshevism," both as propagandistic ploy and sincerely held fear, justified radical countermeasures.[76]

Yet estate owners resorted to more subtle, and over the long term more effective, tactics. Paradoxically they exploited the well-etched divisions among rural laborers that existed despite their rhetoric depicting a community of producers, while less paradoxically they adjusted laborers' incomes so that more workers perceived a common interest with their landlords. Confronting an urbanized environment in which agricultural labor grew increasingly less attractive as a means of livelihood, particularly among the young, estate owners elevated the value of farm work over manual labor in the cities. Although working class opinion rarely intrudes unfiltered into official sources, intimidation alone cannot explain why Pomerania's agricultural laborers, many of whom became the eager recruits of a Socialist-sponsored union at first, succumbed so easily to reaggregation under the direction of estate owners.

The Pomeranian Rural League looked to the top of the ladder for support in its efforts to suppress leftist agitators and strikers, creating armed units drawn not only from the *Freikorps*, but also from coachmen, administrators, artisans, skilled workers, inspectors, and even peasants. Estate owners did not entrust their "day workers" (*Tagelöhner*) with weapons, especially not Polish seasonal workers whom the war had prevented from returning home. All told, the Rural League's unions drew their most committed recruits from skilled and other more settled laborers.[77] The propaganda that the Rural League and its allies addressed to the *Landarbeiter*, or at least those above the "rank" of a short timer, appealed to them not as workers, but rather as property holders, the owners of the means of production. Because relatively little of their income derived from wages, so the League asserted, the term "class" did not apply to them, remaining more appropriate to the wage-earning urban proletariat. While criticizing the DLV's fixation on raising the cash income of workers, and the union's claim that agricultural laborers lived lives of misery, Johannes Wolf asserted that such workers were genuinely small producers whose pigs, cows, and geese and a share of the estate's crop resulted in the same interest in strong commodity prices as their employers.[78]

The Rural League's propaganda described the worker's job as a "vocation" or "calling" (*Beruf*). That term not only dignified his work as above that of mere manual labor compensated by cash wages, but it also recalled its religious roots in Luther's valorizing of secular occupations. Thus, the "Bolsheviks" threatened not only the employer but also his laborer-partner, using their urban ideological poison of "class" to subvert the unity of the countryside. "You have the same interests as the employers," read one Rural League flyer. "If the employer goes under, so do you. If the employer can't give you *Naturalien* [payment-in-kind], then you will starve. Therefore, join the organization which wants to incorporate all of agriculture in one great mass—join the Pomeranian Rural League!"[79]

Discussions as to the propriety of using unemployed urban workers on the land to compensate for the labor shortages that the war created,[80] revealed the degree to which conservative circles insisted on the rural laborer's superiority to his or her "counterpart" in the cities. Such discussion usually deemed city workers unfit for farming because they could not overcome the gulf between wage labor and independent proprietorship. Schooling themselves in the art of growing grain and raising animals, thus living from what they themselves directly produced, would only bring frustration, especially when the acquisition of farming skills enhanced the farmer's standing: "Under no circumstances does the agricultural worker want to remain a wage laborer on the land, for he would stay poor his entire life and would never get anywhere." Moreover, the bond between rural laborer and employer provided the *Landarbeiter* with the means of obtaining "wealth." Employers sold cows cheaply from their own herds to their employees, and they supplied insurance and veterinary care. The experience of urban workers, not to mention such workers' status as outsiders (so these discussions implied) meant that they would not fit in.[81]

The Rural League ceaselessly appropriated the mythic rhetoric of community in opposing the class consciousness that it accused the DLV of instilling.[82] All rural producers, it argued, joined in a common undertaking, that of feeding Germany's population. All confronted the common enemy, the Controlled Economy, which failed to assign proper value to agricultural commodities. What was the DLV doing to counteract that? No real gulf existed between employers and workers because both owned and operated their own concerns. Thus both were equal partners in the enterprise that joined them. The DLV's disruption of that common bond by encouraging strikes alienated farm workers from their real interests and even violated the wishes of the Social Democratic leadership, which did not interpret the right of coalition so extremely.[83] The DLV's failing was not simply philosophical, but moral, for as Dewitz claimed, Marxism treated the relationship between employer and employee as a mere "contract of sale." By contrast, the employees' groups of the Rural League reflected "the personal and ethical relationship of mutual trust" that really existed on the land.[84]

Furthermore, the Rural League cultivated the workers' putative desire for advancement, not merely by manipulating the language of "vocation." It also advocated increasing the percentage of payment-in-kind in the contracts of workers to show that estate owners valued stability over casual labor in their workforce. They thus pegged the largest share of workers' incomes to the market price of key commodities. Prior to World War I, 68 percent of a worker's compensation consisted of payment-in-kind, but by 1924 the percentage increased to 74 percent, according to the more conservative estimate, 89 percent according to the more liberal.[85] Although that percentage declined once again after the stabilization (to 70 percent by 1928), the landowners' strategy contributed to the erosion of the DLV. Despite the DLV's objection that linking incomes to commodity prices represented the landlords' attempt to use the workers for their own benefit,[86] the material "rewards" provided in the permanent worker's contract protected him and his family from the ravages of hyperinflation, making the system a safe economic, as well as political, bet for employers.[87] The landlords rediscovered their appreciation for the loyalty and service of their employees, staging award ceremonies for *Landarbeiter* who received gold, silver, and bronze medals, depending upon the length of their tenure. According to an article in the *Pommersche Tagespost*, the principal mouthpiece of estate owner interests in the province, such occasions bore witness to the harmony that outlived the strikes. There were yet many workers who had toiled on the same estate for twenty, thirty, even fifty years, it reported.[88] The Employees' Groups proved so successful that by 1923 their membership reached sixty-five thousand, and the Rural League's leadership could express with pride that the impulse to strike had completely subsided.[89]

The upheavals of war and revolution endangered the hegemony of big landed property in the Prussian east. Nevertheless, Pomerania's estate owners, and especially its landed nobility, exploited all the resources at their disposal to retain control of their holdings, while reorganizing much of the rural labor force in a way that facilitated the compliance of the estate workers. In Italy at the same time, the militance of proletarianized sharecroppers and landless day laborers exploded to such a degree that "only" Mussolini's fascist *squadristi*, not the Italian state, could protect estate owners against losing control of the countryside.

To be sure, estate owners in the Prussian east, particularly in Pomerania, armed paramilitary troops against the strikers, moving well beyond propaganda or other avenues that imperial party and pressure group politics had once offered. The resort to illegal or half-legal measures to advance their cause could not but bode ill for the long-term survival of the Republic.[90] In Germany, however, the priorities of the moderate left and its pivotal position in government contained the radicalism that would have left the *Freikorps* the "only" wall between Pomerania's large landowners and land reform. Estate owners only helped their cause by utilizing a type of agricultural contract that discouraged the intrusions of working-class consciousness; contracts whose implicit bonding between employers and employees Italian landlords had abandoned more completely than their counterparts in Prussia.[91] Moreover, the myth of rural solidarity gave them ideological legitimation and coherence. Yet because the new government tolerated big agriculture in the name of productivity and restrained its purge of the military and public administration, it severely compromised even the limited goal of organizing farm labor. In the interwar period, the Prussian state government did become a bastion of moderate republicanism, surviving until Papen's coup against it in the summer of 1932.[92] Nevertheless, Pomerania's surviving social hierarchies, its incompletely purged administration, its numerous military garrisons, and its pacified labor force survived as evidence of the German Revolution's limits.

3

Power and Obligation: Social Relations in the Estate Villages After the Revolution

"EVERY SEAT IN God's house was taken, the altar decorated magnificently, not only with flowers as is normal on Sunday, but also with sheaves of grain and various fruits that were placed on both sides of the altar. The singing of the choir surrounded the divine service while the parishioners appeared thankful and festive. It was the celebration of the rural folk, a celebration of the peasantry. . . . For the country dweller it is obvious that during the harvest festival he should have a thankful heart and honor God upon whose blessings everything depends. The thoughts of this day scarcely require much effort from him to come to the surface: they are in his blood and they move his heart. For the true peasant, it is always a disgrace not to observe the harvest festival in church. This double belief, that God gave us the harvest and thus we must thank him, is for him somewhat natural."[1]

This tribute, drawn from a Pomeranian church periodical to depict the "harvest festival" (*Erntefest*), the most important rite of the agricultural calendar, had two complementary purposes. First, it invoked the distinctiveness of rural life, the organic connection between rural dwellers and the land and the deity who blessed both with the harvest. At the same time, the article honored the pious peasant as the backbone of the German Volk. That Pomerania's peasantry, notwithstanding significant local variations, main-

tained a reputation for being the most consistent in their Sunday participation lent credence to the myth so lovingly described in the text.[2] The
solemnity of the harvest thanksgiving, the author explained, further betraying his or her prejudices, escaped the appreciation of those living in the
metropolis. They were simply too far removed from the land to take seriously
the commitments of never-ending work, piety, and rootedness that rural
living imposed upon those most directly tied to it. Other church papers hastened to stress the bonds of community which the hardships of agriculture
necessitated. Those bonds not only transcended class divisions, they also
rendered irrelevant the very language of class itself. "The harvest has come
to an end," chanted one such piece. "The blessings break forth whence God
makes all estates (*Stände*) satisfied, rich, and merry. The God of ages still
lives; one can clearly observe it in so many of his labors of love. Thus we
praise him highly."[3] These papers reminded their readers that the harvest festival was a religious holiday, and that its observance should make full use of
the church's institutional presence.

Nevertheless, the harvest festival also took place beyond the confines of
the Evangelical parish churches, blurring the boundaries between the sacred
and secular to be sure, but reaffirming the themes of community and
common purpose so evident in the church periodicals. Ostensibly secular
periodicals, such as *Die Gutsfrau* ("Lady of the Manor"), a magazine for the
female elite of the countryside, highlighted many of the same issues as the
church newspapers in their articles on the festival, but they went on to
stress the larger obligations of the *Landvolk*: "All rural inhabitants, from the
day laborer to the estate owner, create through their own industry the conditions enabling life in the cities and the work that goes on there. Each
must assume this great responsibility himself, while organizing, calculating
and providing for his own livelihood. Moreover, he must be economical,
and whatever he and his household do not consume themselves he must
whenever possible pass it on to Prussians in modest circumstances, especially to those who are less well off and those who are suffering."[4]

Such populist images of the peasant, community, and calling that were intended to apply to all those involved in agriculture belied the ways in which
the harvest festival reaffirmed the hierarchies in Pomerania's social order. In
peasant villages to be sure, each household took turns hosting the *Erntefest*
in putatively democratic fashion, each designing the centerpiece of the festival, the arrangement of selected shoots of grain known as the harvest
"crown." In the estate villages throughout the Prussian east, however, the
manor house, its lord, and his family served as the focal point of the celebration year after year. Each ceremony disclosed the profoundly religious
connotations of noble dominion known simply as "lordship" (*Herrschaft*),
a feature that Pomerania's rural elite shared with other landed classes, and
artistocracies specifically.[5]

The fullest scenario comes from Count Christian von Krockow, who recalls the harvest festivals of his youth in Pomerania prior to the outbreak of
World War II. Normally, they opened with the congregation of the estate

workers and their families at the village church, dressed in their Sunday best, all prepared to extend the hallowedness of their ritual outward from the chapel door.[6] A procession to the manor house soon followed, led by the estate's steward and other overseers. Upon arrival at the estate, the procession formed a semi-circle around the front stairs of the house where the lord and his family waited. After the steward greeted the lordship on behalf of the group, the overseer presented the lord with the harvest crown; a bundle of rye, wheat, oats, and barley tied together with colorful ribbons. In unison, the estate's "people" then chanted a four-stanza poem praising the lordship and celebrating the harvest as God's miracle, assigning separate stanzas that contained the group's best wishes to each family member. No harvest festival would have been complete without a hymn, so at the instigation of the estate's first inspector, the group concluded by singing the chorale, "Now thank we all our God."

Acts of deference like those that the workers on the Krockow estates performed were by no means unusual. Klaus von Bismarck remembers the words of the song in praise of him: "We wish the young lord Klaus a fully-laden table, a baked fish and a bottle of wine so that he may always be happy."[7] Other songs such as this one from East Prussia implicitly warned the lord who did not farm his lands well. Nevertheless, the very fact that the poem accompanied the presentation of the wreath to the *Gutsherr* suggested that the lord who now received the evidence of the estate's bounty managed his property successfully: "Look upon your harvest wreath, your lordship . . . Our lord is a good lord who also harvests his field, and he is indeed a poor lord who cannot tend to his field."[8]

The harvest festival did not merely rank estate owners over their workers. They also displayed the hierarchies that existed among the workers themselves. The memoir of Liselotte Schwiers, the daughter of a Pomeranian landed family, recalls the ways in which the festival differentiated between German and Polish female workers, for the German women sported black bands on their hats while the Poles wore red.[9] Such distinctions appeared elsewhere in East Elbia, and they showed remarkable staying power. In Mecklenburg, for example, temporary laborers received fewer cigars than the regular employees when it came their turn to accept the estate owner's gifts.[10]

Rituals are supposed to create community by stripping away the social differentiations of everyday life to affirm a measure of equality among those who participate.[11] Such "liminality," as anthropologists term it, clearly did not apply to the ritualistic life of rural Pomeranians, however much the stress on community conformed to the core purpose of rituals: to remind the participants of their common bonds. All the same, the very spirit of community present in the province's celebrations attested to something even more significant: the ability of estate owners to demonstrate their commitment to the general welfare, and even impose it on their villagers. Paeans to Pomeranian estate owners, although undoubtedly conducted with the blessings of heaven, would have been less effective on earth (as measured by their prevalence and longevity) had they not underscored those experiences and values that landowner and rural worker had in common. And for sure, as the harvest festival continued into the evening, with dinner, dancing, and a fair amount of drinking, the everyday social barriers that divided the lordship from his "people" became a little less formidable, intensifying the personal bonds that existed between them.

Again, in a scene typical of East Elbia, the lord took the hand of the senior female employee to open the dancing, while the chief inspector of the estate accompanied the lady of the manor to the floor. The lord's children distributed little bags of candy to the offspring of the workers.[12] Often, amid the shedding of churchlike solemnity and the social inhibitions that such merriment encouraged, the personal interactions between the dominant and dominated mellowed. Thus Ewald von Kleist-Schmenzin, whose extended Junker family controlled twelve estates in the upper Pomeranian county of Belgard alone, temporarily suspended his customary reserve. He not only joined with élan in the drinking and dancing, he listened to his workers' concerns and wishes, albeit with an air of *noblesse oblige*.[13] The workers too often lost their composure, behaving in ways that would normally have been considered unacceptable, such as drinking excessively and brawling.[14] Such release also accorded with the purpose of ritual. The community that the harvest festival sustained arose from the awareness that the survival of all depended on the fertility of the land.

The harvest festival was only one occasion in which estate owners extended themselves for the community around them. Other holidays required their own commemorations. The Silesian nobleman Hellmuth von Gerlach, one of the few members of his caste to break with its conservatism, deplored the prewar Christmas celebrations of his family in which the *paterfamilias* reminded his hands of their sins during the previous year, even as he bestowed gifts upon them. In addition, the workers were expected to kiss the hands of the estate owner's children.[15] Similar yuletide scenarios survived war and revolution. On Christmas eve, Schwiers remembers, her father dispensed gifts to the local schoolchildren before presiding over a similar celebration at the estate house for his employees and the villagers. Toys for the children and cigarettes and practical gifts such as gloves and caps for the adults were the tokens of appreciation that the estate owner felt obliged to give. The gifts could not be distributed until her father had spoken and her mother had accompanied the group on her piano in the singing of "Silent Night." The women crossed their hearts and looked reverently toward heaven while their children hid behind their aprons. The solidly bourgeois origins of Schwiers' parents suggest that the performance of *noblesse oblige* was not confined to the nobility.[16]

To be sure, Pomeranian estate owners could not have relied exclusively on festivals to achieve their goals, for rituals, no matter how crucial to reminding communities periodically of the values they share, are of limited use in the day-to-day exercise of power. Regardless, Pomeranian rituals eloquently attested to the personal quality of the lordship's authority, the maintenance

of which was vital to preserving the estate communities. Agrarian modernization, with its substitution of wage, and mostly seasonal labor for the more
permanent economic bonds between employer and employee, only weakened the traditions of paternalism and deference east of the Elbe.[17] It did not
by any means undermine older patterns of social behavior, precisely because
the unique contractual relationship between estate owners and their permanent employees encouraged deeper social connections. Moreover, because
so many Pomeranian lords resided on their estates and assumed responsibility for the surrounding villages, such traditions persisted, even after the
November Revolution. The authority of estate owners survived with a minimum of conspicuous consumption, but with a maximum concern, at once
self-serving and sincere, for the cohesion of the countryside.

The Estate Community: From the Center to the Margins

The architectural style and furnishings of most manor houses in Pomerania
and the Prussian east spoke to the spartanism that estate owners professed
to value. Most certainly it made sense to transform the virtue of frugality
into a necessity given the straitened circumstances of most estates during the
republican years. Yet Prussian tradition played its role as well. Many estate
owners, and particularly the nobility, emulated the relative austerity that
characterized Hohenzollern absolutism, a habit that partially contributed to
that dynasty's ability to survive longer than the Stuarts and the Bourbons.[18]

To be sure, some manors such as Friedrichstein castle, the East Prussian
residence of the Dönhoff family, displayed the elegance of Italianate rococo.
It was constructed on such a scale that it dominated and integrated the
lakes and extensive gardens surrounding it.[19] The Putbus castle on the
island of Rügen with its rounded Florentine arches, the classicist castle of
the von Behr-Negendank family, the French Renaissance abode of the Heydens, as well as the enormous Baroque manor, Trieglaff, that belonged to the
Thaddens remind us that Pomeranian estates did not want for architectural
distinction.[20] Taken together, they caution us against accepting uncritically
the stereotypical "kraut Junker" (cabbage Junker), Count Eberhard Mölln,
whose son Kai befriends Hanno, the lad who exemplifies the decline of his
once prosperous mercantile family in Thomas Mann's *Buddenbrooks*. The
count's manor house appears in the novel as more like "a small farm, a tiny
valueless property without even a name. The passerby got the impression
of a dunghill, a quantity of chickens, a dog-hut and a wretched, kennel-like
building with a sloping red roof."[21]

Nevertheless, although large enough to accommodate a succession of
guests, most manor houses remained simple and unpretentious, often not
exceeding a single story for those situated on the more modest-sized estates.
Most commonly, they were constructed with nine windows across with the
three in the middle joining to form a gable. When compared to the country
houses or chateaux of the British and French aristocracies, the estate houses
of the East Elbian landed elite seemed modest and altogether rustic.[22]

Nor was this a case of plain exteriors concealing lush interiors: Formality, sophistication, and, if the landowner could afford it, expense graced a few of the manor house's more public rooms, while increasingly in the twenties, manor houses adopted the modern conveniences of electricity and indoor plumbing.[23] Yet here too, ostentation found its limits as families opted generally for a frumpish armchair ease. The receiving rooms of the Dönhoff castle contained elegant tapestries, Dutch paintings, and ornate plasterwork, suitable for displaying the family's distinguished history and current status before visitors. Its private quarters, however, reflected the military-like asceticism that the Dönhoffs practiced in their personal lives, an indication of the family's conviction that their social position carried the obligation of thrift.[24] Ewald von Kleist remembered the plainness of his father's estate house, a one-floor wooden structure whose massive and coarsely-constructed furniture bordered on the shabby. His own estate, although larger and minimally more comfortable, was inconspicuous architecturally.[25] The most prominent feature of noble *Gutshäuse* were the portraits of each family's ancestors and those of the Hohenzollern monarchs (notably Frederick the Great), as well as the mounted hunting trophies, the prized rewards of an equally prized means of recreation.[26] The book collections of the manor houses, although often so limited as to preclude using the term "library" to describe them, did in some cases betray the passing attempt at cosmopolitanism. They extended from international literary classics to contemporary sentimentalism to works conveying the prevailing German Nationalist taste—the writings of Frederick the Great and Ernst Junger to name the most prominent authors.[27]

Yet if luxury, ostentation, and great wealth could not in most instances express power, then the location of the manor houses in the center of the rural universe easily compensated. Often embracing several villages at a time, especially if the landowner owned more than one estate, the estates and their surrounding hamlets legally comprised the local administration for thousands of people until late 1927 when the Reichstag officially abolished them. At least one school and church completed the estate's domain, placing the education of rural youth and the care of the rural spirit, in spacial terms at least, within the estate owner's way.

In Pomerania, manorial districts incorporated over 55 percent of the total area and nearly 20 percent of the population, the highest in Prussia.[28] Although the estate owners no longer held the police and judicial authority that enhanced their power prior to the 1870s, the manorial districts conferred substantial benefit. Not only did the lord retain such responsibilities as supervising elections, but also the isolation of so many manorial districts deprived their residents of the autonomy they would have enjoyed as citizens of the communes, the primary unit of local government. To be sure, the landlord had to assume the public burdens and fiscal obligations, yet given the protest that erupted from conservative circles at the dissolution of the estate districts, the tax load of estate owners likely became greater through merger with the communes than previously.[29]

The estate owner's continuous presence as owner-in-residence solidified his power over his environs, notwithstanding the greater incidence of tenancy west of the Oder where, to name one prime example, the princes Putbus leased most of their seventy-five holdings either to peasants or to members of the bourgeoisie.[30] For Pomerania, the resident landlord emerged as the "norm" by the late nineteenth century, especially for the nobility, a pattern that continued despite war and revolution. Given the skill, discipline, and sophistication that agrarian modernization required, residence was crucial.[31] As a rule, tenants generally enjoyed less economic security than owners and faced considerable discrimination from lending institutions. Lease holders possessed less of a capital foundation than either estate owners or large scale peasants because they could put forth only their inventory as collateral.[32]

Large landlords usually hired administrators, or "inspectors," who managed the day-to-day affairs of the estates and oversaw the work in the fields. Administrators were particularly necessary when the owner possessed more than one estate or when the associational and political commitments of the estate owner did not permit continuous supervision.[33] The Chamber of Agriculture, for example, refused to designate the estate of Hans-Joachim von Rohr-Demmin as a teaching enterprise (thereby allowing it to serve as a training center for future farmers) because his "honorary activities" frequently kept him away from the manor.[34] Nevertheless the major decisions, and indeed the authority, rested with the owners. Even though the inspector sat atop the hierarchy of estate employees, his position beneath the lord was simply presupposed, unless he happened to be a nobleman himself.[35]

The residence of estate owners, particularly Junker families ensconced in Pomerania for generations, invariably extended their leadership of provincial institutional life beyond the major political and economic associations. The activities of Count Fritz Ulrich von Bismarck-Bohlen included not only work on behalf of the DNVP, but also the presidency of the Pomeranian Auto Club, a position he held for several decades.[36] The obituary of Konrad Tessen von Heydebreck, scion of an ancient noble family who died in 1926 after being thrown from his horse, documented an extensive list of commitments that flowed logically from having owned and managed three "model" estates. The Veterans' Association (*Kriegsverein*), the Rural League, the county legislature (*Kreistag*) (including its executive committee), the DNVP, the church and the various occupational *Genossenschaften* would miss him, read the eulogy, as much as the workers, and supervisory personnel on his estates would feel bereft of his direction.[37]

Nowhere did the significance of residence become more evident than in the narrow range of occupations that noble families traditionally considered appropriate for their sons. Conforming to Prussian tradition, all males served in the military barring disability or other unusual impediment, but younger sons counted on a commission in the army or a post in the civil administration.[38] Pomerania's most prominent Junker families included those whose estates were sufficiently numerous to permit even younger sons a landed inheritance. Richard von Flemming, the director of the Pomeranian Chamber of Agriculture throughout the Weimar period, was the sixth son in his family, yet he owned four moderate-sized estates, including his primary residence, Pätzig. Ewald von Kleist, a *Gutsherr* par excellence, was similarly blessed with the 3,500-hectare estate of Schmenzin and four others despite being the second son in his family.[39] Yet as a rule, younger sons expected to serve out their careers in service to the state. The family tree of the Schwerins, Junkers who were prominent in lower Pomerania, reveals the symbiosis that existed between the military and "Junkerdom." The Schwerins' genealogy included 280 officers, as opposed to only six doctors.[40] Forty men of the Borcke family served during World War I, several of them as generals. Thirteen of them lost their lives.[41] "There is an old expression," explained one Pomeranian nobleman retrospectively, "One cannot become a peasant; he must already be one. While it [the saying] does not apply entirely to soldiering, it comes close enough."[42]

Unlike Great Britain, all male offspring of a noble family inherited the title, or the prefix "von," not simply the firstborn son.[43] Yet special responsibilities awaited the eldest male. After a stint in the army or the bureaucracy, he assumed control of his father's property upon the latter's death or incapacity, although he was expected to provide rooms and a share of the estate's yearly profit for his siblings.[44] Increasingly, agrarian modernization demanded that male heirs became inspectors, either to their fathers or to other estate owners, in order to learn the necessary skills before coming into their inheritance.[45] Although a young man standing to inherit an estate could easily consider himself privileged, misgivings could also intrude, even among bourgeois estate owners who might have insisted on more choices. Liselotte Schwier's father had acting in his blood, and on numerous occasions his talent as a thespian surfaced. Yet once the obligation of managing his family's knight's estate beckoned, he obeyed the commitments prescribed for him. "Yes, father would have liked so much to have become an actor," she explains, "but at that time, one could not do that. One became either an officer or a farmer, and that was that!" It was left to his grandchildren, resettled in West Germany after the war, to act on their suppressed inheritance.[46]

The case of Klaus von Bismarck illustrates the pressures that could derail an unorthodox career choice, even though his family did not insist that he follow the usual expectations of a first-born male. Fully anticipating that at least one of his four sons would follow in his footsteps as lord of the Jarchlin and Kniephof estates, Bismarck's father stipulated in his will that his eldest should pursue the profession of his choice; to become a doctor like his uncle on his bourgeois mother's side. Yet his father's untimely death in 1928 forced Bismarck to forgo his plans. Instead he quickly undertook agricultural training so as to assume the burden that had so suddenly fallen to his mother. Only his mother's remarkable success in rescuing the estates from debt despite the agrarian crisis gave Bismarck some latitude. Yet the combination of an uncomfortable relationship with the chief administrator of an estate that employed him, the "synchronization" (*Gleichschaltung*) of the Stahlhelm of which Bismarck was a member, and the expectation of universal military conscription propelled him again into a very Junker-like occupation. He joined the army as an officer.[47]

The Weimar Republic, however, posed a direct challenge to the undeniable, if at times stultifying, security that such a narrow set of options provided, offering one solid explanation as to why so many nobles could not make their peace with the "system." The severe limitations on the size of the German officer corps and the increased competition nobles faced in public administration from the political appointees of the prorepublican parties not only reduced the number of acceptable career opportunities, but also restricted the accustomed avenues of caste sociability. As compensation came the recommendation from a periodical addressed to an aristocratic readership that young nobles pursue careers in occupations such as the Evangelical clergy that most would previously have rejected as unsuitable. Elders sponsored retreats that enabled their offspring to socialize with their own kind, a substitute for the shared experiences and caste cohesion that military and state service once granted. Ultimately the Third Reich's massive rearmament program restored the traditional choice of the military as a viable option for the sons of the nobility, a point that helps to account for the favor with which eastern Prussian nobles at first greeted the Nazi regime.[48]

The attitudes of Pomeranian estate owners, whether bourgeois or noble, toward their property are difficult to characterize as unambiguously premodern. Pomerania's geography and climate, rather than being obstacles to agricultural modernization as such, limited the choices in crops that landowners could successfully grow. Intensification, mechanization, and the search for better strains of seed became increasingly common as landowners struggled to improve their yields in a highly competitive world market. Yet throughout Pomerania and the Prussian east, innovation took time to supplant perceptions that older ways worked best. Ewald von Kleist-Schmenzin eschewed unnecessary risk, adopting machinery only when its worth proved superior to its trendiness.[49] Regret was expressed when estates abandoned their self-sufficiency in food production; when estate-owning families instead bought commodities on the open market because they were produced more cheaply elsewhere. Furthermore, the use of horse-drawn teams did not disappear overnight.[50]

More important, the land represented much more than simply a means of livelihood, and more than a profit-making enterprise.[51] During World War II, Käthe von Normann, the lady of the six-hundred-hectare estate, Barkow, near Greifenberg confessed her astonishment when a left-leaning French prisoner of war assigned to work for her characterized Count von Bismarck-Osten of Plathe as the very paradigm of capitalism, a system he detested. It never occurred to her to see the Pomeranian landowner, a member of the Iron Chancellor's extended family, in that light.[52] Although bourgeois estate owners may well have been more self-consciously capitalist, or at least more disposed to modernize than nobles,[53] they were by no means immune to the mystique of land-owning. Liselotte Schwiers's near idyllic description of life on her family's estate conveys the impression that at least some non-noble *Besitzer* shared the reverence toward the soil that emerges so clearly in the memoirs and autobiographies of the nobility.[54] The estate provided a sense of place, an identification with nature, indeed a *Heimat* that no other residence, no matter how attractive, could offer.

Because the estate represented both a family trust and the bedrock of noble power, there could be no social influence, no political leverage, indeed no nobility at all without land. Even suitable alternative occupations for young noblemen were but substitutes for owning an estate and most appropriate for superfluous sons, despite the importance of such occupations in extending the nobility's influence. The implicit connections between land and power found expression in the periodical *Pommern Adel*, the mouthpiece of the provincial chapter of the Association of German Nobility (*Deutsche Adelsgenossenschaft*). Such sentiments intensified especially after stabilization when the indebtedness of estates began to mount.[55] "We are after all from the land," asserted a lengthy column about the Junkers: "Here lie the roots of our strength, our connection with our native (*bodenständig*) people, [a connection], which has gotten lost in the city that through state service has come to provide economic support for our impoverished members: One can now indeed say that the family who no longer has any land, or who has no other sound (*fundierte*) assets to call its own is not far from the end. Then one has to say as a result that the nobleman who has lost his soil can only count on a few more generations."[56] To extend the logic of that thought one step further raises a telling question: Would that mean that such unfortunate families would become indistinguishable from the bourgeoisie? That noble estate owners often had difficulty conceiving of themselves as "capitalists," despite the quest for profit and their integration in the international marketplace, indicates that "traditional" or "premodern" attitudes coexisted readily with agrarian modernization.

No activity confirmed the relationship between estate ownership and dominion quite like the hunt, a ritual that resumed its importance after stabilization. Unlike Great Britain where a powerful class of tenant farmers fiercely resisted the destruction of their crops by marauding horses bearing aristocratic riders, Pomeranian estate owners retained greater latitude to pursue a sport that brought joy and release to many of them, despite the problems caused to foresters. Although more mindful of conservation than others of his caste, hunting on horseback in the forest brought Ewald von Kleist peace of mind that contrasted sharply to the alienation he felt whenever his business took him to a city.[57] Similarly, other memoirs convey the bonds between the hunters, the animals (both the ones that were ridden and those that were pursued), and nature.[58] Yet the hunt went beyond the experience of the great outdoors. It brought together relatives and caste compatriots in a display of social solidarity; one that reaffirmed the ancient aristocratic right of lordship, the command of fields and forest.[59] Food and entertainment usually followed each outing, the expenses for which comprised a regular item in the estate's budget until economic hardship imposed restraint.[60]

Domination cannot exist without the dominated, however. The power of estate owners shone most clearly in the relatively tranquil character of rural labor relations after the strikes dissipated. Without a doubt, the docility of the estate workers of East Elbia can be exaggerated. Hans Graf von Lehndorff, formerly of East Prussia, recalls the attitude of his grandfather, Elard von Oldenburg-Januschau, a powerful figure in conservative politics, who led the effort to reacquire the estate of President Hindenburg that had fallen into bankruptcy. Even after the November Revolution, according to Lehndorff, Oldenburg treated the workers on his estate as he did his children, denying the relevance of urban labor relations to the countryside. To make his point to a visitor from Berlin, Oldenburg ordered his shepherd to "tell the gentleman here whose Charles you are." "I am the gracious lord's Charles," came the reply.[61] That story imparts a primitive conception of the subservience of estate workers in keeping with Oldenburg-Januschau's well-deserved reputation as a reactionary.

In fact, Pomerania's sparce population and out-migration presented serious difficulties. Until the late 1920s when the agrarian crisis struck with full force, the reports of the Pomeranian Chamber of Agriculture repeatedly complained about the lack of single workers, not to mention laborers with families. Lured by the higher wages, shorter workdays, better housing, greater attractions, and individualism of the cities to which improved transportation exposed them, rural laborers broke their contracts and moved on. The sons of peasants who would normally have signed on for training in the pedagogical academies or enlisted in the military followed suit.[62] Although the largest percentage of the emigrants resettled in Berlin, a considerable number gravitated to Pomerania's own cities and towns, Stettin especially.[63]

Such mobility attested to the waning appeal of country life and farm labor, although it was more evident among younger workers in whom the prospect of unemployment compensation was enticing (or so employers alleged) when no suitable jobs existed in the towns. Moreover, young people valued urban wages more than payment-in-kind, because of the low return on rye and potatoes. Pomerania's beaches especially attracted young women who found better pay and working conditions as household servants to vacationers. Finally the cramped housing of the vast majority of agricultural laborers ill-accommodated the wish for autonomy of young adults.[64] Nevertheless, emigration did not destabilize the position of large landlords, not only because rural hierarchies showed remarkable resilience, but also because on balance, the flight from the land affected regions where estates were less numerous than those with significant numbers of peasants.[65]

The sheer number of agricultural laborers, most of whom worked for the big landowners,[66] provides yet another way of appreciating the importance of estates in Pomerania: According to the 1925 census, workers comprised

43.3 percent (45.2 percent if one includes artisans and other helpers) of those working full-time in the primary sector, as compared to 14.6 percent for the peasantry in all categories of landholding (from five to one hundred hectares). Remarkably, the number of estate laborers actually increased by 8.5 percent over the last prewar census in 1907, revealing a very different trend from the Reich as a whole.[67] Relatively few occupied the top rung of the agricultural laboring class consisting of skilled workers or workers with a high level of responsibility, such as steward (*Hofmeister*), milker, blacksmith, wheelwright, coachman and gardener. The great mass distributed themselves across the three "lower" categories of permanent contract workers receiving payment-in-kind (*Deputatarbeiter*), *Gesinde*, and free laborer.

As was common in the eastern Prussian provinces, the "deputatist" composed the stable backbone of the estate workforce in Pomerania, especially east of the Oder where their ratio to free workers stood at nine to one.[68] Moreover estate owners, especially in Pomerania, not only laid claim to the labor of the deputatist's family, but they also usually expected the deputatist to secure and support additional workers by his own means, known by the difficult-to-translate term *Hofgänger* (auxiliaries). Wives and children of deputatists each received an hourly wage smaller than that of the head of the family. The *Gesinde*, strictly defined as "servants," consisted mainly of unmarried farmhands (*Knechte*) and maids (*Mägde*) under the age of thirty whose compensation included room and board as well as a small wage. Although peasants employed such workers who in turn lived with the peasant's family, most found positions on the large estates. Because many of them became deputatists later, service on the estates assumed continuity over the generations.

At the bottom of the rural hierarchy resided the "free" laborers, short-term workers temporarily housed in barracks and pressed into service in periods of high demand. This category included some whose status approached that of a deputatist, but most in this group maintained few durable ties to their employers, and the relationship between employer and employee was correspondingly distant. Distinctions developed between the free workers who owned their own small plots or lived in the nearest town but worked periodically on the estates as a second source of income, and the truly landless, most of them Poles, who roamed the countryside in search of work. Seasonal workers found employment principally in the sugar beet growing regions of the province, and especially in lower Pomerania where they comprised 60 percent of the workforce.[69]

While before the war, estate owners employed fifty-five thousand Polish workers,[70] the number of *Saisonarbeiter* declined afterward because the Republic restricted the importing of foreign labor.[71] Against the cutbacks, estate owners argued that only Polish laborers could undertake the back-breaking tasks of digging potatoes and harvesting sugar beets, particularly in lower Pomerania where fewer peasants deprived large landlords of a supplemental labor pool.[72] With some success, estate owners exploited exceptions in the regulations, for according to the 1925 census, Pomerania ranked second in the Reich behind Saxony in the use of foreign seasonal workers.[73] Yet the living and working conditions of Polish laborers matched the desperation that forced their migration to Germany in the first place: overpopulation on the land. The substandard, overcrowded, and often filthy quarters of the Polish contingent in which women and children predominated, produced high rates of illegitimacy, infant mortality, and infanticide.[74]

Frequently, estate owners confronted the charge that their hiring of foreigners endangered the national interest, and officials on guard against illegal aliens closely monitored hiring practices.[75] The responses of the landlords betrayed the construction of rank in the countryside, as much the product of the condescension of German estate laborers as of the employers themselves. Polish manual labor was required, estate owners rejoined, because the machinery was unsuitable and periods of high demand, particularly in the sugar beet districts, dictated seasonal employment if the harvest was not to rot.[76] Estate owners further claimed that Germans would not accept such jobs because they entailed constant bending and cutting in nasty weather and because it forced them to live in cramped, impersonal barracks. Employers rejected the use of unemployed German industrial workers, an oft-discussed idea, because such workers disliked farm labor, refused the available housing, and thus did not perform well.[77]

As a result, Polish laborers occupied the very margins of the estate communities, becoming, in fact, the negative reinforcement of those communities. They were condemned to reside there not only because of their nationality, seasonality, and presumed inferiority, but also because of their Catholicism. "Polish and Catholic were synonymous concepts," remarked one pastor, "and resonating in those concepts partly overtly, partly covertly, was a moral devaluation."[78] For the Socialists and Communists, the Poles represented the landlords' quest for cheap labor at the expense of Germans, particularly after the depression set in.[79] Not even the pretense of solidarity existed between Poles and their employers, as Poles were reminded daily of their status as pariahs. Education for their children, unemployment insurance, and public health services were rarely extended to them.[80]

A few Poles, such as Käthe von Normann's farmhand, "the good old Pole" Anton, won their employer's trust: Anton had worked in her village since 1914, had been detained through the war, and had stayed thereafter (she does not explain how). Accustomed to kissing his mistress's hand as was the Polish custom, Anton wept bitterly when the Poles forced Normann to leave her estate forever at the close of World War II.[81] Nevertheless, most Poles escaped the kind of concern that estate owners directed to their permanent employees. Catholic clergymen fretted over the moral development of seasonal workers because, in their view, estate owners did not supervise them properly.[82] The "Polish cattle" who did not return home during the winter as required wandered forlornly in search of work to tide them over, attracting the combined pity and contempt from officials who worried about their potential drain on the public purse.[83] The Polish press routinely cited evidence of mistreatment, including physical abuse: "These poor people who work all day for few wages and an even worse maintenance are beaten with fists, rods and pitchforks by the inspector, and finally by the owner's son, so that a number of people have been injured. But there are not just the beatings. The overseer constantly threatens the people with a loaded revolver and fires it so that he may have fatally shot thirteen persons already." Another report described the brutality exhibited toward Polish workers as having taken on a "mass character, above all in the northern and eastern parts of Germany."[84] Despite the DLV's attempts to organize such laborers,[85] the environment in which the Poles toiled discouraged the shift from diffuse alienation and dissatisfaction to a coherent resistance.

The method of payment for services rendered, which estate owners exploited previously to contain the strikes, continued to separate the *Landarbeiter*. While free laborers settled primarily for wages, only a small proportion of the deputatist contract consisted of cash. Rather, their pay included housing provided at the owner's expense and a small plot of land upon which each worker could grow crops, as well as raise the animals and game that his employer provided. In addition, deputatists received firewood and a fixed share of the estate's crop, and estate owners allowed grazing privileges on the land they set aside for that purpose.[86] West of the Oder, the DLV's pressure succeeded in assigning compensation according to the laborer's performance rather than the landowner's assessment of the worker's family needs.[87] Nevertheless, the deputatist contract cemented an economic relationship between the owner, the deputatist, and the deputatist's family that fostered an unusual degree of dependence.[88]

The cash compensation of permanent workers in Pomerania and the Prussian east, although it improved noticeably under the Republic, lagged behind that of unskilled industrial workers, especially considering the longer hours they devoted throughout the year, twenty-nine hundred as opposed to twenty-four hundred for their industrial counterparts.[89] Together a deputatist, his wife, and one son earned a cash wage of eighty-six pfennigs per hour, or the equivalent of the hourly wage of one unskilled construction worker. Moreover, the demand for adequate housing exceeded the supply.[90] To be sure, the comparison between industrial and agricultural workers might appear inappropriate because the former received no payment-in-kind. Yet measuring Pomeranian farm workers against their counterparts in the west is revealing. The total income of Hessian agricultural workers in the same category averaged 70 percent higher than those in Pomerania throughout the interwar period.[91]

There were other rewards, however. Those workers who did not comprise the flotsam and jetsam of the migrating agricultural labor force could consider themselves an elite, although it is far from clear whether they believed themselves a "labor aristocracy," much less property-owning members of the petty bourgeoisie as the Rural League claimed during the strikes. They included not only the deputatists whose contractual arrangements gave them a vested interest in the estate that could not have been true for those below them, but also the household servants. The precariousness of such an arrangement was evident, given that workers could be fired, particularly on political grounds. Yet the interdependence between such workers and their employers flowed deeply enough to survive periodic tensions. The writer of one Evangelical Church visitation report, struck by the continuity of families under contract from generation to generation, agreed with the argument of Johannes Wolf, the laborer who chaired the Rural League's Employees' Groups: "As a rule, the lordship proves itself responsible for the workers, and in turn, the workers in many cases feel themselves bound to their lordship in a partnership for life."[92] Another village pastor observed that the Zitzewitz family engaged workers whose own families the estate had employed for more than one hundred years.[93]

Indeed Evangelical pastors, although separated by education and station from the lower classes of Pomeranian rural society, serve as effective, if admittedly imperfect, channels for transmitting the attitudes of agricultural laborers, not least because the church committed itself to mediating between the various social constituencies it served. After World War II, pastors who had formerly held parishes in Pomerania often made a point of recalling the feeling of community that seemed to have existed. Noted one, the workers in his parish, because of the income they derived from their animals and their garden economy, could provide advanced training for their children, either higher education beyond primary school or the acquisition of a craft. In his parish, peasants and laborers "built a close village community and willingly subordinated themselves to the fair, and for the most part, able leadership of the *Gutsherrschaft*."[94] Another remarked that all members of his church who were engaged in agriculture referred to themselves as "peasants" (*Bauern*), from the lowliest laborer to the estate owner himself, a comment that suggests a common self-understanding and purpose.[95]

Certainly other recollections betray disagreement with the idyllic picture just presented. They either deny the prevalence of upward mobility or, conversely, admit worker dissatisfaction, even if they agree with the premise that communal bonds indeed existed.[96] As a result, preserving the community against the possibility of its fracture required space for the self-assertion of the dominated. Thus, household servants periodically contradicted their masters' orders if they had been in service long enough to establish their basic trustworthiness, and if the issue of "dispute" was minor. The Krockow family butler, Vietzke, for example, ignored the instruction of the lady of the manor to turn up the heat during a dinner after a winter hunt because it caused him discomfort. That and other seemingly trivial incidents added up to a place of respect in the family's estimation.[97]

The landowners' children played their part in granting the estate's employees opportunities for exercising their skills and gaining authority so as to lend credibility to the myth of "community." Children observed the rules of politeness that required deference to adults, regardless of social station. Some of those children who in their advanced age looked back remembered the practical skills and crafts that their families' servants and *Landarbeiter* taught them. Despite the obsession with social boundaries that governed the outlook of the nobility especially, the respect for manual labor and the value of hard physical work strengthened the belief of estate owners in the interdependence of rural society and the contributions of each member to it.[98]

Friendships between the offspring of estate owners and the children of rural workers not only arose but were considered obligatory. Reaching out to their social inferiors comprised one of the Christian duties that those of higher station performed for those beneath them,[99] corresponding to Johannes Wolf's assertions during the agricultural laborers' strike. Because they coexisted with the hierarchies that structured the lives of their parents, childhood friendships show how the seeming antithesis of hierarchy and community merged in daily life. Liselotte Schwiers would like to have spent the night in the alcove of the worker's cottage that housed her best friend, Erna, the daughter of one of the estate's hands—in the single bed that accommodated six children. Her mother, however, would not permit it, wholly consistent with the decision of other *Gutsfrauen* not to permit their children to dine at a laboring family's table.[100] Such unwritten but strict rules were observed outside Pomerania as well: In Silesia, the estate's park remained off limits to the employees' children except on special occasions.[101] Access to education ultimately reaffirmed the social rank-ordering of the children of employers and employees. The nobility in particular preferred to take on private tutors instead of sending their children to the village school where they would unavoidably mingle with the *hoi polloi*. In any case, the advanced education that noble children received beyond that, the gymnasium and university, was in most cases, well beyond the reach of their playmates.[102] The children of estate owners who attended the *Volksschule* were relatively rare, and one suspects, mainly the offspring of bourgeois proprietors.[103]

Still, the constraints on the landlord's people were as much self-imposed as coerced. In many regions of Pomerania, as well as the Prussian east as a whole, the attitudes of most workers who fell within the orbit of estates could only be described as conservative and entirely in line with the perceptions of rank that most assuredly existed. Witness the value that Grenda, the head coachman on the Dönhoff estate, placed on military service: His time in the army had not only served him well, he thought, it also served in the present as an organizational model for the servants under his "command." In fact in many instances, the deputatists' small and spartan quarters featured lithographs of Jesus praying, a stag in the forest, wedding pictures, and especially photographs of the male family members in uniform.[104] The Dönhoff household staff observed strict rules of hierarchy that regulated even the protocols of dining. The cook and housekeeper ate apart from the kitchen maids, while the assistant coachman dined in the passageway.[105] Dönhoff's descriptions of the way in which the estate's employees insisted upon ranking each other find parallels in other accounts.[106]

Although a high Social Democratic vote persisted throughout the 1920s in the Stralsund district where the leasing of estates was more common, most other rural areas of Pomerania eerily replicated the unpoliticized conservatism that, notwithstanding the November Revolution, had long been evident. "The predominantly agricultural district," stated one church visitation report from the Wollin diocese, "shows a strong adherence to traditional customs. One pays little attention to the reform of all relations since 1918, and the population does not want to know much about it. The majority holds fast to the black, white, and red flag."[107] Another pastor commented retrospectively that the workers in his parish always made him feel at home as he went upon his daily rounds: Despite the anticlericalism of the workers' and soldiers' councils in the towns, the revolution seems not to have affected the rural folk to whom he ministered.[108] A third also confirmed that the councils near his parishes of Gross and Klein Dubberow had achieved but limited success in stirring up the rural labor force, and in fact estate workers nearly drowned a council member who confiscated a pickling barrel from a widow. The workers, he professed, "trusted their pastor more than they did the agitators from the city. As a matter of fact, their growing children were loyal members of the youth association."[109] That prevailing conservatism even infected workers off the estates, such as the Communist road workers who once doffed their hats to the Stahlhelm leader, Rittmeister Bernd von Wedel-Fürstensee.[110]

The ties between the manorial lordship and the estate's employees thus ensured that the solidarity of agriculture, the thematic cornerstone of agrarian propaganda in its confrontation with the Republic, was no mere chimera. Yet what about Pomerania's peasantry? To what extent did peasants conform to the mythic vision to which aristocratic estate owners adhered that presupposed a common purpose and vocation uniting all rural producers; a vision that transcended the differences of class and caste?

Memoirs and official documents betray peasant independence, stubbornness, and a considerable degree of status consciousness that at minimum affirmed their position above the mass of laborers who toiled on the estates. Normally that superiority did not extend into the afterlife because peasants and estate workers were frequently buried together in the same cemetery. Yet more often than not, peasants deliberately sat apart from the *Landarbeiter* at Sunday church services in order to mark their own distinction.[111] If estate employees perpetuated a caste mentality among themselves, Pomerania's peasants took pains to separate themselves from those beneath them. The social distinctions emerged every bit as clearly between peasants and estate owners. The discrete family plots of the *Gutsbesitzer* testified once again to the hierarchies governing the countryside that coexisted with the maintenance of community.[112]

Moreover, conflict between peasants and estate owners erupted frequently over subjects ranging from the right of tenancy on church-owned lands to the quality of representation that peasants received from the Rural League and the Chamber of Agriculture, an issue that would become particularly nettlesome after the onset of the agrarian depression. In many cases to be sure, harmony prevailed and peasants adopted the methods of intensification that the estate owners taught them.[113] In addition, those peasants who derived part of their income as free laborers on the estates could not help but fall to some extent within the orbit of the lordship. Nevertheless, competition often reigned between independent proprietors great and small,[114] and had the number of exclusively peasant villages been larger, so too might have been the challenge to estate agriculture.

As it stood, however, organizations such as the Peasants' League (*Bauern-bund*) and the Peasants' Association (*Bauernverein*) that elsewhere in Germany articulated the interests of small landowners, frequently attacking estate owners in the process, remained underdeveloped and unable to channel peasant resentments into an effective opposition.[115] Thus, the overwhelming presence of estate owners ensured that the rural community could sustain some conflict without risk of upheaval, while the valorization of the peasantry that appeared in so much agrarian propaganda acknowledged its need for recognition, if not its claims to power. Moreover, if that propaganda failed to convince peasants that the established agrarian interest organizations best served their needs, which increasingly became the case during the agrarian crisis, then an important political option remained—voting for National Socialism.

Born to Rule, Born to Serve

The belief in the lord's inherent superiority arose logically and unsurprisingly from the estate owner's role as head of the household, broadly defined to include the surrounding villages.[116] For long-resident Junker families, in particular, their authority came quite simply from God, a view consistent with Pomerania's centrality to the Awakening. Religious life on the Silesian estate of the von Jordans, a noble family of Huguenot descent, consisted of regular Sunday vespers in which every family member carried out his or her designated role, be it playing a chorale on the piano, reading from the prayer book, or reciting the Lord's Prayer.[117] Yet religious observance often took place more frequently than that as Countess Dönhoff's account of her upbringing in East Prussia indicates: Everyone attended the daily morning services in the castle, not only the immediate family, but also the household servants.[118] Daily devotionals were likewise commonplace on Pomeranian estates.[119]

On the one hand, religious practice underwrote the view that God structured human life both hierarchically and communally. Every individual belonged, implicitly at God's behest, to a particular station, and in turn, the maintenance of those social stations assured the ultimate blessing of social harmony. "In the pre-modern world," explains Count Christian von Krockow as he describes the environment of his youth, "there is no equality, but only a rank-ordering of inequality. One is born into it and birth defines one's destiny. Whether one is the oldest or youngest son of his father makes a big difference." That biologically grounded principle applied "equally to the nobleman, the peasant and the hired farmhand [*Knecht*]." Although difficult to accept, hierarchy brought certain advantages: "In such an order, the principle of birth is the means of avoiding conflict: We cannot use human power to dispute that which God or nature preordains."[120]

On the other hand, religion imposed obligations. Not only did the estate owner have to manage his family's lands well, he also had to look after his workers and their dependents, at least the permanent ones. "It was unthinkable," recalls Gerhard von Jordan, "that a lord simply abandon a pensioner or an employee unable to work to his or her fate. Everyone got his living quarters and his payment-in-kind [*Deputat*] for free." Consistent with rural practice, the mentally impaired or otherwise disabled were considered the village's responsibility, not wards of the state.[121] The very goal of avoiding conflict demanded the sort of open handedness that perpetuated the cohesion of the rural community. "The social arrangement by which those who enjoyed privileges were in return expected to exhibit greater concern for society than for their own person," Countess Dönhoff remembers, "was reinforced by the awareness that one was part of a close-knit community.[122] For those landed families who survived the expulsion at the end of the Third Reich, and sought to make permanent their past in memoirs, the evocation of a community lost became the rationale for committing their memories to paper.[123]

In contrast to the sentimentality implicit in the reminiscences of survivors, the estate owners of the Weimar period, most prominently the nobility, confessed more forthrightly the advantages that enforcing their convictions brought to their class. They asserted without hesitation the nobility's inherent fitness to sit atop the rural hierarchy. Thus they made no secret of their distaste for the Republic because the very notions of popular sovereignty and parliamentary government, quite apart from the Republic's expanding urban culture, threatened the integrity and viability of the rural social order. The vehemence with which Ewald von Kleist attacked the strike of the agricultural laborers, for example, accorded smoothly with his belief that landownership secured the nobility's authority. If the strikers, with the Republic's help, had succeeded in violating the rules that governed the use of the land, then the nobility as a caste would have disintegrated, pure and simple.[124] The tension that existed between Klaus von Bismarck's bourgeois mother and his aristocratic grandmother stemmed in large part from the older woman's belief that her daughter-in-law represented the intrusion of alien liberal ideas from Berlin that could only prove threatening to the countryside.[125]

Socialism was an even greater anathema not only because it accompanied the imposition of an alien system, but also because it promised social leveling. The moderation of the SPD provided little comfort: Immediately after the revolution, Elizabeth von Thadden, a committed Christian social activist whom the Nazis executed for her role in the July 20, 1944 plot against Hitler, conducted discussions with Social Democrats from Berlin on such topics as socialization and the status of agricultural laborers. Yet her broadmindedness was conspicuous in its singularity.[126] Jesko's predecessor as patriarch of the Krockow family, Otto Christoph Wilhelm Richard von Wickerau, who became Count von Krockow in 1910, acquired the unflattering, epithet "red count" from his estate-owning peers simply because Friedrich Ebert, the Social Democrat who assumed the presidency of the Republic until his death in 1925, had invited him to discuss the problems of agriculture.[127]

The relationship between the nobility and the state had certainly never lacked ambiguity and tension, especially after the balance of power between industry and agriculture began to shift. During the Kaissereich, the politicization of nobles in response to economic transformation and the spread of mass politics often placed them at odds with the government and tested their loyalty to the throne. Ewald von Kleist, for one, detested Emperor William II for having encouraged urbanism, crass materialism, parliamentarianism, and industrial growth, despite adhering to an instinctual and devout monarchism that he never abandoned.[128]

Nevertheless, the Weimar Republic as the epitome of the modern state more immediately threatened the health of the landbased economy, the foundation of power for estate owners. In theory as well as in practice, it gave free rein to the erosion of traditional values and the unfettered competition of rival interests. The French Revolution and its consequences, charged one writer in *Pommern-Adel*, undermined the patriarchal system that extended from the land to the state. The freedoms the French Revolution proclaimed meant freedom without social connection. The Weimar Republic, the French Revolution's heir, undermined the reverence for authority that saturated the nobility's military ethos.[129] Thus even if nobles found little to praise in the last kaiser, their toasts and prayers rarely forgot to plead for his long life and his restoration to the throne.[130]

Pomeranian Junkers led the way in asserting their inborn fitness to rule their estates, the associational life of the province, and even the state. "Servant of the state, leader of the Volk—here lies the foundation even today for the continued existence of the nobility in general, the defining problem of the younger generation," intoned an article in *Pommern-Adel*.[131] Furthermore, the nobility could be assured that others not immediately within earshot of the estates would acknowledge its leadership. The newspaper *Pommern Stimmen*, an organ affiliated with the German People's Party (DVP), contrasted the "genuine leadership qualities" (*Führernatur*) of the Junkers with those of the bourgeoisie. The premier position of estate agriculture in Pomerania and the dependence of industry and small proprietorship on the landed economy allowed the Junkers' supremacy to continue, despite the November Revolution. The bourgeoisie, the paper argued, could learn much from the Junkers were it not so indifferent or politically divided: "The otherwise shrewd bourgeois with his smart business sense, who is so proud of his economic leadership, who is furthermore inclined to consider himself superior to the Junker, is here [in Pomerania] completely inferior." Unlike the Junkers, the bourgeoisie could not keep the support of their workers.[132]

Increasingly, racial and biological criteria joined with tradition in buttressing noble claims to leadership. To be sure, racism and particularly anti-Semitism became important to the politics of the nobility prior to World War I, as one of the leaders of the Agrarian League, Conrad von Wangenheim, readily exploited it to create a popular base for the right.[133] Yet especially after the Republic withdrew the publicly recognized legal distinctions that formally guaranteed the nobility's special status,[134] race took on more personal meaning and the subject won considerable attention in *Pommern-Adel*. The nobleman could maintain his historical advantages, according to one article, only "if he consciously betters the racial quality of his blood."[135] Social gatherings for young aristocrats designed to educate them as to their position and responsibilities included lectures on the dire consequences of racial mixing.[136]

The fullest statement on the importance of race to the preservation of the nobility came from the pen of Jürgen von Ramin, whose Junker family lost its estate in 1928. Ramin gave expression to the nobility's scarcely concealed anti-Semitism when he attacked the Jews for being at the source of everything that undermined quality, selection, and breeding: democracy, socialism, mass-leveling, materialism, and the dogma of class conflict were all of Jewish provenance. The Jews "want to battle the spirit, the very conception of selection [*Auslese*] when they make Junker a term of abuse," complained Ramin. "The [communist] International," the embodiment of everything Jewish, "is the principal opponent of the concept of selection, the principal enemy of all creative development. It contests the will toward separate national development and wants instead a porridge of humanity (*Menschenheitsbrei*]. It fights the selection of leadership based on ability and wants instead mass elections and plebiscites. It battles the advancement of personality and wants instead to avoid confronting the fact of individual uniqueness. It contests the family and family relations as well as their own unique development. It fights marriage, breeding and morality, as well as all transcendence, all evolution toward superiority [*Spitzenentwicklung*], all that is good, noble, exalted and beautiful. It is the Satan who rebels against God. On this special terrain which is being discussed here, we must first of all summon the moral courage to admit the concept of superiority."[137] Although landed families maintained cordial relations with the occasional Jewish merchant who happened by, or as in the case of Klaus von Bismarck's father, married a woman of partial Jewish ancestry, the "Jew" as the embodiment of the ills of modern civilization proved too attractive a scapegoat to ignore.[138]

The ability of estate owners to exercise their authority, however, needed more than their own convictions, and even more than the disorganization of the peasantry, or the unthreatening worldviews of their employees. The mistresses of the manor (*Gutsfrauen*) and their daughters, perhaps more than their husbands and fathers, gave substance to the putative community of interest that abided on the land. They conveyed the softer side of domination because their work more consistently embodied the obligations inherent in high station rather than simply the privileges. Whereas the lord wielded power in a variety of ways ranging from the use of force to the sponsorship of charity, the lady's role imparted considerably less ambiguity. Indeed, the smooth functioning of the estates and harmony in the estate villages resulted in large measure from the efforts of the *Guts-frauen* who, in the words of the magazine that catered to their needs, were better suited than their husbands to influence the villagers and laboring families.[139]

Pommern-Adel, the Junkers magazine, suggests that the lot of the noble-woman was to have been sheltered and protected by her husband from the unpleasantness of life. As the noblewoman Marie von Roon asserted in an article entitled "The Nobleman and the Woman," marriage involved "comradeship in sorrow and in joy," but also "the chivalrous protection of the beloved woman from the filth of life, above all, the ugly and common." Aware of the modern temptations that attracted young women in particular, Roon counseled young noblemen as to the appropriate behavior upon meeting a "flapper." Despite her wild behavior, he should treat her with respect and reserve, never discussing her various vices behind her back. Instead he should admonish her as to the carriage and attire proper for a noblewoman (*Edelfrau*), and never should he offer her cognac or cigarettes.[140] Furthermore, convention dictated that young officers in the province's numerous garrisons offer themselves as dance partners for single women, whether young and unmarried or older and widowed, at aristocratic social occasions.[141] Yet the roles of women not only reaffirmed the meaning of domesticity, they also extended it beyond the confines of the *Gutshaus*. If the notion of "the entire household" (*das ganze Haus*) incorporated the estate owner as *paterfamilias*, her estate's employees, and the surrounding village(s), then it invoked as well her own unique contribution.

Read the words of Irmgard von der Lühe, Elizabeth von Thadden's biographer, as she describes the world of her subject: "The sale of the rams, the delivery of fish from the sea to the house, harvesting the fruit, the arrival and departure of guests at the exact time. The birthdays of the elderly in the village—cakes, flowers, gifts and a visit—illness in the family of one of the workers, changing governesses, cooking the soap in the wash house and a large laundry—a really large load of laundry!—repairing the giant wooden ice chest [*Kaltmangel*], the construction out of pulley blocks and weights take up an entire room, Christmas preparations for the village—let no one even think of forgetting that!—and early in almost every year under her partial supervision, new living quarters for the workers." What one might be tempted to call a delicate life, plundered the energies of both the mistresses and daughters of the manor.[142]

The lady of the manor directly involved herself in production, primarily that closest to the household economy. She tended the vegetable garden and cared for the fruit trees from whence came the produce for the canned goods that would nourish her family through the winter. She oversaw the

care and feeding of the small animals, including the poultry, educating herself as to the proper treatment for illnesses until a veterinarian arrived.
Toward that end, she could subscribe to *Die Gutsfrau*, at least until that
magazine fell victim to inflation, or *Land und Frau*, the organ of the Rural
Housewives' Association. Both published helpful hints on everything from
grafting fruit trees to keeping bees to identifying diseases in geese. Such
publications kept her abreast of the various rural women's organizations, the
most important being the Rural Housewives' Association, a strongly corporatist organization designed to professionalize rural household work that was
closely affiliated with the Rural League and the Chamber of Agriculture. In
each of its provincial sections, the Housewives' Association subdivided into
specialized areas, each headed by a knowledgeable "adviser."[143] Like her
husband, the lady of the manor aimed to use the most up-to-date means
possible to enhance production.

Moreover, she supervised the household staff, particularly the female
servants. That aegis was not confined simply to improving the staff's com-
petence or making sure that its work was completed promptly and efficiently.
It extended to monitoring the behavior of her employees so as to keep the
pernicious influences of the city from encouraging the staff in immorality.
Young female employees, most of them drawn into service from the surrounding villages, were to keep their quarters clean and their attire properly
washed and ironed; the mistress of the household assured adequate furnishings. She scrutinized her staff's reading habits to assure the acceptability of
what her people digested. Church periodicals supported, indeed championed, the lady's obligation to interfere: Inspect the staff's reading material
often, one admonished, "and throw a bad book into the fire." Give young
girls the same newspapers the family reads and underline only those pieces
deserving of perusal.[144]

If estate owners often assumed a paternalistic concern for the well-being
of their villagers, then the moral and charitable responsibilities of the estate
owner's wife reflected the maternalistic aspect of power. Estate owning in
Pomerania may well have been a male preserve, as few occasions (widow-
hood being an obvious case) allowed the lady to become an owner-
proprietor herself. Despite the patriarchalism that primogeniture reinforced,
her service on behalf of the community transmitted a powerful influence of
its own.[145] The lady's responsibilities took on enhanced significance after
1918, not only because of the social conflict that accompanied the Republic's birth, but also because she acquired an expanded political role now that
women could vote. Marie Luise von Roon, an estate mistress from lower
Pomerania, described the complexities of her position. "It's not wrong," she
commented regarding the extent to which social relationships had become
an issue since the Revolution, "for we are basically very dependent on our
people as they are on us, and Luther himself was very conscious of the
extent to which he counted also on his house servant for his daily bread."
Suggesting that the plague of social unrest had passed from her environs,
she stated, "it is no longer a difficult task to be an estate mother [*Gutsmut-*

ter], the ideal which doubtless most 'proper' rural women adhere to." By contrast, she recalled the tensions of the summer election campaign after the Kapp Putsch. She ventured into the village only afterward. Otherwise, she would have aroused the suspicion that she would pressure the residents to vote her way. Nevertheless, she convened a give-and-take session with the village women, and despite some difficult moments, all left the room together in relative harmony.[146]

In normal times, the *Gutsmutter* ministered to the sick in the absence of a doctor, bringing with her fresh flowers to comfort the afflicted. "In Kniephof and Jarchlin, no child was born, no one died or was even seriously ill," according to Klaus von Bismarck, "without being visited by my mother, who like a nurse gave consolation and advice or performed first aid." The merchant's daughter, the same woman who during the *Landarbeiterstreik* ministered to the worker who had shot her husband, proved fully adept at meeting the matriarchal duties that estate village life imposed.[147] Ladies of the manor read the parish pastor's Sunday sermons to those too old or sick to attend church. During the winter, they even conducted gatherings for the village women, lasting several hours apiece, that combined spinning, the singing of folk songs and hymns, and Bible reading. Each week, the group discussed a different biblical passage, explicating its meaning as their fingers worked.[148] In effect, the mistress's tasks were designed to fulfill the objective that the Rural League assigned to itself: bringing about social reconciliation, and particularly in her case, alleviating the "caste mentality" (*Kastengeist*) that troubled village life.[149]

The bonds between the estates and those dependent on them remained a staple of advice columns directed to an elite female readership; columns that betrayed the subtle connection between hierarchy and community. All is not lost, suggested the *Pommersche Tagespost*, despite the pernicious effects of modern ideas on the villages—despite the fact that young people especially searched for direction. The mistress was therefore obliged to open spare rooms in the manor house for recreation and the instruction of the girls in the village. She would have to work especially hard in breaking down the perceptions of caste differences that divided the offspring of peasants from those of laborers. Otherwise, they would fall into the same pattern that existed in the schools and in confirmation classes. What should she do? She should teach each village girl to assume her "responsibility for the whole." Whether singing songs, reading a book aloud, or giving instruction in child rearing, the trust between the mistress and the villagers could only be strengthened. In turn, that trust would facilitate discussions on religious and patriotic matters, thus giving the *Gutsfrau* the chance to influence her charges.[150] Simply put, the "whole," could not be realized without the lady's instruction.

Naturally the mistress's obligations included raising her own children, although she could expect the help of the household servants, and especially the governesses who presided over her offspring's primary education. Nevertheless, she bore singular responsibility for the development of her daughters who had to learn their social duties as adults directly from her, although here too church periodicals offered advice. Young ladies who found the endless round of parties boring should, like their mothers, visit the sick, assist the local doctor, and read Sunday sermons to the old and infirm. They should also consider hosting "family evenings" at the manor house for workers and their households, affairs that might consist of poetry reading, piano playing, singing folk songs, and lectures on local history. They too should instruct the young in how to select suitable reading matter, thus discouraging them from gravitating toward sensationalist novels. What was the purpose of this exercise? "That all leads to a genuine 'village community' (*Dorfgemeinschaft*) which is talked about so much now. Farm work is hard work. However, these people are there not just for work. Indeed they have their cultural needs too. The possibility for constructive recreation (*einen rechten Erholung*) must be given them. And such family evenings and visits will strengthen the sense of community."[151]

The daughters who remained unmarried, whether by choice or from the lack of acceptable suitors (a common enough problem during the interwar years), could still play the role implicit in the "estate mother" ideal. If their families held sufficient property, they could establish a separate household on one of the adjoining estates where they could raise vegetables, chickens, pigs, and goats. Then too, they could baby-sit for small children, act as the village nurse, or supervise the servant girls and daughters of the rural laborers. In that way, they could utilize their talents and satisfy their desire for independence, very necessary given the allure of the city. Failing that option, there was always the possibility of service in church-run hospitals, orphanages, and other institutions, an honorable tradition among single noble women.[152]

To be sure, even in the areas of moral concern, the responsibilities of the lord and lady of the manor often overlapped. Because both so firmly dedicated themselves to agriculture and to the values of hierarchy, authority, and rootedness that this occupation entailed, little conflict existed between the male and female understanding of the means and ends of social welfare apparent among elites elsewhere.[153] The lady's "sphere" was never so separate and distinct as to exclude him. Indeed, the very concept of "lordship" historically entailed an instructional dimension in that the landowner assumed responsibility for the "moral education" of his dependent peasants.[154] That mission, furthermore, became most evident in his patronage of the village church, a custom that the Reformation initiated and the Prussian General Legal Code (*Allgemeine Landrecht*) of 1794 confirmed. Despite the ambiguities surrounding patronage in the Prussian state constitution of 1920, which seemingly anticipated its dissolution, little happened legislatively to undermine the practice.[155]

Patronage obligated the estate owner not only to maintain the physical structure of the church and manse, but also to the performances of other services. In one case the patron transported his pastor back and forth across a lake in his motor boat so that the cleric could attend to each of his three churches.[156] Other aspects of patronage, however, reinforced the patron's authority in the church. He, or "they" if the church had multiple patrons, headed the parish council and oversaw the appointment of the pastor. Once installed, the cleric could not be removed without the consent of the consistory in Stettin. In some of the more "democratic" cases, the patron allowed the parish council a degree of consent by presenting it with a slate of handpicked candidates for its consideration.[157] Nevertheless, the majority of the parish councils amounted to little more than rubber stamps, "hardly responsible bodies in most instances," according to one pastor's recollection.[158] The mere physical evidence of patronage inside the church testified to the lord's unimpeachable authority: The family pew, complete with velvet cushions, was anchored at the front of the church, raised in such a way that the patron and his family could view the congregation and scrutinize the pastor.[159] The family coat of arms comprised one of the few evidences of decoration in the otherwise austere Pomeranian village churches.[160]

The importance of patronage in Pomerania is difficult to exaggerate. In 1928, sixty-four clergy received appointment to churches in the province, 68.5 percent of them named by a private patron. From 1924 to 1928, an average of fifty-five positions were filled yearly, 60 percent of them by private patrons, slightly over 27 percent by the provincial consistory, and a mere 7 percent by the parishes themselves.[161] Noble patrons, because of their traditions, tended to be more zealous in performing their duties than bourgeois estate owners, although the religiosity of Schwiers's father and the commitment of others like him militate against hard and fast distinctions.[162] For certain, complaints arose from *Pommern-Adel* in the 1920s that the nobility's dedication had declined: "Can anyone wonder that our people don't go to church anymore when the *Gutsherr* and patron fails to go or seldom goes himself. Isn't there the impression, as if the assertion were correct, that the church is only for women?" Lay involvement and particularly the dedication of patrons were now crucial, urged the magazine, in light of the moral degradation and vulgarity emanating from the printed media, the cinema, and the theater.[163]

Yet such jeremiads should not be overemphasized. More often than not nobles accepted regular Sunday attendance as yet another obligation associated with their position in rural society.[164] Evangelical Church authorities would not tamper with the boundaries of ecclesiastical dioceses if doing so would disrupt parish ties to patrons of long standing.[165] The provincial consistory recognized the contributions of Junker families, such as the Thaddens "who for centuries have raised Trieglaff to the very center of Christian life in the Greifenberg synod."[166] Commented another consistorial report, "The Awakening movement of the Below family spreads out from the Seehof estate and even to this day has left its lively impact on the parish."[167] Although a certain Frau von Massow, bearing the name of a distinguished *Uradel* family and patron of the church in the border town of

Rummelsburg had, to the distress of everyone, converted to Catholicism, one visitation report took comfort in the loyalty of other old noble families, such as the Puttkamers and Zitzewitzes: "In their cases, as is the case of large landowners in both church districts generally, I found an Evangelical consciousness, as is true normally for the patronage families with their Prussian traditions. They seem to prove in a gratifying manner their strong Evangelical demeanor and their Evangelical obligations."[168] Another went out of its way to compliment Count von Kleist-Retzow, who was "faithfully and seriously well-disposed to the church."[169] The membership rosters of the provincial synod consisted of such names as von der Goltz, Schwerin, Roon, Gerlach, Knebel, Maltzahn, Borcke, Bismarck, Bonin, Kleist, Heydebreck, Zitzewitz, Puttkamer, and of course, Thadden. The same names appeared prominently in the visitation reports, as each parish's leading personages greeted the commissions.[170] Nobles delivered lectures at superintendents' meetings on such vital subjects as "the contemporary morality question."[171]

Yet here too, the estate mistress both confirmed and softened her husband's sway, primarily in the exercise of her charitable responsibilities. The wives of estate owners, and noblewomen especially, distinguished themselves through leadership in the various church-affiliated women's organizations, particularly the Evangelical Women's League (*Evangelischer Frauenbund*), an association that combined welfare work and educational projects with public initiatives on behalf of "religious-moral renewal."[172] Despite the competition that arose between the secular and religious *Vereine* for their members' time, the involvement of noblewomen paralleled their participation in organizations beyond the church, such as the Queen Louise League (*Königen Luisebund*) or the Rural Housewives Association. In turn, such organizations reinforced the links between the women and the church. *Die Gutsfrau* cheerfully reported the Dewitzes' golden wedding anniversary, celebrated by the *Hausfrauverein*—capped off by a church ceremony featuring their estate's workers and the local shooting clubs in attendance.[173] Service in church-affiliated organizations could become one of the most important commitments for single noble ladies, such as Marie von Kleist, who headed the provincial *Frauenbund* through most of the Weimar period. An unmarried "house daughter" (*Haustöchter*) entrusted with overseeing the estate of her dead aunt, Kleist juggled both family and church responsibilities.[174]

Moreover, such women were supposed to set an example through their generosity, often using the church as the vehicle for their donations. Because she lacked a male heir, Countess von Schwerin suggested to the large Protestant welfare organization, the Inner Mission, that her estate might serve a "Christian purpose" after her death. In return, the provincial Inner Mission could do nothing other than appreciate her grace and generosity, although the very size of the manor house (fully forty-five rooms) involved considerable maintenance costs. The estate, decided the Inner Mission finally, would do nicely as a training school for peasants and workers.[175] The constant presence of estate owners' wives in the lay activity of the Evangelical Church gave moral depth to their role as preservers of both hierarchy and community.

The Politics of Proximity: The Referendum on Expropriation

The political realities arising from the structure of Pomeranian rural social life posed a threat to Weimar, even during the Republic's balmy years. The leverage of estate owners in everyday life meant that their intrusiveness was sufficient to diminish the Republic's most determined attempts at democratization. The referendum in 1926 favoring the uncompensated expropriation of estates belonging to the Hohenzollerns and the ruling families of other German states provides an excellent illustration of the way in which the landlords' direct intervention undercut whatever chances existed for their employees to assert their political independence.

Normally, the secret ballot allowed voters in Weimar parliamentary elections a measure of confidentiality, certainly one good reason that the Social Democratic vote remained relatively high in Pomerania among farm laborers in some regions. Ironically, however, the provisions for direct democracy could under the "right" circumstances discourage the very end they were designed to promote. The constitutional procedures stipulated a two-stage process. First, the initiative (*Volksbegehren*) required that voters who wished that a referendum (*Volksentscheid*) be held register in offices established under the supervision of the Ministry of Interior. One tenth of all qualified voters had to sign the lists in order for the referendum to proceed.[176] In effect then, both stages, but especially the initiative, expected voters to "go public" with their preferences, because either participating or not participating identified the political choice of the voter. Correspondingly, the possibility of social pressure affecting the outcome exceeded that of a regular election.

Sponsored by the Socialists and the Communists in the Reichstag, the expropriation measure spawned the furious reaction of the right all over Germany, a movement that even brought the intervention of the Evangelical Church, an institution that otherwise proclaimed its political neutrality.[177] The right launched a propaganda barrage, one that Pomerania certainly exemplified, to convince voters that the measure constituted nothing less than theft—yet another step toward the bolshevization of the country. *Pommern-Adel* carried Reinhold von Thadden's urging that each nobleman canvas his people, alerting them to the subversive character of the measure that they might likely have supported. The Pomeranian noble "who is once again activating his oft-affirmed loyalty to the hereditary ruling house which he has proven over the centuries," commented Thadden, "has taken up the struggle to defeat the referendum."[178] Yet demagogic appeals to the self-interest of the lower-middle and rural working classes in the name of "property" composed the centerpiece of the propaganda that conservative newspapers and flyers aired, especially to those with little choice but to listen. "The Volk's initiative means a new swindle of the people," blared the headline of one conservative Pomeranian newspaper. "Workers, employees and savers . . . Do you want to allow yourselves to be conned [*beschwatzen lassen*] once again? No signatures on the registration lists!"[179] Another reminded its readers of the appropriateness of the biblical injunctions: "The Seventh Commandment!," screamed the headline. "Thou shalt not steal—that goes for thievery of every estate, even the estate of the king! Therefore, no honest citizen should allow himself to be registered for the initiative, because he would then implicate himself in the planned thievery."[180] In yet another paper, the Rural League placed its own demagogic advertisement denouncing the initiative as having violated the constitutional provisions guaranteeing the inviolability of property, as "expropriation is permitted only on factual, not personal grounds. It is not permitted to dispossess as such the prince or the chimney sweep, the pianist, the day laborer, the teacher or the landed proprietor, etc., etc."[181] The Rural League and Pomerania's conservative press sought to persuade their audience that expropriation, although then limited to the princes, would spread like a contagion if it succeeded. "First the princes, then landed property, then the church, and then finally the home owner," the *Naugard Zeitung* hinted darkly. "So communism attempts to achieve the confiscation of all private property."[182]

Strong suspicions arose thereafter that the right did not limit itself merely to verbal opposition against the left's proposal. Pomerania's Socialists and Communists complained repeatedly to government officials that estate owners made it difficult, if not impossible, for people in their employ to participate. Either the appropriate lists were mysteriously unavailable for registrants to enroll or, so the allegation arose, landowners actually threatened those workers seeking to register with blacklisting and even physical force.[183] Socialists and Communists provided long lists of estate and communal managers, those ostensibly responsible for executing the initiative and referendum according to the Interior Ministry's instructions, who refused to cooperate by sending the registration lists back: "Sabotage is carried out not merely in the relatively open and harmless form of non-acceptance. Rather, one can count on it that in a number of estate districts and communes, the lists are simply not displayed and registry is hindered. Estate laborers and also our party comrades who come from the cities in order to agitate in the countryside were in this regard placed under strict control."[184]

On the whole, county officials and the courts looked skeptically on the left's charges against estate owners, even as they investigated them. A disciplinary court, for example, found in favor of the estate owner Borchert, in Prilipp, an estate village in the Stettin district, who had been accused of threatening to fire those of his workers who supported the referendum. He testified that during a friendly discussion in the field one day, his workers asked for his opinion and he gave it to them. No threat was intended.[185] In

some cases, the county magistrates implied that the procedures for the initiative had been rushed or that the proper instructions had been unclear,
inaccessible, or tardily disseminated.[186] In yet another instance, the magistrate of Bergen county dismissed the complaint of the district labor secretary
in Stralsund against an estate inspector who refused to issue a receipt for
the voter registration list he was given. The inspector questioned the cre-
dentials of the worker who brought the roll to him.[187]

Nevertheless, such incidents also forced the recognition, reluctant to be
sure, of the necessity of official oversight, even if the behavior of the managers in question did not merit disciplinary measures. And although it had
been difficult to distinguish among the truthful, ingenious, or simply disin-
genuous excuses for why registration lists had not been handled properly,
county officers could not avoid punishing managers in egregious cases: The
estate owner von Wißmann, from Falkenburg, for instance, prompted a
recommendation from the county magistrate that he be fined for negligence.
The registration lists under his oversight had somehow been destroyed.
Wißmann insisted that his carelessness had been inadvertent because he did
not believe he had the authority to conduct the referendum. The *Gutsfrau*
came to her husband's defense, claiming that she had withheld his mail,
which included the magistrate's letter of authorization, so that Wißmann
could recover undisturbed from a serious illness. The magistrate only
partially accepted Wißmann's story in response: It had been Wißmann's
duty to delegate his responsibilities effectively in an emergency, he said, and
not assign them solely to his wife.[188]

Whether by subterfuge, fear, or indifference, the referendum to expropriate the princely estates failed miserably in Pomerania. The number of those
who participated in the referendum exceeded by over 67 percent the
number of those who were brave enough to register for the initiative. In
fact, nearly 18 percent of the qualified voters in the province supported the
initiative, well above the required 10 percent.[189] Yet along with East Prussia,
Pomerania ranked the lowest among election districts in the number of
"yes" votes when compared to the total vote of the two leftist parties in the
last Reichstag election of December 1924. Moreover, a significant disparity
arose between the towns and the countryside. In the towns, particularly in
Stettin, those participating in the referendum and voting "yes" exceeded the
left's vote from 1924. Yet in such preponderantly rural counties as Köslin,
Anklam, and Greifenberg, the opposite was the case. In well over two hundred villages, including estate villages, not a single vote was cast for the
referendum, a testimony not only to the conformity and deference that rural
hierarchies induced, but also to the effectiveness of the Pomeranian right's
demagogic appeals to the sanctity of property.[190] The referendum on princely
estates would not be the only occasion in which the entrenched position of
estate owners would bring important political consequences, particularly as
they determined the survival of the Weimar Republic. The efforts of estate
owners to organize themselves and mobilize their villagers not only pres-

aged the strategy of the DNVP's radical leadership after 1928 to undermine the Reichstag,[191] it also spawned a much broader antirepublican protest movement in the process.

Personal Authority and Modernity:
The Compatibility of Opposites

Kazuo Ishiguro's novel *The Remains of the Day* tells the story of an English butler, Stevens, who looks back on his career in the employ of a distinguished landed gentleman. The butler's new employer, a wealthy American, had just granted Stevens a vacation, which allows the latter to reflect on his past. At first, the butler recalls his career with pride, retrospectively basking in the glory of the aristocrat Lord Darlington, whom he once served. As the novel develops, however, less pleasant memories that the protagonist had long repressed struggle to the surface of his consciousness. Among them are his employer's embarrassing pro-Fascist sentiments and his support for appeasement, not to mention the butler's own refusal to confess his love for Miss Kenton, a fellow employee who left the lord's service to marry. The butler now confronts the consequences of his long employ: His loyalty to his employer and his scrupulous observance of the ethos of the occupation he inherited from his father superceded the autonomy that is essential to personhood. Ironically, the butler's new-found self-understanding could only have come about after Lord Darlington's death. The physical presence of the Lord had until then guaranteed the constriction of his employee's identity and independence.[192]

The exercise of power in the modern era, we have been told, has become impersonal and diffuse, concealing its beneficiaries behind sophisticated technologies that operate through language. The very murkiness in assigning agency to those who hold power (if we can even identify them in the first place) ineluctably seduces those who are subjected to power into cooperating in their own subordination.[193] Yet paradoxically, Pomerania, for all of its attempts at agricultural modernization, reproduced older, more personal manifestations of power, the source of which was considerably less ambiguous. Even if we consider the influence of the employer in Ishiguro's work a novelistic exaggeration, it still serves as an effective metaphor for the power of Pomeranian estate owners. That power was immediate, personal, profound, and capable of inducing the consent of those the estate owners dominated through a blend of gentility, charity, and coercion. The hierarchical communitarianism implicit in Pomeranian rituals was but the formal celebration of a personal power that showed extraordinary resilience day in and day out.

Consciously or unconsciously, many of Pomerania's key institutions reinforced the authority of the estates, both by embodying and acting on the myth of the sacredness of rural life. To be sure, those institutions did not reflect the influence of the estate owners in any obvious way, despite the extensive personal and institutional connections that the large landlords maintained. In fact, some were not above criticizing the province's dominant class. Yet ultimately, the values of Pomerania's institutions too closely replicated those of the agrarian elite to allow them to subvert its hegemony. Those values expressed a near virulent outrage at the effects of urbanization, especially the unwholesome lifestyles that the cities fostered.

4

Social Constraints
and Political Limitations:
Pomerania's Evangelical Church

UNDERSTANDING PRUSSIAN HISTORY and particularly Prussian conservatism is inconceivable without examining Prussia's Evangelical Church.[1] The subordination of the Old Prussian Union Church to the state before 1918 when the kaiser acted as its "Supreme Bishop" (*Summus Episcopus*), the dependence of that church on elites, and its notoriously weak roots among the working classes are emblematic of the absolutist and authoritarian traditions for which Prussia is (in)famous. Despite Prussia's significant contribution to the Evangelical opposition during the Third Reich as embodied in the Confessing Church, a new beginning for the Evangelical Church became possible only with Prussia's postwar dissolution.[2] Thus, to focus on the Pomeranian provincial church appears at first glance to yield predictable conclusions, precisely because the pervasive conservatism in the province could not help but affect, and even imprison, that institution.

Yet the Evangelical Church in Pomerania emerges as an ideal subject for understanding not only the diffusion, but also the complexity of the province's conservatism. Despite clear evidence of secularization, the church was a major cultural presence with far-reaching ties to the rural economy and to other institutions that shaped the provincial mentality. The village churches, with their brick or fieldstone construction that paralleled the lack of ornamentation in most manor houses, embraced the collective memory of generations, memories that included hardship and scarcity. Many of the churches that had been rebuilt following the Thirty Years' and Northern Wars in fact either lacked steeples or fashioned them from wood.[3] Parish churches embraced large expanses, particularly in upper Pomerania. They consisted typically of a main or "mother" church with at least one daughter church serving several land communes at a time, as well as embracing manorial districts.[4] Although the parishes constituted the lowest level of administration, subordinated as they were to diocesan superintendents (roughly the equivalent of bishops), the provincial consistory in Stettin, and ultimately to the Supreme Church Council in Berlin, they represented the vital link between the church bureaucracy and the larger society.[5] According to the 1925 census, over 93 percent of Pomerania's population belonged to the province's Evangelical Church.[6]

The elementary schools, however, constituted the most obvious example of the ecclesiastical role in society, both in Pomerania and in Prussia, because they involved the mass education of the young. Until 1918, the public primary school (*Volksschule*) teachers had to teach religious instruction, accept the clergy's supervision of the curriculum, and submit to myriad church-related duties, such as playing the organ and performing janitorial services in the churches. The dream of liberals and Social Democrats during the Second Empire to secularize elementary education, or at least end the division of Evangelical and Catholic pupils into confessionally segregated schools, foundered on the opposition of both churches and the state.[7] In fact, the desire to preserve its public role as a crucial element in the preservation of German culture undergirded the conservatism of the Evangelical Church. Next to estate owners, the Pomeranian provincial church became the most important explicator of the ills of urban civilization, which its press regularly trumpeted, because rural society best sustained the church's cultural mission.

Nevertheless, there was a less predictable side to Pomeranian Protestantism, meaning that its deeply impacted conservatism did not entail unthinking conformity. Ironically, the Evangelical Church threatened to subvert the domination of the big landlords through its formal commitment to remaining "above parties" and its social programs that implicitly contested the interests of estate owners, among them the organization of agricultural laborers and the settlement of bankrupt estates. Its conservatism was thus highly nuanced, containing the potential for independence. Given the absence of other alternatives, Pomerania's church might thus have restrained the reckless demagoguery and right radicalism that characterized elite politics, particularly during the Republic's "end phase." Ultimately, the church's commitment to the rural myth and its formal rejection of party-political entanglements would prove a contradictory and self-defeating combination. Nevertheless, it asserted its autonomy frequently enough to encourage a serious explanation of its workings.

Secularization Defied: Pomeranian Protestantism's Rural Roots

Like their counterparts elsewhere in Germany and in Europe, Evangelical clergymen in Pomerania rung their hands over the evidence of secularization and moral "decline" (indeed the two were inseparable in their minds) that set in, especially in the wake of World War I. They noted the decrease in regular Sunday attendance, or at least its skewing toward disproportionate numbers of women. They had long recognized the indifference, even the hostility, of urban working-class men toward the church, an attitude that resembled that of their compatriots in the cities. That outlook most certainly prevailed in Pomerania's few industrial centers, worrying churchmen of its corrosive effects not merely on religious observance in the towns, but also in the surrounding regions. Radical leftist workers employed in the mills and brickworks in the upper Pomeranian town of Falkenburg, complained the consistory in Stettin in pointing to one example, threatened to expand their influence beyond the city's boundaries. "Church work among the laborers in Falkenburg is thus very important, and should be energetically pursued before it is too late."[8]

In addition, irreligion proved difficult to suppress, even after the Nazi assumption of power brought an upsurge in church attendance in its wake. The synod of Gartz, which oversaw the religious life of a diocese lying along the Oder near Stettin, pleaded for a pastor who could meet the challenge of ministering to the parish of Güstow:

> The majority of Güstow parishioners consist of Social Democratic and Communist workers who even today are not concerned with church and national matters. Church life in the parish which lies firmly on the outskirts of the metropolis [Stettin] has almost completely succumbed. In consideration of the aim of becoming a "people's church" (Volkskirche) and bringing the alienated masses back to the church, it is urgently requested that a minister live in this parish who is up to the task.[9]

Furthermore, churchmen had long understood how the overwhelming presence of estate agriculture and the relative absence of peasant holdings in lower Pomerania led to widespread dechristianization. Although rooted in the oppressive character of serfdom in Swedish Pomerania in which the clergy once read police regulations from their pulpits, the alienation from the church had reached the point where indifference, rather than hostility, prevailed. Explicit antagonism toward the church grew more noticeable, especially among estate laborers, the closer one came to Stettin, most likely because of the left's influence in that city. Yet most workers simply did not care enough to be anticlerical,[10] and in any event, most of them needed Sundays, the only day they had to themselves, to attend to their own plots.[11]

Since the war, however, many Protestants, a disproportionate number of them young men, demonstrated a disturbing, and increasing preference for other forms of camaraderie: sports, the cinema, pubs, and the various vol-

untary associations. The encroachment of "modern ideas" was most noticeable in Pomerania's towns and beach resorts. "Many people from Wollin
travel to the coast on Sundays," complained one visitation report. "They neglect church services and fall under the dubious influences of resort life."
The "unsettling associational life created by secular organizations" clamored
for the attention, even on Sundays, of those who remained behind.[12] Worse
still, many young urban schoolteachers, long frustrated by their proscribed
subservience to the Evangelical pastorate, had grown weary, not only of
teaching religious instruction to their pupils, but also of clerical oversight
in general.[13]

Then came the impositions involved in making a living, such as the petty
commerce that frequently disrupted Sunday services in the towns—commerce that took place with relative impunity now that the Republic
tolerated it. Townspeople attracted to such business instead of going to
church added to the numbers of estate laborers who absented themselves
from services, not only because they needed the time to cultivate their own
crops, but also because in some cases they lacked transportation.[14] An article in one Sunday paper catalogued the forms of competition the church
confronted. The secularization of Sunday had been evident certainly before
the war, it observed, especially among the "little people" employed on the
estates who needed the time for their own devices. Yet it had only acceler-
ated since the Revolution because of the growth of organized sports that
replaced military training in occupying young people's energies. Although
the Weimar constitution preserved Sunday as a day of rest, local authorities
had not only done little to uphold it, they also undermined that custom by
permitting various amusements. Even elections were now held on the sabbath. To be sure, the author admitted, communal governments knew that
the hustle and bustle of such activities were not supposed to disturb the
serenity of church services. In some cases, the Rural League used its influence to preserve the sacredness of the sabbath.[15] Yet curtailing Sunday
commerce proved difficult to enforce given the noise of the rumbling
wagons, the clamor of the repair shop, and the rumble of automobile en-
gines:

> When one today travels to a church visitation a few hours over land, one
> generally sees field work going on where earlier the gendarmes or good
> morality commanded one's observance. . . . Added to this, horse shows,
> menageries, exhibits, agricultural assemblies, political rallies, flag cere-
> monies, patriotic festivals occupy the rural person all day long, Sunday
> after Sunday.[16]

Finally, Pomerania churchmen confronted the alarming number of pastoral
vacancies throughout the province, 21 percent of them in Stettin alone. Although that problem was, if anything, worse elsewhere in Prussia, it had
grown so severe in Pomerania that by 1931, fully 175 positions were open,
110 of them for more than one year. The notable drop in the number of the-

ology students, especially as a result of the war and the competition of other, more secular disciplines, rendered the replacement of retiring pastors difficult at best.[17] The relatively high social standing of Evangelical clergymen, as compared to their Catholic counterparts, further hindered recruitment. According to a survey that appeared in the church press, only seventy-five out of over eleven hundred Prussian theology students in 1926–27 stemmed from peasant, artisanal, or working-class backgrounds. Given that few parents from the popular classes could afford the cost of educating their children toward the pastorate, the Evangelical Church thus deprived itself of a rich source of clerical candidates and an opportunity for improving its relationships with ordinary people.[18] Ironically, church authorities considered pastoral vacancies to be less of a problem in the cities because neighboring parishes often filled the void. The countryside was a different matter, however. There, the dearth of clergymen spelled trouble not only for religious life but for the culture as a whole.[19] Nevertheless, Evangelical Church leaders in Pomerania, and especially the church press, attributed the woes of religious life in the province mainly to the poisonous effects of urbanism and cosmopolitanism.

Such concerns, although ultimately crucial to explaining the church's commitment to rural values and its inability to challenge decisively the hegemony of estate owners, should not belie the degree to which Pomerania remained remarkably *un*secularized. Although the Republic eased the procedures by which individuals could withdraw from the church, and the "free-thinking" movement associated with the left campaigned strenuously to encourage resignations, Pomerania possessed one of the lowest church-leaving rates in Germany.[20] Among the churches comprising the Old Prussian Union, only the border province and Silesia could boast a higher percentage of those regularly receiving communion. A decline in formal Sunday-by-Sunday commitment during the Republic did take place. Nevertheless, statistically speaking, Pomerania remained above average in church attendance, not only in Prussia, but in Germany.[21]

Moreover, the rural areas beyond lower Pomerania remained remarkable for their high level of religious identification and commitment. Church visitations, which the province's two general superintendents conducted periodically to assess the vitality of religious life, constituted major events in village culture, assuming the status of official holidays. The various clubs and associations, especially the nationalist ones, including even the Nazis' paramilitary unit, the SA, showed up in full dress uniform.[22] The decision of Jewish businesses to close on the day of the visitation in Belgard in order to enable their employees to attend church services favorably impressed the commission.[23] Local dignitaries, especially the patrons and elders, comprised the welcoming committees for the visitors, while the parishioners impressed the new arrivals with their religiosity. "Thereby the biblical knowledge of the peasant chairman of the parish council sometimes surprised us," commented one report.[24] Secular conservative publications regularly covered the major events in church life, including visitations, knowing full well the importance of such occasions to their readership.[25]

Notwithstanding the difficulties that their positions frequently entailed, village pastors were considered persons of distinction by virtue of their education and role as ministers, as professionals who deserved the respect of the middling and lower sorts, whose spiritual needs, although inconsistent, nonetheless merited attention. Pomeranian rural life with its isolated villages and small towns was most certainly demanding, especially in upper Pomerania where a single pastor was expected to oversee a parish embracing numerous scattered villages. The roads that connected the hamlets prohibited the use of automobiles and became all but impassable in bad weather.[26] Nevertheless Pomerania's pervasive ruralism helped the province's clergy achieve a degree of prominence that would have been difficult to attain in the large cities. Even in regions such as lower Pomerania where a regular church commitment was rare, visitations received public recognition characteristic of "rural relationships." Not only did the visitation to Anklam receive a welcome consonant with the solemnity that the occasion demanded, but estate owners gave their workers the day off with pay.[27] Evangelical welfare organizations that depended on the dedication of both clergy and laypersons played crucial roles in the delivery of essential services through their hospitals, reform schools, asylums, orphanages, hospices, and old-age homes.

There existed, however, not merely a culture of the Evangelical Church, but also a Protestant culture—one in which Protestant values infused other, seemingly more secular concerns. One of those was nationalism, which elevated Luther and Otto von Bismarck, the Pomeranian son, as the two principal heroes of German history:

> Luther and Bismarck—the peasant's son and the nobleman—both the greatest of all Germans. Both were born in Germany's heartland. Both strove for peace in God and found it. Profound faith and sincerity of conscience, battle-hardened wrath and fearlessness, devotion to duty and restless creative power, family bonding and joyousness in being among one's own people, the depth of feeling and joy in nature, originality and along with it a delicate sensitivity—in these genuine German Protestant qualities stand Luther and Bismarck shoulder to shoulder.[28]

Meetings of diocesan superintendents stressed the importance of the neopietist Awakening to the course of German history. Bismarck, explained one participant, "would never have become the greatest Reich Chancellor if he had not received his decisive religious inspiration in a little upper Pomeranian village from the von Thadden family."[29]

The preservation of the confessional primary school and the continuing loyalty of many of Pomerania's teachers to the Evangelical character of education best demonstrates the tenacity of religious convictions in the province, deep commitments that statistics on regular church attendance by themselves simply cannot plumb. Initially, the Weimar Republic presented the serious prospect of reducing or even eliminating the clergy's role in the schools. Moreover, continuous pressure weighed on the Reichstag to make good on the reformist proposals that had arisen under the Kaiserreich. Successful educational reform would not only have created common schools (*Simultanschulen*) for pupils of all faiths, it would even have sanctioned secular schools that eliminated religious instruction altogether. Both major churches, Evangelical and Catholic, mounted a furious counterattack to defeat those initiatives that would have undermined, or at best compromised, the most visible manifestation of the cultural place of Christianity, the education of youth.[30] In Pomerania as in Prussia, the churches conducted a virtual crusade, appealing to parents of school-age children to demonstrate their commitment to confessional schools. The Evangelical press published articles that were designed to captivate and unsettle— columns that revealed just how deeply religion had come to permeate both the curriculum and the culture of the confessional primary school.

One such piece, composed to frighten Evangelical parents into voting their preference for confessional schools, belabored the limitations of even the common school, the proposed alternative to confessional schools, which still preserved religious instruction. Young students, shaken by the sudden death of a classmate, ask to sing a song beloved by the departed, "Let me go, so that I may see Jesus." Alas, the teacher responds gently, that cannot be done now since this is not the appropriate class hour for religious instruction. "Our school has become a common school," the instructor informs them, and that means that religion is not permitted to impinge on other disciplines. "Religious instruction is only one subject among others," she says. If that is the case, queries one puzzled, but remarkably alert pupil, what will happen if Martin Luther, the father of the modern German language, composer of numerous hymns and folk songs and "the originator of a new theory of the state," is removed from the textbooks? Sorry, responds the teacher . . . only during religious instruction can he be discussed. Well then, when can we sing "A Mighty Fortress," the students ask plaintively, a hymn that has itself become a folk song "that Evangelical and Catholic soldiers sang from the very depths of their souls during the world war"? The answer to that question was certainly consistent with those that preceded it.

Thereafter, the teacher can only answer negatively the increasingly anxious questions of the class: No, the instructor can no longer pray with them before they leave for vacation; no, they cannot sing Christmas carols (except, of course, during religious instruction); no, they cannot even use the word "God" at all except during religion class, just as it is in the French public schools, a less-than-subtle reference to the consequences of republicanism gone wild. But the school has been Evangelical since the Reformation, the students protest. Suppose here and there evidence of wrong belief arises? Should we not then contest it? No, responds the teacher, by now betraying obvious sympathy to the students' concerns. The common school forbids that. "A Volk without God will never be a moral Volk: Ah! But I should not say that either, for we are in a common school."[31]

In most of Germany, the churches won stunning support, a striking indication of the limits of secularization. The confessionally segregated schools remained the norm, a consequence of a badly divided Reichstag's failure to pass reforming legislation. Although religious instruction did not receive the attention it had during the Empire, it nonetheless persisted as a fixture in the curriculum. Clerical supervision most certainly declined; yet with Protestants, clergymen willingly conceded that the primary school teachers ought to be relieved of their church-related chores, even if they rejected the teachers' demand for university training.[32]

Pomerania not only paralleled such trends, it even extended them, not only in the determination with which laypeople defended the Evangelical character of education, but also in the degree to which teachers accepted their "traditional" roles. With much feeling, a rural teacher wrote in a parish newspaper of "the fusion of religious indoctrination with *Heimat*, and its most beautiful realization in the Evangelical confessional school." The entire culture of the school, not simply the hours devoted to religious instruction, was "infused with the Evangelical spirit."[33] Outside Stettin, proper parents overwhelmingly sustained Evangelical education by electing the appropriate candidates to the parents' advisory councils for the schools. Even in the Stettin district, Evangelical schools still outnumbered their alternatives by a wide margin.[34] To be sure, the church contributed to the outcome by appointing pastors who canvassed the province on behalf of the confessional school, giving them leaves of absence to accomplish their duties. Yet the strength of the turnout in response to those clerical initiatives can be taken as a sign that Protestantism, even if only a means of communal identification, maintained very deep roots.[35]

The commitment of laypeople did not end, however, with the parents' advisory committees. It extended to the conduct of their children's teachers and educational administrators. Observe the uproar that occurred in a hamlet near the Polish border over a school supervisor who refused to baptize his son or allow his children to attend religious instruction, who even sponsored free-thinking meetings and advocated nonchurch burials. Evangelical parents, outraged by such behavior, petitioned the DNVP Landtag delegation, the DNVP district chairman, Zitzewitz, and the provincial governor Lippmann, to have the offender removed. A petition with twenty thousand signatures demanded that the school inspector be one who would guarantee "that Evangelical children should be educated in the Evangelical faith."[36] The consitory sympathized with the parents because it considered the consequences of such a disturbance near the Polish border "where every sign of discord among the population must be avoided, not only in the interests of the church, but also those of the state."[37]

Nevertheless the significance of such challenges to the church and to devout laypersons was exaggerated, however disruptive they may have appeared. Despite the obvious restiveness that existed among teachers, especially in the months immediately after the Revolution—discontent that Evangelical authorities sought to pacify by eliminating the most demeaning of their sexton duties—tradition retained a powerful grasp.[38] In 1929, a survey of Pomeranian teachers published in the *Pommersche Tagespost* reported that only 4 out of over 5,700 Evangelical instructors had refused to teach religious instruction, although legally entitled to do so. Moreover, the number of students who formally opted out of religion class was only slightly less impressive: 32 of over 96,000 pupils in the Stettin district, 6 out of over 83,000 in Köslin, and 14 out of over 26,000 in Stralsund.[39]

In 1930, Pomerania ranked second among the Old Prussian Union provincial churches in the number of teachers who still performed the sexton duties assigned to their positions.[40] Not surprisingly, the willingness of teachers to perform these church-related obligations was stronger in the countryside where one-room schoolhouses were more common, than in the towns where church leaders could hardly overlook the "many" teachers whose leftism brought them into conflict with pastors and patrons.[41] Nevertheless in many villages teachers continued to act as cantors at funerals, following an old custom. "In all respects, these practices are still common in the vast majority of rural communities," noted the Pomeranian consistory with notable relief.[42] Teachers displayed their loyalty on several occasions. "The teachers in this diocese," according to the visitation to Schivelbein, "are with few exceptions positive in their attitude toward the church, even if isolated cases are strongly influenced by their organization. They gladly worked toward the success of the visitation's work."[43] The Evangelical clergy in Pomerania served on many school boards, which gave them numerous occasions to air their opinions on subjects ranging from the singing of chorales during school hours and confirmation instruction to school property rights and teachers' salaries."[44]

Yet the influence of the Evangelical Church depended not only on its visibility in the sparsely populated countryside, nor even entirely on the relative lack of secularization in the province. Rather, that institution's partial dependence on the income it derived from land secured it as a necessary fixture, bringing it into daily, more "secular" interaction with the local economy. According to the figures composed at the end of 1932 at the height of the agrarian crisis, Pomeranian parishes possessed over fifty thousand hectares of land attached to both churches and rectories that yielded nearly two million Reichsmarks in cash and over three hundred and fifty thousand Reichsmarks in agricultural payment-in-kind (*Naturalien*).[45] Applications to the Supreme Church Council in Berlin for authorization to fill pastoral vacancies included descriptions of the social composition of the parishioners, the often considerable distances the prospective pastor's children would have to travel to the nearest gymnasium, and the convenience of rail connections, as well as the size and condition of the rectory. Yet they also included an accounting of the quality of the land belonging to the mother and daughter churches in the pastor's care and the income he could expect from it, as well as the proceeds arising from the land attached to the parsonage.

In the case of Größ-Poplow, a parish near the upper Pomeranian town of Belgard, the lease governing church property produced an income from the sale of 2,320 kilograms of rye and potatoes combined, as well as 864 marks in cash. The pastorate's income was to come from 2,100 kilograms in rye and potatoes combined and 910 marks in cash, for a total of 1,961 marks.[46] In Plötzig near Pyritz, rye, wheat, bratwurst, eggs, and a few sheep worth approximately 600 marks total provided the income of the parsonage.[47] For the Old Prussian Union Church, the income from leasing land comprised an important supplement to government grants and the church tax assessed on all who had not formally withdrawn from the church, particularly after stabilization when the income from revised leases approached prewar yields.[48] Yet even that understates the significance of the landed economy for the church, in both Prussia and Pomerania. Not only did inflation permanently and disastrously erode its capital assets, but later on cutbacks in state subsidies and the reductions in the church tax, the consequences of depression, made the church more determined than ever to squeeze a profit from its land. Not a few Pomerania parishes realized more of their income from leasing than from the church tax, a progressive assessment determined by occupation that each parish collected, a point not lost on patrons or parish councils.[49] The council chairman of the parish Juchow, near Neustettin, remarked that land was his church's and pastorate's most important source of income: "Money . . . is no substitute for land. During the inflation, the pastorate lost its cash assets of around thirty thousand marks (and that was all in gold marks!). Its land, however, held its value. In a possible new currency devaluation, the value of one's money could easily be lost again."[50]

The church's place in the landed economy defined the pastor's role. The obligations attached to a country parish were not limited to the more commonly accepted responsibilities of the ministry. They also entailed overseeing, and even personally undertaking, the production of food. To be a *Landpastor* in the truest sense of the word meant not only traveling long distances by bicycle over poor roads to attend to the villages in one's parish or rousing oneself from bed late at night to give communion to the dying. It also involved tending one's garden at six in the morning, and perhaps even becoming an expert beekeeper.[51]

Ultimately, it was the duty of the consistory in Stettin to conclude acceptable parish leases in consultation with the patrons and the parish councils. When the patron himself leased the land, as in the case of the knight's estate holder, Franz Moennich of Schlachtow, near the lower Pomeranian town of Wolgast, his contract revealed both the rent owed to the pastor and the services stemming from the patron's obligation. Not only did the lease require that he deliver one hundred zentners (one thousand kilograms of rye yearly and five liters of whole milk daily at a price 40 percent cheaper than what the closest dairy charged, he was also to provide eighteen round trips yearly to the Klein-Bünzow train station, plus transportation for the pastor in the performance of his various duties.[52]

The ability of the tenant, be he a peasant or estate owner, to produce an acceptable income emerged as the most important criterion, and parishes did not exclude peasants from consideration, particularly if there was no alternative. "By far the largest proportion of the present tenants," commented the provincial consistory of Gröβ-Spiegel, a parish in the Dramburg diocese, "are little people who are protected by regulations governing tenancy."[53] In the interests of maximizing income, church authorities thought it prudent to diversify—to opt for more than one tenant if circumstances warranted, although the group of forty-nine tenants who farmed the pastorate's land in Zettin near Bütow was in all likelihood unusual.[54]

More important, the church valued tenants who mechanized and intensified their production, a clear sign of the widespread commitment to agrarian modernization. The consistory concurred with the parish of Behrendorf in its decision to continue the lease of its patron, Count Behr, not simply because it was difficult to reject his claim in any case, but also because his only rival, a small cottager (*Büdner*) who had been severely injured during the war, could not match the count, either in capitalization or in agricultural sophistication.[55] Yet other concerns intruded as well. One parish council decided to renew its agreement with Count Bismarck-Osten because it would keep his laborers employed when estate bankruptcies drove others from their jobs, and because the peasant who challenged him suffered from alcohol abuse.[56] The provincial and Prussian church leadership intervened in disputes, especially when the parishes themselves could not resolve them, and that intervention became more frequent when estate owners failed to meet their obligations as the agrarian depression deepened.

The social origins and career patterns of Evangelical pastors reinforced the rootedness of the church. A sampling of Evangelical clergymen ordained between the last decade of the nineteenth century and the fourth decade of the twentieth underscores their suitability for the parishes under their care. Most had been born in Pomerania, and those who had not came from other eastern Prussian provinces. Sons of clergymen led those reporting their fathers' occupations. Few certainly could trace their clerical heritage back as far as Hugo Gotthard Bloth, the author of a well-regarded study of the Pomeranian church, whose family tree consisted of three hundred years of Lutheran pastors.[57] Nevertheless a number claimed pastoral heritages of several generations. Sons of primary school teachers and peasants followed at a distant second and third. The remainder consisted variously of officials' sons, usually railroad personnel, estate administrators, and merchants, with one offspring each of a textile worker, gardener, banker, white-collar employee, and industrialist. The strong contingent of pastors' sons signified not only the status of the clergy as solid members of the academically trained middle class (*Bildungsbürgertum*) (all of them, as required, had undergone extensive schooling in university theological faculties), but the social distance a candidate had to travel if he aspired to the pastorate from the ranks of the less educated. One pastor, the son of a peasant, retrospectively confessed his demoralization when he arrived at the gymnasium in the nearest town. Although expected to learn his Latin, he could speak only low German (*plattdeutsch*). Desperately homesick and feeling woefully out of place, he retreated to his village, agreeing to return only after the man who eventually became his father-in-law persuaded him.[58] For the few pastors whose fathers engaged in commerce, the obstacles could be almost as daunting. One cleric recalled his early career in his father's wholesale wine business, one he abandoned for the ministry upon the latter's death. Because he received his diploma from a modern gymnasium rather than the classical variety more typical of divinity students, he was forced to learn Greek and Hebrew before proceeding to his theological studies.[59]

Even more significant, both the training and the careers of Pomeranian pastors linked them to the province's centers of power. Several of them served as military chaplains or traveled a common route for theology students before their ordination, serving as "house teachers" (*Hauslehrer*) to the children of estate owners. In that capacity, they dispensed enough education to allow their charges to avoid the primary school while qualifying for the gymnasium, and in turn, they gained contacts among the local elite that would win them parish churches later. Given the limited career choices open to the children of agrarian elites, especially the Junkers, it is not surprising that few pastors came out of the ranks of the estate owners, a fact of no small consequence to the maneuverability of pastors indebted to landowning patrons. Only when the Versailles Treaty and republican policies increased the competition for the more acceptable occupations were younger sons encouraged to pursue a career in the clergy, yet even that imprimatur produced limited results. The one pastor in the survey with an estate-owning father inadvertently testified to the elder's singularity by remarking that his father expected him to attend the *Volksschule* along with the children of the estate laborers.[60] Nevertheless, the social connections and advanced education of Pomeranian pastors enabled them to assume a relatively privileged position in provincial society. To be sure, pastors' salaries were the lowest of academically trained state officials, which hampered their ability to send their children to secondary schools. Yet their rectories usually testified to their place in the rural world. Although sometimes in need of repair, the pastors' homes were spacious enough to accommodate them and their families.[61]

Evangelical clergymen carried complex attitudes regarding the mission of the church, and particularly its obligations to its parishioners. The characterization of pastors and church leaders as the stooges of noble patrons, as the clerical mouthpieces of reaction, comprised a frequent staple of the Socialist and Communist press in Pomerania. Yet although such descriptions were not entirely unfair, they could acknowledge neither the church's capacity for selective opposition to existing social relations nor the pastors' perceptions of themselves as middling elements in a region without a genuine middle class.[62] In fact diocesan superintendents, although proceeding from entirely conservative premises, worried that the church's status as a state-supported institution had compromised its claim not only to political impartiality, but also to its concern for the welfare of its membership. "The church appears as unsocial," complained one superintendent at a meeting of his colleagues, "as the servant of the ruling classes. One mistrusts it. One has to reawaken good will toward the church, and church members must be brought together again." The educated and property-owning classes who object to paying the church tax "must be told that the church is the last bulwark against Bolshevism."[63] The provincial consistory regularly investigated charges of the right-wing bias in their parish pastors, even if it usually found such complaints exaggerated.

In large part, the caution of Evangelical Church leaders stemmed from their desire to cooperate with amenable republican officials and the Prussian Landtag, however much they disliked doing so. Accommodation assured the "system's" continued legal, financial, and public recognition of the church's place in German culture, a posture that owed much to the upheavals of the November Revolution. Immediately after the church lost imperial protection, it confronted the pronounced anticlericalism of the Prussian Ministry of Culture, the agency most determined to implement policies inimical to church interests, among them the withdrawal of state subsidies and the extension of secular primary education. That interlude forced church leaders to sharpen their political skills, which included mastering the techniques of mass mobilization.[64]

Over the lifetime of the Republic, that strategy reaped handsome dividends. The treaty between the Old Prussian Union Church and the Prussian government concluded in 1931 after extensive negotiations was the concrete result: It guaranteed the public legal status of the church, its property, its funding from the state, and most remarkably, its independence from the Prussian Landtag in all matters of internal administration.[65] Yet the system's good will could never be taken for granted. "Caution is demanded of us," warned General Superintendent Paul Kalmus in 1928 as Pomerania's diocesan superintendents debated the issue, "The Pastors and Politics":

> We must come to terms with the present form of government as the authority ordained by God, and feel our moral obligation in the face of it. . . . Therefore, the greatest restraint is expected of clergymen, so that they do not come into conflict with the complaint desks of the state. Political faux pas (*Entgleisungen*) of pastors can be used by the state against the interests of the Evangelical Church. And punishments against clergy because of such missteps hurt the very circles who stand closest to the church. A united front (*Marschlinie*) is essential.[66]

Thus, accusations against the right-wing proclivities of pastors became notably problematic when they exposed the church's dependence on state funding. Witness the case in 1930 of the pastor from Ramelow in the Kolberg diocese who the SPD alleged proclaimed antirepublican and anti-Semitic views, while at the same time audaciously advocating a yearly three-mark church tax on the households of agricultural laborers. The furor drew the attention of the Prussian Ministry of Science, Art, and Education, which quickly investigated, fearing that the Landtag would intervene. In defending himself, the pastor did not deny his political conservatism: He admitted his opposition to the foreign policy of the late Gustav Stresemann whose program of "fulfillment" accommodated Allied security concerns in return for recognizing Germany's sovereignty. Although he had not disguised his relief at Stresemann's death, the pastor insisted that he had neither called Stresemann a Jew, one of the SPD's charges, nor opposed "the present form of state." As for the tax? If working-class families could pay forty marks a year in dues to the DLV, they certainly could afford to part with a mere three for their parish church![67] Although as that incident makes evident, Pomeranian churchmen expressed their loyalty begrudgingly; practical considerations dictated that their respect be genuine enough so as to avoid biting the feeding hand.

Nevertheless, the material and legal relationship between church and state was by no means the only issue that preoccupied Evangelical authorities. Cultivating and enriching the ties between the church and society that industrialization and urbanization had severely strained drew as much attention as solidifying the links between church and state. Evangelical clergymen in Pomerania, as elsewhere in Germany, understood the institution they represented and embodied as a "people's church," the mission of which was to act as the vehicle of social reconciliation among the classes and as the arbiter of German cultural values. As a result, they insisted repeatedly that secular ideologies could never compromise the assignment of the church to preach the Gospel, because that would compromise the church's character as a *Volkskirche*.[68] The Christian-Evangelical message, proclaimed an assembly of Pomeranian clergymen and laypersons in 1932, would stand on its own terms in effecting social reconciliation without reducing itself to a secular position. This was in keeping with the church's mandate from God.[69]

Preserving such impartiality, however, was less difficult in theory than in practice, precisely because the social context in which the Evangelical Church labored was so one-sidedly nationalist and conservative. Because its roots were weakest among urban dwellers, particularly the urban working class, the church possessed no natural balance among its most committed constituents, even had its clergymen been more diverse politically. The dilemmas of that pervasive conservatism provided grist for discussion among Pomerania's religious establishment. "Our special difficulty lies in the fact that the most loyal members of our church are opposed to the existing form of government," rued General Superintendent Walter Kähler. "No pastor can say: 'The case is closed in my parish, and thus I can speak freely.'"[70] As a result, some feared the consequences of strict neutrality. "Too strong a reserve with regard to the interests of the fatherland," remarked one superintendent, "means that we run the danger of turning off those who until now have been true to the church without winning over others who have not been."[71] Others expressed themselves more forcefully still. The church could not remain neutral in the face of its enemies: "In that case, only decisive opposition is possible. The free thinkers are our greatest enemies, and since Social Democracy in Germany is so favorably disposed to free-thinking, then we can and must battle Social Democracy as well.

Against Communism we must sound the fanfare loud and clear."[72] Although neutrality was never easy in the best of circumstances, the Pomeranian church found its studied impartiality even more difficult to sustain once the Republic's viability became unambiguously open to question.

The significance of private patrons, as well as the estate owners' direct exercise of power in ecclesiastical affairs, composed the most obvious and continuing obstacle to the clergy's desire to remain "above parties." At its most trivial, the patron's pew in front of the church reminded the village pastor of the source of his authority to preach the Word—a real cross to bear. Patrons did not simply attend church casually; many of them, particularly those who headed Pomerania's "old" families, possessed a sophisticated knowledge of theology, no doubt a throwback to the province's neo-pietist heritage when Junker patrons urged their peasants to boycott pastors who were out of step with the Awakening. Thus, patrons felt free to "offer" substantive criticism of "their" pastors' sermons, as well as shuffle their feet or express their disapproval by other means if pastors did not meet expectations. To be sure, the theological positions of the Junker patrons differed: The Kleist-Retzows, to name one example, preferred the "neo-orthodoxy" of Karl Barth, while Ewald von Kleist-Schmenzin adhered to the theological liberalism of Adolf Harnack and Paul Althaus.[73] Nevertheless, from the pastor's point of view, the end result was the same, surveillance. "Even when he mounted the chancel to give his sermon, even as he stood over his parishioners," whom the center aisle of the church divided, men on one side, women on the other, as according to custom, the patron "still looked at him diagonally from above. . . . Pastors come and go, but the *Gutsherrschaft* remains: the evident good will of the lord thus strengthened the authority of the shepherd over his flock who in a conflict would hardly be tended (*die im Konflikt kaum zu hüten wäre*)."[74]

Rural pastors had to adhere to the closely observed social distinctions of the countryside. To be sure, patrons credited their pastors for being the cultivated products of German universities charged with the responsibility for the cultural vitality of the nation. They frequently attested to the cultural significance of the clergy as a bulwark against sectarianism and communism as they sought replacements for vacant positions.[75] Yet although pastors stood above much of rural society, they were by no means the social equals of their patrons. Occasionally, they secured invitations to dinner at the manor house, most often on Sunday after services, but only by themselves, not in the company of neighboring estate owners. Moreover, they could never expect an invitation to the nobles' favorite recreation, the hunt, a slight that confirmed the pastor's status as a member of the middling sort, a *Respektsperson* requiring the deference of the peasants and workers below him, but not of the rural elite. The social position of the pastor's wife was even more ambiguous: Because the mistress of the manor took charge of the church-related charitable and social welfare projects, *Frau Pastor* found herself consigned to a subordinate role in the parish, if she dared to cross paths with her superior at all. On top of that, the long agricultural workday prevented her from ministering to peasants and estate laborers, even assuming that the *Gutsfrau* had not beaten her to it.[76]

Frau Pastor's lack of autonomy was evident in other ways. Visitation reports not only evaluated the future prospects of pastors, but also assessed whether or not their wives properly fulfilled their expected role as helpmeet. "His parsonage breathes of good spirit and his wife stands by his side with understanding," commented one such favorable judgment.[77] In other cases, however, wives suffered equally with their husbands—or even more—if political heterodoxy happened to coexist with less-than-commendable marital circumstances. One pastor under review "unnecessarily emphasizes over and over his democratic and pacifist proclivities, placing himself in opposition to his strongly nationalistic parish, a posture which grates all the more so because of his wife's hysteria."[78] Another who ran afoul of his patron for his near communist political beliefs incurred additional opprobrium because his marriage set an "appalling example."[79]

The living arrangements of pastors' wives, even if they were not beholden to a patron, could become precarious if they were left widows. Witness the example of the seventy-eight-year-old pastor's wife whom the consistory in Stettin sought to evict from the three-room flat she had occupied in the present pastor's house after husband's death. Against the protests of her son who argued that the present pastor still had six rooms for himself and his family, the consistory responded that the widow "is known as a very energetic person, but not one who is easy to get along with." She ought to look seriously for another flat because her husband had been dead for four years. That the church was obligated to support the widow of a pastor who served his parish for twenty-six years, the consistory dismissed as "completely unheard of."[80] If the Evangelical consistory could not accommodate pastors' wives in such cases, then how much greater *Frau Pastor's* dilemma must have been being in the shadow, not only of her husband, but also of the *Gutsfrau*?

Patrons did not limit scrutiny of "their" pastors to the style and substance of their sermons or to the diligence with which they undertook their ministries. Political reliability entered into their considerations as well, so much so that the consistory voiced its concern lest the one-sidedness of the clergy outweigh the transparent benefits of patronage. "In our experience," commented one consistory report, "the adherence of the pastor under consideration to a specific political party or association like the Stahlhelm, for example, has played its part in placement through private patrons."[81] Patrons became the eager sponsors of bitterly anti-Bolshevik pastors from German-speaking communities in the Baltic states who sought repatriation, initiatives that did nothing to undermine the conservative coloration of the majority of Pomerania's rural clergy. Pastors in that position often said the right thing by professing their desire to resettle in a country parish and work toward the resurrection of the German fatherland.[82] If the consistory harbored doubts about the ability of some Baltic repatriates to deliver sermons effectively, the aegis of a powerful patron rendered such reservations irrelevant.[83] If Baltic pastors confronted opposition in their parishes, either because of their lack of familiarity with the local customs or for their flagrant advocacy of right-wing politics, they could anticipate the aid of their patrons. In one such case, a veterinarian who accused his pastor of agitating on behalf of the German National People's Party "found his practice boycotted by the local large landownership."[84] In another instance, the Baltic refugee lacked ministerial initiative and thus did not appeal to many of his parishioners. Nevertheless, the pastor and his wife possessed "a fine general education which in their exchanges with the lordship proves advantageous.[85]

Despite that concern, the wrath of a patron could not help but place the church leadership on the defensive. In the parish of Gross-Jestin in the Kolberg diocese, a conflict arose between a rural pastor and his estate-owning patron, a bourgeois owner, regarding the latter's charge that the pastor harbored communist sympathies. The evidence that the patron presented included the clergyman's celebration of May Day in the marketplace in the company of "the greatest agitators of the rural Volk," his attendance at a Socialist rally before the referendum to expropriate princely estates, as well as his description of Lenin and Trotsky as "model men" to his confirmation classes. Yet while the consistory recognized that the pastor was effective with the "simpler circles" of his congregation, and that the patron had clearly exaggerated his case, only the pastor's advanced age prevented his removal. The consistory criticized his "hostile attitude toward large landownership," his mistrust of the church leadership, and his tactlessness, but let him off with a reprimand because he was nearing retirement.[86]

In another instance, an activist pastor in the parish of Swellin in the Bublitz diocese aroused the ire of his patrons by seeking to broaden the representation of the parish council and objecting to the singing of the *Deutschlandlied* in church. The pastor, his patrons alleged, believed that "the workers give all to the owner, but the owner does nothing for the workers," thus pitting employees against their employers. In the end, the pastor was forced to admit that he had "not always exercised the necessary caution" when he introduced party politics from the chancel. He promised that in the future, he would avoid politics while performing his official duties.[87]

Moreover, the church found it difficult to implement its social agendas, even those that were conservative in their intentions, because of the immobility of rural hierarchies. Recruiting members to the Pomeranian branch of the Evangelical Workers' Association (*Evangelischer Arbeiterverein*, or EAV) provides the first example. Founded in Westphalia in the 1880s, the EAV strove to achieve harmony between Protestant employers and employees, establishing a corporatist body that was "economically peaceful" and non-confrontational, protective of private property, and antisocialist, while remaining above party politics in a way consistent with the Protestant claim to neutrality.[88] After the revolution, however, it endorsed measures that restricted the prerogatives of capital in order to compete with the immediate postwar gains of the trade unions—among them the eight-hour day, the

prohibition against child labor, and the establishment of arbitration committees. On top of that, the EAV sought to extend its protection to
agricultural laborers, advocating the construction of decent housing, a voice
for rural workers on local welfare administrations, improved health benefits, and a presence on arbitration committees.[89]

Not surprisingly, the EAV encountered the opposition of the estate
owners, even as it moved to resist the leftist "threat" in the Pomeranian
countryside. "Here the soil for our work is especially rocky," rued one EAV
report.[90] "Our pastors have worked hard," commented the visitation commission to Belgard, "but unfortunately they have found insufficient
understanding on the land."[91] Some church documents tried to put the best
face on the problems they encountered. The EAV failed to show much ac-
complishment, admitted the visitation report from Bütow, "although the
agrarian working class has in general withdrawn from the Social Democratic organizations and has joined the Rural League, which has thus paved the
way for a harmonious relationship between employers and employees."[92]
Others reflected more depression than optimism. The distrust of church efforts among landowners, noted one of the general superintendents, "has
grown all the stronger as the owners have succeeded, through their powerful influence in bringing their workers to the ballot box to vote German
National (*in deutsch-national Sinne an die Wahlurn zu bringen*)." Churchman
could only concede that the estate owners had effectively co-opted most
estate laborers. "The majority of the workers are integrated in the Rural
League. The leaders [of the Rural League] are politically engaged and
always treat their workers as objects, never as subjects." What was the un-
derlying reason? "Workers on the land are still too much like sheep, who
before long, are brought under control and strung along . . . we find so few
independent souls among rural workers."[93] By 1931 only Mecklenburg, another bastion of estate agriculture, had fewer members in its Workers'
Association among the Eastern Prussian provinces.[94]

The endeavor to resettle the Prussian east with healthy peasant stock,
thus countering the region's depopulation, became another arena in
which Evangelical interests clashed with those of estate owners, despite the
conservative assumptions behind Evangelical policies. Founded in 1929
under the auspices of the Inner Mission, The Evangelical Settlement Service
(*Evangelischer Siedlungsdienst*, or ESD) not only lobbied the Republican
agencies charged with eastern settlement to preserve the Evangelical character of locales under consideration, it also actively encouraged Protestant
settlers to move eastward. The ESD's creation signified the church's growing
concern that agrarian crisis and mounting estate bankruptcies provided opportunities for the spread of Polonism (*Polentum*) and Catholicism.[95]
According to Hermann Schultz, the ESD's head, the organization he led had
no intention of using settlement to challenge large landownership. Rather,
the ESD wanted to increase the number of peasants and contract laborers
so as to prohibit the spread of *Polentum*, implicitly agreeing with the intent
of the existing settlement legislation:

The challenge of settlement for us, however, means the special task of maintaining and strengthening the Evangelical faith. The land east of the Oder can only remain German for the duration if it is Protestant. The construction of an ever greater number of Catholic enclaves can only be avoided by procuring Protestant settlers. The fate of Germany and Protestantism is closely bound to the existence of eastern Germany.[96]

To support the ESD, the church press eagerly espoused the virtues of returning to the land: "Who among us in the nerve-shattering noise of the factories, in the coal mines or elsewhere in the frenetic hustle and bustle of the metropolis, hasn't reflected upon the sunny days of one's childhood on the land in better times when there was still sufficient work?"[97] Despite its commitment, however, the ESD contended with problems that hampered its undertaking, problems that even exceeded those of the Republic's settlement program. They included not only insufficient funding but also the lack of good candidates for farming. As some pastors recognized, even unemployed estate laborers (an increasingly common plight by the early 1930s) constituted poor risks because they were not used to managing on their own. In any case, the income of the estate laborers who still had jobs exceeded that of settlers or small and middling peasants.[98] In Pomerania specifically, the possibility of engaging soldiers discharged from the province's garrisons met with skepticism because "the garrisons lie in the city. Also, the wives mostly come from the city themselves and are ill-suited for agriculture."[99] Then too, the ESD found it difficult to entice Protestants from the west to move east where market conditions and soil quality differed significantly from what they had known.[100]

Worse still, the behavior of the agrarian establishment rendered no easier the task of preserving the Evangelical character of the Prussian east, and Pomerania in particular. The ESD complained bitterly about the "irresponsible agitation of the Rural League" against the construction of settlements for the unemployed, reporting massive opposition from the League and the Chamber of Agriculture. Pomeranian church officials glumly acknowledged that Evangelical interests received less than adequate consideration when estates were divided, particularly when the issue of replacing the landlord's patronage became paramount.[101] As large landowners sought to unload their holdings to escape collapse, they failed to be as selective in their choice of purchasers as the church would have liked, willingly selling to Catholic buyers. The superintendent of Pasewalk in lower Pomerania petitioned the Consistory to engage the Chamber of Agriculture's help in preventing the sale of the Rothenklemp estate to the Catholic Church. If the sale were completed, he warned, Protestant workers, many of whose families had been employed for generations on the estate, would lose their jobs. That in turn would mean the end of the Evangelical school there, as well as the village church: "Then the disappearance of an Evangelical congregation is only a matter of time."[102] Even lords such as Count Eichstedt-Hohenholz who maintained a reputation for being well disposed toward the church were not

above looking to Catholic purchasers if Protestants lacked sufficient financial resources to occupy the estates themselves.[103] Be that as it may, the
number of estates available for settlement dropped precipitously after 1931
when the protection against creditors included in the Eastern Aid (*Osthilfe*)
program gave estate owners less incentive to sell.[104]

Nevertheless, Pomeranian churchmen continued to act as vehicles for the
paternalistic ethos of estate owners, partly by propagating a vision of labor
relations consistent with that of the landlords and partly by permitting the
landlords to speak for themselves in church periodicals. The Sunday press
disseminated the social message of the German Evangelical Church, the
umbrella for all the *Landeskirchen* in Germany, regarding the ethical demands of property and the dignity of work. Decrying the class antagonism
and "materialist spirit" that divided worker from employer, the statement
urged employers to exercise their power wisely, ensuring in particular that
their labor receive decent wages. Labor was not simply a commodity nor an
undifferentiated mass, the proclamation asserted; rather, workers were Volk
comrades "worthy of equality" (*gleichzuachende*) whose spiritual as well as
material needs should be met.[105] Similarly, estate owners stressed the differences between capitalism as they understood it and the human community
on the land: "Capital is demonic if it ruthlessly rides roughshod over
human misery and scorns the Volk community, only to enable the acquisition of profits." By contrast, capital was helpful if used to secure a peaceful
life and ensure possibilities for honorable work: "The health and happiness
of the employee is to us of greater value than a rising rate of return (*Zin-
sertrag*). Concern for the general welfare of our Volk is to us holier than
international capitalist interests."[106] The discourse of community was too
deeply ingrained to allow the church's irritation to become the church's rebellion.

The Sins of the Cities: Sectarianism and Moral Decline

Despite the conflicts that existed between the Evangelical Church and landowners, or more narrowly between Evangelical pastors and patrons, the
church found it impossible ultimately to escape its own need to sustain and
propagandize the rural myth. As an institution with deep roots in rural society, in stark contrast to the cities of the west where it competed far less
successfully against secularism, the church could never identify the landowners as its enemies. Instead, it saw urban civilization and all of its
consequences as its greatest menace. In brief, the cities meant republicanism,
pluralism, mechanization, Americanization, sectarianism, experimentation
in education, and moral decay, particularly in its confusion of the proper
boundaries between the sexes. Such ills, however, did not simply confine
themselves to the cities west of the Elbe that drew people away from the
land, although those urban centers were bad enough. They spread their ten-
tacles eastward, threatening to penetrate the remotest hamlet with their
poison. Because church leaders were accustomed to associating Germany's

strength as a nation with the preservation of a healthy rural life, the threat of the cities, in their minds, was serious indeed.

One of the clearest expressions of the kind of world that the Republic fostered was, in the view of Evangelical Church leaders, the expanded proselytizing of religious sects. Once forbidden to recruit under the Empire, such denominations as the Jehovah's Witnesses, the Church of Jesus Christ of Latter Day Saints (more commonly known as the Mormons), the Baptists, the Seventh Day Adventists, and the New Apostolic Church took advantage of the Republic's constitutionally codified religious neutrality to intensify their missionizing.[107] They showed little hesitation in spreading their message, even in such profoundly Lutheran strongholds as Pomerania. Although the sects could never hope to rival the Evangelical Church there in absolute numbers, cells cropped up in nearly all of the province's cities and towns, while their recruiters made themselves as visible as possible.[108] Ironically, the spread of the sects attested to the pervasively religious climate, especially in upper Pomerania, and the deep religious needs of much of the populace. Oral histories of Latter Day Saints church members from throughout Germany reveal few secularists suddenly transformed into religious believers: Often they explained their conversions, and those of family members, as having resulted from the Mormons' ability to answer nagging questions that the church of their birth failed to satisfy.[109]

The diocesan superintendents of the Evangelical Church admitted as much when they discussed the reasons for the appeal of the sects, especially in the eastern reaches of the province: "That is certainly proof of a strong religious life, but it can also heavily burden the heart," noted one. "The sects can always be found where there is a well-cultivated religious soil," remarked another. Sectarianism drew few followers in such unchurched regions as lower Pomerania and Saxony.[110] Pleas to the Supreme Consistory in Berlin for assistance in finding replacement pastors for parishes without clergymen also indicated how easily the sects could prey on unmet needs. Such parishes were ripe for the enticements of the sects because they lacked a forceful enough presence to counteract them. "Straightaway the church life of this parish would splinter among the sects if a pastor were not there," was a common enough warning.[111]

Then too, parishioners in such circumstances appeared insufficiently sophisticated to recognize "false doctrine" (*Irrlehre*) when they heard it: "The knowledge is so slight that only very seldom can a peasant, day laborer or even an educated man resist the opponent who comes with Bible in hand, although these are for the most part simple people who learn their nonsense with zeal."[112] "The pastorate has frequently observed that simple parishioners are confused by the details of leaflets which they take literally," noted the Consistory regarding the Jehovah's Witnesses, "and they are driven to mistrust of the church and its clergy."[113] Indeed, the Latter Day Saints, to name but one sect, strove for simplicity in conveying their message as a matter of general practice, teaching the meaning of faith, repentance, baptism, and the gift of the Holy Spirit. Delving into the deeper mysteries of the "restoration," the Book of Mormon, and the migration of Hebrew peoples to North America, among the most distinctive elements of Mormonism, either invited incredulity from potential converts to whom such concepts were utterly foreign or imposed the obligation on missionaries to prove their points against those of other faiths.[114]

The recruitment of sectarian missionaries appeared to have the greatest impact among the "little people," those whom the Evangelical Church most wanted to reach in the name of the *Volkskirche*.[115] Although now and then a person of means and high station would gravitate to the sects, the membership of the "new" religious groups tended to draw from the (often unspecified and undifferentiated) lower classes. The Seventh Day Adventist European Conference drew generally from "simple, plain people," with no doctors of philosophy or theology in their midst.[116] "Many of our people are poor," commented the Adventists about their membership in Kolberg, having "no house or farm of their own."[117] Other references were even more elliptical. "The simple witness of a lay person," remarked a superintendent about the New Apostles' services, "are often more effective than great addresses."[118] The sects did particularly well among women, not only because they came to the churches in disproportionate numbers, but also because they were less educated than men. Evangelical clergymen feared especially for the religious choices of single women, while the Mormons canvassed women as being the most effective way to reach their husbands.[119]

Of all the movements, the Mormons came closest to reaching a middle-class audience. According to one former missionary, they operated between the extremes of the "so-called upper classes on the one hand" and "very poor people" on the other, attracting a few middle-class people along with workers in textile plants.[120] Yet here too, the circles in which the Latter Day Saints' missionaries moved were modest. Commented another: "In all the three years I was there I lived in various homes, rented rooms from various homes. I never once found a place where they had a shower, never once knew a person who actually owned an automobile."[121]

What did the sects offer that proved so attractive? For an indeterminate number, material considerations figured to have been at least as important as "spiritual" ones, although we should not succumb to the altogether pointless exercise of precise calculation. On occasion, Mormon leaders warned against giving charity to those who had not tithed, further implying that the depth of the commitment of some extended only as far as the donations they received.[122] Similarly, the Adventists worried that church members were "more interested in being taken care of financially than doing the work of the Lord" and fretted lest requests for contributions from their European branches exceed the means and good will of their congregations, particularly during periods of economic hardship.[123]

What specifically religious needs did the sects fill? For some converts, tragic personal losses such as the death of a parent or close relative impelled them to seek consolation, especially when the established church failed to fill the void in their lives. Indeed for some, intense dreams or visions ac-

companied their search for certainty against the political and social upheavals affecting their lives.[124] Others, however, particularly those who
crossed over to the Mormons, sought emigration to America, not because
they aspired to live in a secular "land of opportunity," but because they believed themselves to be on a fundamentally religious quest. Converts to the
Latter Day Saints understood Salt Lake City, Utah, the Mormon capital and
their intended designation as "Zion," where the "gathering" of the faithful
would occur to build the kingdom of God on earth. German authorities had
long objected to the Mormons on national grounds alone, inasmuch as (according to one report from prewar Saxony) the "fanatical" Latter Day Saints
missionaries, many of them middle class, enticed women and young girls
with the prospect of emigration.[125]

Moreover, the political and economic hardships, especially of the early republican years, brought an upsurge in new members for the sects. The
Adventists enjoyed their best recruiting year in 1923 because of hyperinflation: "The more troubles there are, the more the work of God seems to
prosper," commented the Adventists' American leadership.[126] The sects'
field-workers were better able to cope than the state churches with the "new
standards of living," not least because of the support they received from
their superiors in the United States.[127] Troubled times lent credibility to the
sects' message. "A deeper reason for the spread of sectarianism is the anticipation of the end time," explained a superintendent noting the degree to
which the apocalyptic emphasis of the Adventists, New Apostles, and the
Jehovah's Witnesses appealed to their audiences.[128]

Yet as Evangelical Church officials recognized, together with the sects
themselves, the new religious movements conveyed a sense of community
that their followers could not find in their regular parishes.[129] Lacking
chapels or churches of their own, the sects rented secular meeting places for
their services, be they restaurants, dance halls, or pubs, often having to im-
provise for special rituals.[130] One Mormon from Stettin recalled that his
mother had been baptized in Glambeck lake through a hole in the ice because the Latter Day Saints' meeting hall did not have a font.[131]
Nevertheless, such incidents were memorable precisely because they bore
witness to the commitment of the membership. The Adventists worried
about creating a privileged minority of ministers and tract peddlers, especially because they compensated its personnel for lost income from other
jobs. Yet that too reflected the desire to preserve the solidarity and spiritual
egalitarianism for which the Adventists had been noted.[132]

For the Evangelical clergy, in Pomerania and the Prussian east, the sects
preached a variety of false and even dangerous claims. Some of the sects attacked the idea of a paid, learned, state-subsidized professional clergy as
unbiblical, and by implication, attacked the legally recognized cultural role
of the Evangelical Church as well.[133] While the Jehovah's Witnesses compared the church to Babylon, the New Apostles preached that Jesus worked
only through the living members of their own sect, a doctrine that obviously undermined the mediating roles of the institution and its pastors. For

the Evangelical clergy, every individual through his or her own faith sacralized the world, a notion entirely consistent with Luther's concept of the "priesthood of all believers." Yet not everyone was entitled to serve as a pastor, who needed the requisite academic training to prepare him for his central task—the public proclamation of the word of God to his parishioners.[134] Moreover, the Adventists observed their sabbath on Saturday while the Baptists rejected infant baptism outright. The Mormons could never escape their reputation as polygamists, although they had long since abandoned the practice.[135]

Ironically given the concern they engendered, one could scarcely consider the new religious movements politically offensive. When they confronted political questions at all (usually when those questions were thrust upon them), their answers ranged from conservative to naive. Not surprisingly, they interpreted political events through the lens of salvation history. Although hostile to Bolshevism, indeed having gone so far as to praise Germany as the last bulwark against the Soviet system, the Adventists insisted that their primary mission had to do with "things eternal," thus securing the opportunity to preach freely. Their leadership's attitude toward Hitler once the Nazis achieved power revealed qualified gratitude that the denomination was allowed the liberty to do its work.[136] An indeterminate number of Mormons joined the Nazi party while their American missionaries found it difficult to criticize Hitler. The Führer stood for self-sacrifice and motherhood, and he appeared at first to be supportive of the Mormons' work.[137] One Mormon looking back on his career recalled that many church members with whom he came in contact did not believe that the Nazis would harm the Jews, maintaining instead that God called Hitler to lead them back to Palestine.[138] The New Apostolic Church moved beyond benign neutrality to outright support for the Third Reich.[139]

Regardless, some of the sects espoused positions that put them at odds with prevailing cultural mores. The Adventists rejected military service, particularly in combat positions. The Jehovah's Witnesses, however, went to such extremes as to push them completely beyond the pale of respectability. They not only denied the trinity, they also refused obedience to secular authorities. Thus they rejected both military service and the performance of secular oaths. Their pacifism, it was feared, rendered their listeners less willing to perform their duties to the Fatherland. Their eschatological conviction that the present order was soon to collapse rendered separatism the only logical course of action.[140] Devout Lutherans especially, who valorized the state as a regiment ordained by God—a necessary vehicle for containing evil in the world and allowing the church to preach its message, could not tolerate them.

The American origins of many of the sects drew fire as well, and not just because their foreignness accounted for the peculiarity and extremes of their theologies. Rather, America exhibited a variety of ills ranging from unsanctioned violence to crass materialism. Mormon missionaries, all but rare exceptions American and often having learned their German on the boat coming over, found themselves answering questions about Chicago gangsters and the putative wealth of other Americans as often as they discussed their founder, Joseph Smith, or defended themselves against the stereotype of being polygamous.[141] Their watches, cameras, and clothes and the strength of their dollar, especially during hyperinflation, attracted criticism, even from German church members.[142] In fact, the church considered purchasing a mansion in Berlin for its headquarters, but it feared that the Latter Day Saints would be compared negatively to "those Jews" from Poland, Russia, England, and the United States who allegedly bought properties in the best neighborhoods.[143] Although the sects appreciated the freedom to preach that the Weimar Republic gave them, in contrast to the repression of the Kaiserreich, all steeled themselves against the resistance they would likely confront in securing permission to hold meetings in public places. They endured the interruptions of ministers from the state church who were determined to refute "false doctrine". In one such case, an Evangelical pastor spoke out during a Mormon service in Kolberg, attacking Joseph Smith as an epileptic and fanatic. Not satisfied with assaulting the good name of the Latter Day Saints' founder, the intruder accused the Mormons of believing that Adam was Christ and that the savior in turn had many wives.[144]

Because the Jehovah's Witnesses provoked the greatest animosity, the Evangelical press and the provincial consistory launched conspiracy theories to explain their theology and even their very existence. The Witnesses, according to one such article, were motivated not by religious commitment or spirituality, but rather by political considerations. They eagerly positioned themselves to take advantage of a people whom war, defeat, and revolution had demoralized. Moreover, because the Witnesses turned their followers against the existing order, they did the work not only of the Bolsheviks, but especially "international Jewry," whom American money generously financed. Both the Russian and German Revolutions bore the Witnesses' signature. The Jewish influence among Socialists and Democrats (the sort of people who desired a confessionally neutral republic in the first place) underscored the seriousness of the threat that good Protestants had to meet head on. Like the Socialists and Jews, the Witnesses mocked European Christian culture, and thus they destroyed the very foundations of the German nation.[145]

The intrusions of the Catholic Church provoked only slightly less antagonism that those of the sects. Not only did the Protestant attitude reflect the deep religious cleavages in German society as a whole—cleavages that did much to sustain religious identity in numerous regions. Catholic activity also threatened to undermine the near uniformly Protestant character of Pomerania and the other border areas in the Prussia east. "We are continually focusing our attention on this danger which lies in the eastern portion of our province at the same time it threatens the fatherland," remarked a consistory report in the mid-twenties, "because there Catholic Polonism is at work gradually in putting Pomeranian land in the hands of Poles."[146] How was it possible for Catholicism to arouse such anxieties? According to an Old Prussian Union Church survey conducted in 1925, some Catholics migrated from the west to take up civil service jobs on the railroads and in the customs and welfare bureaucracies, as well as the post. They comprised the physical evidence of the Center Party's key position in the Prussian governing coalition. Compounding those numbers were the Catholic settlers whom the provincial consistory accused of creating closed Catholic enclaves partially from divided estates, a subject that, as we have already recognized, produced considerable exasperation among churchmen with landowning patrons.[147] Then came the Polish laborers whom Protestant estate owners employed against the interests of their own church, because of their docility, their willingness to perform the chores that Germans would not do, and their low susceptibility to leftist recruitment.[148] "The guilt of Catholicism for the collapse of our Volk makes itself palpable," commented a superintendent in this connection.[149] Polish laborers, agreed the Pomeranian consistory, invited the intrusions of "Roman Catholic propaganda," and that only reinforced the expansion of Polonism.[150]

In turn, the presence of Catholics, however limited their numbers may seem from a distance, induced their church to provide the necessary support—priests, teachers, hospitals, and religious orders dedicated to welfare work, all of them from the Protestant perspective at least lavishly funded. The survey alleged with dismay that Catholic settlers were expected to hire only Catholic workers in return for receiving church-sponsored loans in order to buy their land. In addition, Evangelical authorities believed that the Catholic Church pressured couples in mixed marriages to rear their children Catholic, and that Catholic teachers subverted the once totally Evangelical composition of many schools in the border areas. Most galling of all, the survey noted that even Protestant doctors often referred their patrons to Catholic hospitals. These developments could not have been anything other than unsettling to Evangelical Church leaders who condemned the "national unreliability" of Catholics, especially those residing close to the Polish border. "Which position . . . the Catholic Church has taken toward *Polentum* shows itself clearly in the fact that Catholic priests agitated in favor of Poland" in the upper Silesian plebiscite.[151]

The encroachment of other denominations into Pomerania represented for the Evangelical Church the wages of the republican "system." The religiously neutral state guaranteed the right of foreign sects to spread their "false doctrine," while the pivotal position of the Center Party at the Reich and Prussian levels lent new legitimacy to Catholicism, encouraging Catholics and the Catholic Church to occupy traditionally Protestant regions, despite their negative implications for the survival of German culture. Given the linkages that Protestant clergymen envisioned between their identity as Pomeranians, Prussians, and Germans on the one hand, and the Reformation on the other, notions of religious pluralism within a common citizenship appeared entirely foreign. Such diversity characterized the city to be sure, but it contradicted the spirit and substance of "community" in the east. Yet if the sects and Catholicism were but two symptoms of the Republic's inadequacies, the social liberalization of the 1920s that clergymen perceived as the unfortunate, if logical, consequence of cosmopolitanism was even worse. It undermined the permanence, stability, common moral bonds, and close-knit character of rural society, the essence of the rural myth. It especially called into question the patriarchalism of Pomeranian country life, blurring the accepted boundaries between male and female. Although moral concerns sat high on the agendas of Evangelical churches throughout Germany in the twenties, they resonated deeply in Pomerania because the province's agrarian environment seemed well suited to the sort of values that urbanism undermined.[152]

Throughout the Weimar period, Pomeranian church periodicals launched a sustained attack against the evidence of widespread moral degradation that they perceived. High suicide rates, alcoholism, and high crime rates, particularly among the youth, drew their share of coverage. Reporters intended not simply to convey the "facts" as they understood them, but to grab their readers' attention with colorful and imaginative "this-is-what-will-happen-if-it-gets-much-worse" scenarios. Alcohol abuse, for example, produced a poem entitled "Alcohol speaks," printed in the shape of a cocktail glass that invited one to succumb to progressive degeneration sip by sip. When the reader-drinker arrived at the last line of the poem, he or she learned the irreversible fate of alcohol consumption: "So I [alcohol] nourish the fire, while you drink and drink until you slink to the very depths of hell!"[153] Similar to the treatment accorded the issue of religious instruction and the status of the confessional primary schools, Evangelical newspapers extensively criticized pedagogical experimentation that promoted individualism at the expense of instruction that stressed the dependence of human beings on their maker. Complained one article, educational theory that cultivated the "ideal of personality," a notion that had been gaining acceptance over the previous century, bowed to the Enlightenment's idols of nature and human reason. It celebrated human autonomy while neglecting to convey the moral and religious values that "assert the claim that God has upon us and on the world he created."[154]

Yet the multiform evidence of eroding sexual morality, the result of the war and the Republic's more liberal climate, was the most worrisome concern of the church press. The greater tolerance of pornography, sexual expressiveness in the fine arts, prostitution, relationships without marriage, a divorce rate that seemed to soar out of control, and abortion all menaced what the church determined was the bedrock of German culture and nationhood, the nuclear family and the appropriate gender roles assigned to each member.[155] The "germ cell" of the nation, as one Sunday newspaper implied, consisted of the father-bread winner and mother-homemaker surrounded by numerous disciplined, handsome, and obedient children. Consistent with the fear of conservative circles as to the consequences of the declining birthrate for Germany's future as a world power, another periodical commented that a married couple without children is like the sun without its rays. It is a dubious sign of our times that the joy of having children has so often disappeared, that one finds at most one to three children in a family. How tragic it becomes when illness or war takes away the only child, or when the only child is spoiled and warped, and therefore turns out badly. Too late do parents come to realize just how shortsighted they have been.[156]

Although all but invisible in the church administration, synods, and of course the pastorate, women assumed pronounced significance in the Evangelical Church's conception of the proper moral universe. Because the church connected a healthy moral order with national resurgence (or conversely, moral collapse with national decline), the female contribution was vital to Germany's recovery from defeat. "Today the other [the woman] stands at the forefront of our Volk's difficult battle of destiny" as a source of consolation and welfare, commented one parish newspaper.[157] The responsibilities of Evangelical women included not only the care of the home and tending to the children, but also the maintenance of an ethical and Christian climate, so necessary to ensuring that future generations could sustain a revitalized Germany. By extension, awakening and sustaining a Christian life in the parishes depended on her engagement in church-sponsored welfare work and ministering to the sick: "As the mother is the center piece of the family, so a lively parish will only emerge where women are also alive."[158] Another commended the work of the Ladies Aid (*Frauenhilfe*) in ways that clarified the linkages between well-defined gender roles and German reconstruction:

> Our precious Evangelical church has an especially important task to perform in the rebuilding of our Volk, one which cannot be left to the pastors alone. We therefore call upon our dear Evangelical women, as guardians of our deepest religious riches, faith, love and moral purity, to cooperate in making our church parishes vital; thereby supplying our Volk with the religious and moral power necessary for renewal.[159]

Consistent with her significance as *Landesmutter* for the Pomeranian right, the departed empress Auguste Victoria, who suffered and died in exile, appeared in the church press as the Evangelical *Hausfrau*'s paradigm. Articles described her as the archetypal caring mother, closely supervising the moral development of her children, pious and deeply committed to church work. "We value the Kaiserin's life and work," memorialized one article. "What an example she has left to us as a mother in the narrower circle of her family, and as the mother of her country for the wider circle of our Volk comrades."[160] Not surprisingly, neither male church leaders nor pastors considered women equal partners, and the degree of cooperation that church-sponsored women's organizations received depended on whether the hierarchy viewed them as subversive or supportive of "traditional" gender roles. Even a noble woman such as Marie von Kleist complained about the lack of support she received from church leaders, one of the few instances when the clergy felt secure enough to spurn the intrusions of the landed elite. They were more inclined to favor the less emancipatory Ladies Aid.[161] Nevertheless, the very importance that the church assigned to women's fulfilling their proper roles rested on the assumption that fundamental gender differences justified separate spheres for men and women.

The sins of the cities contraposed the Evangelical Church's vision of intact and partriarchally structured Protestant families contributing to the moral regeneration of the Volk. The church's obsession with sexuality, particularly its misuses, did not merely express prudery, however tempting it is to look on it as such. Rather, ecclesiastical fixations underscored the Evangelical conviction that diversity, indeed disorder, in sexual relationships assaulted the very structures of power—that power that not only resided in the patriarchal family as the foundation of society, but also extended to other institutions embracing the body politic. The cities, according to one article, represented modernization above all, and that in turn meant godlessness. Moreover, "rootless" and "homeless" migrants who "lacked their own soil" filled the industrial centers, creating unemployment and suffering. The belief in progress and the worship of machines had led to the destruction of culture. Marriage and the family, according to church periodicals, were in shambles, while divorces, suicides, and free love proliferated. No one observed the ten commandments any longer.[162] Although all cities acted as breeding grounds for the disease of immorality, Berlin stood as the very paradigm of corruption. "Whoever has to travel to Berlin these days," harped one piece, "will rightly wonder about the picture of public immorality." Every street car and train station displayed pornography and blatant prostitution. "Can any father or mother still remain composed if they let their growing children travel to the city?"[163] Finally, urbanization brought with it the blurring of gender roles: Not only were more women working, thus jeopardizing the man's role as bread winner, they were also participating in activities that the church press believed even men should shun: Instead of staying home and playing their proscribed roles as guardians of morality, lamented one Pomeranian superintendent, women as well as men now frequented the local pubs.[164]

The clearest expression of the Evangelical version of family life and the ills that constantly beset it came in an article entitled appropriately enough "The German Family," written by the Brandenburg superintendent, Otto Dibelius, which the Pomeranian church news carried. Factories now claimed the work of men and women alike, he complained, and children living in the metropolis felt more at home on the streets than in the dark, cramped living quarters of their parents. "The metropolis has destroyed the old family morality," especially because families residing in the city no longer attended church. Was it still a family, asked Dibelius rhetorically, when one married without having a dwelling and furnishings of his own, "when children are unwanted guests who make one's entire existence impossible? . . . The material and spiritual power of a people stands and falls with the family." What sort of conditions best sustained the family? "A little house on a small piece of land—that is and remains the goal of parents who are raising children." Such an arrangement would obviate women's work outside the home (which Dibelius condemned), for even if a wife needed to produce extra income, she could attend to her little plot while minding her children. In any case, the setting Dibelius suggested was more conducive to offspring becoming obedient, rather than turning into children who knew no authority, "the consequences of which lay before the eyes of everyone." Moreover, it would sustain the piety that was so desperately needed. "A new generation who can bring us a future and a new life to our fatherland must arise from us in obedience and piety from the bosom of the family! God send us parents who recognize their great sacred responsibility!"[165]

The freedom to forge an identity of one's own, apart from the strictures of family and "normal" roles, grounded the objections of churchmen to urban life and its consequences. Most obviously, the burgeoning associational life undermined the family's primary claim on each individual and its status as the bedrock of social life. The *Vereine*, lamented one piece, resulted in the "destruction of that widely-famed and beautiful German family life. . . . Associations do have a justification for their existence, but let's do away with all association insanity (*Vereinsmeierei*), for it kills the German family spirit." In the family lay "not only the mysteries of creation, but also those of maturation and growth." Associations for youth especially, the article added, ought to extend the family, not undermine it.[166] In addition, moral turpitude resulted from the desire for self-fulfillment and personal satisfaction rather than one's obligation to family and Volk. No wonder the institution of marriage was in shambles; no wonder there were calls for its legal weakening from liberals and the left: "All these wishes, demands, and strivings," claimed the press, have arisen under the influence of the cosmopolitan atmosphere, where economic emergency, the emancipation of women, and above all, a pestilent *Weltanschauung* combined with the strong lust after sensual pleasure has provided fertile ground for them. . . . Marriage is not an arrangement of enjoyment dedicated to the pacification of self-serving demands for happiness. Rather, it is a natural and spiritual life partnership which, resting in the dissimilarity and need for completion of man and woman, has been established to realize one's full humanity.[167]

The blurring of boundaries could also be seen in the movement of women into jobs once reserved for men, in the spread of contraceptives, in the vocal if ultimately unsuccessful demands for the decriminalization of abortion, and in the declining birthrate.[168] The drive for sexual equality in employment, complained one article, resulted in the "masculinization" of women with its dire consequences for the normal female spheres of church, family, and morality.[169] The church press described abortions as the product of individualism, subjectivism, and "personal considerations of convenience" (*Beguemlichkeitserwägungen*).[170] The low birthrate was ascribed not to poor economic conditions, but to the lack of trust in God as the creator of all life, to the desire for personal enjoyment, and to the vanity of women who strove to preserve their beauty, thus sparing themselves the pain of childbirth. Women did not bear the exclusive right to control their own bodies, concluded another piece, "rather the Volk also has the right to see that children are born. The sale of contraceptive devices must be punished severely."[171]

Such pieces highlight the emotionally charged and ambiguous position that women played in church periodicals, for the very diversity that was emerging in women's roles paralleled the larger conflict between deeply held values about the "traditional" family and those of a rapidly urbanizing society. On the one hand, the image of the mother, or woman's proper and assigned role, appeared frequently to magnify the contrasting vices of life in the cities through her virtue. In one article, a young urban mother weeps because her bitterly anticlerical husband has forbidden her to attend church services. One night after coming home and catching her in prayer, he slays her and then kills himself because he cannot live with his shame.[172] In another piece, written during the occupation of the Ruhr, the image of the "regal woman" arises, flowers adorning her hair, attended to by her adoring son. Alas that vision is only a memory, rued the article. Instead, its author claimed, one in twenty men has a venereal disease and the proportion of women suffering that sexually transmitted affliction is even worse. Thereafter, the article documented other woes contributing to a national crisis, thereby linking the collapse of personal morality with Germany's loss of power: politicians who appeal to the masses, the rampant power of money, Germany's bondage to external enemies, and the sinking of the *Mittelstand.* "Let us think of the plain words of the regal woman whom we spoke of at the beginning: good can only come from good." Despite those "positive" feminine images, however, women often assumed the principal responsibility in church periodicals for the putatively urban vices that consigned the nation to ruin.[173]

Taken together, the array of moral concerns that found public expression undermined the Pomeranian church leadership's official posture of political even handedness. Cultural liberalization won its strongest support among the Socialists and Communists, who, although far from being totally consistent, were nonetheless well-publicized advocates of everything from reducing or eliminating religious instruction in the schools to decriminalizing abortion and homosexuality. They even sponsored architectural modernization to celebrate urban living—the very thing the Pomeranian church so resolutely denounced.[174] Churchmen feared the replication of Bolshevism in Germany if such experimentation came to fruition. Bolshevism meant not merely a radically new government (the Weimar parliamentary system was troublesome enough), but a thoroughgoing transformation of power relationships in the spheres of sexuality and gender, the arena where male and ecclesiastical authority traditionally overlapped.[175] Moreover, because "proper" gender roles and sexual behavior defined rural life, rural life itself was in mortal danger. Church periodicals regaled their readers with the Soviet Union's destruction of religious life, as well as the sanctity of marriage and family, through its prohibition of religious instruction, its elimination of strict laws against divorce, its state-run kindergartens, and even its tolerance of polygamy. Perhaps Bolshevism would not come through a revolution, implied one paper, but its destructive potential resided in the German left's entire cultural program.[176]

The only alternative to this state of affairs, of course, was the preservation of the rural culture and population "without which the Volk as a whole has no future." To that end, right religion was crucial. Rome, after all, declined because of its empty villages and low birthrate: "The more our *Landvolk* divest themselves of the quiet strength that comes from Sunday observance and the Sunday service in church, the faster the germ of infection does its work. The land suffers from it primarily, but so too does the Volk in its entirety."[177] As a consequence, the church converged with the landed elite in both propagating and personifying the rural myth—the nobility because the myth gave legitimacy to its domination, the church because the countryside, despite evidence of slippage, provided that institution with its most hospitable surroundings. The cities gave the church sufficient grounds to attack urban civilization, even without the social pressures that confined Pomeranian clergymen. The obvious inconsistencies in the position of the Pomeranian church would undermine its resistance to the political realignment that took place as the agrarian depression deepened.

Remembrances of the dead in Pomeranian church periodicals elicited reflections as to the stability, tranquillity, rootedness, and indeed supremacy of rural life. "The simple man in the *Großstadt* has virtually nothing left," asserted an article. "Not even his grave belongs to him. After twenty years, the last vestiges of his being are cleared away. One no longer knows his place (*Stätte*). On the land, however, one does not forget the dead so quickly." Graves were well cared for and usually covered with flowers in anticipation of family visits after Sunday services. A rich folklore reminded potential villagers that the interred would not smile on the disruption of their places of rest. The removing, even touching, of the flowers on a grave would result in physical maladies, or worse still, the sudden emergence of the dead person's hand to reclaim his or her rightful property.[178]

Would rural society in the east survive so that the dead would not be forgotten? The structural weaknesses of Pomeranian agriculture, not to mention the contingencies of the world economy lent poignancy to such a question. Yet the most articulate and well-placed spokespersons of the rural myth, the estate owners and the Evangelical clergy, would see to it that Sunday services continued to anchor rural culture, and that the graves in so many village churchyards would remain focal points of family and community.

II

A WORLD COLLAPSES

5

Pomeranian Estate Owners, the Rural People Movement, and the Young Plan Referendum

ALTHOUGH POMERANIA'S LANDED elite remained unchallenged in its local environment, its economic position, like that of farmers elsewhere in Germany, grew increasingly precarious, particularly after hyperinflation and the Ruhr crisis necessitated the stabilization of the Republic's currency. Whereas previously the most heavily indebted of the agricultural enterprises could repay their obligations and modernize their production with inflated currency, stabilization demanded higher taxation and interest rates as the Republic struggled to acquire revenue to sustain the value of its money. On top of that came higher social welfare contributions and the importing of food from abroad as the artificial barriers of inflation disappeared. Immediately following stabilization, the government encouraged banks to make cheap credit available to farmers to boost agricultural production and rectify the decline of the war years. Yet the primary sector grew increasingly less attractive as an outlet for commercial investment. The mounting evidence of crippling indebtedness was such that banks would risk only short-term loans at high rates of interest.[1] From there, the problems of agriculture multiplied, as did the political response to those problems.

From Weakness to Disaster:
Pomeranian Agriculture After Stabilization

As we have seen, the problems of eastern Prussian agriculture arose in part from the outcome of the postwar settlement that included the loss of its markets further east. That compounded the problems caused by the erosion of profit margins through higher wages, high freight costs, and competition from imports. On top of that, the declining status and chronic difficulties of agriculture in the poststabilization period signified unpalatable novelties. The changing political context in which agrarian interest associations operated worked to the detriment of farmers, and especially estate owners, who had long been accustomed to governmental favor. Compared to the Second Empire, the Republic presented a more competitive environment in which agrarian claimants lost at least as much as they won. Weimar not only accorded a significant voice to organized labor, which sought to placate its urban working-class constituents with inexpensive food, obviously the most significant change from the prewar period when labor had been kept at arms length. It also took seriously the proposals of industrialists committed to export who advocated bilateral trade agreements as the principal means of expanding their international markets. Bilateral agreements entailed lowering the barriers against foreign livestock and foodstuffs in return for opening markets for German manufactured goods. The end result was greater competition for German agriculture.

The trade treaty concluded with Poland in 1929 after nearly two years of negotiations was a prime example of Weimar economic policies that the primary sector interpreted as hostile to rural interests, especially in the Prussian east where Poland's legitimacy as a nation reconstituted in the postwar settlements enjoyed even less acceptance than elsewhere in Germany. Initially proposed against the vehement objections of highly placed agrarian spokesmen, including Martin Schiele, the German National minister for nutrition and agriculture in the cabinet of Wilhelm Marx, the accord was finally achieved at the behest of the government of Hermann Müller. That coalition, which came to power in May 1928, clearly articulated the interests of export industry and organized labor, for it extended from the SPD on the left to the DVP on the right. In fact, both exporters and labor pressed for trade liberalization in the first place, not only because Poland promised a market for finished goods and cheaper food for urban working-class consumers (a prime consideration for the SPD), but also because the ongoing tariff war with Poland brought a sharp decline in orders for German products and thus unemployment. Polish agricultural products, especially pork and live pigs, entered Germany to challenge German farmers who produced both in abundance. By the fall of 1930, several months after Heinrich Brüning had replaced Müller as chancellor, the treaty was a dead letter, having failed to win ratification in the Reichstag.[2] Yet it and similar bilateral treaties contributed to the myth of an agrarian community uniformly victimized by antagonistic interests, and to the frenetic politicization of that community in its own defense. The implications of that politicization stretched far beyond the Polish treaty's lifetime.

It is absurd to claim that the position of organized agriculture, particularly that of large landowners, was so weak as to exclude it from power altogether. The sheer size of the German primary sector and the protectionist climate worldwide made agriculture impossible to ignore politically, because advocates of free trade, including many of Germany's leading economists, found their recommendations limited by the realities of an increasingly ugly and depressed international marketplace.[3] The restoration of the tariff on cereals in 1925 and the subsequent enhancements to it ultimately raised the price of grain in Germany to 250 times its world market value.[4] In addition, the infamous pork barrels that Weimar governments instituted to prevent eastern agriculture's collapse, of which the Eastern Aid (*Osthilfe*) program stands out as the most profligate, comprised yet another example of agriculture's reserves of strength. Such palliatives demonstrated the need of successive governments to pacify eastern agriculture as a reward for enduring the Republic's trade and export policies.[5]

Nevertheless, regardless of the favors bestowed on German grain production, the demands of an export-based economy and the political leverage of urban Germany threatened to marginalize agriculture, especially after 1927–28 when the precipitous decline in commodity prices worldwide transformed an already precarious situation in the countryside to outright disaster. Mechanization and the expanded use of chemical fertilizers once encouraged industry to tolerate the insistent and repeated demands of agrarians for tariff protection, but only as long as the rural sector proved able to purchase the products that industrialists manufactured. That forbearance ended, however, when the combination of domestic stabilization and international collapse eroded the purchasing power of rural Germany. Subsequently, farmers large and small felt the pressure of leading industrialists who expected them to increase efficiency and cut costs instead of lobbying for government subventions, not to mention the resistance of consumers who begrudged any increases in the price of food. The regional and confessional fragmentation of agricultural interest representation made it doubly difficult for the primary sector to air its case. As a result, the growing impoverishment of farmers turned their scarcely suppressed hostility toward the Weimar Republic to open rebellion against it.

Pomerania's agrarian leadership viewed the competition among interest groups as an indication of the Republic's implacable hostility toward the countryside and as justification for casting every policy measure as a threat to the viability of the east. Arguably the province's most forceful and articulate spokesman, Hans-Joachim von Rohr-Demmin, the owner of an estate of over 1,200 hectares who could trace his ancestry back to the colonization period,[6] described the Republic's unemployment compensation program as constitutive of a broader, revolutionary agenda to destroy rural society. The unemployment insurance program that passed in October 1927 encouraged young farm laborers to migrate to the cities, he maintained.[7] Even if they could find no work, they could be assured of compensation equal to the income they would have earned on the land. Do not blame landowners for hiring Poles, Rohr warned. They had little choice but to look eastward for their labor pool because German workers left in such large numbers. Pomerania's farmers, reluctantly and inadvertently to be sure, would become the agents of historical regression. The Poles would be at the banks of the Elbe in one hundred years, thereby eradicating one thousand years of German history in the east. Rohr could not resist drawing an invidious comparison between Weimar's treatment of agriculture and the impact of the Bolshevik Revolution on the Soviet countryside, the best example of "what a politics of brutality against the rural population, one grounded in the instincts of the urban masses, can bring forth." The German peasantry thus increasingly lagged behind the "mass of humanity in the large city. Fatefully in this mass of humanity it loses its ties to Volk, Heimat and state." The result, according to Rohr, was the spread of pacificism, the decline of heroism and morality, and the triumph of the perverse.[8]

In Pomerania, the inherited limitations of climate and soil magnified the liabilities that crippled other rural areas, and they help to explain why that province led the Prussian east in the vehemence of the right radicalism that developed. Pomerania's primary crops, rye and potatoes, not only found fewer consumers willing to buy them (or products made from them), they yielded even less of a profit once market prices dropped, despite the sub-ventions supporting them. Those deficiencies grew more extreme when the weather failed to cooperate at the same time that farmers tried desperately to expand production to compensate for their losses. Too much rain and hail decimated the crop of 1927, but even the conditions of the previous two years had been far from optimal. Nor did the weather improve signifi-cantly in the years following. In 1930 a severe drought gripped much of the province and proved especially devastating in the regions with the poorest soil that could only produce rye and potatoes.[9] The drought exacerbated the already heavy pressure of lending institutions on Pomeranian peasants and large landowners as they grasped for repayment of their loans, eager to re-alize a return on their investment before their clients collapsed.[10]

Month by month, estate owners individually, as well as collectively through the Chamber of Agriculture, set forth a litany of woes that beset the Pomeranian countryside, hardships that were in place well before the fall in prices. They included high freight costs, the loss of markets farther east, the politically induced decline in the supply of cheap Polish labor at harvest time, high costs for the construction of living quarters for estate laborers and other farm buildings, the shortage of credit at affordable rates of inter-est, the low demand for machinery, and finally the high taxes needed for social insurance expenditures and the local schools. All converged to create resentment and profound desperation.[11] An estate possessing slightly under 500 hectares that one Chamber report offered as an example, paid 4.35 marks her hectare toward social insurance before the war. By mid-1927, however, that figure soared to 14.41 marks per hectare.[12] The rural crisis hit

Pomerania's border regions especially hard. If those areas did not receive help, particularly cheaper credit, the Chamber insisted, the only winners would be the wildlife or the Poles, "who have cut us off from our natural economic basis, Danzig and West Prussia."[13] Always eager to present itself as the voice of all Pomeranian agriculturalists, the Rural League complained of the importing of foreign meat and animals for slaughter, especially from Poland, as well as (in its view) the loose veterinary regulations that permitted it. The peasant or farm laborer who derived part of his income from raising swine and growing potatoes found himself losing out in competition with pigs and potatoes brought in from the east.[14] Then, too, the peasants suffered from the high costs of domestic labor owing to negotiated wage settlements and the allegedly easy accessibility to unemployment compensation: "Peasant proprietors put forth spirited complaints that local manpower can hardly be obtained even in winter, in contrast to previous times." Workers who lost their jobs at a sugar factory that shut down either found work on neighboring estates or drew unemployment. Warned the Chamber, this would only increase the demand for foreigners.[15]

The evidence of economic hardship spread much like an inoperable cancer. As early as 1926 and 1927, the magistrate of the upper Pomeranian county of Stolp reported that only 35 of the 120 estate owners in his district could afford to pay Reich income taxes. The percentage of peasant holdings that could meet their obligations was even less, as 1,500 of the 12,000 to 13,000 farms in the Stolp county paid their contributions.[16] At the same time, Pomerania ranked highest per hectare among the Prussian provinces after Schleswig-Holstein in the severity of its indebtedness. Moreover, by early 1929 its total debt far surpassed one billion marks, ranking with East Prussia as one of the two worst among the eastern Prussian provinces.[17] Crippling indebtedness affected the estates most profoundly. By 1931–32 the net income per hectare (15 Reichmarks) of estates in the central part of the province fell well below their interest burden of 60 Reichmarks per hectare, for a difference of 45 Reichmarks. In eastern Pomerania the gap grew wider, revealing a difference of 57.3 Reichmarks per hectare between net income and interest owed. By contrast, the largest peasant holdings, at least in the central portion of the province, operated slightly in the black.[18]

The nonpayment of taxes paled in comparison to the bankruptcies and compulsory auctions that multiplied once agrarian debtors could no longer meet their obligations to their creditors. In 1924, only nine properties were sold in bankruptcy auctions, reflecting the immediate impact of stabilization. By the end of 1928, however, fully 98 had met that fate, while during the first nine months of the following year, 117 farms were placed on the auction block. According to a Chamber of Agriculture report, more enterprises would have faced the same fate except that their creditors discovered the futility of staging bankruptcy auctions. Much like squeezing blood from a turnip, some creditors realized, auctions yielded too little to compensate for their losses. Moreover, despite the possibility of sale for settlement, estate owners especially found it difficult to unload their estates because of their marginal value. "The market for estates," noted the report, "has almost ceased to function." "If that were not the case," it commented dryly, "then the flight from the land would also to a large degree overtake the estate owners." Even the owners of healthy enterprises could not find buyers.[19]

In a province that depended so completely on the primary sector, the mournful evidence of the depression's devastation was overwhelming and inescapable. The loss of tax revenue meant in turn the poorer maintenance of public health and higher rates of infant mortality, the wages of bankruptcy and, of course, unemployment.[20] By 1930, the persistent complaints of landowners regarding the shortage of certain kinds of workers ceased altogether as farm bankruptcies created the unusual phenomenon of unemployment among agricultural laborers, although suspicions abounded that the hiring of illegal Polish labor by estate owners caused as much unemployment as estate liquidation. Even married estate administrators, once heavily in demand, could no longer find work.[21] The programs of Chancellors Heinrich Brüning and Kurt von Schleicher to resettle the unemployed on bankrupt estates not only confronted the hostility of estate owners who convinced themselves that such attempts meant a restructuring of rural social relations,[22] but settlements in general faced chronic underfunding and the lack of candidates qualified for farming. Merchants in the towns and villages who relied on their rural customers withered on the vine. Widespread bankruptcies of stores owned by Jews and Christians alike took place, remarked Marie von Kleist. Despair became pervasive. Kleist agreed with the Chamber of Agriculture's assessment: If any estates remained in the hands their old owners at all, she commented, it was because the owners found no one willing to purchase them.[23]

Pomerania's limited industry suffered as well, particularly in its center, Stettin, where the shipbuilding and lumber industry lay in the doldrums.[24] The interdependency between industry and the countryside became a relationship of mutual misery, as a meeting of Pomerania's industrialists in the spring of 1930 made abundantly clear. In addition to the complaints that arose against burdensome taxes, social insurance and wages higher than those in other countries, Pomerania's industrialists grieved over their struggle to realize a profit and East Elbia's very existence. Eastern Prussian industry found it difficult to compete with the west, one industrialist insisted, because industrial wages at home had crept upward during the postwar period, thus militating against the production of lower priced goods that lower wages would have permitted. Unemployment unavoidably resulted. Moreover, agriculture needed to recognize the dire need of industry for assistance, because the domestic market was of special importance to the province's industry, and agriculture amounted to industry's largest customer. The same speaker constructed a telling comparison to dramatize the impact of the high number of industrial jobless: "What would it mean for agriculture if [it lost] 11,000 jobs like Pomeranian industry has lost? It would mean the employees of two hundred large knights' estates. The downsizing that industry has undergone is comparable to the shutdown of perhaps one-fourth of all the large estates in the province."[25]

The crisis by no means left Pomerania's peasantry unaffected, even though their lower indebtedness and slightly greater solvency usually rendered them less vulnerable to foreclosure than estate owners. From the beginning of October to the end of November 1930, however, the Chamber of Agriculture reported that forty-one holdings, all but seven of them possessing fewer than 100 hectares, had been liquidated by compulsory auction. Over the entire year, 159 holdings totaling 61,023 morgen (15,255 hectares) had been dissolved by auction, while another thirty-four totaling 24,344 morgen (6,086 hectares) were in receivership. The Chamber admitted that this particular wave of auctions affected peasants more than estate owners.[26]

The *Pommersche Tagespost* carried the denunciations of peasants against the neglect of the republican system. In one such case, a peasant named Jandren attacked the Communists, Socialists, and Democrats for consistently sabotaging aid to agriculture since stabilization by encouraging foreign competition and rejecting further tariff protection. What was the aim of these parties?, he asked rhetorically. It was simply to take property from the peasants, "to willfully realize the Marxist mania for equality (*Gleichmacherei*)." The DNVP's proposals to raise tariffs benefiting agriculture and to increase aid to the east should be enacted, Jandren demanded, so as to ensure that "the labor of the peasant and agricultural laborer would be protected against foreign competition and as a consequence be made profitable."[27] In fact, by 1931 duties against agricultural imports from Poland, Pomerania's principal bugabear, exceeded those of the tariff war of the mid-twenties,[28] the result of organized agriculture's residual political impact.

The massive government assistance package to the east, however, the Eastern Aid program that owed its largess to the pliability of Hindenburg and Brüning, did little to east the distress of peasants. The political connections of estate owners resulted in the circumvention of institutions such as the Prussian State Land Bank (*Preussenkasse*) that would have assumed the responsibility for overseeing the program because estate owners perceived them as inimical to their interests. Those connections ensured that the lion's share of the funds allocated for debt relief went to salvage big landed property. Indeed the generosity of *Osthilfe* toward East Elbia contrasts markedly to the deflationary parsimony that otherwise characterized the economic policies of Brüning's chancellorship.[29] For the Prussian east as a whole, the nearly thirteen thousand estate owners benefited disproportionately from the *Osthilfe* measures. Over 5 percent of them were reorganized while fully 81 percent drew tax abatements, protection from foreclosure, and reductions in interest. Only 2 percent of medium-sized peasant holdings obtained support, while small peasants received next to nothing.[30] Such blatant inequity provoked the widespread resentment of peasants against the favoritism bestowed on estate owners, anger that would exacerbate the radicalization of small producers.

Initially, the *Osthilfe* decrees extended only to the extreme eastern portions of Pomerania, primarily the border regions of Bütow and Lauenburg. Nevertheless, the president of the provincial Chamber of Agriculture, Richard von Flemming-Pätzig, along with other prominent agrarian representatives, influenced Hindenburg to amend the program to cover the entire East Elbian region. The success of Flemming's appeal embodied in the *Osthilfe* decrees of March 1931 resulted in 110 million Reichmarks alloted for Pomerania instead of the mere 20 million promised in the original legislation.[31] The program was administered through the Rural Commission (*Landstelle*) in Köslin, a corporation placed under the direction of none other than Johann Georg von Dewitz. In turn, the commission answered to the *Osthilfe* Commissar and Hindenburg.[32] It acted on the recommendations of committees formed to assess the worthiness of those large landed properties applying for debt relief. The agricultural schools took responsibility for processing peasant claims.[33] By the fall of 1932, 5,398 Pomeranian farms had fallen into receivership, nearly 4,000 of which were valued at less than 40,000 marks. Another 8,678 were so deeply in debt as to rule out the possibility of ever regaining their solvency, the principal criterion for coming under *Osthilfe*'s protection. The number of protected enterprises rose the further east one traveled, most likely the reflection of poorer soil and thus the reliance there on rye and potatoes. In the former Stralsund district, only 704 properties ended up in receivership, as opposed to 2,177 in Stettin and another 2,517 in Köslin.[34]

The lack of specificity in the Chamber's data as to the number of agrarian holdings liquidated in compulsory auctions reveals its leadership's sensitivity to the prospect of dissension among its members over the impact of the crisis and the distribution of aid. From 1924 through 1932, it reported, fully 1,008 Pomeranian holdings had been dissolved through forced auctions, most of them the result of the agrarian crisis that hit after 1927. The Chamber used its report to demonstrate the consequences of republican failures, but it made no effort to distinguish between the absolute number and proportionately of estates and peasant holdings that succumbed. Moreover, the Chamber produced no analysis as to the holdings Eastern Aid might have spared.[35] The Rural League proved equally touchy. According to its figures, the losses for estates from July 1930 to July 1931 significantly outstripped those of peasants, 8 percent of their combined holdings as opposed to only 1 percent for the peasantry. Yet the League hastened to add that the volume of land in estates as opposed to peasant holdings lessened the significance of estate losses.[36]

Amendments to the *Osthilfe* regulations granted heavily indebted owners generous protection from their creditors that limited the liability, particularly of estates, once the rescue program covered the entire province. Up to 50 percent of an owner's debt could be stricken without the agreement of those whom they owed, and repayment could be delayed if the requirements of the next harvest demanded it.[37] Hard-pressed estate owners, including Count von Bismarck-Bohlen, took advantage of those stipulations to pull themselves out from under a mountain of debt. Bismarck's wife, Viktoria (Tola), who during the winter of 1932 moved to Berlin while her children attended school there, informed her landlady that she could not pay her monthly rent of 250 marks because the terms of receivership governing the family's entailed estate prohibited such payments except to the immediate family.[38] *Osthilfe* thus created a class of aggrieved people whose complaints revealed the extent to which estate owners helped themselves to the state's largesse. The victimized included not only Pomerania's creditors and peasants who perceived an obvious bias in the distribution of government assistance, but, as we shall see, even the Evangelical Church.

Nevertheless, although *Osthilfe* might very well have disproportionately protected estate owners from foreclosure and compulsory auction, allowing Junker families in particular to hold on to their property, estate owners remained anything but effusive in their gratitude. Rather, they condemned the program as irrelevant to the restoration of agriculture's health. Even before the Eastern Aid law went into effect, the principal voices of Pomeranian agriculture expressed considerable skepticism that the proposals under discussion would alone suffice. For Flemming, the recovery of profitability was crucial: "We strive not for the periodic reduction of interest rates through subsidies, but rather decreasing them through forgiveness (*Entschuldung*). The conversion of debt must therefore be tied to lowering the debt burden." To add to that modest request, Flemming called for the construction of railroads and the reduction of freight rates, particularly in the border regions.[39]

After *Osthilfe* went into effect, the government's efforts met with even less approval, a judgment that the program's increasingly expansive generosity did little to silence.[40] It could only have been galling to estate owners that much of the program's funding came from the export-based League of German Industry (RDI), whose desire to restore the viability of agriculture contained its scarcely concealed condescension toward the primary sector's glaring failures.[41] Complained Rohr candidly, the *Osthilfe* program only pulled the healthy enterprises down with the bankrupt ones. What good would aid do when it was merely taken away again through high interest rates and unfavorable trade treaties that disadvantaged German farmers? "Down with the false doctrine about invading the world market," he argued, "The well-being of a nation lies not in money but in self-creation (*im Schaffen in sich selbst*)." The competition of Danish butter, Hungarian cattle, Russian eggs and rye, along with high interest payments crippled German farmers to the point that the government dole could not save them. The only sensible solution, stated Rohr, was a tariff policy like Great Britain's, a nation that barricaded its borders against foreign imports and consumed only what its own farmers produced.[42] Stung by the criticism of agrarian mismanagement, the Chamber of Agriculture denied that the incompetence of farmers lay at the root of agriculture's problems. The agrarian crisis arose instead from high interest rates, high wages, the border settlements that Versailles imposed, and the Republic's import policies.[43]

Given Pomerania's agrarian-conservative heritage and agriculture's troubled status among republican policy makers at the top, such antirepublican sentiment should not be surprising. As Rohr charged, the Weimar system itself was so thoroughly antagonistic to the needs of agriculture that the party composition of its ruling coalitions mattered little.[44] Hostility toward the Weimar "system" was but the logical outcome of a profound malaise that pervaded the mentality of Pomerania's agrarian elite. The early years of the Republic had certainly not been pleasant for estate owners as they confronted the continuation of the Controlled Economy, the restiveness of estate laborers, and a new *Staatsform* that removed many of the props that enhanced the influence of estate owners. Nevertheless, large landowners retained their estates, disciplined their workforce, and maintained their leadership of the Pomerania's political and economic associations, having done so through a combination of physical presence, cooptation, and counterrevolutionary violence that they evoked at will. The hardships after stabilization did not merely reawaken their antirepublicanism, which had scarcely lain dormant anyway. Rather this time the state of the rural economy, and the Republic's putative toleration of it, threatened to impoverish Pomerania altogether.

The rhetoric of agrarian leaders achieved apocalyptic proportions. In 1931, the director of the province's Agrarian Cooperative Society (*Landwirtschaftliche Genossenschaft*), Dr. Geer, expressed the increasingly held view that Pomerania stood "in the midst of an economic-cultural as well as national struggle between being and non-being (*Sein oder Nicht-Sein*)." The county magistrate, Eugen von Brockhausen, one of the association's long-time leaders, compared the current rural predicament with that of the Caprivi era in that it was not just a market crisis but a "life crisis." Already during the last century, Brockhausen argued, Pomerania began to lose its markets to cheap grain imports from elsewhere. The rapid industrial growth of the west and its higher wages slowly marginalized eastern agriculture. Unlike industry that could organize trusts and syndicates to protect its position, he stated, agricultural producers as mere individuals had no power to fix prices. Worse still, they wrestled with higher production costs, demands for higher wages, and sinking prices for the commodities that they produced.[45] How then could Pomerania's primary sector defend itself? Brockhausen's reference to Caprivi, whose trade policies spawned the founding of the Agrarian League in 1893, was certainly apt. As a demagogic response to economic crisis, the Agrarian League's successor in Pomerania would more than prove its mettle.

Political Pressures: The Dissolution of the Manorial Districts and the Left's Resurgence

As devastating as Pomerania's disintegrating economy appeared, troublesome political developments accompanied the economic downturn and contributed to the siege mentality, particularly of estate owners. The resurgence of the left came at the very moment that collapsing prices and poor weather took their toll. In December 1927, following years of political conflict, the Reichstag approved the dissolution of the manorial districts, thus permitting the incorporation of estate villages into the nearest communes. Passed over the vehement objections of the DNVP, the measure formally ended a local administrative anomaly that perpetuated the power of big landlords over their "people."[46] In fact, given the logistical problems that arose, which included the assumption of new tax burdens by both the communes and manorial districts, dissolution took some time to complete. Moreover, an escape clause protected the integrity of estates whose distance from the closest commune was too far to warrant consolidation. Such exceptions would thus dissipate the legislation's impact at crucial moments in the mobilization of the rural right: A number of manorial districts lay too far from the nearest election district, in the opinion of county magistrates, to allow consolidation.[47]

Nevertheless, estate owners were aggrieved because the newly-created entities of local government not only entailed the potential loss of political influence, but also an increase in taxes that they could ill afford.[48] One bourgeois landlord, Georg Wussow, who in 1917 purchased the 232 hectare estate, Stadthof, from the Borcke family, protested the dissolution as an undeserved punishment. The property lay in poor condition when he assumed control of it, he said, its buildings run down and its inventory stripped—a meaningless adjunct estate (*Nebengut*) that for years failed to realize a profit. After a few hard years, he put the estate on sound footing while earning a modest living for himself, his wife, and five children. Now he was threatened with ruin.[49]

The *Pommersche Tagespost* published doleful accounts of estates forced into compulsory auction because of Weimar's exhorbitant tax increases and agriculture's loss of political influence, proof positive of Weimar's hostility toward the primary sector. Such accounts were not loathe to include a touch of demagoguery as in the case of a tenant farmer, the grandson-in-law of a Maltzahn, whose employees and peasant neighbors suffered from the bankruptcy sale of his estate's assets: "The suits have been tied together with string and red labels hang from the three pigsties. These pigs could fetch wages for the "people" in a regular sale. Yet today Herr Flamm [the executor] will swing his gavel and perhaps the happy cattle dealer from Kallies who comes as his faithful companion will get the swine. In any event, the peasants and laborers don't have enough money to participate in the bidding themselves."[50]

Moreover, the Reich and Landtag elections of May 1928 that produced the first SPD-led national government since 1923, the coalition of Hermann Müller, confirmed the left's growth against the "traditional" right's decline, both nationally and regionally. In Pomerania, the SPD gained 30.2 percent of the vote, nearly 6 percent above the party's performance in 1924, while the Communists gained slightly. By contrast, the DNVP's share dropped to 41.5 percent, down from the 49 percent it won previously. Although still preeminent in the province—the DNVP sent nine delegates to the Prussian Landtag as opposed to only six for the SPD—the German Nationals suffered a clear setback from which they would never recover.[51] Nationally, the DNVP's losses, many of them to the "moderates" of the newly formed Christian National Peasants and Farmers' Party (CNBLP), who hoped a national agrarian party could win concessions for agriculture by bargaining within government, set in motion that party's simultaneous radicalization and disintegration. The assumption to the party's chairmanship of the virulently antirepublican, Alfred Hugenberg, a move that enjoyed broad, although not unchallenged, support from Pomerania's rural leadership, exacerbated the flight of agrarian interests nationwide that, in contrast to Hugenberg, preferred a double strategy of negotiation and opposition.[52]

The left's "Indian summer," which lasted until the collapse of the Müller government in March 1930, emboldened the DLV to accelerate its efforts at recruitment in the Pomeranian countryside, despite its earlier defeats, by pressing for higher pay.[53] The Employees' Groups of the Rural League, charged the Socialist newspaper *Volksbote*, had done little to improve their members' wages, which still lay well below those of industrial workers. The supposedly impartial local arbitration committees, the paper alleged, repeatedly ruled in the landlords' favor.[54] As the agrarian crisis deepened, the Rural League redoubled its efforts to convince workers of their communal ties to their employers against the purely "materialistic instincts" of the DLV.[55] Typically, its message sang of the uniqueness of social relations on the land, the naturally close ties between employer and employee in their joint endeavor, a relationship cemented by their common identity as property owners. According to the Rural League, the DLV represented nothing other than "the tow-line (*Schlepptau*) of metropolitan interests" in its attempts to inculcate notions of class struggle. Its ways of thinking undermined the estate workers' effort to better their economic position, which could only come about through the struggle to raise the status of agriculture as a whole. Accordingly, "the struggle on behalf of the vocational spirit among employers and employees," was "the struggle for the Reich of the future."[56] Although the DLV never seriously threatened the primacy of the Employees' Groups, who ultimately won formal recognition through the courts, the pressures of the agrarian economy, coupled with the left's apparent revitalization, rendered estate owners more intransigent than ever.

Peasant Wars and Junker Initiatives

Despite the economic and political pressures weighing on them, Pomerania's agrarian elites proved anything but helpless to meet those challenges. The mushrooming rural crisis prompted estate owners to do what they had always done: propagandizing vehemently in defense of agriculture, organizing across class lines, and invoking the rural myth against hostile urban interests. That agenda placed Pomerania's Junker leaders on Hugenberg's side, at least until Nazi successes after 1930 caused some of them to regret the consequences. Indeed that increasing radicalism exploited the communal ties embedded in the Pomeranian countryside, thus ensuring that the unity of agriculture was no mere ploy of estate owners, but the reality borne of estate agriculture's deeply-rooted influence and the lack of viable alternatives to that power. Pomeranian rightist militance would continue to make use of the constitutional provisions that encouraged popular democracy, the initiative and referendum. In turn, however, the elevated politicization of estate owners, mortgaged as it was to Hugenberg's national strategy, resulted in the acquisition of a new and potentially dangerous ally, the National Socialists, a party that asserted greater independence from elites than seen previously.

The first attempt of Pomeranian estate owners after stabilization to rally their troops against the Republic built upon the radical undertaking in Schleswig-Holstein, the Rural People (*Landvolk*) movement, while significantly modifying that movement's populist anti-elitism. Beginning in January 1928, the Rural People movement, embracing chiefly the Schleswig-Holstein peasantry, coalesced in a series of mass demonstrations that demanded higher tariffs to protect meat and dairy products, cheaper credit, and a reduction in social welfare payments. As the protests gathered momentum in the spring and summer, spreading across north and eastern Germany, the rallies grew even more militant as the protesters attacked banks and government offices, while refusing to pay their taxes. In most cases, the antirepublican and right radical tenor of the Rural People movement weakened the better established mouthpieces of German conservatism, the DNVP and the National Rural League. In fact, the DNVP's performance in the May elections evidenced not only the left's surge, but also the popular right's rage. The "rural people," who were frustrated by the high cost of the grain that they used to feed their animals, the direct result of estate agriculture's influence, had grown just as disillusioned with those who claimed to represent them as with the Weimar "system" itself.[57] In Pomerania, however, peasants and farm laborers comprised the shock troops in the Rural League's army as the latter organized antirepublican demonstrations. Pomerania's estate owners, as was customary, remained the generals. Those exercises provided the spade work for the elite's increasingly demagogic and reckless assaults against the "system" that in the end provided National Socialism with its crucial entrée into Pomeranian rural politics.

As the Rural People movement won supporters outside Schleswig-Holstein, the Prussian Ministry of Interior alerted its field administration to curb demonstrations whenever possible. To no avail.[58] Protests in Pomerania surfaced by early March 1928 and continued into the following year, not only in response to the outbursts in Schleswig-Holstein and the grievances those articulated, but also to the disastrous harvests of the previous two years. Although not nearly as violent as others, those protests conveyed an ugly, demagogic tone, and because they cut across rural class lines in calling for the refusal to pay taxes, they showed a degree of collective militance not often witnessed. Remarked the president of the Köslin district, Kurt Cronau, the demonstrations in the upper Pomeranian towns that took place on March 3 would have been unheard of normally for a population more noted for its "authoritarian sensibilities" (*Autoritätsgefühl*) than its rebelliousness. Between thirty and forty thousand farmers (*Landwirte*), shopkeepers, and artisans came together to express their anger as the precarious rural economy victimized them all. The Stahlhelm and other nationalist organizations accompanied them.[59] A demonstration of forty-four hundred persons in Pyritz convened at the behest of the Rural League's estate-owning leadership, von Wedel and Blankenhagen, demanded the end of public auctions for the nonpayment of taxes, the reduction of social insurance contributions, the elimination of the competition from big-city business, and an adjustment in the rent tax.[60] Over and over again, demonstrations numbering in the thousands brought all rural producers together, their feverish reaction to their common emergency.[61]

Such rallies arose from the initiative of the Pomeranian Rural League, as well as the DNVP and other nationalist associations. Frequently they featured speakers from Schleswig-Holstein in an effort to seal the unity of Pomeranian agricultural producers under the Rural League's aegis. Although the assemblies convened in the name of peasants and farm workers, the estate owners who comprised the leadership of the provincial Rural League directed the protests, and like one of the Rural League's directors, von Oertzen, they recklessly invoked the example of Schleswig-Holstein.[62] "The peasants fight for the freedom of their soil," exhorted a speaker at one such rally in Belgard. "The cry which has come from Schleswig-Holstein to shake up the Pomeranian *Landvolk*" won the appreciation of Ewald von Kleist, who organized the affair in that upper Pomeranian town.[63] As the president of the Stettin district summarized some time later, the Rural People movement was not an independent force in the province, and the speakers who came from Schleswig-Holstein appeared at meetings that the Rural League organized: "One noticed that the current leaders of the Rural League were also at the head table," he commented about one such rally in Lauenburg. "It was also observed that entry permits to a closed assembly were distributed by the office of the German National People's Party. In Pomerania the Rural League and the German Nationals have obviously understood that they should seize upon the Rural People movement and use it for their own purposes."[64] Likewise, his counterpart in the Köslin district regretted the lack of peasant leaders who, in his view, properly appreciated the Rural League's bias in favor of estate owners and who possessed enough autonomy to form organizations that faithfully articulated peasant interests. He attributed that to the lack of peasants of Old Germanic stock, particularly in the border regions, the sort of peasants who were traditionally proud of their independence.[65]

To be sure, the reports of provincial officials revealed divisions among Pomerania's agriculturalists.[66] In some cases, the local chapters of the Rural League and the DNVP expressed their discomfort with the peasant radicalism that the Schleswig-Holstein protests conveyed, especially their blatant resort to illegality and violence. Furthermore, the Rural League's reputation both nationally and locally as the preserve of estate owners compromised its best efforts to speak for the entire countryside. Remarked the county magistrate of Anklam, a Rural League-initiated rally that drew up to two thousand met with the disapproval of peasants, and even some large holders, who objected to the Rural League's arrogance and intransigence, particularly its continuing refusal to negotiate wage agreements with the DLV. "Especially the peasant population of the county," he stated, "maintains without exception a calm and thoughtful disposition, and it cannot be denied that now more frequently than earlier, a distancing from the large landownership will result in such cases, as their natural economic interests often demand."[67] Moreover, peasants seemed less eager to protest than estate owners, according to Cronau of Köslin, given that "as a rule, (they) are far more cautious and discreet when it comes to investment, the use of artificial fertilizers, the renovation of their buildings and the renewal of their inventory."[68] Thus, they were less burdened by indebtedness than the large landownership, although as he noted, their advantage was rapidly disappearing.

Nevertheless, to be a remarkable degree the Rural League succeeded in mobilizing a broad cross section of Pomeranian rural society because economic misery threatened all enterprises and the lack of effective representation independent of the Rural League meant that peasants and workers had no other vehicle through which to voice their growing rage at the Republic. The Peasants' Association (*Bauernverein*), founded at the turn of the century as a counterweight to the Agrarian League, did exist in Pomerania, occasionally holding demonstrations that expressed considerable resentment at the advantages that estate owners received from the Rural League. Yet Pomeranian peasants could not produce leaders with broad enough support from their ranks across the province to form a serious institutional alternative.[69] In any event, common hardship militated against a permanent rift between peasants and estate owners, notably in areas with extensive potato cultivation. Even if the peasants accumulated fewer debts than estate owners, their income according to Cronau of Köslin still fell below that of unskilled workers.[70] Plummeting pork prices affected both peasants and agricultural laborers alike, while the sinking value of the potato prompted the concern of both estate owner and peasant.

Pomeranian peasants focused more of their attention on dairy and cattle prices while estate owners fretted about the return on their grain sales. Yet even that difference in emphasis, which split farmers enough to weaken agrarian protest nationally, in Pomerania produced no fundamental divergence in interest between peasants and estate owners.[71] The shortage of labor affecting large peasant holdings most in need of supplemental workers, particularly young girls, not only prevented the extension of animal husbandry, it in many cases forced those peasants to reduce their herds altogether.[72] The county magistrate of Bütow called his superior's attention to the "interest solidarity" that the Rural League exploited; one that would not easily fracture. For the profitability of large holdings rested on the potato, "and here peasant and estate owner interests merge completely since between pork and potato prices, a clear and generally recognized dependence exists. As for the interests of the agricultural working class, this group too is first and foremost interested in the structuring of favorable pork and potato prices, and will at least not turn away from the demands which the Rural League has made."[73]

It should come as no surprise that in some cases, estate laborers participated less from a spontaneous solidarity with their employers than from the landlords' power of suggestion. Estate owners sympathetic to the Rural League left nothing to chance, providing incentives for their "people" to take part in the demonstrations: Nearly all estates in the county of Bublitz, for example, gave their employees and their wives the day off with pay provided that they attend the demonstrations of the Rural League. Those who refused risked a reduction in their income. Thus, 70 percent of those attending were workers.[74] Yet repeatedly, county officials remarked that the demonstrations would not have occurred in the first place had not economic hardship intervened to inflame rural discontent. Even in regions where the Rural League encountered disapprobation from its local chapters, officials nervously wondered whether that relative moderation would continue.[75]

The Rural League sought the broadest possible popular audience for its demagogy. Its rallies drew not only peasants and farm laborers, but also members of other occupations who suffered as a result of the agrarian depression. They were occasions which seethed with antagonism toward the cities. One such demonstration in Naugard, which drew seven thousand persons, included artisans and small shopkeepers whose businesses the agrarian depression jeopardized, as well as land owners with holdings of various sizes. The program featured speeches by representatives of all classes and occupations, including an estate laborer who obligingly sympathized with the plight of estate owners unable to offer higher compensation because of the poor economy: "If agricultural workers in this economic situation fail to stand behind their employers, then that would be like being on the high seas in a sinking ship, hindering rescue operations and saying to the ship's captain that it served him right that he should drown." An estate owner named Fassbender pointed his finger at the common enemy as he attacked the duty-free imports of frozen meat that competed with German pork: "It is a false economic policy that gives into the supposed necessities of those who live in the cities. Agriculture is the custodian of the fatherland's soil, and we should not permit its impoverishment and that of its workers."[76]

Another rally of five thousand in Cammin convened fishermen, artisans, and small shopkeepers, as well as farmers. The platform synthesized a cornucopia of demands reflecting the diversity of interests among those in attendance. The list included a tariff and trade policy that supported the domestic market, not foreigners or international capital. No imports of food-stuffs that Germany herself produced were to be permitted, especially fish, potatoes, and Polish pigs. The rally insisted on affordable interest rates, the reduction of property and rent taxes, as well as the curtailing of unemployment compensation and the competition from department stores. Last but not least, the platform addressed the needs of estate laborers, likewise an effort to diffuse the criticism that the Rural League had drawn for refusing to negotiate pay increases. The platform proposed "that the farmer be put in the position of paying wages which the hard labor of the agricultural laborer who knows no eight-hour day deserves. Only when agriculture can again make a profit; only when its products are sold for a price that is commensurate with the work that goes into them, can the farm laborer demand and receive the wage that is owed to him and which will willingly be granted; only then can his standard of living, including his housing and clothing, equal that of an industrial worker."[77]

The pervasive dissatisfaction that the rural demonstrations signified over-lapped with the tenth anniversary of the provincial Rural League in 1929. Demagoguery abounded during the Rural League's commemoration ceremony as speaker after speaker, representing the diverse wings of the agrarian right, contrasted peasant virtues with the ills of urbanism that threatened the demise of rural life. With Field Marshal von Mackensen and the Stahlhelm in attendance, the county magistrate and president of the German Chamber of Rural Municipalities (*Deutscher Landgemeindetag*), Dr. Günther Gierecke, who was one of the driving forces behind the CNBLP as well, urged his listeners to "save the German village" as he attacked international capital and the encroachment of government bureaucracy on the autonomy of the village, an obvious condemnation of the dissolution of the manorial districts. The rural population had to fight back, he exhorted, not in the spirit of the individual, but in the spirit of the entire Volk; that is, in the traditional Prussian way. Rural people should raise their children according to the Prussian virtues of loyalty to the fatherland and adherence to the Christian faith. The chair of the Rural League's Employees' Group, Johannes Wolf, continued to articulate the corporatist arguments that had so characterized his opposition to the strikes, waxing eloquently regarding the League's "fusion of employers and employees." He concluded expansively that the ability of the Employees' Group to bridge class conflict locally should serve as a model for the entire German Volk.

No one in attendance, however, could outdo the keynote speaker, the Rural League's director, Rohr. Referring to the organization's revival in response to the Rural People movement, Rohr told his listeners that in early 1928, "it happened for the first time that official politics moved away from the metropolis and turned toward the broad countryside, a success for the Rural League's united front." Yet sensing that the "victory" was but temporary given that class antagonism everywhere was stronger than ever, Rohr assailed the pro-urban and export premises of the Republic. He argued that the importing of frozen meat had to be curbed, that the trade treaty with

Poland be revoked; and that the high prices for industrial goods, which particularly burdened farmers, be reduced. Moreover he asked rhetorically: "Is it just that the peasant has to pay three times as many taxes as the salaried worker with the same income; that industry gets back the peacetime tariff but not agriculture; that the peasant is tormented until he bleeds with meat inspections, but not the importer of foreign goods?" Rohr raged at the "false helpers," who in seeking to establish settlements in the east in order to weaken estate agriculture, wanted to drive a wedge between large and small holders. In any event, he claimed, "the colonizers are led into a life of hunger while simultaneously ten thousand peasants are driven from their soil, a resurrection of serfdom in new form."[78] That someone of Rohr's heritage should have spoken of the oppression of serfdom illustrates how desperation allowed Pomeranian estate owners the inconsistencies of demagogy. The meeting concluded with Rohr's attack on the escalating "slavic flood" infiltrating Prussia, and a defiant chorus of the *Preussenlied.*

The demonstrations called in sympathy with the Rural People movement provided not the only indication of frustration in the Pomeranian countryside. Disruptions of public auctions where bankrupt farms were sold to pay off the owners' creditors also occurred, affairs in which the Rural League repeatedly aided and abetted the popular rage. Unlike the gatherings that endorsed the Rural People movement, these protests, which extended into the 1930s, accompanied the attempts of banks to call in their loans in response to the high volume of agrarian debt. Yet here too, deeply rooted peasant symbols rallied land owners with holdings of various sizes. In one such protest that took place in March 1931, 120 farmers, large and small, appeared in the peasant village of Grapzow in Demmin county to prevent the sale of a property and its assets because of unpaid taxes. The group formed a parade and hoisted a black flag, a replica of the one used during the Peasants' War of 1524–25, while singing the *Deutschlandlied* as they marched.[79] Similar incidents took place in the county of Usedom-Wollin. At another foreclosure, the authorities could not complete the auction "because no offer was made for the items being sold."[80]

Some of those episodes became violent. The auction of the assets of the estate lease-holder Herud in Grabitz drew five to six hundred landowners and workers who shouted catcalls and sang the *Deutschlandlied* to prevent the sale. The Rural League in Bergen, according to the county magistrate in Rügen, "obligated its entire membership to take part in the liquidation sale of the inventory, but not to make any offers." The auctioneer managed to sell one plow over the cacophony, but the bidder for a second one, not to mention the auctioneer himself, was forced to seek refuge in the manor house away from the angry crowd. Ultimately, several persons, including a laborer and the tenant himself, received prison terms for their roles in the disturbance.[81] Although county magistrates could not identify those causing the violence as Rural League members, they nonetheless acknowledged that the League pressured its members to attend.[82] At minimum, the Rural League granted few concessions to subtlety, circulating flyers throughout the province that threatened the ostracism of anyone who cooperated with, or otherwise took advantage of, the auctions.[83]

Lest the coercive and manipulative capacities of the Rural League be exaggerated, we should acknowledge the evidence of genuine unity, as well as the unforced expression of grievance that the compulsory auctions engendered. The agrarian crisis proved at least as effective in suppressing class tensions in the countryside as in exacerbating them, invoking instead the myth of a rural community bound together in a common vocation. At a public sale in the county of Greifswald, a gathering showed its solidarity with the victimized tenant farmer: "After a longer wait, the majority went as guests into the farmhouse where all who gathered together, large and small holders, tenants and even estate laborers unanimously agreed that it would be an intolerable insult if, as members of this vocation (*Berufskollegen*), they became a party to exploiting their colleague's distress by seeking to acquire cheap inventory in the compulsory auction. Moreover, farmers were no longer to allow a dealer onto their property who participates in this way. Clearly, the unconditional will to decisive unity came forward from all."[84]

Rural hardship promoted rural solidarity against those who became the agents of the Republic's discrimination against agriculture, and thus it became possible for the province's agrarian interest organizations to describe the crisis as one of undifferentiated misery. The Chamber of Agriculture reported the remarks of an agitator at a public auction in Randow county who articulated the predicaments of his audience, as though speaking for each rural class: "When the farm that has been in our family for generations is put up for sale, when I as a laborer lose my job on an estate, or when I as a settler forfeit my down payment and everything else, then I no longer shrink from believing that it is worse here than it is in Russia."[85]

The demonstrations that the Rural League either organized directly or simply encouraged proved worrisome enough to provincial officials responsible for monitoring the political impact of the agrarian crisis, not least because of their own exasperation with republican policies that undermined agriculture. Raise prices for swine, potatoes, and grain, insisted one, and right radicalism would disappear.[86] Yet the politicization that the Rural People movement stimulated provided additional opportunities for right-radical spin-offs that formed independently of preexisting conservative associations. The most prominent of these was a new political movement that had shown its determination all across rural Germany to profit from popular mobilizations, the National Socialist German Workers' Party (NSDAP). In Pomerania, surveys of county magistrates turned up little evidence of widespread Nazi success, although the party distributed its literature across the countryside and organized rallies.[87] Even though Hitler himself wished that his party would keep its distance from the Rural People movement, National Socialists appeared in exercises closely associated with it. They also attended the demonstrations against compulsory auctions, going so far as to instigate the violence against buyers and auctioneers.[88]

Increasingly, officials emphasized the collaboration between the NSDAP and the Rural League at those demonstrations, especially after the Reichstag elections of September 1930 when the party's fortunes soared.[89] Ominously, that collaboration included the extension of military training to university students in preparation for a civil war with the left. The Stahlhelm cemented its ties with right-wing student organizations so as to avoid losing the initiative to "other political and ideological (*weltanschaulichen*) organizations, namely to the National Socialist Student League." As early as March 1930, three summer camps given over to military exercises had been established in Pomerania.[90]

That the Nazis attempted to benefit from the politicization of others was only logical given the party's modest presence in Pomerania up until then. Although Hitler had been hospitalized in the lower Pomeranian town of Pasewalk for his war injuries, subsequently a point of symbolic value for Pomeranian Nazis, the party's growth in the province provided little encouragement. Founded in 1922 in Stettin, it established a number of urban cells across the province, while its activists courted estate laborers in the countryside. The party's membership in Stettin consisted of a motley assortment of occupations, including several doctors, a wealthy peasant, a merchant, and a railway employee. Yet it was forced to go underground after the arrest of Hitler for his part in the Munich Putsch of November 1923. Thereafter it had difficulty regaining its momentum, even after 1925 when the party was once again legalized. Its first leader, the Greifswald professor and rector Theodor Vahlen, attracted notice only because of his incompetence and his frequent conflicts with the judicial system.[91]

Nonetheless, even after Walter von Corswant, a nobleman and knight's estate owner with roots in the region surrounding Greifswald, replaced Vahlen, the party's fortunes improved little, suffering as they had in rural areas elsewhere in Germany from a lack of funding, coordination, and consistent attention from the movement's national leadership. The Pomeranian party's target audience of agricultural workers, peasants, and small proprietors, reliable conservative constituencies that, according to Corswant, opposed social democracy on economic grounds, awaited effective propagandists to entice it away from the DNVP. Yet the Nazi movement's national leadership concentrated mainly on wooing the urban working classes.[92]

Despite Corswant's leadership, estate owners in particular remained distant, keeping their loyalties firmly within the German National camp. In mid-1927 a number of magistrates still reported that no Nazi group had organized in their jurisdictions, despite Governor Lippmann's belief that Nazi extremism deserved official concern.[93] The Nazis possessed neither the rural organization they would call into being nationally in the spring of 1930, the "Agrarian Apparatus" under Walter Darré,[94] nor even a headquarters located in the capital until 1931 when the Greifswald lawyer Wilhelm Karpenstein replaced Corswant as Gauleiter. The latter contented himself during his tenure with conducting party business from his estate.[95] The movement even lacked newspapers or journals to propagate its message. Several attempts to establish them immediately after its founding either went bankrupt or achieved limited success. Its first permanent newspaper *Die Diktatur*, which was based in Pyritz, did not appear until 1929. The Stettin organ, *Die Parole*, commenced publication the following year. Be that as it may, the agrarian depression caused enough despair as to provide the Nazis with an opening, especially through the collective efforts of the right to dramatize the rural predicament.

The decision of the right to exploit the constitutional provisions for popular referendums allowed its adherents in Pomerania to extend their antirepublicanism beyond the demonstrations at government offices, in market squares and at foreclosures. That broader engagement first came in 1929 as a result of the right's revulsion after the announcement of the Young Plan, the internationally negotiated agreement that rescheduled Germany's reparations payments for a period of fifty-nine years. Although the maximum Germany would be forced to pay was 2.4 billion marks, considerably less than the 132 billion which the victors originally set, the Young Plan unleased a storm of protest on the right, providing the DNVP's new national chairman, Alfred Hugenburg, with an opportunity to organize an antirepublican coalition. The National Rural League, the Stahlhelm, the National Socialists, and the Christian National Peasants and Farmers' Party (CNBLP), the new party spawned in the wake of the Rural People movement and the DNVP's divisions, organized a referendum to block the ratification of the Young Plan, a clear attempt by the most radical members of the coalition to bury the Weimar "system" under a wave of popular indignation.[96]

The unity of the anti-Young Plan crusade received a jolt when in August 1929, Hugenberg and the Nazis on the National Referendum Committee inserted a paragraph mandating that all officials responsible for the plan be put on trial for treason. This was too much even for the agrarian organizations associated with the referendum, such as the CNBLP and the National Rural League, then under Martin Schiele's leadership. At the same time, both organizations were in the midst of forming a coalition of agrarian interest groups in the "Green Front" that sought concessions from the parliamentary "system" that Hugenberg categorically rejected. The divisions within the front help to account for the referendum's ultimate failure. Arguing that Hugenberg's intransigence would produce few tangible results for a sector in dire straits, those "moderate" voices commanded broad support.[97] In Pomerania, however, the Hugenberg strategy of militant opposition dominated, thanks in large measure to Hugenberg's association with the Rural League's director, Rohr. Following Hugenberg's takeover of the DNVP in the autumn of 1928, Rohr engineered the removal of the moderate estate owner Hans von Schlange-Schöningen, from the leadership of the provincial DNVP, a foretatste of the unenviable position Schlange would later assume as commissar of *Osthilfe* when his "moderation" discredited him with many estate owners.[98] Schlange's successor, Georg Werner von Zitzewitz, a Junker who had long been active not only in the DNVP but in paramilitary politics as well, showed no such hesitation in endorsing the Hugenberg course.[99] Thus locally, the Rural League and the DNVP joined forces, and the Pomeranian Rural League, like Rural League chapters elsewhere in the Prussian east, became Hugenberg's lance.

Unlike the referendum on princely estates, when officials evinced skepticism toward complaints arising from the conduct of estate owners, the Young Plan referendum presented far less ambiguity as estate owners exercised their power to the fullest. To be sure, some of the province's most prominent German Nationals, including one of its representatives to the Prussian Landtag, Walter Graef from Anklam, a supporter of the party's trade union wing that Hugenberg expelled,[100] opposed both the proposed referendum and Hugenberg, as did (less surprisingly) Pomerania's Democrat governor, Lippmann. Lippmann received declarations of support for the Young Plan from officials, professors, and teachers who owed their positions to the Prussian government, the center-left composition of which survived until Franz von Papen's coup of July 1932.[101] Nevertheless, the sentiment overwhelmingly favored Hugenberg's extreme antirepublicanism, not only among estate owners, but even among county magistrates who curtailed their support of the referendum only under pressure from above.[102] Impressively Pomerania's right marshaled its forces through rallies, flyers, and newspaper advertisements against the latest manifestation of the "Paris tribute." Prominent landowners and the leaders of such nationalist associations as the Stahlhelm, the Queen Louise League, and the Fatherland Women's Association joined the Chamber of Artisans in condemning the Young Plan.[103] The DVP newspaper, *Pommern Stimmen*, opposed the initiative, but recognized that bourgeois opposition to the Hugenberg course could not compete with the German Nationals who flooded the countryside with literature while convening numerous rallies. "We have no press on the land, nor the means to send out speakers to every county. We cannot come up with many ten thousands of marks for advertisements, flyers, auditoriums and brass bands."[104] Moreover, the preponderance of newspapers in the province that not only affiliated with the DNVP, but also supported the referendum, made it difficult for alternative positions to win a hearing. Even many of the official county newspapers (*Amtsblätter*), supposedly the neutral purveyors of government policy, scarcely remained impervious to the anti-Young Plan fervor. Rather, their biases prompted subsequent investigation by the Prussian government.[105]

Support for the referendum came from what might at first glance seem to be surprising quarters. Ewald von Kleist-Schmenzin, who detested Hugenberg—the latter's corporate empire, wealth, and urbanism stood for everything the Junker despised—endorsed both the anti-Young Plan crusade and the treason clause, outraged by what he took to be the Allies' impossible reparations demands. Because of his prominent role in the Main Association of German Conservatives, a staunchly Prussian organization closely affiliated with the Pan German wing of the DNVP, he became yet another vehicle through which Pomeranian estate owners cast their lot with the antirepublican extremes.[106] Kleist publicly condemned the twelve DNVP Reichstag deputies who rejected the party's position on the treason clause.[107] Indicative of the overlap between religion and politics in the province, Evangelical pastors contributed their share as signatories of anti-Young Plan petitions, as bystanders at rallies, and even as communal or manorial district managers responsible for obtaining signatures in support of the referendum.[108]

The rhetoric of the anti-Young Plan crusade came replete with the language of victimization that not only stressed the plight of the adult population, but also the nation's children, who would find themselves saddled with decades-long obligations that foreigners had imposed on them. The burden of paying reparations, according to the Young Plan schedule, would fall on the heirs of the present generation until 1989.[109] "Should the liquidation (*Ausverkauf*) of Germany continue?" asked a headline in the *Tagespost* rhetorically. Underneath, a cartoon featured "gentlemen" from the United States, England, France, and even Poland greedily snatching German assets while the top-hatted creditor who represented them demanded reparations. "Away with the Young Plan!" read the caption; otherwise all Germany would be producing for the benefit of foreigners.[110]

"Enslavement" claimed the chair of the DNVP, Georg Werner von Zitzewitz, as he described the Young Plan to two rallies at which he spoke: "Our people who are already crammed together in a tight space, buckling under the weight of the chains of slavery, will then harvest the fruits of their hard labor only for the world's victorious powers."[111] The Young PLan threatened to reduce the German people to the status of a "helot Volk" whose national sovereignty faced elimination. A record existed, he commented, that should have discredited the policy of cooperating with the entente powers. Ten years of fulfillment had yielded only disappointment and misery. Our children, he complained, will wonder subsequently why we sacrificed their life chances by knuckling under to Allied demands. Zitzewitz impugned Lippmann's patriotism because, consistent with the Prussian government's own policy, the provincial governor refused to endorse the anti-Young Plan initiative and instead prohibited the participation of civil servants in the referendum. His attitude, Zitzewitz maintained, contradicted the responsibilities that came with Lippmann's office as leader of a border province. Zitzewitz closed one of his speeches with an unashamedly populist appeal, one typical of organized agriculture's claim to speak for the whole: The struggle against the Young Plan would guarantee "the possibility of existence and upward mobility of the German worker." Only a healthy economy, that is, one unburdened by reparations payments, would fund the social programs that the working class desired. By contrast, meeting the terms of the Young Plan would only bring further unemployment.[112]

Here, too, estate owners progressed beyond leaflets, advertising, and rallies, championing the initiative and referendum to such an extent that the Prussian field administration in the province could scarcely deny its painful impact on those who needed the landlords for their livelihoods. Most strikingly, the dissolution of the manorial districts did not discourage Pomeranian estate owners from wielding their economic power with élan, even though some county officials moved the registration away from the manor houses or banned lobbying by estate owners and their inspectors while the registration took place.[113] To be sure, complaints arose from proreferendum supporters in some counties that the dissolution of the manorial districts and the creation of larger communities meant that residents traveled longer distances to register, particularly in the fall when the roads became difficult to traverse.[114] Nevertheless, such inconveniences interfered little with the pressure, subtle or otherwise, that Pomerania's agrarian elite readily utilized.

Sometimes estate owners disguised their intentions, or at least cast them in a more benevolent light, by performing "valuable" services. Chauffeuring their employees to the registration centers was a common enough occurrence. According to the testimony of a teacher near Greifswald, one knight's estate owner, von Storch-Schmoddow, used the harvest festival to cajole his employees, driving them to the registration locale on the day it opened.[115] Others "generously" permitted an afternoon off for workers who had not yet registered so that they could do so.[116] The solicitude extended in another case illustrated the convergence of estate owner self-interest and obligation that feminine concern made credible: Even a church-run poorhouse for women could not escape the lobbying on behalf of the anti-Young Plan effort. One resident "was brought here [the registration center] in a coach by Miss von Köppen from Zürkvitz." Because the prospective registrant could not write herself, "Miss von Köppen volunteered to guide the old woman's hand."[117]

Most of the time, however, the intrusions of estate owners made no pretense of gentility or subtlety. At minimum, they called on the nationalist associations not only to campaign for the initiative, but also to circulate the registration lists beforehand so that no villager would lack the "opportunity" to sign.[118] Or they deputized the supervisory personnel on their estates, persons who were not so legally authorized, to act as official registrants. In the commune of Swantow in Bergen county the communal manager, an estate owner, allowed his "secretary," who in reality was his inspector, to register voters in a building situated near the manor house. Instances like these inadvertently revealed how little had changed procedurally despite the dissolution of the manorial districts.[119]

Worse still, estate owners warned of job forfeiture if they did not secure the expected cooperation, and their employees understood completely the consequences of refusing to participate in either the initiative or the referendum. There was no question, asserted one report, that the estate owners used every possible means, including the threat of firings, to achieve the highest number of registrations: "The same picture goes for all rural communes in which the large landowner has spoken out in favor of the popular initiative. The workers have the feeling that they must choose between economic injury and registering for the initiative. It is understandable that they opt for the latter course. That also explains why many workers who are organized by the free trade unions have registered as well." The same source reported that landowners confiscated literature favoring the Young Plan, while "*Amtsvorsteher* von Behr-Negendank in Kavelsdorf, according to old and sick people, delivered the news by private auto to the registration center."[120] Other reports were more circumspect, yet damning nonetheless. The county magistrate of Rügen could not officially confirm reports that the administrators of the vast Putbus estates twisted the arms of the estates' employees. Yet absolute proof had been hard to come by, he explained, mainly because the workers had been too frightened to testify.[121] There were ways to be sure in which workers could vent their disgust. Some reports noted not only a decline in the number of votes from the initiative to the referendum, but also the relatively high number of "no" and invalid votes cast in some districts against the referendum. Because the latter promised greater confidentiality and voters could secretly choose between yea or nay, some took advantage of that slight leeway. Nevertheless, summarized the president of the Stralsund district, the pressure from landowners convinced even those workers sympathetic to the left to register for the initiative and intimidated many to favor the referendum itself.[122]

Together with their exploitation of the Rural People movement, the estate owners' crusade against the Young Plan cemented alliances among Pomerania's right-wing organizations that in turn brought about the Nazi movement's integration into the political constellation that most Pomeranians accepted as respectable.[123] Indeed, paralleling the national alliance that existed between the Nazis and the right, Pomerania's rural elite showed little reserve in joining with the Nazis at the provincial level. The "working committees" that the right established to coordinate the campaign fused the efforts of right-wing parties and organizations alike, while both the Nazis and Stahlhelm troops shouted down speakers at anti-Young Plan meetings who opposed the referendum.[124] The community of purpose across the right extended so far as to include the Queen Louise League, forming a seamless web of interconnecting organizations that large landed property dominated.[125]

To make the most of their opportunity, Pomeranian Nazis relied not only on homegrown agitators. They also imported major party figures, such as Wilhelm Frick, who obliged with attacks on Stresemann, the Republic's "Marxist" foreign policy, its "Jewish" financial program, and the ban on the Stahlhelm in Prussia and the Reich.[126] Gregor Strasser also appeared. One of Hitler's most trusted lieutenants, Stasser at the time enjoyed enormous prestige as he built the regional apparatus that would bring electoral victories.[127] To well-attended rallies in the upper Pomeranian towns of Köslin and Stolp, occasions that attracted the Stahlhelm, Strasser contrasted the "old German state" with the corruption of the present system. "Today the German Volk is considered nothing but the rabble at every foreign policy conference for Czechs and Slovaks. The old German state fulfilled its task to protect the saver, but the German Republic, by contrast, has permitted the theft of the Volk's entire savings by the Jewish banks."[128]

Raising a theme that would appear in the future, Strasser professed his respect for established religion and morality, a position in accord with the province's reigning ethos. Basic morality, he claimed, had seriously declined, because republican policies harmed religion. Novels and films romanticized divorce, one obvious indication of degeneration. Indicative of the way in which the Nazi party's anti-Semitism attached itself to the issues of economic, political, and moral decline, Strasser sprinkled his remarks with attacks on Jews and Jewishness, elevating Jews as scapegoats for Germany's comprehensive predicament. The Berlin police chief, Bernhard Weiss, received condemnation for suppressing right radicalism, while Strasser noted smoothly in passing that Weiss's father was once a synagogue director. Moreover, Strasser accused Rudolf Hilferding, the finance minister in the Müller cabinet, of allying with "Jewish banks" and international capital instead of defending "the pensioner, the peasant, or the unemployed." He concluded by alluding to Hilferding's status as "without confession," thus connecting the minister with the Republic's erosion of religion and morality.[129]

To be sure, the tensions that complicated the anti-Young Plan movement nationally appeared in Pomerania as well. They would grow even more pronounced after 1930, once the Nazis conclusively demonstrated their political viability. Yet the potential impact of the alliance continued to cause concern among local republican officials: As the president of the Köslin district conveyed to Lippmann in August 1929, the Young Plan initiative resonated deeply within an embittered population. Although at this point, he observed, National Socialism was relatively weak, the spiraling number of bankruptcies could well drive estate owners into the arms of the Nazi movement, jeopardizing the survival of the Republic. Because of their standing in their communities, others most surely would follow their example. The Stahlhelm, whose leadership lay in the hands of estate owners, and the Nazis forged close ties in a collaboration that increased the Stahlhelm's strength. "One is permitted to make the point that a few of the large estate owners who are active in the Stahlhelm's leadership are moving closer and closer to the National Socialists," he fretted, "so that in these cases one can expect a radicalization of the Stahlhelm."[130] Subsequent events would prove that commentator correct.

The Stahlhelm was not alone in encouraging a meeting of the minds between the agrarian elite and National Socialism. Other *völkisch* organizations, a prime example being the Artaman League, not only enjoyed the sponsorship of estate owners, but also encouraged and facilitated Nazi agitation. Having emerged first in Saxony in the mid-1920s, the Artaman League drew its name, meaning "renewal," from the old German to designate a new type of youth organization built on voluntary labor and arising from the "primordial power of the *Volkstum*." Because it celebrated blood and soil, the overlap between it and the Nazi movement in both ideology and membership was considerable.[131] It trained young people on landed estates for several years, after which time the trainees received their own holdings. Over the short term, estate owners expected that the continuing influx of such candidates, most of them sons of peasants and estate administrators,[132] would replace the Polish seasonal workers whose entry the Republic restricted. By 1929, seventy Pomeranian estates employed some two hundred candidates for settlements, and the provincial Rural League expected to at least double that number by the following year.[133] Pomeranian officials quickly grew suspicious of the League, especially during the Young Plan campaign, believing that the young estate workers spent more of their time lobbying for the referendum and for National Socialism than working on the farms.[134] At minimum, the membership of estate-owning Artaman League members such as Behr-Negendank-Kavelsdorf and others in organizations such as the Stahlhelm that *were* participating in the anti-Young Plan initiative gave good grounds for suspicion.[135]

Other than a dramatic improvement in the condition of Pomeranian agriculture, few prospects existed for diffusing the roaring tornado of antirepublican activity, as yet another magistrate from the Stettin district confirmed. Perhaps the Nazi party had not performed well in the last Reich and Landtag elections, he noted, but the climate had changed significantly in the fourteen months since. The party's agitation increased, particularly under the aegis of the Nazis' principal agent in the countryside, Emil Tät, an Artaman League member who worked for the knight's estate owner Kolbe. Earlier, the magistrate explained, one could not ascertain the Artaman League's political leanings beyond its vaguely *völkisch* pronouncements, but since Tät openly divulged his sympathies, that ambiguity evaporated. The Young Plan campaign had become the catalyst for the self-assertion and convergence of all rightist forces in his district. Although he did not believe that agriculture was in as perilous a state as Schleswig-Holstein, he worried that a worsening economy would enhance the Nazis' prospects. The report suggested that the radicalism of National Socialism might succeed if it divided the popular classes from the elites. Would those who had so smoothly incorporated the diverse elements of Pomeranian rural society under their leadership now lose them to the Nazis? "At any rate, with respect to the very strong political contradictions in the county of Anklam," the magistrate opined, "one can see that a fair amount of bitterness over the one-sided interest and large estate owner politics of the DNVP is spreading within the broad and thoroughly German National circles of the peasantry and the *Mittelstand*. It is possible that these dissatisfied elements will turn to the radical ideas of the Hitler movement and the National Socialist Workers' Party [sic]."[136]

That magistrate was correct in discerning the risks inherent in the traditional right's strategy. The Rural League's ability to organize populist protest depended on the cohesion of its membership. Yet among all categories of the League's members—estate owners, peasants, employees and free professionals—its numbers dropped significantly in the poststabilization period. By 1931, only 1,943 estate owners would be registered for the League, down from 2,604 in 1924. Similarly, the number of peasants would show a decline from 37,140 in 1924 to 32,335 in 1931. In 1925, the Employees' Groups counted 46,708 members. By 1931, however, they would reveal a loss of over 10,000. Be it simply the unwillingness to pay dues when cost cutting appeared essential or frustration with the inability of the Rural League to benefit for its members, the League's claim to speak for the whole was weakening.[137]

Notwithstanding that magistrate's sensitivity to the diversity within Pomeranian conservatism and his cogent analysis of the political divisions that propelled antirepublicanism, the agrarian mobilizations of 1928 and 1929 percolated at the behest of organizations that estate owners dominated. The agrarian elite had thus far succeeded, not only because the province lacked other channels that better expressed populist grievances, but also because the interests of all agriculturalists coalesced more than they diverged. Especially the potato's key position in the rural economy materially underwrote the unity that Pomeranian daily and ritual life cyclically recreated and reenacted. Furthermore, Pomerania's agrarian interest groups provided an associational nexus through which the Nazis gained visibility, recognition, and respect, necessary attributes if the party expected to attract Pomerania's disaffected. Just how much the Nazis would prosper became clear soon after. Although the arrival of fascism to the German countryside came later than in Italy, it would now appear with a vengeance.

6

Fluid Boundaries: Pomeranian Conservatism and the Nazi Onslaught

ON NOVEMBER 17, 1929, voters across Prussia elected representatives to the state, county, and municipal parliaments. Overlapping with the preparations for the Young Plan referendum, these elections gave some indication of the Nazi party's growing appeal. Although it remained small, the Hitler movement noticeably increased its share of the electorate. In Pomerania, the party received slightly under thirty-five thousand votes as compared to the nearly thirteen thousand votes it won in the Prussian Landtag election in May 1928. Nevertheless, Pomerania ranked only seventh in the Prussian state in the percentage of voters attracted to National Socialism, as the German National People's Party, although with difficulty, retained its leading position. The DNVP delegation to the provincial Landtag composed from the results of the elections consisted of thirty-one members. Estate owners, including prominent noblemen, comprised over forty percent, as opposed to just four representatives for the NSDAP. The SPD came in second with twenty-four delegates.[1]

To be sure, the election campaign gave the German Nationals grounds for unease, but not because of the Nazi presence. Rather, the DNVP fixated on the splinter parties, most notably the CNBLP, which it feared would enlarge its support at the German Nationals' expense, generating more opposition to the Hugenberg course, particularly from resentful peasants.[2] The unity of agriculture could only sustain itself, insisted the Rural League, if estate owners turned against their few renegade compatriots. Only then could they retain the trust of peasants and workers: "Outsiders among the large landowners are more dangerous and harmful than this or that misguided worker or peasant. The more strongly estate owners themselves reject such people in their own ranks, the greater will be the cohesion between large and small."[3]

In addition, confusion reigned regarding the DNVP's relationship to the "National Rural People" slate which, despite the DNVP leadership's assurances to the contrary, some German Nationals failed to recognize as having the sanction of the German Nationals' provincial leadership. The lack of coordination between the Rural People and the DNVP, not to mention the competition of the CNBLP, cost the DNVP close to seventeen thousand votes.[4] Yet the full consequences of the support that Pomeranian estate owners bestowed on Hugenberg's radicalism, as well as the Nazis' own agitation against the Young Plan, would not become evident until the Reichstag elections ten months later.

When those elections took place, the result of the decision of Chancellor Brüning to overcome a budgetory stalemate, the outcome was nothing less than shocking. Nationally the National Socialists garnered six million votes over the mere eight hundred thousand it obtained two years before. It became the second largest party in the Reichstag after the Social Democrats. Building on the party leadership's decision to campaign more strenuously in the countryside, the Nazis performed particularly well in rural, Protestant areas in the north and east, capitalizing effectively on the populism of the Rural People movement. The magnitude of the Nazi achievement, however, surprised even its most fervent supporters who previously saw little to encourage them. Although all the major parties, including the Center and the Social Democrats, suffered significant reverses, the nonconfessional parties of the bourgeois center and right, especially the DNVP, came away as the biggest losers.[5] The German Nationals suffered one of their worst defeats in the Pomeranian election district, losing over 130,000 votes as compared to 1928, most of them switching to the Nazis. Only in the Köslin district did the DNVP retain its lead, yet there too the German Nationals incurred major losses, an unfavorable omen for the future.[6] The Nazis' stepped-up campaigning during the previous months in anticipation of the referendum and the parliamentary elections had paid enormous dividends.[7]

The September 1930 elections magnified the concerns that had been building within the provincial administration since the emergence of the Rural People movement and the Pomeranian Rural League's demonstrations. At the request of their superiors, county magistrates produced extended commentaries that explained how such a major realignment could have occurred, although only those from the Stettin district survive. In their view, the Nazis had become the reservoir that drew together a diffuse, diverse, and disenchanted populist coalition fed up with the Weimar government and disappointed with the inability of the Rural League to mitigate the agrarian crisis. Peasants, pensioners, agricultural workers, civil servants, and white-collar employees transferred their allegiance to the Nazi party, contributing to the NSDAP's near exclusive status as a political movement that cut across class lines. The province's urban lower middle classes, because their own well-being depended so heavily on agriculture, supported the Nazis as easily as people in the countryside: "The urban shopkeepers and artisans who in this county are very closely connected to agriculture likewise see no way out of their desperate situation and have allowed themselves to be influenced by the unusually strong propaganda of the radical parties," explained the county magistrate from Labes.[8] Moreover, conforming to the national trend, the Nazis tended to draw the young and the previously nonvoting, those without firm party ties, because the Nazis' status as political outsiders allowed them to escape the responsibility for unpopular republican policies. Noted another county magistrate, albeit condescendingly, the Nazis appealed to the unpretentiousness of the rural population, providing voters with the convenient scapegoats of Marxists and Jews.[9]

The analyses of county officials demonstrated a sophisticated grasp of the complexities of the Nazis' success, and particularly the party's potential for redirecting popular energies away from the tutelage of the agrarian elite. The financial support for the party's campaigns drew mainly from the fees collected from attendees at party rallies, not from abroad or from elite sources at home, as had frequently been charged. "In any case, it cannot be established," insisted one magistrate, "that donations for the election campaign flowed to the party from wealthy bourgeois circles."[10] Some of the party's leaders, including its Gauleiter, Walter von Corswant, and one of its district leaders, Bernd-Bogislaw von Enckewort, were estate owners, thus contributing to the NSDAP's chameleon-like social character. Nevertheless, the party's membership was decidedly populist. According to a list of Nazi local and county leaders from two of the province's three districts comprised in the fall of 1930, the Hitler movement drew some of its personnel from the urban and rural working classes (a construction worker, a coachman, and various farm workers, for example), but it relied primarily on such lower-middle-class occupations as cabinet maker, book seller, hotelier, cigar merchant, pastry shop owner, hair dresser, railroad employee, and office assistant.[11]

Furthermore, several officials remarked that most estate owners continued to follow the German Nationals, especially the "old" families such as the Schwerins, Borckes, and Kolbes, or in some cases the splinter Conservative People's Party, yet another group of DNVP secessionists who objected to Hugenberg's ties to the Nazis.[12] The Nazis did particularly well among Artaman League members who eked out a living on estates that had been dissolved.[13] In addition, the Nazis won the allegiance of peasant members of the Rural League who had grown sympathetic to their cause. The peasant Blödhorn in Wustermitz drew special mention for his ability to persuade other villagers to support the Hitler movement. As the chairman of the Rural League's county group in Cammin and once an adherent of the DNVP, Blödhorn had until that moment remained politically passive. In fact, the German Nationals, the quintessential political voice of estate owners, sustained most of their losses in the countryside, an indication that the shifting political alignment contained the possibility of weakening the position of estate owners.[14] A passionate commitment to the Nazi movement among peasants in some regions went hand in hand with their deep antagonism toward estate agriculture.[15]

Some of the reports lent credence to the suspicion that the social and political climate was rapidly changing. The populist upheaval in the province, they noted, occurred partly because major disparities had arisen in the assistance extended to rescue hard-pressed farmers. Commented the county magistrate from Usedom-Wollin, favoritism toward estate owners figured as heavily in his district as the conviction that the Young Plan would bring additional economic hardship: "Credit is distributed without sufficient controls so that a few large landowners [among them an estate owner named Lefevre] obtain 250,000 marks without having to put up any collateral. This capital has been totally lost. The compulsory auction which was initiated against Lefevre's estates had to be canceled because of the costs arising from it. Now, seizure has every bit as unpropitious an effect as improper distribution [of credit]. All the same, it is impossible in the present emergency to repay the fertilizer bill all at once should the farmer be pressed by continuous sharp warnings." Nevertheless, the burden, he concluded, fell much harder on the small holders than on the large, "against whom all coercive measures are pointless because of their high indebtedness."[16] How widespread was the resentment to which that official alluded? Did the election results signify a rebellion of "lower status groups" against "long-established village and agrarian elites?"[17]

Although mindful of the conflicts within Pomeranian agriculture, the reports of local officials reveal the deeper connections, and not simply the divisions, among the aggrieved. They communicate the strong impression that the outcome of the Reichstag campaign in Pomerania was but the result of the estate owners' own militance; one that flowed logically from the character of provincial social relations. If most large landowners remained loyal to the DNVP, they proved anything but militantly hostile to the Nazi party, as the county magistrate of Saatzig recognized: "In all probability, an *active* intercession on behalf of the National Socialists by large landowners in this district hardly took place. Nevertheless, in many cases one can describe the position of large landowners toward the National Socialists as a system of benevolent neutrality."[18] Moreover, some estate owners, including men bearing the prominent names of Puttkamer, Wedel, Enckewort and Kalckreuth cast their lot with the Nazis, effectively enough in some instances as to contribute to the party's electoral breakthrough.[19] Although they comprised but a minority of large landowners and particularly the nobility, their decision suggests at minimum that the electoral

achievements of the NSDAP resulted from discontent at all levels of Pomeranian society, and not simply from a populist "rebellion" against agrarian
elites. The Nazis' attacks on the Weimar "system" found widespread agreement among the bourgeois parties, with the exception of the Center and
the DDP, as well as the press—not surprising given the latter's conservatism and its opposition to the Young Plan: "This support is so pervasive
that the impact of countless articles, especially on the politically naive (*Un-
geschulte*) can only have been that they saw their sole salvation as lying
with the politics of the Nazis."[20]

In addition, the radicalization of estate owners committed to Hugenberg's
uncompromising antigovernmentalism, as the Young Plan campaign so
powerfully illustrated, encouraged the rest of the countryside to move in a
similar direction. At minimum, the divisions between the pro-Hugenberg
radical majority in the provincial DNVP and the moderate minority who
abandoned the German Nationals for the CNBLP and other splinter parties
"confused those who had formerly voted for the DNVP," according to the
magistrate from Usedom-Wollin. "The preparations for the [Young Plan]
referendum provided very effective help to the National Socialists and they
comprised a trial run for the election itself."[21] "It is to be accepted," commented another, "that the majority of the voters in Pomerania are relatively
easy to incite in questions which can be called national."[22] To be sure, the
disappointment of small and middling peasants with the Rural League and
the DNVP did figure heavily in the NSDAP's emergence. Yet according to
these sources, it was a disappointment "that must therefore have operated
all the more radically when in recent years the political parties and interest
associations agitated with increasing harshness and recklessness against the
'present system' and every republican government. The lack of any practical achievements and the increasing radicalization of the DNVP must have
inevitably driven rural dwellers, who are normally unpolitical and accustomed to thinking only in narrow economic terms, into the arms of the
extreme party, the NSDAP."[23]

What had the Nazis done to assure the estate owners' "benevolent neutrality"? Were estate owners unaware that the discontent they boldly
exploited contained the potential for backfiring against them? The answers
lies in the message that the party employed to mobilize supporters in the
province. Despite flourishes of radicalism of the sort that Pomerania's elite
found altogether discomfiting, the Nazis' rhetoric concentrated most of its
fire on the common rural enemies, the Weimar Republic and especially the
left, while deploying symbols that were sure to resonate at all reaches of the
province's hierarchies, outside of the urban working-class left. Behind the
scenes, the party strengthened its alliances with the "respectable." Consistent with the strategy it practiced elsewhere in Germany, the NSDAP
tempered those elements of its promiscuous ideology that resonated poorly,
utilizing instead those themes that more effectively addressed local concerns. In Pomerania, that strategy meant playing to the rural myth, the core
elements of which rural elites best articulated, pressing the party's claim that

it was better able to ensure social harmony, preserve right religion, and resurrect agriculture without unsettling the hierarchies that the province engendered.

Radicalism and Respectability: The Spread of Nazi Influence

Through the first eight months of 1930 as the September elections approached, the Nazis, as they had done elsewhere, increased their visibility in Pomerania. Party rallies featured as speakers such up-and-coming local talent as the Greifswald lawyer Wilhelm Karpenstein, who would replace Corswant as Gauleiter the following year. In a speech entitled "Dictatorship by the stock exchange or a Hitler Dictatorship," which he delivered in May to a rapt audience of SA men in Stargard, Karpenstein denounced Germany's victimization by international and alien forces. The NSDAP, he argued, wanted a new state that combatted the "class spirit," a theme thoroughly in line with the party's oft-stated goal of a harmonious Volk community that would replace the present social fragmentation. "We are a revolutionary movement, an explosive force," he asserted, also a common enough Nazi *leitmotif.* Yet he but murkily defined the targets of revolutionary overthrow, steering away from any direct reference to local hierarchies: "We fight against the domination of the purse, against the party machines. Today the state has become a colonial administration for foreign banking houses. Germany is no longer free in its work to which every human being has a right. That is the consequence of the republican-democratic form of government (*Staatswesen*)." The Versailles *Diktat* contributed its share to Germany's predicament, according to Karpenstein, because it had transformed the Germans into the slaves of "American financial monarchs."[24]

Although determined to appeal to lower-middle and working-class elements, the party took care to reach those higher on the social ladder as well. Vitally interested in the countryside where the political power lay, the Nazi movement by no means neglected the province's commercial and industrial centers, knowing their importance to the rural economy. In Stettin, the NSDAP's newly formed Industry and Trade Committee held its first meeting in the spring of 1930. That affair featured an address by Gottfried Feder, ironically one of the authors of the NSDAP's original radical program that vaguely alluded to the overthrow of the capitalist system.[25] His audience consisted of 120 invited guests, "including leading men from the Stettin business community," according to the party's newspaper, *Die Parole,* an audience whose size the city's police confirmed. Even if the content of Feder's remarks remained unexplicated in those reports, the purpose of the meeting clearly emerged: to establish an ongoing relationship between the party's committee and the local business establishment.[26]

Relations between the Nazi party and the Stahlhelm, however, evinced noticeably less harmony. Despite their common maneuvers before the Young Plan referendum, their differences, particularly over the restoration of the monarchy, one of the Stahlhelm's primary objectives, remained close to the surface.[27] The tension became evident in a remarkable exchange of letters between the Nazi Gauleiter Corswant and the Stahlhelm's leader Bernd von Wedel-Fürstensee, which the *Pommersche Tagespost* published in May 1930. Despite Wedel's plea for unity, Corswant rejected a permanent alliance between the NSDAP and the Stahlhelm because, in the Nazi view, the Stahlhelm was national but not sufficiently social: "Just as for us National Socialists a socialism based on international or anti-national foundations has no credibility, so there can be no nationalism built on anti-socialist foundations." Against Wedel's insistence to the contrary, Corswant complained that the Stahlhelm's ties with the German Nationals compromised the former, because the narrow class interests for which the DNVP spoke and that party's rapidly eroding electoral constituency rendered the Stahlhelm ill suited to social reconciliation, the primary Nazi objective. Nor could the Nazis support the restoration of the monarchy.[28] Over the summer, the Stahlhelm leadership forbade its members double membership in its organization and the NSDAP, a reaction to the Nazis' own refusal to countenance dual allegiances, only to see some Stahlhelm cohorts resign rather than comply with the injunction. All the same, the Stahlhelm's leaders, believing that the Nazis could not ignore the need to preserve unity on the right as the Reichstag elections neared, waited for the party to "finally cease its continuing attacks against the Stahlhelm, recognizing that our strength lies only in firm cohesion."[29]

The Stahlhelm's equivocation mirrored the fluid boundaries between the emerging National Socialist movement and the better established organizations of the Pomeranian right. The crossover of members from the Stahlhelm to the SA and to the Nazis paralleled the open sympathy with which many estate owners greeted the Hitler movement. In fact, Wedel's response to Corswant stressed the desirability of avoiding friction precisely because so many of his people belonged to the party, or at least expressed sympathy toward it. Furthermore, Wedel's protests that the Stahlhelm was every bit as anti-Marxist, antiliberal, anticapitalist, and procommunitarian as the Nazis emphasized how much a common discourse linked the two sides.[30] The "paramilitarization" of the countryside like that of the revolutionary years, proceeded apace against the attempts of the republican interior minister Severing, to contain right radical groups capable of a second Kapp or Munich putsch, until Brüning dismissed him.[31] "It is an open secret," according to one official source, "that there isn't a single estate in Pomerania which hasn't been furnished with weapons, nor a single association which doesn't have arms at its disposal and hasn't held military exercises." The intention, continued that observer, was to aid the National Socialists even outside of Pomerania in states like Thuringia, which the Prussian government considered annexing in order to defuse the growing Nazi presence there. "One should not leave Hitler in the lurch in Thuringia," remarked the observer as he relayed the prevailing sentiment, "and we must be armed just in case."[32]

The issue that provided the greatest potential for disrupting the alliances between agrarian conservatism and National Socialism was the party's suspicious position on large landownership. The Nazi agricultural platform that began to circulate in Pomerania after the Young Plan referendum focused heavily upon the injuries done to the peasantry whom the Nazis believed to be the backbone of the Volk. While the party program acknowledged the "special and necessary tasks" of large estates, it emphasized the creation of a "healthy proportion" of small, medium, and large holdings, a vision that presumably did not yet exist. Moreover, consistent with its vague desires to effect "land reform," language that would most certainly trouble estate owners given its "socialist" connotations, the party insisted on the state's right to approve the sale of "Ground and Soil" (*Grund und Boden*), forbidding the mortgage of landed property to private lenders. Furthermore, the party claimed the state's right of dispossession in several circumstances, some of them not particularly threatening (for example, property owned by non-Germans), but some of them more so, including the "irresponsible use" of property defined as not serving the "maintenance of the Volk."[33]

Indeed, the party's reputation was more extreme than its agrarian program suggested. The "socialism" in its name conjured up near Bolshevik visions of expropriation and dispossession that would not spare even the most modest proprietor. The parties of the right, the DNVP and the DVP, as well as the Rural League, all of them eager to appeal to the "little people," called the Nazis enemies of the peasantry and lower middle classes. What would the Third Reich look like?, asked the DVP's newspaper, *Pommern Stimmen*, rhetorically before the elections. Peasants would lose their own soil. Their land would be confiscated without compensation. Home ownership would no longer exist as the government would nationalize housing. Civil servants would find themselves pressured to join the Nazi party, while producers as a whole would soon be victimized by the Nazis' bias toward consumer cooperatives.[34]

Nevertheless, the Nazi party's emerging rural strategy demanded that it reassure its audience that it affirmed the inalienable right of private property. The party downplayed its reputation for advocating radical social experiments so as not to offend those whom it could ill afford to irritate. When the Rural League accused the Nazis of wanting to "expropriate the land from the rural dweller," the party protested that it advocated only the dispossession of speculators, Jews, and "traitors." The NSDAP explicated the "socialism" in the party's name so as to differentiate the movement from the Marxist left, denying that the party amounted to Bolshevism in disguise, and it repeatedly avowed its commitment to the preservation of private property.[35] Subsequently, Wilhelm Karpenstein, although less solicitous of estate owners than others among the party's provincial leadership, included them in his list of victims whom republican policies, Jewish banks and other unnamed outside forces created. He accused the SPD of hating the knight's estate holder, the factory and brickworks owner, who no longer had anything to call their own.[36] Similarly, Karpenstein reassured industry and commerce that the party rejected collectivization. Instead the NSDAP, according to its understanding of ancient Germanic law and the Prussian General Legal Code, advocated private property as long as it remained immobile, and as long as the property owner used it in the best interests of the larger community. Private property was not a "thing," an object of speculation or exploitation by individuals unconcerned with its capacity to nourish the Volk and its *Heimat*.[37]

Even if the party's rhetoric remained suspiciously vague, there were still those like Gauleiter and knight's estate owner Walter von Corswant, himself of ancient noble pedigree, who by their decision to support National Socialism reassured their listeners. Shortly before the September 1930 elections, Corswant insisted that the Nazis endorsed private property, "including the right of him who inherits it, so long as he has acquired it through creative labor." That was a qualification perhaps, but a qualification that would not have offended rural proprietors who most likely understood themselves as eminently "creative." Private property acquired through bank and stock exchange speculation, usury, and the like, explained Corswant, belonged to the state. The Nazi party would dispossess owners of that kind of property when it took the helm because the owners had "stolen their assets both from the state and from the German Volk."[38]

Other estate owners, such as von Wedel-Parlow, who cast their lots with the party, did not address the issue of property directly but instead denounced the common enemy, the Republic. Germany's future, Wedel claimed, lay in the underpopulated east, yet the Prussian east had fallen into disarray because of misguided republican policies. The Nazi party demanded that capital be redirected to bread and work, asserted Wedel: "Now all German assets have been mortgaged to foreigners for which the Social Democrats and the German Nationals ought to be blamed."[39] Nazi rallies drew large numbers of farm laborers, including the SPD voters in their ranks, who received transportation courtesy of their employers.[40]

Remarkably, the DNVP's losses in September 1930 would not deter most of the Pomeranian agrarian leadership from pursuing a broad antirepublican front. Thus, they adhered to the strategy of Hugenberg himself, who used the election outcome to intensify the DNVP's opposition to Brüning and the ineffective farm policies of the agriculture minister, Martin Schiele, as well as to the Socialists' domination of Prussia.[41] Yet ominous signs of Nazi dissatisfaction with its junior partner status appeared. Following the elections, the Pomeranian NSDAP, consistent with the party's tendencies nationally, asserted Hitler's claim to the sole leadership of the right. Moreover, it attacked the DNVP's repeated compromises with the Weimar system through its on-and-off participation in republican cabinets. The German Nationals proclaimed "positive cooperation" with the Nazis, sneered the party press, while spinelessly serving as a government party; giving into rule by Ebert and Noske during the November Revolution, voting in favor of the Dawes Plan, and supporting Hindenburg for the presidency without realizing that they provided "the hated system with a strong foundation under the tottering frame of its power."[42] By implication, the Nazi party had not so compromised itself.

Behind the scenes, however, the Nazis collaborated with the DNVP, continuing the policy they adopted the previous year. Immediately after the elections, the party instructed its representatives in the Stettin city council to ally with the German Nationals in a "national fractions-community," in order to expand its possibilities.[43] The following spring, the Nazis joined with the traditional right to oppose the attempts of local governments to raise taxes in compensation for lost revenue.[44] The realities of power in Pomerania, notwithstanding the Nazis' astonishing electoral successes, still required coalition-building. The NSDAP's pragmatism would only encourage the provincial establishment to take advantage of the Hitler movement.

The Italian experience persuaded some estate owners that for all of its ambiguities, Nazism represented but a variant of Fascism. Prominent Pomeranians, among them Rohr and Wedel-Fürstensee, visited Mussolini on separate occasions, coming away impressed by the Duce's hostility to "international Marxism" and his corporatist programs to end class conflict.[45] Social snobbery intervened as well. Whether or not Rohr shared Hugenberg's belief in a meritocracy composed of men with education, talent, and property is unclear. Like Hugenberg, however, he wanted to exploit the Nazi movement, despite his belief that its members were poorly qualified to govern. Although recognizing the ideological compatibility between himself and Nazism, he chose not to join the party, in part because of the "untruthfulness and substandard quality of a great number of [the party's] subordinates."[46] Regardless, allying with the Nazis could only have seemed logical, because many nobles had long considered populist politics a justifiable risk. The vision of the "unity" of agriculture enmeshed in the social relations of the countryside proved serviceable in the past, and it would be necessary in the present if Pomeranian agriculture expected to do its part in undermining the hostile Weimar "system."

The Stahlhelm referendum held in August of the following year brought another opportunity for an antirepublican surge. Claiming that the Prussian Landtag no longer reflected the popular will as expressed in the Reichstag elections, and hoping to undermine the Prussian government so as to render Brüning less dependent on the SPD, the Stahlhelm lobbied for the state parliament's early dissolution.[47] During the spring and summer, the Pomeranian right converged under the Rural League's aegis, seeking signatures to initiate the referendum, while attacking the "Marxist-dominated" Prussian government in the province's largely compliant press. The consequences of Prussia's current political alignments, complained one such newspaper advertisement, were cultural, "the disintegration of morality, a growth in Marxist-sponsored heathenism, the fight against God, family and marriage." In addition to representatives of the Stahlhelm, the signatories included the Employee's Groups of the Rural League as well as the Rural League itself, the Bismarck and Queen Louise Leagues, the German

Women's Order of the Red Swastika, the DNVP, and the National Socialists.[48]

Likewise, the Stahlhelm, the Chamber of Agriculture, and the Rural League organized assemblies, many of which incorporated the National Socialists, striking the familiar themes of agrarian demagogy: the moral corruption and misguided policies of the "Marxist" republic; the insufficiency of existing aid programs to the east; and the common professional objectives that united all rural producers, including the agricultural laboring class. The accommodation that existed between the Rural League and the Nazis, as one magistrate observed, enabled the party to expand and deepen its presence in the countryside.[49] At a meeting of the Chamber of Agriculture, Flemming reiterated the pervasive conviction that the problems of agriculture originated elsewhere; in the burdensome reparations payments, in high taxes and interest rates, in the low prices fetched by domestically produced crops (especially rye and potatoes), and in a trade policy that permitted the entry of cheaper foreign commodities.[50]

Speakers at other rallies attempted to convince estate workers that neither the Socialists nor the Republic had significantly bettered their condition despite their initial promises. An improvement in their status would result only through "a national trade and economic policy which once and for all must guarantee to our German east honorable prices for honorable work." Such a policy, furthermore, would "put the employer in the position of letting his workers share in the profitability of his enterprise." That could not happen, however, as long as the "Marxists" remained in power, especially in Prussia.[51] Stahlhelm gatherings cemented their cause with the power and appeal of religion: "The Stahlhelm will succeed in convincing those who still distance themselves from the selfless will of the old front soldiers. It will win them over," argued one of the group's district leaders, von Bredow, "only if it holds to its firm faith in God and the justice of the German cause." The Lord's Prayer and Luther's hymn, "A Mighty Fortress," concluded the occasion.[52] Along with condemning the left's neglect of the lower middle classes and agriculture, another convocation denounced the SPD's hostility toward Christianity, which had encouraged over two million to leave the church.[53] Likewise, Nazi meetings conjoined attacks on the "pacificism, unbelief, and godlessness" of the Prussian government with evocations of past Prussian heroes, verbal assaults against Jewish capital, and appeals to a "socialism" grounded in the Volk community rather than class hatred.[54]

Few rightist rallies neglected to stress the disparity between the popular will and the Prussian government. The ubiquitous Rohr repeated the refrain that Marxism intended to destroy German agriculture but noted that "Marxists" could not have gotten away with their inimical policies without the help of the bourgeois parties. The National Opposition, he asserted, would no longer permit the kind of political compromises that had proven so damaging; it would end the system altogether: "So will our struggle prevail against red Prussia, in faith and in the hopes which we have placed in our national leaders, Hugenberg and Hitler." It was high time, he affirmed, that the state of Frederick the Great be rid of the red flag fluttering over it.[55] At a meeting of the Rural League's Köslin district group, even the estate owner von Gerlach's business report extolled the unity of agriculture while chiding the Brüning government for having failed to recognize the "great groundswell (*Gärung*)" that had taken place on September 14.[56] To be sure, the mobilization in Pomerania should not obscure the mistrust and suspicion that existed at the state level among the participants in the initiative. Yet that dissension had little practical effect in the eastern Prussian hinterlands as the agrarian crusade against the Republic mounted.[57]

As in the Young Plan episode, numerous charges arose that estate owners pressured their employees to register for the Stahlhelm initiative. Naturally, the Social Democrats took up their rhetorical arms against the "unbelievable terror of the referendum supporters," the large landowners, officers, pastors, and other minions who compelled estate laborers to join their pernicious crusade against the Republic.[58] Yet again, even though official investigations found such complaints exaggerated or beyond confirmation at times, they nonetheless revealed the personal interaction between large landowners and their employees that undercut the will and ability of workers to abstain from the Stahlhelm campaign. The most common means for assuring a good turnout at the registration centers was transportation that the estate owner or his administrator provided, accompanied frequently by additional inducements or rewards, such as time off from work. For example, von Richter, an estate owner from Rügen county informed his people that they should register for the initiative, facilitating their decision by loading them onto his horse-drawn wagon. After all had signed the list—the estate owner himself registered last in order to ensure that all his employees complied—he distributed corn, beer, and cigarettes to his male employees while his mother dispensed sweets to the women.[59] Then too, the wives and daughters of owners or estate administrators assisted the elderly and illiterate, not only driving them to the registration sites, but signing for them too.[60]

Other workers were not so fortunate as to receive gifts or other sorts of kindnesses: In some cases employers bore down on their female employees sufficiently to induce tears, or others prevailed on their staffs by propagandizing among their children.[61] Summarized the president of the Stettin district: "On the land, the Stahlhelm as much as possible authorized those personalities who could exercise their influence because of their economic position. Actually, in many cases but especially through the large estate holders, direct pressure was put upon their economic dependents to induce them to sign the registration lists. In specific instances, this pressure also had not inconsiderable success when one compares the results of the Reichstag election and the numbers appearing on the current registration lists."[62]

Even the failure of the Stahlhelm referendum could not dampen Pomerania's radical antirepublicanism, as the rhetoric emanating from the Rural League's leadership made manifest. Rohr's address, "A World Is Collapsing in the East," to a DNVP rally in the fall of 1931 decried the countryside's persecution by alien forces. Not content to limit his analysis to the economy alone, Rohr described the rural catastrophe as an unmitigated cultural disaster with profound consequences for the fate of the German nation. He attacked the Republic for having imported agricultural commodities, thereby undermining the desired end of agricultural self-sufficiency. Moreover, he complained, the rural population had been saddled with higher prices for manufactured goods, a threefold increase in taxes, higher interest rates, and an eleven hour workday for every man, woman, and child. "International commerce has triumphed over the peasant and has driven us to the point where once again we have lost our freedom in food production . . . Not the world economy," continued Rohr, "but the peasant and his labor are the foundation of all healthy economics." What have the Republic's policies meant for Pomeranian agriculture? he asked: "Similar to the peasants of China and India, the peasants [here] and their families perform an unending measure of unpaid work and do it all for scanty nourishment and the illusion of property ownership." The continuation of the Marxist republic, insisted Rohr, would result in Soviet-like conditions that in turn would destroy Germany.

Similarly, Rohr's vision of politics, and more narrowly the theory of government that he derived from it, situated rural society and especially the peasantry at the center. The very definition of political maturity implicit in his conception asserted the primacy of a healthy rural community. Industrialization, international capitalism, and the cities seemed not merely peripheral to the development of nations; rather, their cultural by-products destroyed nation-states altogether: "Populations move from a nomadic existence to statehood with their peasantries. Nevertheless, every state in the world is being shaken to its very foundations by a new modern nomadic life which thinks only of money; one which in its rootlessness, childlessness and faithlessness dispenses with all *völkisch* principles. This nomadism that again undermines the state, stands against the peasantry as well." Exhorted Rohr in conclusion, "Let us save Prussia and Germany from the hands of nomads!"[63]

The Nazi party's growing appeal, however, proved sufficiently intoxicating as to embolden the NSDAP to distance itself from the traditional right, this despite the tenuous and conflict-ridden reconfirmation of the National Opposition in Bad Harzburg in October. The Chamber of Agriculture elections, held throughout Prussia in the fall of 1931 and the winter of 1932 served notice of the Hitler movement's determination to transform its alliances with the traditional right into instruments of its own political control. In Pomerania the NSDAP followed suit. Its press assaulted the chamber leadership for its "unpolitical" posture and timidity toward the government, and its failure to benefit its members. Its advocacy of agricultural intensification—pressing for wheat and milk production to meet consumer demand—brought only the rising indebtedness of farmers to international capital.[64]

Moreover, the NSDAP not only criticized the hefty compensation that Chamber officials received at a time when its dues burdened the hard-pressed peasant, it also derided the overlapping leaderships of the Chamber and the Rural League, a thinly veiled assault against the elitism of organized agriculture in Pomerania. The party press alleged that the Chamber's director Richard von Flemming, as well as other estate owners, received commercial credit from the district bank at an 8.5 percent interest rate. Peasants on the other hand paid from 12 to 18 percent, or even as much as 120 percent for loans to cover taxes in arrears, because they lacked the requisite influence. The party agitated for a new chamber leadership that would "shatter the old clique economy."[65] The novelty of the NSDAP's strategy threatened to upset rural unity. According to one peasant from Bütow, the Rural League had always named the Chamber executives without calling elections, and the Chamber fairly represented all agriculturalists. Only the democratic peasants' groups would benefit from the Nazis' new demand.[66]

Because of the Nazis' obstreperousness, the Rural League's leadership, Rohr and Oertzen, sought to co-opt the Hitler movement by opposing Flemming's reelection and proposing Rohr as president instead. They placed the National Opposition above loyalty to the Chamber's long-standing leader, who in recent months had objected to Hugenberg's obdurate opposition to Brüning. Flemming, they believed, overcommitted himself to the ineffective governmentalism of Schiele and Hans von Schlange-Schöningen, formerly the provincial chair of the DNVP and now the commissar of *Osthilfe*. Moreover, Flemming appeared too comfortable negotiating in Berlin, too skeptical of the wisdom of the Hugenberg course, and thus too moderate to appreciate the radical sentiments prevailing at the grass roots.[67] Flemming denied the criticism against him, and in so doing he underscored the extent to which *Osthilfe*, despite its abuses, failed to appease Pomeranian militants. Rather than being too willing to tolerate the system, he had only commended Schlange for preventing foreclosures, restraining creditors, and removing the Preussenkasse from administering the aid program.[68] Nevertheless, Flemming confessed his fear that the Rural League had grown too dependent on the Nazis, an obvious reference to the League's rightward drift nationally since the Reichstag elections.

In response, Rohr and Oertzen maintained that only the complete rejection of governmentalism would keep Nazi-sympathizing rural producers loyal to the League and Nazism itself subordinated. Flemming's reelection, which did not have the Nazis' support, would only cause the National Opposition's fragmentation. Rather than succumbing to the Nazis as Flemming implied, they sought to avoid a repeat of the National Rural League's capitulation when in December Werner Willikens, Darré's deputy, became one of the organization's four presidents. Rohr took heart in the Nazis' failure to achieve a majority in elections across the province in contrast to their victories elsewhere: "We are the only Rural League that has taken steps against the Nazis. . . . Of all the Rural Leagues outside of Hesse, we have had by far the best chamber election in the Rural League sense. On the contrary, Silesia and Brandenburg are in a wretched state, and East Prussia is at the very least worse off. During the National Rural League's presidential election, we were the only provincial chapter that did not cave in to the Nazis, while the National Rural League's leadership capitulated to the Nazis exactly like it did in the face of the *Landvolk* party." Rohr admitted that the Nazis could "severely disappoint us," but he took comfort in his conviction that rural voters were returning to the DNVP in large numbers. Ironically, the Nazis refused to back Rohr's bid to unseat Flemming, thus assuring Flemming's reelection by default.[69]

The party did not stop with the Chamber of Agriculture, however. It also went after the leadership of the Rural League, especially Rohr, an estate owner who had not stinted in his commitment to the National Opposition, nor opposed the Hitler movement whose "basic ideas" he described as "not far" from his own.[70] The party press claimed that during Rohr's tenure, the Rural League produced few practical solutions to the agrarian crisis other than bemoaning the inadequacies of *Osthilfe*.[71] Moreover, party flyers aimed at the peasantry and working class assailed Rohr for hiring Polish workers at a time when German estate laborers were being laid off: "To us, the youngest most honorable horse boy is better than Herr von Rohr who employs Polish reapers even in winter, who is supposed to have hired them only recently. As a result, he had to let go three German laborers because of a shortage of work. What then remains of our honest struggle against the importing of Polish pigs if the highest ranking official of the Rural League substitutes two legged Polish workers for German laborers?"[72]

In anticipation of new elections for officers of the Rural League, the NSDAP challenged Rohr because he would not permit an election based upon proportional representation; that is, one that would enlarge the voice of the increasing numbers of pro-Nazi peasants who were tired of the Rural League's ineffectiveness: "Up until now, Herr von Rohr has sought to use every means possible to avoid taking the strength of National Socialism into consideration in the composition of the Rural League. The election may well be a storm signal for him. It is high time that in Pomerania too, the Rural League should unconditionally fall in behind the leader of the new Germany, Adolf Hitler." Despite those attacks, Rohr survived as director until the summer of 1933.[73]

The presidential elections in the spring of 1932 confirmed the seemingly irreversible right radical drift. Nowhere in the Reich was it clearer than in Pomerania just how much the Nazi party siphoned its electorate from the DNVP, and just how much Hitler's campaign for the presidency drew sustenance from voters who had chosen the incumbent Hindenburg when he ran for his first term in 1925.[74] More to the point, Hitler's very candidacy for president signified a major defeat for Hugenberg's strategy of a united right radical assault force against the Republic under the DNVP's leadership. Although the DNVP and the Nazis jointly refused to endorse an extension of Hindenburg's term, they could not agree on a common candidate.[75]

In the first provisional election held on March 14, Hitler bested Hindenburg in two of the three provincial districts, losing by only two thousand votes in Stralsund. The candidate of the Stahlhelm and the DNVP, Theodor Düsterberg, drew significant numbers in Pomerania, although his national average of slightly less than 7 percent had not been competitive. Yet Hitler benefited handsomely from Düsterberg's departure from the presidential race; Hindenburg did not.[76] During the runoff election one month later, Hitler won all three districts outright, beating Hindenburg by well over 100,000 votes in the province at large.[77] The Nazis added to their successes in the elections later on in April for the Prussian Landtag, garnering over 450,000 votes, compared to the German Nationals' 176,000. That comprised one of the party's best performances in the Prussian state where, as a whole, the Nazis commandeered 36.6 percent of the popular vote.[78] The Landtag's failure to represent the popular will, the justification for the Stahlhelm referendum, had now been effectively remedied.

That Hindenburg, the very archetype of the Prussian values that Pomeranian estate owners treasured, should have met with such rejection, attests to the depth of rural alienation. The president's association with the Republic's failed policies, and in particular the inability of the *Osthilfe* package with which Hindenburg had been so intimately associated to remedy the condition of Pomeranian agriculture, obviously undermined his standing. Moreover, the pro-Hugenberg position of so many estate owners, not to mention their generally tolerant view of Hitler and the Nazi party, produced a backlash against Hindenburg that was extreme, even when compared to the other eastern Prussian provinces.[79] That such radicalism might make it more difficult for estate owners to orchestrate the politics of the countryside seemed less worrisome than retreating from the more urgent objective of undermining the Republic. In January 1932, as the presidential elections approached, Jürgen von Ramin, whose family's losses help to explain his position, spoke firmly in favor of Hugenberg as the heir apparent to the "Christian-Prussian tradition." In answer to the criticism that the DNVP had not been effective under Hugenberg's leadership, Ramin airily responded that such a remark was but a "typical parliamentary and supremely short-sighted observation."[80]

Privately, the results of the presidential election and the strategy of the National Opposition created conflict and confusion among some estate owners, according to one unnamed moderate source from the Stralsund district who believed that the future of the German Nationals resided in abandoning the National Opposition and becoming a wholeheartedly government party. Under their breath, those estate owners criticized Nazi demagoguery, for the party made promises to workers that it could not fulfill. Worse still, it seemed to them that the DNVP suffered by competing with the Nazis in stirring up the population. Hugenberg, according to this source, enjoyed "no great personal favor" among large landowners who would have much preferred a party leader "from the eastern German nobility." Hugenberg's tactics, furthermore, "resonated little with the rural mentality (*Denkweise*). They are too petty bourgeois and commercial." The bankruptcy of the DNVP's strategy, this observer believed, should have been obvious even to extreme rightists such as Rohr, one of the most vocal supporters of a united opposition against the "system."[81]

In fact, the competition between the Stahlhelm and the SA persisted throughout 1932 as the Nazis continued to erode the Stahlhelm's membership, revealing a dynamism that the old right could no longer muster independently. That rivalry became a source of internecine quarreling within the NSDAP itself, as Wilhelm Karpenstein sought to undermine the new SA leader Hans Friedrich, a former Stahlhelm commander who switched his allegiance to the Nazis.[82] For some Stahlhelm leaders, collaboration with the Nazis brought obvious dangers, "because the Nazis suffer from the arrogant presumption that they alone want to be the saviors of the German Volk."[83] The "Border Patrol" (*Grenzschutz*), the anti-Polish civilian defense unit with close ties to the Reichswehr, remained the preserve of loyal Stahlhelm members and their Junker commanders, while the SA for the most part kept its distance.[84]

In many districts, however, Stahlhelm locals vented their dissatisfaction with their national and provincial leadership for supporting Düsterberg instead of Hitler in the presidential campaign, thereby dividing the national front. Entire locals dissolved themselves in order to join the Nazis.[85] Just before the first round of balloting, in fact, Wedel was forced to resign as the Stahlhelm's head, because Hitler refused to allow the Stahlhelm to lead military exercises with the SA or to discourage Stahlhelm members from changing their affiliation to the Nazis.[86] Those developments encouraged the party to press its advantage by underscoring the Stahlhelm's lack of social commitment. Several months after the presidential election, for example, the NSDAP press accused Stahlhelm troops of acting as scabs in a forestry workers' strike near Gollnow. Even though the workers did not earn enough to feed their families, that article charged, their German Nationalist employer wished to lower their wages further. The Stahlhelm's role in the affair rendered it "like all other workers' associations with a German National stamp. The helping hand it lends is not for the benefit of the worker who perhaps looks for protection from such an organization, but purely for the benefit of the managers without regard for the differences in their social character."[87]

Moreover, after Hindenburg replaced Brüning with Franz von Papen as chancellor in May 1932, dissension erupted between Pomerania's most militant estate owners and the DNVP on one side and the Nazi movement on the other. For most of Pomerania's agrarian leadership, Papen's "cabinet of barons" meant the long sought-after authoritarian replacement for Weimar, which unlike its predecessor favored agriculture. Indeed Papen's tax reductions, import quotas, and ban against the auctioning of bankrupt property justified that confidence.[88] For the Nazis, however, Papen represented yet another obstacle to a Hitler-dominated government. Locally, the party's impatience only increased with its performance in the July Reichstag elections, when it virtually doubled its share of the electorate over 1930, while the DNVP declined further.[89] As a result, the Nazis assailed the elitist and anti-social character of Pomerania's establishment and its unwillingness to step aside for the party with the broadest popular appeal. After all, charged speakers at one Nazi rally before the November 1932 elections, the Papen cabinet amounted to nothing more than a club embracing lords and barons who had been asleep for ten years while a new movement to save Germany had overtaken it.[90] In addition, the NSDAP press charged employers belonging to the DNVP with having fired their employees who switched to National Socialism: "German National employers take work and bread from National Socialists purely for the purpose of demonstrating their economic power, just to show an employee who thinks differently how dependent he is. . . . The reactionary advocates of class warfare are equal to the Marxists in their methods. Just as the Marxist system tosses unpopular officials out onto the streets, so the employers in the DNVP use economic terror against their employees."[91]

The NSDAP's unwillingness to support the Papen cabinet caused frustration and anxiety, even among estate owners who supported the National Opposition. As the November 1932 Reich and Landtag elections approached, Georg Werner von Zitzewitz-Groß-Ganzen, who in addition to leading the provincial DNVP served as a delegate to the Prussian Landtag, urged a DNVP rally to back the government. Not only did it rule "above party," without parliament and without the cooperation of the Center Party, it had also destroyed the Prussian government, the last major SPD stronghold. The "black and red corruption" had ended. Despite a counterattack by the Nazi speaker who accused the German Nationals of pursuing a "policy of illusion," Zitzewitz chastised the Nazis' demagogy and lack of principle.[92]

Yet no estate owner more forcefully denounced the Nazis than Ewald von Kleist-Schmenzin, whose reservations regarding Hugenberg had turned to open dismay at the failures of the National Opposition. For him, the Nazi movement represented Marxism, social leveling, revolution, and irreligion that would produce the destruction of traditional elites and their legitimate claim to rule. Distressed by the favor that the Nazis found among his fellow large landowners, he urged them to recognize the error of their ways before it was too late. That Kleist's own radical antirepublicanism, aristocratic elitism, and anti-urbanism had only exacerbated the dilemma of the Pomeranian establishment seems to have escaped him.[93]

Although acknowledging the claims of many German Nationals that Kleist did not represent the views of the majority, the Nazi party press used Kleist as evidence of the DNVP's calumny. The German Nationals and particularly the DNVP press, it claimed, maligned the SA as nothing more than "a bunch of mercenaries (*Landesknechthaufen*)" and such pro-Nazi worthies as Count von der Goltz as being insufficiently willing to defend Pomerania's borders against the Poles. Moreover, the DNVP charged that the Nazis had not done enough to fight the "tribute slavery" of Versailles. All told, trumpeted the Nazi press, the desperation of the German Nationals, the result of the DNVP's inability to withstand the Nazi onslaught, put it in league with the SPD as Nazi opponents.[94] The Nazi press labeled Hugenberg as nothing more than "a Hitler copy" who could no longer recognize that National Socialism, not the German Nationals or the left, drew the middle and working classes.[95]

If Pomeranian Nazis assiduously belabored the narrow constituencies and elitist composition of their opponents on the right, they took special umbrage at the sneering condescension that drifted toward them from establishment circles. "German National stab-in-the-back politics," the party press complained when Countess von Bredow-Seefeld attacked Hitler in the fall of 1932 for inciting a civil war. The Nazis, she asserted, possessed only average "intellectual capacity (*Denkvermögen*)," despite their "inner temerity." Although she accused the Social Democrats of causing most of the violence in the province, seemingly a defense of the Hitler movement against similar charges from the left, the party professed its resentment at her cool and arrogant hauteur.[96]

We have seen Pomeranian officialdom testify that the anti-elitism of the Hitler movement encouraged the province's popular element to desert the DNVP. Yet despite the backbiting that characterized the relationship between the NSDAP and the traditional right, especially after the autumn of 1930, the party's rhetoric more consistently alighted on the symbols and expectations that the right held in common. Notwithstanding notable exceptions, the Nazis conformed to the expectations and values of the population in general, including estate owners; and whenever possible they downplayed the social revolutionary implications of their propaganda. The relative "moderation" of the NSDAP, along with the unacceptability of cooperating with the democratic system, caused most estate owners to consider exploiting National Socialism instead of opposing it. The Nazi characterization of Hugenberg as a "Hitler copy" pointed to the common bonds between Nazism and Pomerania's traditional right.

The most prominent issue that the Nazis pursued in their Pomeranian campaigns was their hatred of the left, which they carried to the extreme of street violence that did not exist in their contests with the German Nationals. If the Stahlhelm and the SA battled verbally for supremacy, there was little of the bloodshed between them that appeared in Pomerania's towns, the principal base of the left. Consistent with its behavior throughout the Prussian east, the SA refrained from assaulting the institutions that most embodied conservative power, instead employing its violence against the Socialists and Communists.[97] The conflicts between the Nazis and the left amounted to battles between enemies, not family quarrels.

The antileftist appeals of the Nazis sought to secure the party's populist base while assuaging the misgivings of estate owners. To do so, they highlighted the intrinsic evils of "Marxism," its antinationalism and its doctrine of the class struggle that violated the hierarchical, communitarian, and nationalist ethos of most Pomeranians. "The most powerful destroyer of the energies of the Volk is Marxism," claimed *Die Parole*, "because it is the most active in influencing the formation of political opinion and in mobilizing the unused strength of the Volk, the manual working class, for its own ends."[98] On the other hand, the party press and its speakers stressed that the leftist parties turned their backs on what was supposed to have been their central objective, the political and social elevation of the working class. The Social Democrats betrayed the working class beginning with the Revolution of 1918, claimed one agitator, despite their promises of "peace, freedom, and bread." They delivered Germany to the tyranny of the stock exchange and the international marketplace in coalition with the liberal parties. Gustav Stresemann's policy of "fulfillment," which the Social Democrats endorsed, led to Germany's dangerous dependence on foreigners that in turn brought unemployment, economic collapse and misery: "The promises of 1918 have not been fulfilled. . . . Liberalism and Marxism are not a system of idealism, but one of materialism."[99] The Nazis intended to improve the condition of the working class by integrating it with the Volk community, not segregating it by class. The party proposed to reward performance rather than laziness, "creative" work rather than the "rapacious" work of the stock exchanges and speculators. All citizens would have the same rights, but also the same obligations. All those who worked hard, including workers, would receive pensions, health coverage, and rights of inheritance.[100]

Moreover, anti-Semitism assumed pronounced significance, not only because of its integration with the party's antileftism, a common theme in party agitation in other parts of Germany, but also because of its potential for personifying the sources of Pomerania's misery and deflecting attention from the sins of estate owners.[101] Not only did the NSDAP highlight the putative similarity in aims between the Jews and Karl Marx, it also identified the Jew as the convenient scapegoat, the symbol of all the oppressive forces that weighed on the Prussian east: the Republic, the left, international capitalism, and the Versailles "tribute." "Bolshevism or German Freedom" were the choices, according to the theme of a rally in Bütow. The international "money power" of the Jews operated behind the left and the Weimar parliamentary system. High taxes and interest rates proletarianized the peasantry and artisans, while the Young Plan, the by-product of Social Democracy, benefited only big international capital. At another assembly, the claim arose that Germany slid into difficulty beginning in 1868, the year the Jews obtained civil rights. Thereafter, their influence in the press and on the Kaiser as well as their prominence in the Social Democratic movement and international finance came to endanger the nation's vitality.[102] Like Marx's destructive notions of class struggle and international solidarity, claimed another party agitator, the Jews oppressed workers: "As Faust sold himself to Mephisto, so the entire working class has signed itself over to the aims of the Jewish world economy." The Nazis thus proposed to end reparations, take over banking, and end the dictatorship of finance capital.[103] Marx may have rejected private property, but his basically "bourgeois attitude" prevented him from fully realizing his goal, argued another ironically, if a bit curiously. Germany suffered the consequences: Marxism had done nothing more than enlarge the power of capital, especially cosmopolitan capital, which Jews dominated.[104]

In particular, the party tailored its appeals to agricultural workers whose status the left had sought to equalize with that of industrial workers. In so doing, it not only used agitators who came from that class, it also sounded the corporatist themes that the Rural League once successfully employed during the *Landarbeiter* strike. The 1918 revolution betrayed agricultural laborers, asserted the farm worker, Karl Jobski, from Rügen. The SPD's desire to create a "Jewish-Marxist world state" has deprived the worker of even the opportunity at a job. The NSDAP would integrate "the farm worker in the Volk community following the principle: Justice also for the poorest of our Volk comrades."[105]

The left combined with Jews provided the primary targets for National Socialism, especially regarding racial questions. The Hitler movement used its press to elaborate on its positions. Although racial theory *per se* did not figure prominently in the NSDAP's speeches and flyers, it occasionally appeared in the party's more "learned" and considered explanations of its platform, those it formulated to correct what the NSDAP believed were the left's and right's misinformation campaigns. Marx believed in the blending (*Verschmelzung*) of peoples to achieve uniformity, asserted *Die Parole*, because he was himself a Jew. Likewise, Marx wished for the destruction of the Prussian state because he did not believe in having a state at all: "With this mush of humanity, with the contamination of nordic blood, comes simultaneously the victory of materialism over idealism. Humanity then ripens enough to give itself up as slaves to the master of materialistic thought, ripe enough for the world republic, ripe enough for the Jewish world kingdom!"[106]

For as much as the Nazis claimed to be radical, populist, and anti-elitist, their pronouncements, particularly on unions and the status of the working class, more often reinforced than assaulted existing property relations, describing alternatives to the contrary as Marxist, and therefore Jewish. According to one agitator, both Marxists and Jews sought domination through organizing the masses on behalf of "social equality" and "equal wages." Moreover, Jews ruled in both Germany and the Soviet Union. Socialization as practiced in the USSR eliminated small producers while creating big enterprises, an experiment that had failed utterly. By contrast, the Nazis intended that the worker be put once again in possession of his own property and soil, a feat that would be accomplished by encouraging factories to situate in villages. The same propagandist expressed the party's preference for its own corporatist union, which would allow workers representation but eliminate the pressures toward equality in income: "The worker will no longer be allowed to dictate how much the employer can pay. A bakery apprentice who sits opposite his master on a committee will know what his master earns. He can no longer dictate what the master himself deserves."[107]

The party took pains to stress that it did not oppose unionization in principle. In fact it sought improvement in the education and livelihood of workers so they would become full members of a harmonious Volk community that would forever abolish class divisions and the conflict they spawned. According to *Die Parole*, the NSDAP intended only that the trade union idea be purged of Marxism, the ideology of conflict promoted by Jews.[108] The consequences of that "purge" for the independent working-class organizations that permitted workers at least some degree of leverage against their employers would become clear enough once Hitler assumed power.[109]

The seamless web of Marxism, liberalism, international capitalism, and the Jew allowed the party to transcend the contradictions in the social bases it strove to win over by presenting a unified, conveniently identified source of woe. Yet the Jew could also appear in more modest settings, away from the lofty if pernicious heights of the international economy, especially in Nazi propaganda aimed at the Pomeranian peasantry. In that case, the NSDAP exploited the more traditional stereotypes, although not neglecting to connect them with the larger forces afflicting the countryside. One such example in a paper rife with anti-Semitism made its point in a poem entitled "The Destiny of the Peasantry:"

> "Very rare is capital
> and in agriculture all the more so.
> True friends are still not there.
> Only Nathan the money lender is nigh,
> his face full of cunning sympathy.
> He approaches the hardpressed man,
> benevolently offering him a sum of money
> at a year's fixed term.
> Yes, you poor German peasants;
> truly you are to be pitied!"[110]

We have seen instances in which the Hitler movement, in criticizing estate owners and the Stahlhelm for their "unsocial" behavior, targeted sources of misery closer to home, particularly the elites. Nevertheless, aside from linking the DNVP to the failed policies of distant cabinets that lacked sympathy for agriculture, the Nazi party less often equated the sins of the estate owners with those of the major enemies, the left and the Jew. Even when Nazi rallies tried to capitalize on the anger of peasants and estate laborers, they usually did so by damning the Republic and "Jewish Marxism." The party's most prominent peasant leader, Blödhorn, indicated as much to a rally in the spring of 1931, after announcing the huge crossover of peasants and farm workers to the movement. Tired of burdensome interest rates and unable to pay off the banks, the peasants no longer wanted to be slaves to capital and the parliamentary system, he exclaimed. The estate laborer was also being dispossessed, "in that he can no longer obtain work and bread from his employer." Only the Jews have profited. By contrast, the

Nazis offered relief. They intended to imprison those who charged more than 5 percent interest and hang those who took their capital out of the country.[111]

In all other respects, the party kept its positions consistent with, although not necessarily identical to, those of the province's elite. Like the leadership of the Rural League, the party minimized, and even denigrated, the impact of *Osthilfe* as a package of "half measures," a kind of unemployment compensation dispensed by an overweening bureaucracy. It echoed the agrarian leadership's emphasis on the recovery of profitability while demanding moratoriums for farmers and their creditors, a significant reduction in interest rates, and the elimination of reparations. It too advocated increasing animal husbandry so as to reduce Germany's dependence on imported butter. Even though the party recommended cutting back on the production of rye, potatoes, and sugar beets, it did so in the name of creating a self-sufficient economy that would put agriculture on its feet again while meeting the needs of consumers. No longer, the party insisted, would Germany be disadvantaged by the world market or the logic of "international Jewish capital."[112]

Moreover, the party took pains to limit its offensiveness regarding an issue that estate owners found threatening, especially as two of the last three Weimar governments, Brüning's and Schleicher's, singled out bankrupt estates as potential areas of settlements. To be sure, Gauleiter Karpenstein advocated settlement as a means of extorting land from estate owners.[113] Yet the Nazi press softpedaled the issue, denying that the party's settlement program would penalize large estate owners in another version of the "agrarian Bolshevism" of the "system." Although the press attacked the German Nationals for having no coherent settlement policy at all, and admitted that some of the nonviable estates would be divided to benefit estate laborers with serious prospects of becoming successful peasants, it proposed that the majority of settlements be placed in suitably drained marshes and moorlands.[114] At no point did the party cease to defend its claims the guardian of private property or to deny that its socialism was equivalent to Bolshevism. For the Nazis, socialism meant neither equality nor the elimination of private property; rather it symbolized the party's desire to construct a genuine property-owning national community out of the wreckage of class conflict and the Marxist ideology that celebrated it.

In the cultural realm, the Nazi movement spoke the language of traditional Prussian values and celebrated Frederick the Great as the party's exemplar of duty to the nation. "The SA leadership has been based on the spirit of Prussian Potsdam," claimed a speaker to a rally near Bütow. "The only man who is suitable to lead the German Volk is Adolf Hitler. He is imbued with the same spirit as King Frederick the Great who once spoke the words, 'The king is the first servant of the state.'"[115] Immediately before the Stahlhelm referendum, the party press negatively compared the Prussia of Weimar with Prussia's more glorious past, while connecting prominent Nazi slogans with the putatively traditional and communal Prussian spirit:

"Once the [Prussian] state was what it was supposed to be—a human community that from the king down to the miller recognized one law: the law of solidarity with the state, the law which we National Socialists acknowledge in the formula, "Community use before individual use."[116]

To a meeting of the Rural League in March 1932 in the heat of the presidential race, Gauleiter Karpenstein maintained that the new state arising from the ashes of Weimar would sustain the land, making it the centerpiece of the economy. The new state would relieve the land of the external pressures of finance capital: "From the tradition of the old Prussia with its founding principle, 'I serve,' will arise a new great consciousness of the state(*Staatsgesinnung*)." He concluded that National Socialists combined the socialism of Moeller van der Bruck and the state consciousness of Frederick the Great.[117]

Despite the Nazis' expropriation of the Prussian past, and particularly the hallowedness of land as the anchor of that tradition, important differences remained between the party and the "old" right, among them the place of the monarchy once Weimar was destroyed. For Rohr, a revitalized Prussia and a renewed Germany could come about only through a restored Hohenzollern monarchy because that institution anchored the Prussian inheritance: "As long as Prussia exists, the Hohenzollerns are her monarchical house. This belief is but a part of our faith in Prussia and Germany generally."[118] Karpenstein on the other hand scrupulously ignored the subject altogether. Moreover, the old right clung to a "smaller German (*kleindeutsch*)" view of Prussia that clearly subordinated the rest of Germany, a perspective that was intended to preserve the hegemony of its brand of conservatism. During the presidential campaign, the DNVP asserted that it was the only party that could "consciously lead the struggle for a Prussian Prussia," because it was the bearer of true conservatism and Protestantism. "Whoever thinks primarily in "greater German (*Groß–deutsch*) terms cannot think Prussian!"[119] Karpenstein, by contrast, insisted that the strength of Prussia could be realized only in the unity of north and south, thus refusing to endorse Prussian particularism.[120]

In addition, differences arose between the racism of the old right, particularly its noble core, and that of National Socialism, although neither side ventured into lengthy theoretical discussions in the heat of campaigning. They confined themselves to the "practical" issues that preoccupied the electorate. Among themselves, however, the Junkers maintained that purity and blood were of paramount importance in the face of mass leveling. Yet, consistent with their self-image as "natural" leaders, they linked racial purity with the preservation of the hereditary nobility that was in turn urged to mix only with its own kind and improve its fertility.[121] Obviously, given their propensity for attacking the "reactionary" cliques of the old elite, the Nazis adhered to a considerably more expansive notion of racial purity—assigning it to the Volk as a whole, especially the biologically natural leaders among them, rather than one hereditary caste. Traditional leadership, in other words, figured more centrally in the Junkers' conception than in that of the Nazis, hardly surprising given the NSDAP's diffuse populist composition and the Junkers' decided preference for exclusivity. That significant difference in emphasis bespoke of future conflicts as to who would dominate the coalition of the right during the Third Reich.

Nevertheless, if the Nazis proved determined to press their own meanings in response to the terms "Prussia" or "race," they remained cautious on religious matters, a sound strategy given the depth of religious practice and identity in the province. The NSDAP contended that "a deep moral power" motivated it, namely the obligation of every member to submit to the duty commanded of all National Socialists, the preservation of "order and justice." Service to the Volk and nation and the future of its children testified to the selflessness that governed party principles.[122] The NSDAP criticized liberalism and Marxism for questioning the state's obligation to protect religious life "as the strongest source of strength of our Volk community." Officially, the party guaranteed all confessions religious freedom so long as they did not violate the "sensibilities" of the Volk, because like National Socialism, Christianity taught the virtues of self-sacrifice and the individual's responsibility to the whole, while combating the "Jewish-materialistic spirit."[123]

The blatant anti-Christianity that some party leaders exhibited, notably Heinrich Himmler and Alfred Rosenberg, and the tendency of pagan fringe groups such as the Tannenberg League to affiliate with the Nazis, forced the Nazis to defend themselves against the charge that they were hostile to religion. Such accusations, they insisted, were nothing but lies. "We National Socialists know very well that a state cannot exist without religion," asserted one Nazi leaflet. "Religion is the foundation of ethics and morality." As a consequence, the party fully supported confessional schools and religious instruction, wholly in accord with Pomeranian commitments: "We demand teachers for our children who will teach religious instruction so that children remain faithful and obedient to their parents."[124] "National Socialism demands not the absence of religion, but rather a strong religious education in the schools," claimed a speaker at a rally near Bütow. "It shouldn't happen that a teacher says to the children at grace that they'd better not let the potatoes get cold."[125]

For certain, the party exhibited potentially worrisome tendencies, including the somewhat inconsistent disposition to rigidly separate "confessionalism" from politics. While Christianity might well continue to be the "foundation of ethics and morality," religious divisions undermined the Volk community the Nazis wanted to establish: "A German who on confessional grounds alone withdraws from Germans of another confession, or even uses confession as a weapon against the German struggle for freedom, does severe injustice to his own blood."[126] Nevertheless, when the party reached for specific examples, it usually pointed to the Catholics, not only because the Center Party allied with the Social Democrats as one of the original partners of the Weimar coalition, but also because the apparent cohesion of "political Catholicism" ran counter to national unity.[127] There is no question that the ambiguities in the Nazi position would become all too evident during the Third Reich. But for the moment, attacking Catholicism would not have sounded offensive to the pervasively Protestant political culture of Pomerania, and it might well have assuaged those who remained leery of the NSDAP because of its south German Catholic origins.[128] It certainly capitalized upon the anti-Polish feeling that existed, especially in the border regions.

Beyond the promise to defend religious schools, the party reached for symbols that resonated deeply in the population, particularly the peasantry, to illustrate just how much the Marxist republic threatened to devastate rural culture. The Communist party (KPD), it claimed, not only wanted to raise German children without religion, it also planned to kill clergymen if it took power.[129] The choice lay between the "swastika and Soviet star," insisted another party tract: "Do you want your Christianity to be spat upon and shamed by idlers and the dregs of humanity, or your village church be turned into a cinema like in Russia?" Not only would Jews in the politburo tell the peasant what and how much to produce, they would place him in a collective and dissolve his family: "Only the Third Reich will make the peasantry, and with it blood and soil, the cornerstone of the Nation! Fight for self-sufficiency in food produced from our own soil, and reject the importing of every ounce of foreign food! Fight for God and family!"[130] A clearer statement as to the vital connections between economy and culture, so important to the self-understanding of Pomeranian rural society, could scarcely be found.

Cooperation along the right drawing upon the discourse that the Nazis and conservatives shared never ceased, despite the squabbling that frequently erupted. Nazi assemblies did not hesitate to incorporate compliant dignitaries, including even the exiled kaiser's fourth son, Prince August Wilhelm. The prince stressed that only Hitler could reawaken Germany after its terrible defeat: The German Volk, united in 1871 under the empire, he explained, still had not inwardly become one nation. Thus after the stress of war, disintegration set in quickly. Only Hitler had again seizer upon the idea of the Volk community, he claimed, the reason that the Nazi party now gathered millions under his banner. A new German nation was in the making.[131] Provincial officials monitored the further evidence of militarization that appeared on Pomerania's estates, as SA men, ostensibly in the employ of estate owners to bring in the harvest, were suspected of combining sport and military exercises. Rumors abounded that the Brown shirts campaigning for the July 1932 parliamentary elections distributed leaflets to the countryside at the estate owners' behest. The Socialist newspaper *Volksbote* charged that all over Pomerania, workers were suddenly being pulled from their jobs and transported to Berlin to aid in the general strike that the Nazis sponsored with the Communists.[132] Ever fearful of Nazi populism, Ewald von Kleist-Schmenzin grew appalled by the attitudes of his comrades, such as Hans von Wedeymeyer-Pätzig, who supported Papen's ongoing negotiations with Hitler to bring the latter into the government.[133]

Until the "seizure of power," that misleading phrase used to describe Hitler's assumption of the chancellorship in January 1933, Pomeranian estate owners continued to define the political and cultural agendas that the National Socialist movement addressed. Although the party that principally spoke for their interests, the German Nationals, disintegrated from its internal contradictions, a collapse that produced misgivings among some estate owners once the Nazis' intention to dominate the right became clear, preserving the National Opposition seemed the best way of destroying the hated Republic. In any event, the attitudes of estate owners toward the Nazis, which ranged from benign neutrality to outright support, radicalized the rural population that came to see the Nazis as the logical and more effective heir to the DNVP. To be sure, the ability of estate owners, regardless of the disagreements among them, to maintain their hold on key positions, ensured that the NSDAP's ambition to command the Pomeranian right remained but a wish, not yet the reality. Ironically, however, the catastrophic consequences of agrarian elite conservatism resided in ensuring that the estate system and rural hierarchies worked to the NSDAP's advantage, creating a mutually reinforcing radicalism that doomed the Republic and facilitated a fascist alternative.

Succumbing to Right Radicalism: The Evangelical Church Relents

The extent of Pomeranian conservatism's bankruptcy becomes more apparent with the Evangelical Church, an institution that strove to distance itself from political partisanship and especially right radicalism. Throughout the 1920s, church leaders often conveyed their suspicions of *völkisch* movements, most notably the Tannenberg League, because they rejected the Old Testament as "Jewish."[134] The anti-Christianity prevalent among the Nazi party's national leadership seemed, in clerical minds, not only intrinsically objectionable but also continuous with the worst aspects of the *völkisch* movement and the secularization of the Weimar period. Shortly after the Reichstag elections of 1930, when estate owners uttered comparatively few misgivings about the Nazis, the church press appeared guarded, uncertain as to what to make of the party's support of "positive Christianity" on the one hand and its vituperative attacks on the Old Testament on the other. As one column put it, one wished "that the patriotic enthusiasm one finds in them [the Nazis] were combined with a firm foundation in the Evangelical faith. Then indeed the future would belong to them; then and only then would they become truly German."[135]

Moreover, the agrarian crisis not only damaged the church severely, but also graphically exposed the weaknesses of its dependence on estate-owning patrons. The decline in government support and the loss of revenue generated by the church tax was but partial evidence of the straits into which the church had fallen. On top of that, it experienced a dramatic drop in the income that tenants paid to farm church lands as individual proprietors either struggled to keep themselves from bankruptcy or collapsed outright.

Construction and renovation projects faced postponement or cancellation as landowning patrons failed to contribute, and even meeting such incidental costs such as paying the moving expenses of a pastor became the subject of appeals to the Supreme Consistory in Berlin.[136] The provincial consistory had to assume the burden of maintaining such ancillary charitable undertakings as a home for single or sick Protestant women, including pastors' daughters. The local estate owner could no longer sustain the foundation itself.[137]

Nevertheless, the *Osthilfe* measures treated the church and its parishes as a low priority, refusing to grant debts owed to them the same status as other public obligations. Thus parishes and their pastors confronted their creditors with rapidly dwindling resources. By July 1932, the loss of income from the church tax and land leases came to over 437,000 Reichmarks, roughly one-half of that in income from leases.[138] Of all the churches in the Old Prussian Union, the problem was most evident in Pomerania, especially in the purely estate villages where the church had been unable to diversify the tenants who farmed its land. In the church district of Greifswald-Land, for example, the parish leased 315 morgen (79 hectares) to a knight's estate for 4,250 marks per year, but the latter's debt, to that point over 6,000 marks in rent and 1,400 marks in church taxes, remained unpaid. After putting continuous pressure on the estate's trustee, the consistory could wrest only 500 marks.[139]

Records of the Old Prussian Union Church reveal much about the scandal of *Osthilfe*, particularly its favoritism toward the large estates. They note, for example, the belated but nonetheless angry refusal of hard-pressed East Elbian peasants to pay their church taxes on the grounds that estate owners had already won that "privilege" months before.[140] Objected the president of the Pomeranian church, Dr. Wahn, "It is hard for the parishes to take the fact that parishioners have to pay the church tax which necessarily means a considerably lower standard of living than some of the larger proprietors who are protected from their obligations."[141] Moreover, the record conveys the combination of mounting desperation and rage with which church officials confronted trustees and other institutions that seemed more concerned to grant undue protection to estate owners than to the churches whose cultural significance to the east should have, in their view, been utterly transparent. They describe "near-Bolshevik" conditions in country parishes, especially in the estate villages where, in many cases, parish income had all but ceased.[142] "The procedures of the trustees are impossible and give rise to exasperation," protested Wahn: "Estate owners who pay not one pfennig in church taxes or rent, and thus let the pastor go hungry, can spend the winter in Italy attended by their servants. They are given twelve hundred marks for their necessary livelihood, and in special cases, are allegedly granted up to eighteen hundred marks. The entire profit from the harvest is reputedly needed for the safeguarding of the next harvest, and in this way, these enterprises are again made viable (*wieder auf die Höhe gebracht*) without regard for their creditors."[143] Complaints of this nature continued, even into the Third Reich.

Nevertheless, despite the utterance of genuinely felt grievances, such frustration never extended so far as to question Pomeranian hierarchies, only the fairness with which assistance was allocated. Consistent with its past behavior, the church articulated its resentments in ways that conformed fully to the rural myth: The major sources of the Protestant predicament, it maintained, lay elsewhere; in the cities and in the Republic itself. Despite the church's claim to political neutrality, the behavior of many pastors and loyal parishioners only confirmed the conservatism of the church's overall political direction. Evangelical pastors could usually be found delivering benedictions at Stahlhelm gatherings, no surprise given the paramilitary group's specific commitment to safeguard Christianity as well as the right-wing affiliations of most clergymen.[144] But as the Nazi party took hold, not a few of them sanctified that movement as well, prompting the consistory to review charges of political bias. The spiraling politicization of the last years of the Republic placed the consistory on the horns of a difficult dilemma: It asserted that pastors, like all other citizens, possessed the civic right to their political positions and it insisted that its clergymen were obligated to speak on public issues that directly affected the church. Yet the consistory also warned that pastors could not advocate a specific party-political line in the direct performance of their duties, such as delivering sermons from the pulpit.[145]

Could the church really uphold such a fine distinction in the pervasively conservative Pomeranian countryside, particularly when the public issues that concerned the church placed it unambiguously in the conservative camp, and especially when the right's politicization captivated most of its lay people? The Prussian church elections of November 1932, which would choose representatives to the parish and provincial synods, begged such questions strenuously. They directly introduced the politics of the outside into the church administration. The "German Christians," a new and explicitly pro-Nazi faction, which had received the endorsement of the party press, won a creditable share of the ballots cast. Although both the Nazi party and the German Christians denied that they politicized the church, their slogans called for a genuine *Volkskirche* that would not only defeat Marxism and liberalism, but it would also sweep away the narrow class-bound church (*Standeskirche*) of the DNVP-affiliated church leadership.[146]

Pomeranian superintendents scarcely concealed their ambivalence toward the German Christians. On the one hand, church leaders could not ignore the Nazi movement's inroads among their parishioners, much less the excitement and vitality that the party and its German Christian affiliates manifested. On the other hand, they could not deny the less desirable consequences of that right radical surge. Nazi dominated church synods might further alienate left-leaning laypersons whom the church wanted to lure away from the Marxist parties. Moreover, the Nazis' insistence on unconditional obedience to the will of the Führer suggested the incompatibility between the oath required of church officers and the claims of the party. Finally, the German Christian leadership gave few grounds for comfort when its pre-election gatherings attacked the church administration, while politicizing church doctrine.[147] The pressure on the leadership grew even more irresistible after the strong performance of the German Christians in the parish elections.

Specific examples bring concreteness to the painful realities that undercut the intentions of church leaders to remain politically neutral. In response to a complaint from the SPD paper *Vorpommern*, located in Stralsund, the consistory investigated the activity of one pastor Kurt von Puttkamer from Rakow who allegedly made antirepublican remarks during his Sunday sermon. At the conclusion of the investigation, the consistory admitted that the sermon's content came dangerously close to politics and it communicated its warning to the pastor. Nevertheless, the consistory's report qualified its findings, noting how in a relatively short time, Pastor Puttkamer had won the confidence of his congregation. "If we certainly do not want to endorse the position of the sermon which has come into question," the consistory admitted, "so we must also call attention to the fact that the parish, composed to an important degree from large and smaller peasants, as well as large landowners, doubtless agreed wholeheartedly with the sermon's disputed position. . . . Whether the members of the parish from the working class who as estate laborers belong to the parish, or perhaps a teacher, took offense at the sermon, we do not know."[148]

Witness also the case of Pastor Pecker from Bütow, accused of criticizing his local government for favoritism toward Catholics and Poles, particularly Poles who bought German land. Pecker was already well known for his anti-Polish and pro-Nazi convictions, having spoken at a party rally prior to the 1930 elections where he attacked Polish encroachments and anticipated the Nazis' coming to power as an event that would "bring order to the fatherland."[149] In his own defense, the pastor admitted his utterances but noted their consistency with the views of "all national circles in the border county" who objected to the democratic leanings of the authorities. The consistory looked closely at several of Pastor Pecker's accusations of favoritism, including his complaint that the government bought musical instruments for Catholic school children rather than investing in the maintenance of German landownership. Although the consistory found that the pastor too easily accepted rumors, it concluded that it was not in his nature to spread them: "His conduct thus appears in a gentler light; Pastor Pecker is an enthusiastic friend of German nationhood (*Deutschtum*) who with ardent love sees his parish which lies directly on the Polish border, and his homeland as well constantly threatened with Polish propaganda." The consistory warned him soberly to be cautious about political matters in the future.[150]

The consistory found it equally difficult to chastise the pro-Nazi leanings of pastors, especially after 1930 when so many lay persons flocked to the Hitler movement. In fact, the party membership of the infamous Pastor Pecker could not be too severely faulted given that he likely influenced his parishioners less than the unemployed youths who agitated on the party's behalf. That the rural youths of his parish, the sort of constituency with whom the church sought strenuously to cement its ties, were pro-Nazi as well placed Pecker in an appropriately mitigating context.[151] Pastors frequently responded to leftist accusations by asserting that socialism had no appeal for their congregations. When *Volksbote* charged a pastor in Naugard with having permitted Nazi and Stahlhelm demonstrations during memorial services, the pastor's superintendent answered acerbically that the left's "hostility toward the church" (*kirchenfeindlichkeit*) and its godlessness aroused no sympathy among the workers there. The socialist attitude, he asserted, was but an urban attitude.[152]

To be sure, the commitment to party-political neutrality did prevent the Evangelical leadership and the church press from becoming as rancorous as so many estate owners in their opposition to the Republic. Thus, they practiced evident restraint even when they saw fit to praise social or cultural trends to their liking, such as the move away from the less authoritarian child-centered pedagogy that found favor during the 1920s, particularly in urban areas. Warned the paper for the ecclesiastical district of Anklam, the church should stand aside from party-political conflict to avoid compromising its institutional and theological integrity: "Its word must remain the word of the church and not that of a party."[153] Similarly, the leadership of the Evangelical Women's League repeatedly cautioned its members against excessive politicization, although without notable success: "Everything falls under the rubric, Heil Hitler," complained Marie von Kleist, "and that can often become a stumbling-block (*Klippe*) for the DEF." Nevertheless, she stressed to her group that political involvement should not compromise the League's "inner sincerity."[154] Such warnings would become the *leitmotif* of the church's pronouncements in the months and years following the Nazi takeover when the German Christians sought to conform German Protestantism to Nazi organizational and racial principles.

All the same, the Nazis' trepidation, evident in the party's desire to avoid offending the established bourgeois institutions and associations whose support it needed, produced strategies to which the Evangelical Church could scarcely object. Fortunately, sighed its press, good sense prevailed against *The Myth of the Twentieth Century*, Alfred Rosenberg's tract that posited the incompatibility of Christianity and Nazism. "It must thankfully be recognized," according to one paper, "that the great majority of the National Socialists stand on the soil of Christianity, and in as much as they are Protestant, they are remaining true, and will remain true, to our church."[155] Explained one clergyman, formerly of Belgard, the Nazis' local leadership was comprised of "loyal members" of the Evangelical Church, lending sustenance to his own belief that one could be both a good Christian and a good German.[156]

In addition, the Nazi movement, according to the church press, directed most of its energy against the very source of Weimar secularization, the left: "In several cities in our province, the National Socialists have performed valuable service in the struggle against the Free Thinkers. Otherwise, we could experience the same thing with National Socialism as with the SPD in which unfortunately free thinking is the official *Weltanschauung*, at least among the leadership, while the Religious Socialists are utterly without influence."[157] The press noted that the party condemned prostitution, smut, and abortion, while calling the new government that took power on January 30, 1933, "the last chance which has been given to our Volk to master the huge dangers which threaten it," the last opportunity to contain "the red flood."[158] The Nazi campaign against atheism, both before and after the party took power, proved so successful in the eyes of the clergy that even communist youth, once bitterly anticlerical, returned to the church.[159]

Moreover, pro-Nazi pastors not only lent legitimacy to the movement by taking part in party demonstrations, they also interpreted the party's message as "authentically" Christian—revealing the fluidity between Protestant nationalist convictions and right-wing politics. One Pastor Müller, who spoke at a Nazi-sponsored "field service" in Anklam, suggested to his listeners that "positive Christianity" meant daily self-sacrifice modeled after the apostles of Jesus. The rebirth of Germany demanded inner strength. Pastor Müller's remarks accorded well with an assembly that thereafter stressed not only Hitler's continuity with tradition, but also the party's perpetuation of the struggle of World War I in its attacks on the "gold international," the stock exchanges and finance capital.[160]

The surrender of the Evangelical Church underscores the ease with which Nazism flowered in Pomerania in the soil of rural conservatism that estate owners so assiduously cultivated. The case of Pomerania helps to explain why conservative elites overcame their reservations to Hitler's appointment as chancellor, especially when he would head a cabinet with but two Nazi members. The hostility of Pomeranian estate owners toward Weimar induced most of them to see the advantages of perpetuating the National Opposition more consistently than the disadvantages. Evangelical clergymen, the other major source of sustenance for the rural myth, more dependably recognized the Nazi movement's Janus-faced qualities, because they claimed political neutrality. Yet they too remained trapped in their conservatism and as a result, they succumbed to the belief that Nazism coexisted with Christian-conservative values. Now that the Nazis had come to power, however, would they continue to respect those to whom they owed so much of their success?

Epilogue

Pyrrhic Victory:
Pomeranian Conservatism in
the Third Reich

AFTER A LONG, frenetic, and complex series of negotiations, President Hindenburg approved the formation of a new cabinet on January 30, 1933. Its new chancellor became none other than the "Bohemian Corporal," Adolf Hitler, whom the old Field Marshal detested. Indeed Hitler's appointment was not the first choice of the German conservative "establishment," consisting of high-ranking officials and military officers, industrialists, and estate owners, who preferred an authoritarian system that exploited, yet subordinated, the populist energies of the National Socialist movement. Nevertheless, given the disappearance of popular support for the parties that normally articulated the interests of elites, the "establishment's" options had grown decidedly limited, promoting conflict among its members as they determined the best way out of the late Weimar political crisis. Ultimately, conservative elites could not construct an authoritarian system without the mass backing that the Nazi party offered. A remark attributed to Alfred Hugenberg at Hitler's ascension, "the greatest stupidity of my life," clearly betrayed his unease at the prospect of the latter alternative, which included a new leader whose contempt for conservatives Hugenberg had personally experienced.[1]

To be sure, the new cabinet consisted of a majority of conservative appointments, including Hugenberg as the minister of agriculture and economics who in turn took the portfolios of several key Prussian ministries and the post of *Osthilfe* commissar. Moreover, Hugenberg named

Hans-Joachim von Rohr as his state secretary. As members of a government that unified the elements of the antirepublican right, the two personified the "wisdom" of the National Opposition. Yet, although the Nazis received but three appointments, the cabinet's final composition came about without the DNVP leader's consultation. As a consequence, the control of the police in the Reich and Prussia wound up in the hands of the Nazis who envisioned a more overtly partisan use of repression than Hugenberg was prepared to allow.[2] Conservative elites, badly fragmented among themselves, saw their "alliance" with the Nazis as grasping for the lowest common denominator. The goals that conservatives and the Nazi movement agreed upon, the elimination of Weimar, eradicating of the influence of organized labor, expansionism, and the ridding of the restrictions of Versailles, comprised an explosive package of negativity that over the long term would exacerbate Nazi radicalism. Franz von Papen's assertion that the new cabinet effectively "framed in" Hitler was as much an expression of nervousness as it was of confidence—an act of desperation that feared that an authoritarian solution without the Nazis would either risk civil war or allow the left to exert political influence once again.[3]

Nevertheless the new government, to resort to an admittedly stale metaphor, represented the chickens coming home to roost. Conservative elites had been unable (and unwilling) to accommodate the Republic's parliamentarization of political life. Moreover, they even found its "above parties" corporatism inadequate to their needs, particularly after the onset of the depression.[4] The logrolling among the major interest groups and particularly, negotiating with the left incurred the steady, if uneven, reduction of elite influence. Moreover, it reduced the possibility of a Germany that would dominate the continent because the Socialists stood for high welfare expenditures and low military budgets.[5] The resignation of the Papen cabinet in November 1932, the result of its narrow base of support, and the threat of "reparliamentarization" under Papen's successor, Kurt von Schleicher, prompted the furious counterattack of elites alarmed at Schleicher's overtures to the trade unions, his cabinet's proposed work-creation projects, and especially his plans for settling bankrupt estates. In fact, the vehemence of the agrarian reaction to Schleicher's settlement program, a repeat of the episode that precipitated the fall of Heinrich Brüning, pulled the rug out from under Schleicher. His unacceptability to estate owners rendered a Hitler chancellorship all but unavoidable.[6] Even apart from the issue of eastern settlements, the National Rural League found little to praise in the general. At Rohr's bidding, the League withdrew its support from Schleicher's cabinet because it failed to institute a ban against the importing of foreign butter, that organization's transparent attempt to satisfy peasant dairy producers.[7] Even Hindenburg preferred the plebeian "corporal" to a Reichstag whose investigations into the *Osthilfe* scandal—investigations the Nazis incidentally encouraged—threatened his reputation and that of his family.[8]

And how had the Nazis become a political force in the first place if not through the politicization of estate owners whose powerful place in the countryside and virulent anti-Weimar radicalism shaped itself into the Frankenstein who in turn created the Nazi monster? In Pomerania and the Prussian east, there were those who objected to the National Opposition's volatile amalgam of elite and popular politics because they feared for the future hegemony of elites and the established institutions of rural life. Such stalwarts among the nobility as Ewald von Kleist and the leadership of Pomerania's Evangelical Church counted among them. Nevertheless, hatred toward the Republic and all that it represented neutralized the voices of moderate conservatism that struggled to be hard, emblematic of the dilemma that beset East Elbia as a whole. Those voices arose too late and too timidly to become credible.[9] Ambivalence characterized the attitude of the majority of Pomerania's elites until the end of the Third Reich. On the one hand, the Nazis attacked the political dominance of estate owners and the cultural role of the Evangelical Church. On the other hand, the Third Reich's assault against Versailles and its destruction of the left, an extremely brutal undertaking in Pomerania,[10] met with at least tacit acceptance. Pomeranian estate owners, especially the landowning nobility, exemplified the indivisible blend of consent and dissent found among conservative elites generally.[11]

The Nazi regime's reluctance to undermine estate agriculture, the economic foundation of rural social hierarchies, comprised one major reason that Pomeranian estate owners remained off balance.[12] The Nazi party depended on its "alliance" with conservative elites to stabilize the new government and carry through the regime's burgeoning rearmament program, an indebtedness made more onerous by the nobility's contributions to the military and to the civil administration, suitably purged of leftists, Center Party adherents, and Jews.[13] The regime discovered also that its campaign to boost agricultural production so as to make the Reich less dependent on imports that absorbed valuable currency, and more self-sufficient in its ability to feed itself, could only come about if Germany's largest producers remained intact. Ironically, the Third Reich came to a similar conclusion to the one the Majority Socialists had drawn fifteen years earlier, although the consequences, of course, differed markedly. The disruptions of World War I on the supply and distribution of food, and the social upheavals that resulted, discouraged both left and right from instituting significant land reform.[14]

As a result, the privileging of the peasantry that the Nazi party promised before its accession to power, as well as the aggressive settlement programs that party radicals touted against a rural elite they despised, dissipated sufficiently so as not to be a major threat to estate owners. Both the Hereditary Farm Entailment (*Erbhofgesetz*) and the Reich Food Estate (*Reichsnährstand*) promulgated to preserve a healthy peasant stock produced at best limited gains owing to the priority invested in rearmament. Moreover, they often contradicted the peasants' own best interests as they perceived them.[15] To be sure, the *Erbhofgesetz* did not bring the reversal of the Republic's policy on entailed estates that many nobles expected. In fact, a new law in 1938 eliminated the remaining entailed estates, fully one-third of those that existed in 1918. Yet, the entailment law subjected peasants to a degree of regulation that most found unpalatable, even if their heavy debts otherwise qualified them for the law's principal benefit, protection from dispossession.[16] If peasant production served the interests of preparing Germany for war, such as that devoted to the cultivation of sugar beets, then the regime did favor peasants over the interests of large landowners. Nevertheless, the persistent labor shortages that rearmament engendered caused widespread resentment, whatever advantage peasants acquired otherwise.[17]

For the first five months of the regime's life, Hugenberg's ministry became a "bully pulpit" on agriculture's behalf, and against the demands of consumers and the export industries. The minister advocated the unilateral introduction of quotas to protect agricultural commodities, drastic cuts in interest rates, the freezing of farm foreclosures (thus once and for all protecting estates from settlement projects that capitalized on bankrupt estates), and the guarantee of high prices for farm products. Not only was agriculture, according to Hugenberg's scheme, to be the cornerstone of the German economy, it would also justify an intensive program of autarky. Hugenberg's most dramatic success came in the 600 million Reichmarks representing the state's contribution toward paying off farmers' debts. Although Hugenberg was forced to resign by the end of June 1933, the result of his weak political base, the bitter opposition of industrialists, and his disastrous performance at the London Economic Conference, his successor, Walter Darré, pursued similar policies.[18]

Remarkably, the *Osthilfe* program with all its blatant inequities bestowed its largess on eastern estate owners until it was phased out in late 1936 after agrarian profitability improved. Despite the mounting indebtedness of peasants throughout the 1930s, which should have prompted the concern of a regime whose leading party made the peasantry the centerpiece of its propaganda, the regime's need for cereals and potatoes encouraged its tolerance of inequities in the distribution of aid.[19] Thanks to declining production costs (the result of falling prices for farm machinery), as well as to rising prices and the reductions in interest payments on debts, the income of estates rose.[20] The aggressive attempts of the Reich Food Estate to assure good incomes for farmers while delivering food to consumers at reasonable prices favored big producers over small ones in some respects, exactly the opposite of Darré's intentions.[21] Thus, the regime's wholly conflicting aims of giving pride of place to the peasantry, expanding the German population in the east, and securing adequate food supplies could only be reconciled through the brutal colonization of Poland and the western regions of the USSR, not to mention the economic penetration of the Balkans.[22]

Despite its expedient concessions to large landownership, the Nazi regime's political and cultural challenges caused genuine frustration, particularly to many of Pomerania's oldest families whose domination of provincial associational life comprised but a natural extension of their social hegemony in the countryside. After maintaining its autonomy longer than the National Rural League and others among its provincial branches, the Pomeranian Rural League found itself "synchronized" (*gleichgeschaltet*) soon after Hugenberg's resignation. That initiative arose less from Pomerania's disgruntled peasantry than from a decision on high—from Walter Darré, who named Blödhorn as Rohr's successor despite Rohr's complaints as to the blatant illegality of his removal. Blödhorn summarily dismissed most of the Rural League's county leaders, replacing them with new faces from the peasantry.[23] Ironically, the constitution of the new Rural Peasant Estate (*Landesbauernstand*) not only stipulated that the representative from the agricultural working class to the leadership council had to belong to the Rural League's Employees' Groups, it also incorporated the Rural League's self-description as the single voice of all agricultural producers. Nevertheless, although such allowances reflected the corporatism to which both Pomeranian conservatives and Nazis adhered, the Nazis' determination to remove the "reactionary clique" from the province's civil administration and agrarian interest organizations produced real enough results as did the *Gleichschaltung* of the Stahlhelm.[24] The perception of having been shunted aside persisted despite the housecleaning that occurred in the provincial Nazi party hierarchy after the Röhm Purge in June 1934. To prepare the political leadership and state administration for war, a process that required the cooperation of provincial elites, even the party's radical leader, Wilhelm Karpenstein, had to resign.[25]

"Synchronization" proved even more disruptive to the Evangelical Church, whose leadership had evinced greater reserve toward the Nazi movement than the leaders of organized agriculture. The German Christians, whose highly politicized religious revival had so concerned the Pomeranian church leadership when the Nazi-sympathizing movement first made its mark in the previous fall's parish elections, increased their campaigning after the seizure of power. Like their cohorts elsewhere in Prussia, the German Christians capitalized on Hitler's explicit endorsement of their attempts to bring the church into conformity with the national Awakening, winning by a sizable margin in the hastily called parish elections of July 1933. The provincial synod, once the bastion of Junker patrons and conservative church hierarchs, now contained a majority of German Christians, many of them extraordinarily young. Nazi newspapers that in previous elections urged their readership to drive the DNVP's influence from the church administration in the name of creating a *Volkskirche*, simultaneously reminding readers of the proper registration procedures and eligibility requirements,[26] trumpeted the new synodical majority as having come from all classes. The old leadership, including the two General Superintendents Kalmus and Kähler, was retired, replaced by the young German Christian Bishop Karl Thom, the self-styled grandson of Pomeranian peasants whose new ecclesiastical title reflected the movement's commitment to the Führer principle.[27]

The "Church Struggle" (*Kirchenkampf*), as the conflict surrounding the Evangelical Church came to be known, embraced two consecutive, but bla-

tantly contradictory facets. It consisted first of the German Christian attempt to create a unified and Nazified "Reich church" under the German
Christian Reich Bishop, Ludwig Müller, out of the loose federation of
German regional Evangelical churches, including the Old Prussian Union.
In so doing, the German Christians expected to enhance the ability of insti-
tutionalized Protestantism to play an important cultural role in the
formation of the "new" Germany. Second, however, the Church Struggle
comprised the effort of the Nazi regime, one that became increasingly evident as the regime distanced itself from conservative elites, to secularize
German life and undermine the institutional impact of both major
churches, Evangelical and Catholic.

The initiative of the German Christians not only bitterly divided the laity
and clergy throughout the Third Reich; it also invited the regime's persistent
and negative intervention in church affairs that extended well beyond the
German Christians' evanescent successes. In fact, by the fall of 1935, the
Reich church project collapsed, placed in receivership under the newly ap-
pointed Reich Minister for Church Affairs, Hans Kerrl. Kerrl's task was to
depoliticize and suppress the internal church conflict that had created in-
numerable problems for the regime, including the discontent of its
conservative allies, widespread popular disaffection, the rejection of the
courts, and much unfavorable foreign media coverage. The hostile reaction
that the German Christians drew in Great Britain, in particular, whose tolerance the regime considered crucial to the success of its anti-Versailles
foreign policy, was especially worrisome.[28] Yet the never suppressed desire
of radical Nazi party members to eradicate the cultural influence of Christianity proved over the long run more difficult to contend with. The Nazi
regime achieved considerable success in deconfessionalizing the primary
schools in regions where creating confessionally mixed schools was possible. Even though the party's efforts to eliminate religious instruction and
remove Christian symbols from the schools provoked enough popular hostility to force its retreat in many instances, conservatives could only bemoan
the steady erosion of a Christian-based culture that smacked of "Bolshevism."[29]

In Pomerania, the German Christians and the regime's secularization
campaign attracted support, including the outspoken endorsement of some
estate owners. Yet the attempts of the German Christian-dominated provincial synod and consistory to carry out the centralization of the Reich Bishop
and the insertion of an "Aryan paragraph" in the church constitution generated vocal support for the oppositional Confessing Church. The
anti-German Christian movement took shape with the formation of the Pastors' Emergency League in the fall of 1933 and coalesced into a rival
institution with theological substance during its synod in the Westphalian
city of Barmen the following spring.[30] In addition to that of many pastors,
the sentiment of patrons from Pomerania's oldest families lay clearly on the
side of the Confessing Church, and in fact Reinhold von Thadden and
Stephanie von Mackensen joined its first provincial "Council of Brethren"

(*Bruderrat*).[31] Such behavior effectively illustrated the growing inner distance from the regime and sense of betrayal that increasingly shaped the attitudes of the province's rural elite. The Pomeranian opposition demanded that Bishop Thom end the "red revolution" that upset the "peace of the church," namely the takeover of local church administrations by the "Bolshevik hurly-burly" (*Treiben*) of German Christian district leaders and their henchmen.[32]

The case of Pastor Reimar from a parish in the Belgard diocese, home to the Kleist family, demonstrated the clergy's and the nobility's disenchantment with the regime's church policies. Pastor Reimer, an inveterate conservative who had aroused the ire of local Nazis even before 1933, bitterly resisted his removal, demanded by the local Nazi leadership and two bourgeois estate owners. Moreover, the pastor refused to hang the swastika from the church in honor of the chancellor's birthday. His defiant act won the endorsement of none other than Ewald von Kleist-Schmenzin, himself under the Gestapo's surveillance for his openly expressed animosity toward the Nazi regime. Indeed, Kleist lost the protection he received under *Osthilfe*, a punitive measure that could have resulted in the foreclosure of his estates had he not sold one of them for settlement to keep his creditors at bay.[33]

After the defeat of the Reich church, when the Ministry for Church Affairs endeavored to undercut the Confessing movement by refusing financial support for theology students sympathetic to the Evangelical opposition, many old-line patrons in Upper Pomerania, including the Thaddens, Kleists, Bismarcks, and Wedemeyers, sponsored independent Confessing Church seminaries. One of them sprouted under the direction of the emerging theologian, Dietrich Bonhoeffer, one of the few pastors to associate with the conservative underground later. Bonhoeffer's most ardent supporter, Ruth von Kleist-Retzow, introduced the young theologian to her granddaughter, Maria von Wedeymer, who eventually became Bonhoeffer's fiancée. In extreme cases, patrons even supplied food to pastors whose salaries had been stopped. Like many of their counterparts elsewhere in the Prussian east, membership in the Confessing Church conveyed for many noble families their belief that Evangelical Christianity permeated the foundations of the Prussian-German polity, and that those foundations could not be eradicated without inviting disorder.[34]

The regime's distancing from the Reich church and Nazism's increasingly overt anti-Christianity disappointed the province's German Christians, most of whom strove sincerely to dedicate the church to the national renewal while maintaining the religious integrity of the Gospel. A distinctly "moderate" lot, at least when compared to their more politicized and racist brethren elsewhere,[35] most of them, including Bishop Thom, disassociated themselves from the movement following the infamous "Sports Palace" rally that took place in Berlin in October 1933. At that affair, radical German Christians condemned the Old Testament as "Jewish," championed the segregation of non-Aryan Christians, and demanded the transfer or removal of all pastors in opposition to the Reich church.[36] Subsequently resigned to an uncomfortable neutrality, and often ostracized by the most militant Confessing Church pastors, former German Christians grew dismayed as local Nazi party officials regularly interfered with the church's charitable and welfare activities. Exiled to West Germany after the war, some took to writing long explanations for their politics after Hitler's accession, conveying their disillusion at Nazism's having used them and contesting the dominant view of the early postwar era, that of the Confessing Church's heroic opposition to the German Christians' "false teaching."[37]

Conflicts with the regime and its German Christian surrogates intensified the discordant feelings of oppositional pastors, even if spokesmen on their behalf exaggerated their favor toward Nazism to keep them from the Gestapo's scrutiny. For some, the Reich church represented a foreign intrusion into the Evangelical faith, a virtual recatholicization. Pastor Damrow from Tonnin sermonized against Reich Bishop Müller, implying that his regime amounted to little more than a papacy that true Christians would do well to reject, regardless of the regime's obvious merits.[38] In March 1934, the consistory intervened with the Reich Bishop on behalf of Pastor Lettan in the Stargard diocese, who was accused of circulating a leaflet critical of the German Christian *Gleichschaltung*. According to the consistory, however, the pastor believed strongly in a partnership between church and state toward the revitalization of the Volk. Furthermore, the pastor took pains to assure the consistory that he intended his circular not as a criticism of the Nazi regime, but simply as an expression of concern over the state of internal church affairs. Local Nazi authorities, argued the consistory, attested to the sums that Pastor Lettan contributed to party rallies and to "procuring a party banner." Let the matter drop, concluded the consistory, now that the pastor had given all the necessary assurances of his loyalty to the Third Reich.[39]

Pomeranian pastors persisted in proclaiming their loyalty even as Nazi party radicals attacked the church from outside. The German Faith Movement, a party-sponsored attempt to create a new religion out of German mythology to supplant Christianity, caused stupefaction among pastors who otherwise considered themselves committed Nazis. Such was the case of Pastor Freidrich Schauer from Pütte, a member of the Pastors' Emergency League and the Confessing Church, whose county magistrate intervened to defend him against party charges of disloyalty. Pastor Schauer had been disabled during the war and his heroism at the front earned him an Iron Cross, first class, the magistrate explained. During the course of his career, the pastor emerged as a vigorous opponent of Marxism and ultimately a fervent supporter of National Socialism. His wife was active in the Nazi women's movement and his son belonged to the Nazi Jungvolk. The German Faith movement, however, forced the pastor to condemn an enterprise that he believed contradicted his own mission and that of the Third Reich.[40]

Laypeople also refused to remain silent in the face of the party's anti-Christianity, despite the conservatism that otherwise caused most of them to accept the Third Reich. Committed parishioners in Tempelburg complained of the repeated denigration of the church, including the disruption of Sunday services, the propagation of anti-Christian propaganda, and even the anti-Christian burials that the party conducted on behalf of its departed members. Popular resistance to such Nazi initiatives, even among those who were normally indifferent to the church, arose in that largely peasant and worker community.[41] Popular opposition was common, particularly in regions with a strong confessional identification, either Evangelical or Catholic, where protests constituted an expression of social solidarity against the party's egregious violations of local mores.[42]

Yet, in many instances, opposition continued to induce profound misgivings that occurred more as the product of dismay than anger. In 1939, two Pomeranian pastors, both of them party members since 1932, drafted a lengthy memorandum bemoaning the regime's anti-Christian course. Up to 1936, they remarked, the relationship between the church and the Nazi party had been relatively harmonious. Afterwards however, the party's anti-Christianity caused nothing but division. Of particular concern to the two pastors was the behavior or a certain "Junker" Wimmer, who criticized the clergy for sabotaging the anti-Semitic Nuremberg Laws, as well as the law for the "Prevention of Genetically Diseased Offspring," otherwise known as the Sterilization Law. The pastors claimed that the population at large, including most Nazi party members, objected to the new course of the local party leadership, especially its efforts to disrupt family life by deluging members of the Hitler youth with anti-Christian propaganda. The cohesion of the Volk community, argued the pastors, was becoming unglued.[43]

Despite the divisions that the Church Struggle generated, and despite the bewilderment and disillusion that increasingly saturated the outlooks of opponents of the regime's religious policy, the Third Reich's "successes" effectively contained Pomeranian conservatism, be it that of estate owners or of clergymen. The muted reaction of Pomeranian estate owners, especially the nobility, to Nazi rule contrasts markedly to their vehement, militant, and well-coordinated politicization against the Weimar Republic. Like their counterparts elsewhere in the Prussian east, the improving condition of agriculture, the career opportunities for sons that rearmament and the expansion of the army entailed, and the undermining of Versailles convinced most that whatever its liabilities, the regime provided notable relief from its predecessor. The viciousness of the Röhn Purge, which claimed the lives of prominent conservatives along with the SA leadership, and Hitler's assumption of the title Führer upon Hindenburg's death, disturbed some who rued the spreading dictatorship.[44] Yet the palpable revulsion among the nobility generated little more than a fragmented opposition that produced few alternatives capable of achieving broad support.

To be sure, considerable variation arose in the degree to which the Pomeranian nobility bonded with the Third Reich. Many noblemen welcomed National Socialism without reservation and, like Jürgen von Ramin and Carl Friedrich Ludwig von Behr, endorsed its antileftist and racial policies, including eugenics, in the *Deutsches Adelsblatt*.[45] Some, like Alexander von Woedtke who lost his ancient noble estate in 1929, found their way into the SS.[46] Hans Peter von Heydebreck, who in September 1933 succeeded Hans Friedrich as head of the SA, lost his life during the Röhn Purge, sacrificed ironically to Hitler's determination to prevent the "second revolution" that the anti-elite "Brown Shirts" demanded.[47]

Other noble families in Pomerania and elsewhere in the Prussian east, however, spawned conspiratorial opposition to the regime, especially once the threat of war became palpable. Although not opposed in general to the broad outlines of Nazi foreign policy, some nobles realized that the regime's recklessness threatened Germany's destruction in a catastrophic war. Such circles overlapped with those emerging in the bureaucracy and in the officer corps itself.[48] From the Sudenten crisis in 1938 to the climax of the conservative resistance on July 20, 1944, the final failed assassination attempt against Hitler in the Führer's East Prussian headquarters, East Elbian estates facilitated clandestine contacts among nobles dismayed by the regime's adventurism, its party cronyism, and its cultural radicalism. The most famous of these groups, the Kreisau Circle surrounding the young Silesian nobleman, Helmut James von Moltke, was also the most programmatic, eschewing acts of violence against the regime in favor of constructing a future constitution for Germany once National Socialism collapsed.[49] Knowledge of the numerous plots concocted against Hitler, however, as well as close personal ties to those connected with them, characterized the political activity of many Junkers until the July 1944 attempt backfired.[50] Nearly a third of those executed for their part in the coup attempt were nobles, and they included such prominent Pomeranians as Ewald von Kleist and Elizabeth von Thadden. Fifteen Pomeranian nobles, including Hans-Joachim von Rohr-Demmin, spent time in prison for their association with the assassination plot.[51]

Nevertheless, regardless of the significance of the July 20 plot as the founding myth of the Federal Republic of Germany—as the "other" Germany that provided the moral foundations of postwar democracy—the conservative underground failed to destroy the Third Reich. Its weaknesses attested more forcefully to the absence of categorical opposition to the regime among conservatives themselves than to the lack of popular support or to the insufficient encouragement of Germany's enemies.[52] Similarly, the reaction to National Socialism from most Pomeranian nobles appeared equally compromised—colored by resentment and revulsion to be sure, but ultimately checkmated by agreement with much that Nazism offered. The Weimar "system" absorbed the brunt of their hostile politicized energy, so much so that allying with National Socialism became their only remedy. Neither the Pomeranian nobility nor Pomeranian estate owners generally reckoned that the outcome would be a ruinous war that would engulf the rural community they sanctified and defended. The sad vigil of the Krockows in their estate's park personified the legacy of Pomeranian right radicalism.

Notes

Introduction

1. Christian Graf von Krockow, *Die Stunde der Frauen. Bericht aus Pommern 1944 bis 1947. Nach einer Erzählung von Libussa Fritz-Krockow* (Stuttgart: Deutsche Verlags-Anstalt, 1988), 60–61. Libussa's mother Elly, herself a Puttkamer, married Jesko after the death of her first husband Otto Christoph von Wickerau, Count von Krockow, in 1928.

2. Ibid., 239–50.

3. The view that Germany diverged from Western European norms achieved its high-water mark in the 1970s among the so-called "Bielefield School" of West German historians, especially Hans-Ulrich Wehler and Jürgen Kocka. One of the best examples of this historiography is Hans-Ulrich Wehler's *Das Deutsche Kaiserreich 1871–1918* (Göttingen: Vandenhoeck and Ruprecht, 1973). The most thoroughgoing critique of the *Sonderweg* thesis is that of David Blackbourn and Geoff Eley, *The Peculiarities of German History: Bourgeois Society and Politics in Wilhelmine Germany* (Oxford: Oxford University Press, 1984). For an analysis and survey of the "Bielefeld" historians, see Roger Fletcher, "Recent Developments in West German Historiography: The Beilefeld School and Its Critics," *German Studies Review* 7(1984): 451–80. The field is still wrestling with the implications of Blackbourn and Eley's criticism. For illustrations, see Charles Maier, *The Unmasterable Past. History, Holocaust, and German National Identity* (Cambridge, Mass., and London: Harvard University Press, 1988), especially chapter 4, who finds some merit to the *Sonderweg* argument, and Detlev J. K. Peukert, *Der Weimarer Republik: Krisenjahre der Klassischen Monderne* (Frankfurt am Main: Suhrkamp, 1987), who dispenses with it altogether. As for the singularity of Nazism, see Michael Burleigh and Wolfgang Wippermann, *The Racial State. Germany 1933–1945* (Cambridge and New York: Cambridge University Press, 1991), especially the concluding remarks on pp. 304–7. They find the concept of "Fascism" inadequate as a characterization of the Third Reich, especially when confronting its racial core.

4. An "estate," according to imperial and Weimar censuses, contained a minimum of 100 hectares (1 ha. = approximately 2.5 acres), or roughly 250 acres.

5. For a recent work that effectively stresses German agriculture's political weight, despite the primary sector's economic problems, see Heinrich Becker, *Handlungsspielräume der Agrarpolitik in der weimarer Republik zwischen 1923–1929* (Stuttgart: Franz Steiner Verlag, 1990). The percentage of those who worked the land was just as high in France during the same period, but France's industrial base lagged considerably behind that of Germany. See Maurice Larkin, *France Since the Popular Front. Government and People, 1936–1986* (Oxford: Clarendon Press, 1988), 2–12.

6. See Richard Bessel, "Eastern Germany as a Structural Problem in the Weimar Republic," *Social History* 3, no. 2(1978): 199–218. During the Weimar period, the

eastern Prussian provinces, often referred to as "East Elbia," consisted of Branden-burg, East Prussia, Saxony, Pomerania, Upper and Lower Silesia and the Border Province, which included the remainder of Posen and West Prussia. I will use "East Elbia," "Prussian east" or "eastern Prussian provinces" interchangeably.

7. For a discussion of the various properties of myth, see I. M. Lewis, *Social Anthropology in Perspective. The Relevance of Social Anthropology*, 2nd ed. (Cambridge, London, New York: Cambridge University Press, 1976), 120–24.

8. See Thomas Childers, "The Social Language of Politics in Germany: The Sociology of Political Discourse in the Weimar Republic," *American Historical Review* 95, no. 2(1990): 331–58. Childers stresses the importance of corporatist identity and values as a means of political mobilization in interwar Germany.

9. See the seminal work of Hans-Jürgen Puhle, *Agrarische Interessenpolitik und Preussischer Konservatismus im Wilhelminischen Reich (1893–1914). Ein Beitrag zur Analyse des Nationalismus in Deutschland am Beispiel des Bundes der Landwirte und der Deutsch-Konservativen Partei* (Hannover: Verlag für Literatur und Zeitgeschehen, 1966). For discussions of the ideology of agrarian romanticism in Germany, consult Kenneth Barkin, *The Controversy over German Industrialization, 1890–1902* (Chicago and London: University of Chicago Press, 1970); Klaus Bergmann, *Agrarromantik und Großstadtfeindschaft* (Meisenheim/Glan: Verlag Anton Hain, 1970); and George Vascik, "Agrarian Conservatism in Wilhelmine Germany: Diederich Hahn and the Agrarian League," in *Between Reform, Reaction and Resistance. Studies in the History of German Conservatism from 1789 to 1945*, eds. Larry Eugene Jones and James N. Retallack (Providence and Oxford: Berg Publishers, 1993), 229–60.

10. A study that describes the preservation of implicitly antiurban and anticommercial values in older American farm communities is that of Hal S. Barron, *Those Who Stayed Behind. Rural Society in Nineteeth Century New England* (Cambridge and New York: Cambridge University Press, 1984).

11. *Die Reise nach Pommern. Bericht aus einem verschwiegenen Land* (Stuttgart: Deutsche Verlags-Anstalt, 1985), 30.

12. See Peter Manstein, *Die Mitglieder und Wähler der NSDAP 1919–1933. Untersuchungen zu ihrer schichtmäßigen Zusammensetzung* (Frankfurt am Main, Bern, New York, Paris: Peter Lang, 1988); Detlev Mühlberger, *Hitler's Followers. Studies in the Sociology of the Nazi Movement* (London and New York: Routledge, 1991); and especially Jürgen Falter, *Hitlers Wähler* (Munich: C. H. Beck, 1991). A summary and analysis of recent scholarship can be found in Wolfgang Schieder's article, "Die NSDAP vor 1933, Profil einer faschistischen Partei," *Geschichte und Gesellschaft* 19, no. 2(1993), 141–54; and Peter Stachura's piece, "National Socialism and the German Proletariat, 1925–1935. Ole Myths and New Perspectives," *Historical Journal* 36, no. 3(1993): 701–18.

13. See Jürgen Falter, "The Two Hindenburg Elections of 1925 and 1932: A Total Reversal of Voter Coalitions," *Central European History* 23, nos. 2/3(1990): 225–41; and Falter and Michael Kater, "Wähler und Mitglieder der NSDAP. Neue Forschungsergebnisse zur Soziographie des Nationalsozialismus 1925–1933," *Geschichte und Gesellschaft* 19, no. 2(1993): 155–77.

14. Falter, *Hitlers Wähler*, 179–86.

15. For the beginnings of such a discussion, see Shelley Baranowski, "The Sanctity of Rural Life: Protestantism, Agrarian Politics, and Nazism in Pomerania during the Weimar Republic," *German History* 9, no. 1(1991): 1–22.

16. Works that are crucial in this regard are Alexander Gerschenkron, *Bread and Democracy in Germany*, rev. ed., with a new forward by Charles Maier (Ithaca and

London: Cornell University Press, 1989); Barrington Moore, *The Social Origins of Dictatorship and Democracy* (Boston: Beacon Press, 1966); and Karl-Dietrich Bracher, *Die Auflösung der Weimarer Republik. Eine Studie zum Problem des Machtverfalls in der Demokratie*, 3rd ed. (Villingen/Schwarzwald: Ring-Verlag, 1960). See also Andreas Dorpalen, *German History in Marxist Perspective. The East German Approach* (Detroit: Wayne State University Press, 1985), 358–464, for a cogent summary of East German analyses of Nazism as "state monopoly capitalism." The most recent synthesis of Weimar history, Heinrich-August Winkler, *Weimar 1918–1933. Die Geschichte der ersten deutschen Demokratie* (Munich: C. H. Beck, 1993), makes much of the Junker contributions to the appointment of Hitler as chancellor.

17. Until recently, book-length treatments of the East Elbian landed elite consisted mainly of Lysbeth Muncy's still valuable *The Junker in the Prussian Administration Under William II, 1888–1914* (Providence: Brown University Press, 1944), and Walter Görlitz's apologia, *Die Junker: Adel und Bauer im deutschen Osten; geschichtliche Bilanz von 7 Jahrhunderten* (Glücksburg: Ostsee, C. A. Starke, 1956). Fortunately the tide is turning. Such newer works as Robert Berdahl's *The Politics of the Prussian Nobility. The Development of a Conservative Ideology 1770–1848* (Princeton: Princeton University Press, 1988); Francis L. Carsten's summary statement, *Geschichte der preußischen Junker* (Frankfurt am Main: Suhrkamp, 1988); Robert G. Moeller, ed., *Peasants and Lords in Modern Germany. Recent Studies in Agricultural History* (Boston, London, Sydney: Allen and Unwin, 1986); Klaus Heß's *Junker und bürgerliche Großgrundbesitzer im Kaiserreich. Landwirtschaftlicher Großbetrieb, Großgrundbesitz und Familienfideikommiß in Preußen (1867/71–1914)* (Stuttgart: Franz Steiner Verlag, 1990); and Hanna Schissler's "Die Junker. Zur Sozialgeschichtliche und historischen Bedeutung der agrarische Elite in Preußen," *Preußen in Rückblick*, eds. H. -J. Puhle and H. -U. Wehler, Sonderheft 6, *Geschichte und Gesellschaft* (Göttingen: Vandenhoeck and Ruprecht, 1980), 89–122, represent a surge of interest in the Junkers representing a long overdue attempt to explore the implications of Hans Rosenberg's seminal article, "Die Pseudodemokratisierung der Rittergutsbesitzerklasse," in Hans Rosenberg, *Machteliten und Wirtschaftskonjunkturen: Studien zur neueren deutschen Sozial-und Wirtschaftsgeschichte* (Göttingen: Vandenhoeck and Ruprecht, 1978), 83–101, first published in 1958. Although part of Berdahl's work deals with life on the estates as a foundation for his discussion of the political ideology of the eastern Prussian nobility, we still lack local studies that deal extensively with the social environment in the estate villages.

18. Although often used to cover all eastern Prussian estate owners with the noble prefix "von," the term "Junker" more aptly applies to those nobles with origins in the German colonization of the east from the twelfth through the fourteenth centuries. I use "Junker" mainly to refer to those Pomeranian families who were legitimately *Uradel* (ancient nobility), opting for the broader term "nobility" when I mean to include Pomeranian families ennobled after 1400. I am thus following the distinction set forth in the *Genealogisches Handbuch des Adels, Adelige Häuser* A (the directory of families who were noble before 1400) and B (families ennobled after 1400) published by the Deutsches Adelsarchiv (Limburg, 1951–). My use of "estate owners" or "agrarian elites" refers to all those who owned landed property of one hundred hectares and more, noble and nonnoble.

19. See, for example, William Sheridan Allen, *The Nazi Seizure of Power. The Experience of a Single German Town*, rev. ed. (New York: Franklin Watts, 1985); Johnpeter Horst Grill, *The Nazi Movement in Baden 1920–1945* (Chapel Hill: University of North Carolina Press, 1983); Richard Hamilton, *Who Voted for Hitler?*

(Princeton: Princeton University Press, 1982); Rudy Koshar, *Social Life, Local Politics and Nazism. Marburg 1880–1935* (Chapel Hill and London: University of North Carolina Press, 1986); Jeremy Noakes, *The Nazi Party in Lower Saxony 1921–1933* (London: Oxford University Press, 1971); Geoffrey Pridham, *The Nazi Movement in Bavaria 1923–1933* (New York: Harper & Row, 1973); and Zdenek Zofka, *Die Ausbreitung des Nationalsozialismus auf dem Lande. Eine regionale Fallstudie zur politischen Einstellung der Landbevölkerung in der Zeit des Aufstiegs und der Machtergreifung der NSDAP 1928–1936* (Munich: Kommissionsbuchlandlung R. Wolfe, 1979). The term "local notables" is Hamilton's.

20. Despite the whirl of controversy surrounding this work, David Abraham's *The Collapse of the Weimar Republic. Political Economy and Crisis*, 2nd ed. (New York: Holmes and Meier, 1986), provides a fruitful way of analyzing the relationship among the various elites and between elites and the Nazi party as Weimar disintegrated. Ian Kershaw, "Introduction: Perspectives of Weimar's Failure," in *Weimar: Why Did German Democracy Fail?*, ed. Ian Kershaw (New York: St. Martin's Press, 1990), 24–25, notes that Hitler's appointment was not "inevitable." Rather, he was named because conservative elites had run out of political solutions since they did not have the mass base they needed. See also Martin Broszat, *Hitler and the Collapse of Weimar Germany*, trans. Volker Berghahn (Leamington Spa, Hamburg, New York: Berg Publishers, 1987), who describes the narrowing options beginning in the fall of 1930. Again, conservatives faced the dilemma of wanting to construct an authoritarian alternative to Weimar, but they lacked the mass support to do so without the Nazis.

21. See Ralph Gibson and Martin Blinkhorn, eds., *Landownership and Power in Modern Europe* (London: HarperCollins, 1991), 14–15; Jonathan Powis, *Aristocracy* (Oxford: Basil Blackwell, 1984), 50; and Otto Graf zu Stolberg-Wernigrode, *Die unentscheidene Generation. Deutschlands Konservative Führungschichten am Vorabend des Ersten Weltkrieges* (Munich and Vienna: R. Oldenburg, 1968), 188–89, 168–205.

22. See my essay, "Continuity and Contingency: Agrarian Elites, Conservative Institutions and East Elbia in Modern German History," *Social History* 12, no. 3(1987): 285–308.

23. Studies that emphasize the anti-elitism of the Nazi movement, and even the weakening of elites, include Peter Fritsche's *Rehearsals for Fascism. Populism and Political Mobilization in Weimar Germany* (New York and Oxford: Oxford University Press, 1990); Peukert's *Die Weimarer Republik*; Henry Ashby Turner Jr., *German Big Business and the Rise of Hitler* (New York and Oxford: Oxford University Press, 1985); and Richard Bessel, "Why Did the Weimar Republic Collapse?," in *Weimar: Why Did German Democracy Fail?*, 120–52. The diminishing ability of German elites to control popular politics has also figured prominently in the critique of David Blackbourn and Geoff Eley. See in particular Eley's *Reshaping the German Right. Radical Nationalism and Political Change after Bismarck* (New Haven and London: Yale University Press, 1980).

24. The criticism of the "Bielefeld School" has always objected to the vision of popular dependence on elite machinations implicit in the work of such historians as Wehler and Puhle. In an article, "German History and the Contradictions of Modernity," in *Society, Culture and Politics in Germany 1870–1930: New Approaches*, ed. Geoff Eley (forthcoming, Ann Arbor: University of Michigan Press), Eley draws heavily on Michel Foucault's theories of power to critique Wehler's *Deutsche Gesellschaftsgeschichte*, two volumes of which have appeared.

25. For examples, see Gerschenkron, *Bread and Democracy*, 71–88, 113–32, 145–48, and Wehler, *Das Deutsche Kaiserreich*, esp. 78–141, 171–82.

26. The effectiveness of deference and patronage as explanations for the staying power of landed elites looms large for other European nobilities as well. See Gibson and Blinkhorn, *Landownership and Power*, 8–14, and Anthony L. Cardoza's recent article on the Piedmontese nobility, "The Long Good-Bye: The Landed Aristocracy in North-Western Italy, 1880–1930," *European History Quarterly* 23, no. 3(1993): 323–58.

27. See Heβ, *Junker and bürgerliche Groβgrundbesitzer*, who forcefully makes the case for the good health of large estates during the Kaiserreich, 215–312.

28. See the remarks of Dick Geary in *Weimar: Why Did German Democracy Fail?*, 197–98.

29. Consult David Cannadine's impressive synthesis, *The Decline and Fall of the British Aristocracy* (New Haven and London: Yale University Press, 1990).

30. See by contrast Abraham, *The Collapse of the Weimar Republic*, especially 308ff., who sees the shifting balance of power between the two major wings of German industry, resulting in the political primacy of heavy industry, as decisive in producing a Nazi-led government.

Chapter 1. Foundations of Continuity

1. For an analysis of the historiographical treatment of Germany since World War II and suggestions for future conceptualization, see Michael Geyer and Konrad Jarausch, "The Future of the German Past. Transatlantic Reflections for the 1990s," *Central European History* 22, nos. 3/4(1989): 229–59.

2. *Pommern. Ein Bildband der Heimat mit 159 Fotografien*, Kultur und kunstges- chichtliche Einleitung von Klaus Granzow (Frankfurt am Main: Verlag Wolfgang Weidlich, 1983), 21.

3. In the summer of 1989, *Pomorze zachodnie zawsze polskie* appeared painted on the side of the ruins of a sea gate in Szczecin that Frederick William I constructed in the eighteenth century.

4. Iwo Cyprian Pogonowski, *Poland. A Historical Atlas*, rev. ed. (New York: Hip- pocrene Books, 1988), 66, contains a map of Poland as it existed under King Bolesław III (1102–1138). Bolesław's realm which included the western Slavs ex- tended well beyond the Oder River to the west, beyond even Rügen Island.

5. For this view, see Klaus-Dietmar Henke, "Der Weg nach Potsdam-Die Al- lierten und die Vertreibung," in *Die Vertreibung der Deustchen aus dem Osten. Ursachen, Ereignisse, Folgen*, ed. Wolfgang Benz (Frankfurt am Main: Fischer Verlag, 1985), 48–69, and especially Andreas Hillgruber, *Zweierlei Untergang. Die Zerschla- gung des Deutschen Reiches und das Ende des europäischen Judentums* (Berlin: Corso bei Siedler, 1986). Hillgruber's argument that the Allies' dismemberment of Prussia allowed the Soviets into eastern Europe was a prominent issue for the conservative side of the *Historikerstreit*.

6. *Pommern. Ein Bildband*, 18–20; Francis L. Carsten, *The Origins of Prussia* (Oxford: Clarendon Press, 1954), 1–27; Oskar Eggert, *Geschichte Pommerns* (Glück- stadt/Elbe: Buchdruckerei Gerhard Rautenberg, 1961), 9–35; and H. W. Koch, *A History of Prussia* (London and New York: Longman, 1978), 1–22.

7. Excellent surveys of Germany in the Middle Ages include Alfred Haverkamp, *Medieval Germany 1056–1273*, 2nd ed., trans. Helga Brown and Richard Mortimer (New York: Oxford University Press, 1992); Horst Fuhrmann, *Germany in the High Middle Ages c. 1050–1200*, trans. Timothy Reuter (Cambridge, London, New York:

Cambridge University Press, 1986). For Pomerania's history, see Eggert *Geschichte Pommerns*, 35–45, and *Pommern. Ein Bildband*, 19.

8. Eggert, *Geschichte Pommerns*, 57–58; Koch, *History of Prussia*, 51–52.

9. Eggert, *Geschichte Pommerns*, 57–73.

10. Tadeusz Białecki, Magdalena Mazurkiewicz, and Adam Muszyński, *Podziały Administraczyne Pomorza zachodniego w latach 1800–1977* (Szczecin: Wydawnictwo Institut Zachodnio-Pomorskiego, 1970), 7; Martin Wehrmann, *Geschichte von Pommern*, rev. ed. (Würzburg: Verlag Wolfgang Weidlich, 1982), 286.

11. Eggert, *Geschichte Pommerns*, 46–47; *Pommern. Ein Bildband*, 20.

12. "Lady bug flee, father's in the war, mother is in Pomerania, but Pomerania is burned to the ground. Lady bug flee!" See *Pommern. Ein Bildband*, 20.

13. For the formation of the Prussian Union Church, see Robert M. Bigler, *The Politics of German Protestantism. The Rise of the Protestant Church Elite in Prussia, 1815–1848* (Berkeley, Los Angeles, London: University of California Press, 1972), 37–50, and John E. Groh, *Nineteenth Century German Protestantism. The Church as Social Model* (Washington, D.C.: University Press of America, 1982), 34–42. Although the new church did not fulfill the monarchy's desire for a confessional union of Lutherans and Reformed, it paralleled the administrative consolidation that the Hohenzollerns pursued in the political arena.

14. Christian Graf von Krockow, "Gutshaus und Pfarrhaus," in *Das evangelische Pfarrhaus. Eine Kultur-und Sozialgeschichte*, ed. Martin Greiffenhagen (Stuttgart: Kreuz Verlag, 1984), 228.

15. Hermann Schmidt and Georg Blohm, *Die Landwirtschaft von Ostpreussen und Pommern 1914/18–1939* (Marburg/Lahn: Johann-Gottfried-Herder Institut, 1978), 6.

16. Ibid., 4, 6; Erich Murawski and Erwin Stein, *Pommern. Das Grenzland am Meer* (Berlin-Friedenau: Deutsche Kommunal Verlag, 1931), 68.

17. Schmidt and Blohm, *Die Landwirtschaft von Ostpreußen und Pommern*, 6; Murawski and Stein, *Pommern*, 68.

18. Murawski and Stein, *Pommern*, 23.

19. "Schädigung der Wirtschaft des Regierungsbezirks Stettin durch die Grenzziehung im Osten," in Dopierała *Ekonomiczne i Demograficzne Problemy Pomorze zachodniego w świetle Niemieckich. Materialów źródłowych z Lat 1926–1932* (Poznań: Institut Zachodni, 1955), 160.

20. Murawski and Stein, *Pommern*, 66.

21. Ibid., 69.

22. Eggert, *Geschichte Pommerns*, 78. For the influence of the military on civilian officialdom, see Alf Lüdtke, *Police and State in Prussia, 1815–1850* (Cambridge, New York, Port Chester, Melbourne, Sydney: Cambridge University Press, 1989).

23. See the recollections of Klaus von Bismarck, *Aufbruch aus Pommern. Erinnerungen und Perspektiven* (Munich and Zurich: Piper, 1993), 115–16.

24. Schmidt and Blohm, *Die Landwirtschaft von Ostpreußen und Pommern*, 7, 9–10.

25. Krockow *Reise nach Pommern*, 84–85; Wolfgang Marzahn, *Erinnerungen an Hinterpommern* (Leer: Verlag Gerhard Rautenberg, 1971); and Arthur Noffke, *Unvergessenes Pommern. Erzählungen aus Pommern* (Leer/Ostfriesland: Verlag Gerhard Rautenberg, 1976), 58.

26. Theodor Fontane, *Effi Briest* (New York: Penguin Books, 1983), 66.

27. Walter Treichel, *Ostland Pommern. Streiflichter aus Wirtschaft, Kultur and Politik* (Berlin and Stettin: Verlag der Nahe Osten, 1935), 33. As Celia Applegate points out in *A Nation of Provincials. The German Idea of Heimat* (Berkeley, Los Angeles, Oxford: University of California Press, 1990), 1–19, the meaning of *Heimat* is ulti-

mately elusive, yet it suggests a deep emotional connection with a place that translations such as "homeland" or "home town" cannot convey.

28. Schmidt and Blohm, *Die Landwirtschaft von Ostpreußen und Pommern*, 13; Martin Golling, *Der Pflanzenbau in Pommern. Grundlagen, Entwicklung und Bedeutung*, in Kurt Holder-Egger, *Die Gartenbau in Pommern* (Giessen: Wilhelm Schmitz Verlag, 1963), 22–26.

29. Schmidt and Blohm, *Die Landwirtschaft von Ostpreußen und Pommern*, 16.

30. Krockow, *Reise nach Pommern*, 144.

31. Ibid., 63–64; Schmidt and Blohm, *Die Landwirtschaft von Ostpreußen und Pommern*, 78–80.

32. For good introductions to the intensification of agriculture in Germany before World War I, see J. A. Perkins, "The Agricultural Revolution in Germany, 1815–1914," *The Journal of European Economic History* 10(1981): 71–118, and Shearer Davis Bowman, *Masters and Lords. Mid-19th-Century U.S. Planters and Prussian Junkers* (New York: Oxford University Press, 1993), 42–78, who argues that the Junkers bested Southern planters in agrarian modernization. The notion that the Junkers were backward stemmed primarily from Gerschenkron, *Bread and Democracy*, who connected the Junker insistence on tariff protection with the inability to modernize.

33. *Niekammer's Landwirtschaftliche Güter-Adreßbücher*, vol. 1, *Pommern* (Leipzig: Reichenbach'sche Verlagsbuchhandlung, 1921) is more than just an address book. It contains information not only about the possession of utilities, but also the size of holdings, the number of livestock and farm equipment, and the net profit subject to the ground tax, as well as such ancillary enterprises as distilleries and sawmills.

34. Krockow, *Reise nach Pommern*, 77–78; H. W. Graf Finck von Finkelstein, *Die Entwicklung der Landwirtschaft in Preussen und Deutschland 1800–1930* (Würzburg: Holzner Verlag, 1960), 156–57; Manfred Jatzlauk, "Agrarische Untersuchung über die Entwicklung der landwirtschaftlichen Großbetriebe in Deutschland zwischen den beiden Weltkriegen," *Wissenschaftliche Zeitschrift der Wilhelm-Pieck-Universität Rostock* 38, no. 7/8(1989): 36–42. See also Detlev Zimmer's article on several generations of the Helldorff family, "Soziale Lebensläufe und individuelle politische Biographien. Das Beispiel der Familie von Helldorff (Haus St. Ulrich), *Zeitschrift für Geschichtswissenschaft* 40, no. 9(1992): 834–52. For a discussion of agriculture as contributing to, rather than hindering, economic development, see Michael R. Haines, "Agriculture and Development in Prussian Upper Silesia, 1846–1913," *Journal of Economic History* 42(1982): 355–84.

35. See by contrast Ilona Buchsteiner, "Großgrundbesitz in Pommern zwishen 1871 und 1914. Soziale und ökonomische Veränderungen als Ausdruck der Integration des Adels in die bürgerliche Gesellschaft," *Zeitschrift für Geschichtswissenschaft* 37(1989): 329–36, who argues that bourgeois estate owners were more eager than were nobles to modernize, at least before the war.

36. Bismarck, *Aufbruch aus Pommern*, 42–43.

37. "Geschichte der landwirtschaftlichen Schule Demmin," *Unser Pommernland. Monatsschrift für das Kulturleben des Heimat* 12, no. 4(1927): 144–46; "Die Landwirtschaftliche Schule Treptow (Rega)," in the same journal, 13, no. 5/6(1928): 198–99.

38. Bismarck, *Aufbruch aus Pommern*, 75.

39. See the remarks of Klaus von Bismarck regarding his father-in-law, Hans von Wedemeyer, who had little incentive to modernize as a result of the soil conditions on his estate, *Aufbruch aus Pommern*, 78–79, and Hainer Plaul, *Landarbeiterleben im*

19. Jahrhundert. Eine volkskundliche Untersuchung über Veränderungen in der Lebens-
weise der einheimischen Landarbeiterschaft in den Dörfern der Magdeburger Börde unter
Bedingungen der Herausbildung und Konsolidierung des Kapitalismus in der Landwirts-
chaft. Tendenzen und Triebkräfte (Berlin: Akademie der Wissenschaft der DDR
Zentralinstitut für Geschichte. Veröffentlichung zur Volkskunde und Kulturgeschichte, Band 65, 1979).

40. In addition to Bessel's "Eastern Germany," see also Hans Raupach, "Der inter-
regionale Wohlfahrtsausgleich als Problem der Politik des Deutschen Reiches," in
Die Staats-und Wirtschaftskrise des Deutschen Reichs 1929/33, eds. Hans Raupach,
Dietmar Keese, Wilhelm Treue, Ursula Hüllbürch, Rudolf Vierhaus and Werner
Conze (Stuttgart: Ernst Kett Verlag, 1967): 13–34, Frank B. Tipton, Jr., *Regional*
Variations in the Economic Development of Germany during the Nineteenth Century
(Middletown, Conn.: Wesleyan University Press, 1976); and Georges Castellan, "Zur
sozialen Bilanz der Prosperität 1924–1929," in *Industrielles System und politische*
Entwicklung in der Weimarer Republik, eds. Hans Mommsen, Dietmar Petzina, Bernd
Weisbrod (Düsseldorf: Droste Verlag, 1971), 104–11.

41. Treichel, *Ostland Pommern,* 12.

42. Ibid., 7–11. See Murawski and Stein, *Pommern,* 70, for the overall effect of the
territorial settlement on trade.

43. Dopierała, *Ekonomiczne i Demograficzne Problemy,* document no. 15, 85–105.

44. Dopierała, *Ekonomiczne i Demograficzne Problemy,* 257.

45. Dopierała, *Ekonomiczne i Demograficzne Problemy,* 165–81; Treichel, *Ostland*
Pommern, 12.

46. Treichel, *Ostland Pommern,* 7–11.

47. Robert Thevoz, Hans Branig and Cecile Lowenthal-Hensel, *Pommern 1934/35*
im Spiegel von Gestapo Lageberichten und Sachakten, vol. 1 (Cologne and Berlin: G.
Grote'sche Verlagsbuchhandlung, 1974), 193–96; Dopierała, *Ekonomiczne i Demog-*
raficzne Problemy, 256.

48. See Bessel's remarks in "Eastern Germany as a Structural Problem," 217–18.

49. See J. A. Perkins, "Dualism in German Agrarian Historiography," *Comparative*
Studies in Society and History 28(1986): 287–306. Heinrich Kaak, *Die Gutswirtschaft.*
Theoriegeschichtliche Untersuchungen zum Agrarwesen im ostelbischen Raum (Berlin
and New York: Walter de Gruyter, 1991), takes the standard view.

50. See the analyses in Hess, *Junker and bürgerliche Großgrundbesitzer,* 22–100,
and Becker, *Handlungsspielräume,* 53–60.

51. J. Conrad, "Agrarstatistische Untersuchungen, IV. Der Großgrundbesitz in
Pommern," *Jahrbücher für Nationalökonomie und Statistik. Dritte Folge* 10(1895), 707.

52. Perkins, "Dualism," 297.

53. Ibid., 289; Conrad, "Agrarstatistische Untersuchungen," 717–23; Becker,
Handlungsspielräume, 69. Thirty percent of the land in lower Pomerania was in state
hands during the Weimar period. According to Heß, *Junker und bürgerliche Groß-*
grundbesitzer, 52–55, over 50 percent of the total land area was in the hands of
estate agriculture in the Stralsund district.

54. Thevoz, et al., *Pommern 1934/35,* 213.

55. Heß, *Junker und bürgerliche Großgrundbesitzer,* 87.

56. Krockow, *Reise nach Pommern,* 126; Golling, *Pflanzenbau in Pommern,* 41–52;
and Bismarck, *Aufbruch aus Pommern,* 91.

57. See Rosenberg, "Pseudodemokratisierung," 84–89. Rosenberg intended to
write a social history of the Junkers but did not complete it.

58. See Berdahl, *Politics of the Prussian Nobility,* 278, who notes the nontypical

character of bourgeois estate owners. For a good example of a work that depends heavily on the view that the German bourgeoisie was "feudalized," that is, the bourgeoisie could not escape the permeation of aristocratic values throughout society, see Fritz Stern's biography of Bismarck's Jewish banker Bleichröder, *Gold and Iron. Bismarck, Bleichröder and the Building of the German Empire* (New York: Vintage Books, 1979). The "feudalization" argument which, has been strongly integrated with the *Sonderweg* thesis, has come under heavy attack in recent years. See Lothar Machtan and Dietrich Milles, *Die Klassensymbiose von Junkertum und Bourgeoisie. Zum Verhältnis von gesellschaftlicher und politischer Herrschaft in Preußen–Deutschland 1850–1878/79* (Frankfurt am Main: Verlag Ullstein, 1980), who exclude a discussion of the self-understanding of the Junker-bourgeois ruling class altogether. Consult especially David Blackbourn and Richard J. Evans, *The German Bourgeoisie. Essays on the Social History of the German Middle Class from the Late Eighteenth to the Early Twentieth Century* (London and New York: Routledge, 1991), particularly the essay of Dolores L. Augustine, "Arriving in the Upper Class. The Wealthy Business Elite of Wilhelmine Germany," 46–86. She has written another piece on the same theme, "Very Wealthy Businessmen in Imperial Germany," *Journal of Social History* 22(1988): 299–321. For other important recent work on the German bourgeoisie, see *Bürgertum im. 19. Jahrhundert. Deutschland im europäischen Vergleich*, 2 vols., ed. Jürgen Kocka (Munich: DTV, 1988), and Larry Eugene Jones and Konrad Jarausch, *In Search of a Liberal Germany. Studies in the History of German Liberalism from 1789 to the Present* (New York, Oxford, Munich: Berg Publishers, 1990).

59. For the origins of the Junkers, see Berdahl, *Politics of the Prussian Nobility* 14–43; Francis L. Carsten, *Geschichte der preußischen Junker* (Frankfurt am Main: Suhrkamp, 1988), 9–54; Muncy, *The Junker in the Prussian Administration*, 3–40, as well as Hans Rosenberg, "Die Ausprägung der Junkerherrschaft in Brandenburg-Preußen," in *Machtelite und Wirstschaftskonjunkturen*, 24–82.

60. See William Hagen's critique of Prussian history in his series of articles, "How Mighty the Junkers? Peasant Rents and Seigneurial Profits in Sixteenth-Century Brandenburg," *Past and Present* 108(1985): 80–116; "Working for the Junker: The Standard of Living of Manorial Laborers in Brandenburg, 1584–1810," *Journal of Modern History* 58, no. 1(1986): 143–58; "The Junkers' Faithless Servants: Peasant Insubordination and the Breakdown of Serfdom in Brandenburg-Prussia," in *The German Peasantry. Conflict and Community in Rural Society from the Eighteenth to the Twentieth Centuries*, eds. Richard J. Evans and W. R. Lee (New York: St. Martin's Press, 1986), 71–101; "Seventeenth-Century Crisis in Brandenburg: The Thirty Years' War, the Destabilization of Serfdom, and the Rise of Absolutism," *American Historical Review* 94, no. 2(1989): 302–35.

61. The literature on this subject is enormous. See in particular, Berdahl, *The Politics of the Prussian Nobility*, 77–157; Hans-Ulrich Wehler, *Deutsche Gesellschaftsgeschichte*, vol. 1; *Vom Feudalismus des Alten Reiches bis zur Defensive Modernisierung der Reformära 1700–1815*, vol. 2, 71–90, 140–77, 409–28; and *Von der Reformära bis zur industriellen und politischen 'Deutschen Doppelrevolution' 1815–1848/49*, 27–53, 145–74 (Munich: Verlag C. H. Beck, 1987); and Hanna Schissler, *Preußische Agrargesellschaft im Wandel: Wirtschaftliche, gesellschaftliche und politische Transformationsprozesse von 1763 bis 1847* (Göttingen: Vandenhoeck and Ruprecht, 1978). Hartmut Harnisch's work, *Kapitalistisch Agrarreform und Preußische Agrargesellschaft im Wandel. Agrarhistorische Untersuchungen über das ostelbische Deutschland zwischen Spätfeudalismus und bürgerlich-demokratischer Revolution von 1848/49 unter besonderer Berücksichtigung der Provinz Brandenburg* (Weimar: Hermann Bohlhaus

Nachfolger, 1984), views the impact of the reforms on the peasantry more positively. For a helpful critical analysis of recent scholarship, particularly Harnisch's work, consult Josef Mooser, "Preußische Agrarreformen, Bauern und Kapitalismus," *Geschichte und Gesellschaft* 18, no. 4(1992), 533–54.

62. Heß, *Junker und bürgerliche Großgrundbesitzer*, 81–100.

63. Ibid., 82.

64. Ibid., 101–214.

65. Carsten, *Geschichte der Preussischen Junker*, 60–61, 65.

66. Ibid., 85. See Hagen. "The Junkers' Faithless Servants," who sees the Brandenburg peasantry in a very different light.

67. Carsten, *Geschichte der preussischen Junker*, 94.

68. Buchsteiner, "Großgrundbesitz in Pommern," 330–31.

69. Vorlage für den Kreistag, undated, Rejencja Koszalińska, no, 84, Wojewódskie Archiwum Państwowe Koszalin (hereinafter cited as WAPK-RK with file number). Judging from this document's location in the file, I place it sometime in 1919. The Kreistag commission that produced this report included one Zitzewitz and two Puttkamers, both prominent Junker families in the county of Rummelsburg.

70. Buchsteiner, "Großgrundbesitz in Pommern," 331. For some general remarks about leasing in Pomerania, see Jatzlauk, "Agrarstatistische Untersuchungen," 37.

71. "Die Fideikommiße in der Provinz Pommern," *General Anzeiger Stettin und die Provinz Pommern*, 72, no. 271 (30 November 1920); Conrad, "Agrarstatistische Untersuchungen:" 716. See also, Becker, *Handlungsspielräume*, 5; Heß, *Junker und bürgerliche Großgrundbesitzer*, 104–5. *Die Fideikomißbesitzer in Preußen vor, während und nach der Auflösung. Unter Berücksichtigung des schwebenden Reformsbestrebungen* (Berlin: Verlagsbuchhandlung Paul Parey, 1929), 5–6, found in Vorpommersches Landesarchiv Greifswald, (hereinafter cited as VL followed by the file number), Rep. 38d Karlsburg, no. 650. According to this study, there were 1,347 entailed estates in Prussia in 1919. Only one-half of them had been dissolved by the date of this book's publication.

72. This observation is drawn from my survey of over sixty of the most prominent families, most of them Junkers, using the *Güter-Adreßbuch der Provinz Pommern*, 1914, and *Landwirtschaftliches Adreßbuch der Rittergüter und Güter des Provinz Pommern*, 1921.

73. See Theodor Häbich, *Deutsche Latifundien. Ein Beitrag zur Berichtung unserer Vorstellung von der bestehenden Verteilung des ländlichen Grundeigentums* (Königsberg: Gräfe und Unzer, 1930), 134–37, who provides the official Reich statistics from 1925 on the size of agrarian holdings, and a list of Pomerania's latifundia drawn from the 1928 estate address book.

74. Krockow, *Reise nach Pommern*, 150. The same was true for Silesia. See Gerhard von Jordan, *Unser Dorf in Schlesien* (Berlin: Siedler Verlag, 1987), 44.

75. Hans-Olaf von Rohr, *Bodentreuer Adel. Eine Statistik mit Zwei Landkarten* (Berlin: Verlag von Georg Stilke, 1936), 36–37. Rohr focused on estates established before 1800 prior to the mass influx of bourgeois purchasers.

76. Georg Plenske, "Pommerscher Adel," *Unser Pommernland* 8, no. 4, April 1923, makes the case that the Pomeranian nobility was mainly an ancient one stemming from the colonization period.

77. Krockow, *Reise nach Pommern*, 19.

78. Berdahl, *Politics of the Prussian Nobility*, 24–28.

79. A complete prosopography of the East Elbian nobility has yet to be written. Such an undertaking goes well beyond the objectives of this study. I have confined myself to some preliminary, yet I hope useful, suggestions in this section. I have worked back from a listing of over three hundred noble families with coats of arms found in *Pommern-Adel. Nachrichtenblatt für die Mitglieder der Landesabteilung Pommern der Deutschen Adelsgenossenschaft* 1, no. 12 (1 March 1926), to more detailed information on noble marriages in *GHdA*, Freiherrliche Häuser, Gräfliche Häuser, and Adelige Häuser A and B. The *GHdA* emphasizes family lines as they have developed from the late eighteenth century to the present. Further details on family genealogies before then can be found in the *Gothaisches Genealogisches Taschenbuch*. Heinz Reif's *Westfälischer Adel 1770–1860. Vom Herrschaftsstand zur regionalen Elite* (Göttingen: Vandenhoeck and Ruprecht, 1979), and Gregory Pedlow's *The Survival of the Hessian Nobility 1770–1870* (Princeton: Princeton University Press, 1988), provide the sort of prosopographical treatment that the Junkers lack.

80. This confirms the findings of Rüdiger von Treskow, "Adel in Preußen: Anpassung und Kontinuität einer Familie 1800–1918," *Geschichte und Gesellschaft* 17, no. 3(1991): 34–69 for the Treskow family, although in the case of some Pomeranian families such as the Puttkamers (the baronial line), the gap was rather narrow.

81. GHdA, Adelige Häuser A, XVII (1983), 515–99.

82. GHdA, Adelige Häuser A, XVII (1983), 141–98.

83. GHdA, Adelige Häuser A, XI (1971), 340–92; GHdA, Freiherrliche Häuser, A VIII (1971), 199–225.

84. GHdA, Adelige Häuser, A VIII (1966), 379–89.

85. GHdA, Adelige Häuser A, XVIII (1985), 99–101, Gräfliche Häuser, II(1955), 144–47; Adelige Häuser A, XV (1979), 46–53; Adelige Häuser A, XVIII (1985), 379–87.

86. GHdA, Adelige Häuser B, XV (1984), 257–66; Adelige Häuser B, I (1954), 85–94. The Knebels' *Stammvater* was ennobled in 1806, while the Enckewort patriarch was ennobled in 1663.

87. Spouses selected by the von Borcke family, for example, consisted of a Lehndorff, a prominent East Prussian family, and a Dohna (Silesia), Gräfliche Häuser A VII(1973), 75–80.

88. According to Krockow, *Reise nach Pommern*, 132, the name "Jesko" was so common in his family, as were marriages with either the Zitzewitzes or especially the Puttkamers, that his family had to refer to relatives by their estate, rather than by name so that the reference was clear.

89. Klaus von Bismarck, *Aufbruch aus Pommern*, 28.

90. GHdA, Freiherrliche Häuser, V (1962), 224–45; X (1977), 264–73.

91. Jobst had been a close friend of one of Libussa's older brothers.

92. Krockow, *Stunde der Frauen*, 18–24. See Berdahl, *Politics of the Prussian Nobility*, 23–28; and Reinhold Brunner, "Landadliger Alltag und primäre Sozialisation in Ostelbien am Ende des 19. Jahrhunderts," *Zeitschrift für Geschichtswissenschaft* 39, no. 10(1991), 998, on the importance of family tradition.

93. Wealth being defined as the possession of at least ten million Reichmarks in assets and one hundred thousand marks per year in income. See Dominic Lieven, *The Aristocracy in Europe 1815–1914* (New York: Columbia University Press, 1992), 57–73.

94. Heß, *Junker und bürgerliche Großgrundbesitzer*, 56–73, especially table on p. 61.

2. Continuity Survives Revolution

1. For an introduction, see Bigler, *Politics of German Protestantism*, 125–55; Groh, *Nineteenth Century German Protestantism*, 247–53, chapter 3; and Hartmut Lehmann, "Pietism and Nationalism: The Relationship between Protestant Revivalism and National Renewal in Nineteenth-Century Germany," *Church History* 51(1982): 39–53.

2. Berdahl, *Politics of the Prussian Nobility*, 247–63. For a piece that emphasizes the way in which the Awakening congealed the anti-absolutist sentiments of the Junkers, as well as enabling them to establish a popular base that would later serve them well, see Christopher M. Clark, "The Politics of Revival. Pietists, Aristocrats, and the State Church in Early Nineteenth-Century Prussia," in *Between Reform, Reaction and Resistance*, eds. Jones and Retallack, 31–60.

3. For Bismarck's conversion, see Ernst Engelberg, *Bismarck. Urpreuße und Reichsgrunder* (Berlin: Siedler Verlag, 1985), 183–206; Otto Pflanze, *Bismarck and the Development of Germany*, vol. 1, *The Period of Unification, 1815–1871* (Princeton: Princeton University Press, 1990), 48–53; and Lothar Gall, *Bismarck. The White Revolutionary*, vol. 1, *1815–1871*, trans. J. A. Underwood (London, Boston, Sydney: Allen and Unwin, 1986), 23–34.

4. Cited in Marzahn, *Erinnerungen an Hinterpommern*, 10–11.

5. Clark, "Politics of Revival," 60. Berdahl's *Politics of the Prussian Nobility*, chapter 4, discusses the development of a conservative ideology to parallel the Junkers' politicization. For the development of Bismarck's own career after his conversion, particularly his newly acquired appreciation for building a mass base, see Gall, *White Revolutionary*, vol. 1, 35–87.

6. Wehrmann, *Geschichte von Pommern*, 299.

7. My view differs from that of Geoff Eley who, contrary to Hans-Jürgen Puhle, sees the East Elbian nobility as having been profoundly reluctant to give in to mass politics until the SPD victories in the 1912 elections forced a change in tactics. After 1912, according to Eley, the aristocracy became "Pan-Germanized." See Eley's essay, "Conservatives and Radical Nationalists in Germany: The Production of Fascist Potentials, 1912–28," in *Fascists and Conservatives. The Radical Right and the Establishment in Twentieth-Century Europe*, ed. Martin Blinkhorn (London: Unwin Hyman, 1990), 50–70.

8. Shelley Baranowski, *The Confessing Church, Conservative Elites and the Nazi State* (Lewiston and Queenston: The Edwin Mellen Press, 1986), 51. For an account of Reinhold von Thadden's career, see Werner Hühne, *A Man to be Reckoned with: The Story of Reinhold von Thadden-Trieglaff* (London: SCM Press, 1962).

9. Eggert, *Geschichte Pommerns*, 73; "Die Oberpräsidenten der Provinzen Brandenburg, Pommern und Sachsen 1868–1918," and "Die preußischen Oberpräsidenten der Weimarer Republik als Verwaltungs-elite," in *Die preußischen Oberpräsidenten 1815–1945*, ed. Klaus Schwabe (Boppard am Rhein: Harald Boldt Verlag, 1985), 83–103, 183–217.

10. Lysbeth W. Muncy, "The Prussian *Landräte* in the Last Years of the Monarchy: A Case Study of Pomerania and the Rhineland in 1890–1918," *Central European History* 6(1973): 305–15.

11. Klaus Saul, "Der Kampf um das Landproletariat. Sozialistische Landagitation, Grossgrundbesitz und preussischer Staatsverwaltung 1890 bis 1903," *Archiv für Sozialgeschichte* 15(1975): 180.

12. Siegfried Ramm, "Die Landwirtschaftskammer für die Provinz Pommern zu Stettin," *Baltische Studien* 47(1960): 137–49.

13. For discussions of the anti-elitism of the populist right, see Eley's, *Reshaping the German Right*, and David Blackbourn, "Between Resignation and Volatility. The German Petite Bourgeoisie in the Nineteenth Century," in *Shopkeepers and Master Artisans in Nineteenth-Century Europe*, eds. Geoffrey Crossick and Heinz-Gerhard Haupt (London and New York: Methuen, 1984), 35–61, *and* "Peasants and Politics in Germany, 1871–1914," *European History Quarterly* 14(1984): 47–75.

14. The Anti-Socialist Law was lifted in 1890. Eric D. Kohler, "Revolutionary Pomerania, 1919–20: A Study in Majority Socialist Agricultural Policy and Civil-Military Relations," *Central European History* 9(1976): 255.

15. See Athar Hussain and Keith Tribe, *Marxism and the Agrarian Question*, vol. 1, *German Social Democracy and the Peasantry 1899–1907* (Atlantic Highlands, N.J.: Humanitites Press, 1981), 72–101 and *The German Worker. Working Class Autobiographies from the Age of Industrialization*, trans. and ed. Alfred Kelly (Berkeley, Los Angeles, London: University of California Press, 1987), 204–29; and Saul, "Kampf um das Landproletariat, " 163–208.

16. Saul, "Kampf um das Landproletariat," 197. For a view different from mine—one that stresses the limits of coercion in imperial German elections, see Margaret Lavinia Anderson, "Voter, Junker, *Landrat,* Priest: The Old Authorities and the New Franchise in Imperial Germany," *American Historical Review* 98, no. 5(1993): 1448–74.

17. Frieda Wunderlich, *Farm Labor in Germany 1810–1945. Its Historical Development Within the Framework of Agricultural and Social Policy* (Princeton: Princeton University Press, 1961), 20–22.

18. Prezydent Policji w Szczenie, Wojewódskie Archiwum Państwowe w Szczecinie (hereinafter cited as WAPS), folder 44, contains official correspondence regarding emigration from Pomerania. For a more general discussion, see Klaus Saul, "Um die konservative Struktur Ostelbiens: Agrarische Interessen, Staatsverwaltung und ländliche Arbeitsnot. Zur Konservativen Landarbeiterpolitik im Preußen-Deutschland 1889–1914," In *Deutscher Konservatismus im 19. und 20. Jahrhundert. Festschrift für Fritz Fischer zum 75. Geburtstag und 50. Doktorjubilaum* (Bonn: Verlag Neue Gesellschaft, 1983), 139–40.

19. Richard Bessel, *Germany after the First World War* (Oxford: Clarendon Press, 1993), 10; According to the *Landwirtschaftliches Adreßbuch der Rittergüter and Güter* (1921), XII–XIII for Pomerania, over 20,000 horses, 167,000 head of cattle, 40,000 sheep, and 795,000 pigs were lost.

20. Wehrmann, *Geschichte von Pommern*, 321–27. Consult also Robert G. Moeller, *German Peasants and Agrarian Politics, 1914–1924. The Rhineland and Westphalia* (Chapel Hill and London: University of North Carolina Press, 1986), especially 47–51, and "Dimensions of Social Conflict in the Countryside," *Central European History* 14(1981): 142–68, as well as Bessel, *Germany after the First World War*, 212–19.

21. Wehrmann, *Geschichte von Pommern*, 325.

22. See Bessel, *Germany after the First World War, 238–39.*

23. Konvent Evangelischer Gemeinden aus Pommern, Evangelisches Zentral archiv (Berlin), Bestand 46 A, no. 188 (hereinafter cited as EZA followed by collection).

24. Bessel, "The Formation and Dissolution of a German National Electorate from Kaiserreich to Third Reich," in *Elections, Mass Politics, and Social Change in Modern Germany. New Perspectives,* eds. Larry Eugene Jones and James Retallack (Cambridge and New York: Cambridge University Press, 1992), 399–418, esp.

404–5. For a relatively recent synthesis of the revolution, see Ulrich Kluge, *Die deutsche Revolution 1918/1919. Staat, Politik und Gesellschaft zwischen Weltkrieg und Kapp-Putsch* (Frankfurt am Main: Suhrkamp, 1984).

25. For a summary and analysis of the revolution in Pomerania that emphasizes the strength of the counterrevolution against it, see Andrzej Czarnik, *Stosunki polityczne na Pomorzu Zachodnim w okręsie republiki weimarskiej 1919–1933* (Poznań: Wydawnictwo Poznańskie, 1983), 13–42 and 63–103.

26. Carsten, *Geschichte der preußischen Junker*, 156–57.

27. Becker, *Handlungsspielräume*, 107–114, describes how land reform evolved into settlement. See also, Heinrich-August Winckler, *Von der Revolution zur Stabilisierung. Arbeiter und Arbeiterbewegung in der Weimarer Republik 1918 bis 1924* (Berlin/Bonn: JHW Dietz Nachf., 1984), 84–89.

28. Bessel, *Germany after the First World War*, 201.

29. Ibid., 201–12. For an excellent discussion of the agricultural laborers' strikes in general, see Martin Schumacher, *Land und Politik. Eine Untersuchung über politische Parteien und agrarische Interessen 1914–1923* (Düsseldorf: Droste Verlag, 1978), 296–314.

30. Kohler, "Revolutionary Pomerania," 266; William L. Patch, Jr., *Christian Trade Unions in the Weimar Republic, 1918–1933. The Failure of "Corporate Pluralism"* (New Haven and London: Yale University Press, 1985), 50–51.

31. Schumacher, *Land und Politik*, 294.

32. Otto Braun, *Von Weimar zu Hitler*, 2nd ed. (New York: Europa Verlag, 1940), 52, 54; Wunderlich, *Farm Labor*, 33–41; Winckler, *Von der Revolution zur Stabilisierung*, 84–89; Schumacher, *Land und Politik*, 189–215.

33. For the fullest account of the *Landarbeiterstreik* in Pomerania, see Jens Flemming, *Landwirtschaftliche Interessen und Demokratie. Ländliche Gesellschaft, Agrarverbände und Staat 1890–1925* (Bonn: Verlag Neue Gesellschaft, 1978), 277–97.

34. Centralrat der Provinz Pommern to Landwirtschaftsministerium, 9 July 1919, Geheimes Staatsarchiv, Abteilung Merseburg (hereinafter cited as GStA), Rep. 87B, Ministerium für Landwirtschaft, Domänen und Forsten, no. 281; Streikbericht, under cover letter from the Landbund to Oberpräsidium Pommern, 1 August 1919, VL, Rep. 60, no. 2418. In one case, the strikers returned to work upon hearing that their employer would honor their contract, including eight marks a day in cash and the ten-hour workday.

35. Abschrift der Verhandlungsniederschrift der Besprechung, 29 June 1920 über die Lage in Pommern und Mecklenburg, Reich Ministry for the Interior, Bundesarchiv, Abteilung Potsdam (hereinafter cited as BA followed by the file no.), Reichsarbeitsministerium, no. 2313, bl. 71–78.

36. Centralrat der Provinz Pommern to Landwirtschaftsministerium, 9 July 1919, GStA Merseburg, Rep. 87B, Ministerium für Landwirtschaft, Domänen und Forsten, no. 281.

37. See Bessel, *Germany after the First World War*, 210–11.

38. VL, Rep. 83d (Karlsburg), no. 724/1; Landrat Landkreis Greifswald to Oberpräsident Pommern, 26 November 1919, VL, Rep. 60, no. 2419.

39. Landrat Greifswald, Anmeldung von Schnittern für das Jahr 1921, 3 December 1920; Landrat Franzburg to Oberpräsident Pommern, 12 March 1921, both found in VL, Rep. 60, no. 2421.

40. Kohler, "Revolutionary Pomerania," 264–66. The DLV drew disproportionately in lower Pomerania.

41. Aufruf an die Landarbeiter! Kreistrauensmann des Deutschen Landarbeiterverbandes, published in Kreisblatt of Stolp Land County, no. 14, 10 March 1920, WAPK-RK, 285a, document 15. The DLV wanted workers to observe the ten-hour day in return for obtaining higher wages, but some workers disregarded this appeal. Regierungspräsident Stralsund to Ministerium der Innern, 22 September 1919, VL, Rep. 60, no. 2419. Often the DLV was not in control of its members, in part because of its leadership's youth.

42. Die Stellungnahme des Pommerschen Landbundes zur Arbeiterfrage. Rede vor dem Ausschuβ für Arbeiterfragen, 10 May 1919, GStA Merseburg, Rep. 87B, Ministerium für Landwirtschaft, Domänen und Forsten, no. 329.

43. Staatskommissar für öffentliche Ordnung to Ministerium für Landwirtschaft, Innern and Reichspräsident, 19 June 1920, Ministerium der Landwirtschaft, Domänen und Forsten to Oberpräsident Pommern, 12 April 1921, Abschrift der Verhandlungsniederschrift, BA Potsdam, RAM, no. 2313, bl. 65–66.

44. Landrat Franzberg to Regierungspräsident Stralsund, 19 November 1919; Landrat Anklam to Oberpräsident Pommern, 10 December 1919, VL, Rep. 60, no. 2419; Polizei Präsident Stettin to Oberpräsident Pommern, 26 June 1920, VL, Rep. 60, no. 2420.

45. Staatskommissar für öffentliche Ordnung re: Landarbeiterstreik in Pommern, 19 June 1920 to Prussian Min. für Landwirtschaft, Domänen und Forsten, Innern, Reichspräsident, BA Potsdam, RAM, no. 2313, bl. 65–66; Der Vorsitzende der Kreisausschusses Stolp, 5 July 1920, BA Potsdam, RAM, no. 2313, bl. 108–10; Landrat Lauenburg in report to Regierungspräsident Köslin to Staatskommissar für Sicherheit und Ordnung (Int. Min.), 6 July 1920, BA Potsdam, RAM, no. 2313, bl. 114–15; Staatskommissar für öffentliche Ordnung to Reichskanzlei, 18 November 1920, re: Greifswald, BA Potsdam, RAM, no. 2313.

46. Kohler, "Revolutionary Pomerania," 254–55; Flemming, *Landwirtschaftliche Interessen*, 61. See J.A. Perkins, "The German Agricultural Worker 1815–1914," *Journal of Peasant Studies* 11(1984): 3–27, for a discussion of the transformation of the rural labor force.

47. Marie Wegner, *Die Lage der Landarbeiterinnen* (Leipzig: Felix Dietrich, 1905), 20; Karl Müller, *Die Frauenarbeit in der Landwirtschaft* (M. Gladbach: Volksvereinverlag, 1913), 41, 46. The forthcoming dissertation of Bernd Kölling (Trier), "Zwischen Unterordnung und sozialem Protest: Landarbeiterstreiks in Deutschland und Italien 1880–1925. Eine vergleichende Sozialgeschichte," promises a more detailed discussion of the strikes as the workers' rational response to the long term modernization of agriculture and the homogenization of the rural labor force.

48. The source of the quotation in Abschrift, Pommerscher Landbund to Ministerium für Landwirtschaft, Domänen und Forsten, 21 May 1919, GStA Merseburg, Rep. 87B, Ministerium für Landwirtschaft, Domänen und Forsten, no. 329. Similar remarks are found in Vermerk über das Ergebnis der Besprechung im Reichsministerim der Innern betr, den Landarbeiterstreik, 6 June 1920, BA Potsdam, RAM, no. 2313, bl. 68; Landrat Pyritz to Oberpräsident Pommern, 30 June 1919, WAPS-RS I, no. 10456.

49. Th. Witthorn, Rittergut Parchow auf Rügen to Oberpräsident Pommern, 11 July 1919; Streikbericht with cover letter from Rural League to Oberpräsident, Pommern, 1 August 1919, VL, Rep. 60, no. 2418.

50. Jordan, *Unser Dorf*, 7–8, notes that one of his family's workers became a socialist during his wartime service, and temporarily assumed a certain cheekiness as a result.

51. Höhne, *Man to be Reckoned With*, 26, mentions that social relations on the Thadden estate remained harmonious, even after the revolution.

52. Bismarck, *Aufbruch aus Pommern*, 18.

53. Reise nach Stettin-Labes, 6–9 June 1919, GStA, Rep. 87B, Ministerium für Landwirtschaft, Domänen und Forsten, no. 281. This document notes that one of the primary agitators in this district had been in a Russian prisoner of war camp for four years, where Bolshevism had won him over.

54. Czarnik, *Stosunki polityczne*, 22, 63–102.

55. Ibid., 66. Kolberg's workers' and soldiers' council tried to remove the councillor Nikolaus von Gerlach, but the Peasants and Farm Workers council voted for his restoration.

56. See Arno J. Mayer, *Politics and the Diplomacy of Peace-Making 1918–1919* (New York: Alfred A. Knopf, 1967), 229–83, for a discussion of Germany as a potential bulwark against Bolshevism, both in the eyes of the Provisional Government and the Allies. According to Becker, *Handlungsspielräume der Agrarpolitik*, 95–114, the creation of the Reich Ministry for Agriculture and Nutrition by early 1920 that centralized agricultural policy making at the Reich level was a crucial step in eliminating the Controlled Economy and magnifying estate owner interests.

57. Czarnik, *Stosunki polityczne*, 50–51. For a clear discussion of the DDP's collapse nationwide in particular, the result of its alienating its electorate on Versailles, and its attempts to build bridges to the SPD, see Larry Eugene Jones, *German Liberalism and the Dissolution of the Weimar Party System 1918–1933* (Chapel Hill and London: University of North Carolina Press, 1988), 55–80.

58. Pomerania's notoriety in suppressing the strikes is seen in a volume of literature, including Carsten, *Geschichte der preussischen Junker*, 158; Kohler, "Revolutionary Pomerania:" 267–93; Flemming, "Die Bewaffnung des 'Landvolks.' Ländliche Schutzwehren und agrarischer Konservatismus in der Anfangsphase der Weimarer Republik," *Militärgeschichtliche Mitteilungen* 2(1979), 18–24; and Schumacher, *Land und Politik*, 294–314. Abschrift Landrat Kolberg, 28 July 1920, GStA Merseburg, Rep. 87B, Ministerium für Landwirtschaft, Domänen und Forsten, no. 288, called attention to the consequences of roving free booters.

59. Czarnik, *Stosunki polityczne*, 32–34, Flemming, "Bewaffnung des 'Landvolks'," 21–22.

60. Kohler, "Revolutionary Pomerania" 283–85; Czarnik, *Stosunki polityczne*, 38–43.

61. Czarnik, *Stosunki polityczne*, 91. This was true despite the drastic reduction in the number of noble county magistrates in Prussia as a whole. See Jane Caplan, *Government without Administration. State and Civil Service in Weimar and Nazi Germany* (Oxford: Clarendon Press, 1988), 46.

62. Czarnik, *Stosunki polityczne*, 91.

63. Ibid., 86–90.

64. Ibid., 91. See Caplan, *Government without Administration*, 45–46, and "Der preußische Oberpräsidenten der Weimarer Republik:" 190–91, 199.

65. Verzeichnis der Landwirtschaftlichen Kreiskommissionen der Provinz Pommern; Verzeichnis der der Landwirtschaftskammer für die Provinz Pommern angeschlossenen Vereine, *Landwirtschaftliches Adreßbuch der Rittergüter und Güter der Provinz Pommern*, xvii ff.

66. See the entry on the National Rural League (Reichslandbund), 1921–1933 in *Lexikon zur Parteiengeschichte. Die bürgerliche und kleinbürgerliche Parteien in Deutschland (1789–1945)*, eds. Dieter Fricke et al., Bd. 3 (Cologne: Paul Rugenstein, 1985), 688–712.

67. On the organization of the Rural League, see Flemming, *Landwirtschaftliche Interessen*, 217 ff; *Pommersche Tagespost*, 9 no. 102 (12 April 1919); 9, no. 105 (15 April 1919); 9, no. 119 (30 April 1919); 9, no. 126 (13 May 1919).

68. Flemming, *Landwirtschaftliche Interessen*, 223.

69. Heidrun Holzbach, *Das "System Hugenberg." Die Organisation bürgerlicher Sammlungspolitik vor dem Aufstieg der NSDAP* (Stuttgart: Oldenburg, 1981), 109–11. For the formation of the "Employees' Groups," see Flemming, *Landwirtschaftliche Interessen*, 220.

70. Flemming, *Landwirtschaftliche Interessen*, 281, notes the discrepancy between the amount of dues paid and the benefits given out by the yellow unions, indicating the significance of "outside" funding from the Rural League.

71. *Pommersche Tagespost*, 20, no. 121 (24 May 1930), contains a report on the decision of the Landesgericht Frankfurt/Oder recognizing the wage agreements between the Rural League unions and the estate owners.

72. Niederschrift über eine besprechung betreffend Stellungnahme zum Pommerschen Landbund, 3 February 1921; Erklärung des Deutschen Landarbeiter-Verbandes, Berlin betr. seine Stellungnahme zur Arbeitnehmergruppe des Pommerschen Landbundes, 26 February 1921; Niederschrift über eine Besprechung betreffend Tarifverträge in der pommerschen Landwirtschaft, 15 March 1921, all found in BA Potsdam, RAM, no. 2314, bl. 117–19, 133–34, 143–44.

73. For Wolf's background, see Patch, *Christian Trade Unions in the Weimar Republic*, 51.

74. "Muss sich der Landarbeiter einer Organisation anschliessen?" (1919), BA Potsdam, RAM, no. 2314, bl. 35–43.

75. See the editors' introduction, *Landownership and Power in Modern Europe*, eds. Ralph Gibson and Martin Blinkhorn (London: HarperCollins Academic, 1991), 5–6.

76. Bodo Scheurig, *Ewald von Kleist—Schmenzin. Ein Konservativer gegen Hitler* (Oldenburg and Hamberg: Gerhard Stalling Verlag, 1968), 36–37.

77. Flemming, "Bewaffnung des 'Landvolks'," 19; Amrei Stupperich, *Volksgemeinschaft oder Arbeitersolidarität. Studien zur Arbeitnehmerpolitik in der Deutschnationalen Volkspartei (1918–1933)* (Göttingen and Zürich: Muster-Schmidt Verlag, 1982), 47.

78. "Muss sich die Landarbeiter einer Organisation anschliessen?," BA Potsdam, RAM, no. 2314, bl. 34–43.

79. Abschrift, Pommersche Landbund to Minister für Landwirtschaft, Domänen und Forsten, 21 May 1919, GStA Merseburg, Rep. 87B, Ministerium für Landwirtschaft, Domänen und Forsten, no. 329.

80. Ulrich Herbert, *A History of Foreign Labor in Germany, 1880–1980. Seasonal Workers/Forced Laborers/Guest Workers*, trans. William Templer (Ann Arbor: The University of Michigan Press, 1990), 121–26.

81. "Stadtische Arbeiter auf Land," *General Anzeiger* 72, no. 15 (18 January 1920); Jahresbericht der Arbeitnehmergruppen des Pommersche Landbund (1925) with cover letter of 21 January 1926 from Johannes Wolf to Lippmann, BA Potsdam Re 1, Reichslandbund, no. 247. Insurance coverage came through the mediation of the Rural League.

82. Flemming, *Landwirtschaftliche Interessen*, 291.

83. *Pommersche Tagespost* 8, no. 360 (29 December 1918); 9, no. 126 (13 May 1919).

84. Dewitz to Wehrkreis-Kommando II, Stettin, 10 December 1923, BA Potsdam 61 Re 1, Reichslandbund, no. 247.

85. See Wunderlich, *Farm Labor in Germany*, 111, regarding increases in the percentage of wages consisting of payment-in-kind, and especially, Flemming,

Landwirtschaftliche Interessen, 292, Flemming's analysis of the Rural League stresses the ability of estate owners to persuade the *Landarbeiter* that their interests were diametrically opposed to those of urban workers.

86. Deutscher Landarbeiterverein, "Wer gefährdet den Wirtschaftsfrieden in den pommerschen Landwirtschaft?" 17 March 1921, VL, Rep. 60, no. 2421.

87. Jens Flemming, "Landarbeiter zwischen Gewerkschaften und Werksgemeinschaft," *Archiv für Sozialgeschichte* 14(1974), 404.

88. 9, no. 251 (9 September 1919).

89. Dewitz to Wehrkreis-Kommando II, Stettin, 10 December 1923, BA Potsdam, 61 Re 1, Reichslandbund, no. 247.

90. For this view, see Flemming, "Die Bewaffnung des 'Landvolks'," 7–29.

91. See Anthony L. Cardoza, *Agrarian Elites and Italian Fascism. The Province of Bologna 1901–1926* (Princeton: Princeton University Press, 1982), 245–386; Frank M. Snowden, *The Fascist Revolution in Tuscany 1919–1922* (Cambridge: Cambridge University Press, 1989), Part I; as well as Eley's comparative insights in "Conservatives and Radical Nationalists in Germany," 55–56.

92. For a study that recognizes the limits of reform in Weimar Prussia while rejecting the teleology that reduces the Republic to a mere prelude to the Third Reich, see Dietrich Orlow, *Weimar Prussia 1918–1925. The Unlikely Rock of Democracy* (Pittsburgh: University of Pittsburgh Press, 1986).

3. Power and Obligation

1. "Deutsches Erntedankfest," *Gemeindeblatt für das Kirchspiel Grossmöllen*, 7, no. 10 (October 1933).

2. EZA, Frageboden zum kirchlichen Brauchtum, Sammlung hist. Ostgebiete; Report on General Visitation to Anklam, 26 May to 14 June 1926, EZA, EOK Pomerania VI, no. 59; Report on General Visitation to Schivelbein, 6–22 May 1931, EZA, EOK Pomerania VI, no. 53. Regular church attendance, and the vitality of church life in general, tended to be at their lowest in purely estate villages with large numbers of estate laborers.

3. "Im Herbst," *Heimatklänge. Kirchliches Monatsblatt für die Synode Greifswald-Land*, 9, no. 1 (October 1924).

4. "Erntedankfest," *Die Gutsfrau*, 11, no. 1 (October 1922).

5. For appropriate references, see note 19 in the Introduction. Berdahl, *Politics of the Prussian Nobility*, 10–11, provides a full definition of *Herrschaft* that beautifully relates "lordship" to a discussion of the lord's personal authority and the ownership of land.

6. Krockow, *Reise nach Pommern*, 117–20.

7. Bismarck, *Aufbruch aus Pommern*, 86.

8. Hans Graf von Lehndorff, *Menschen, Pferde, weites Land. Kindheits-und Jugenderinnerungen* (Munich: Biederstein Verlag, 1980), 176.

9. Liselotte Schwiers, *Das Paradise liegt in Pommern* (Munich: Droemer Knaur, 1989), 118–19.

10. Alfred Kelly, *The German Worker*, 277–78.

11. For the communitarianism inherent in rituals, see the highly influential works of Victor Turner, especially *The Ritual Process. Structure and Anti-Structure* (Ithaca: Cornell University Press, 1969), 94–130; *Dramas, Fields, and Metaphores. Symbolic Action in Human Society* (Ithaca and London: Cornell University Press, 1974), 231–71. In my opinion, Turner overstates the social egalitarianism that occurs during rituals.

12. Krockow, *Reise nach Pommern*, 119–20; Gerhard von Jordan, *Unser Dorf*, 60.

13. Bodo Scheurig, *Ewald von Kleist-Schmenzin*, 42–43.

14. Bismarck, *Aufbruch aus Pommern*, 86.

15. Ursula Susanna Gilbert, *Hellmuth von Gerlach (1866–1935). Stationen eines deutschen Liberalen vom Kaiserreich zum 'Dritten Reich'* (Frankfurt am Main: Bern; New York: Peter Lang, 1984), 24.

16. Schwiers, *Das Paradise liegt in Pommern* 39, 54, 48–50. Schwiers's great-grandfather had been police chief in Stettin from 1832–68, while her grandfather leased land from the royal domain. Her memoir covers the years between 1910 and 1925. For a similar description of Christmas gift-giving, see Lehndorff, *Menschen, Pferde, weites Land*, 43.

17. In referring to rural rituals, Berdahl, *Politics of the Prussian Nobility*, 70–71, following Pierre Bourdieu, suggests that such obvious paternalism and the personal relationship that spawned it declined with the spread of capitalist agriculture, only to receive more formal codification under the pressure of modernization in a conservative ideology. Yet the Pomeranian case suggests the compatibility of "traditional" rituals, personal authority, and agrarian transformation.

18. See the extended comparisons explicit in C.B.A. Behrens, *Society, Government and the Enlightenment. The Experiences of Eighteenth-Century France and Prussia* (New York: Harper & Row, 1985).

19. Marion Countess Dönhoff, *Before the Storm. Memories of My Youth in Old Prussia*, trans. Jean Steinberg (New York: Alfred A. Knopf, 1990), 5, 14–15.

20. *Pommern. Ein Bildband*, photograph nos. 99, 144, 146, and 148.

21. Thomas Mann, *Buddenbrooks*, trans. H. T. Lowe-Porter (New York: Vintage Books, 1961), 406. The original German edition was published in 1901.

22. *Pommern. Ein Bildband* provides a photograph (number 29) of Schloss Barnow-Rummelsburg belonging to the Puttkamers. Krockow, *Reise nach Pommern*, 165.

23. Ibid., 166; Jordan, *Unser Dorf*, 23–24.

24. Dönhoff, *Before the Storm*, 134–41. For the intergration of military values and aristocratic lifestyles, see Lieven, *Aristocracy in Europe*, 190–91.

25. Scheurig, *Ewald von Kleist-Schmenzin*, 12, 48–49.

26. Ibid., 48; Krockow, *Reise nach Pommern*, 167; Brunner, "Landadliger Alltag," 996.

27. Bismarck, *Aufbruch aus Pommern*, 57; Krockow, *Reise nach Pommern*, 168; Scheurig, *Ewald von Kleist-Schmenzin*, 48.

28. Prussian Minister of the Interior: Denkschrift über die Durchführung der Auflösung der Gutsbezirke (1929), GStA Merseburg, Rep. 169D, Preußischer Landtag, IVb, no. 11, Bd. 2.

29. Horst Möller, *Parlamentarismus in Preußen 1919–1932* (Düsseldorf: Droste Verlag, 1985), 473–97; "Auflösung der Gutsbezirke?," *Pommersche Tagespost* 16, no. 213 (10 September 1926).

30. *Landwirtschaftliches Adreßbuch der Rittergüter und Güter der Provinz Pommern, 1921*. A preliminary listing of the Putbus holdings can be found in the index, which can then be used to access each estate in the directory itself.

31. Krockow, *Reise nach Pommern*, 150–51, suggests ironically that patriarchalism was given a new lease on life by the new demands of farming.

32. Verband Vorpommerscher Gutspächter to Reich government, Prussian government, Reichstag and Landtag, 27 August 1927; Oberpräsident Pommern to Finanzministerium, 8 December 1927. Both found in GStA Merseburg, Rep. 151C, Finanzministerium, no. 11513.

33. Bowman, *Masters and Lords*, 27, argues that the hiring of inspectors permitted the nobility to assume a status comparable to English country gentlemen and Southern planters, in that nobles could be actively engaged in the management of their estates without having to do manual labor.

34. Niederschrift über die 14. Sitzung des Ausschusses für Güterbeamte der Landwirtschaftskammer Pommern, 10 September 1925, 5–6, GStA Merseburg, Rep. 87B, Ministerium für Landwirtschaft, Domänen und Forsten, no. 13425.

35. Jordan, *Unser Dorf*, 81.

36. In fact, VL Rep. 38d, Karlsburg, no. 2054 includes Bismarck-Bohlen's correspondence with Mercedes Benz.

37. *Pommersche Tagespost* 16, no. 156 (6 July 1926); GHdA Adelige Häuser A, XIV (1977), 206–22, contains the Heydebrecks' genealogy.

38. Brunner, "Landadliger Alltag": 1010.

39. My data on Flemming was culled from the *Landwirtschaftliches Adreßbuch*, 1921, and GHdA, Adelige Häuser A, XVIII (1985), 99–101, Gräfliche Häuser, II (1955), 144–47, Gräfliche Häuser, VIII (1976), 114–19; Scheurig, *Ewald von Kleist Schmenzin*, 32.

40. Eggert, *Geschichte Pommerns*, 76.

41. "Die Familie Borcke und der Kreis Regenwalde," *Unser Pommernland* 16, no. 7/8(1931): 261–64.

42. Friedrich Karl von Zitzewitz-Muttrin, *Baustein aus dem Osten. Pommersche Persönlichkeiten im Dienste Ihres Landes und der Geschichte ihrer Zeit* (Leer: Verlag Gerhard Rautenberg, 1967), 15.

43. Werner Mosse, "Adel und Bürgertum im Europa des 19. Jahrhundert. Eine vergleichende Betrachtung," in *Bürgertum im 19. Jahrhundert. Deutschland im europäischen Vergleich*, vol. 2, ed. Jürgen Kocka (Munich: DTV, 1988), 288–89.

44. VL Rep. 38d Karlsburg, no 649, includes the legal agreement surrounding the dissolution of Karlsburg as an entailed estate in 1929. The agreement includes the stipulation that the estate will pass to Bismarck-Bohlen's son, Theodor, with Theodor's obligations to his younger siblings in turn.

45. Bismarck, *Aufbruch aus Pommern*, 75–88, gives an account of his career as an estate administrator; Jordan, *Unser Dorf*, 44; Scheurig, *Ewald von Kleist-Schmenzin*, 32. Kleist administered his grandmother's estate for a time.

46. Schwiers, *Das Paradies liegt in Pommern*, 74.

47. Bismarck, *Aufbruch aus Pommern*, 73–83.

48. Krockow, *Reise nach Pommern*, 217; Reg. Rat. von Borcke, Stettin, "Adel, Kirche, Vaterland," *Pommern-Adel. Nachrichtenblatt für die Mitglieder der Landesabteilung Pommern der Deutschen Adelsgenossenschaft* 3, no. 12 (1 March 1928); *Pommern-Adel* 2, no. 7 (1 October 1926), contains a report on the *Jungadelfreizeit* in Lindenfelde near Demmin.

49. Scheurig, *Ewald von Kleist-Schmenzin*, 43.

50. Dönhoff, *Before the Storm*, 66; Krockow, in *Reise nach Pommern*, 32, notes that horses were still extensively used to pull equipment.

51. Brunner, "Landadliger Alltag," 1009–10, characterizes land as a "status symbol," which, although true, understates its overall importance.

52. Käthe von Normann, *Tagebuch aus Pommern 1945/46* (Munich: DTV, 1962), 30.

53. So suggests Ilona Buchsteiner in "Großgrundbesitz in Pommern," 329–36.

54. *Das Paradies Liegt in Pommern*, passim.

55. See the *Lexikon zur Parteiengeschichte*, Bd. 3, 430–43, for a brief history of the *Adelsgenossenschaft*. It catered primarily to Germany's middling and lower

nobility. Although it was interconfessional, its fulcrum lay in the Prussian east.

56. "Die junge Generation des Adels und ihre Verantwortung vor der Geschichte," *Pommern-Adel* 2, no. 11(1 February 1927).

57. See Cannadine, *Decline and Fall*, 361–62; Scheurig, *Ewald von Kleist-Schmenzin*, 47.

58. Krockow, *Reise nach Pommern*, 171–78; Dönhoff, *Before the Storm*, 52–53, describes the toughness that she and her siblings liked to display in the face of injuries they inevitably suffered when riding horses.

59. Krockow, *Reise nach Pommern*, 176–78.

60. Jordan, *Unser Dorf*, 149–51; VL Rep. 38d Karlsburg, no. 126, consists of a record of the household expenses of the Bismarck-Bohlen estates.

61. Lehndorff, *Menschen, Pferde, weites Land*, 139–81, esp. 176.

62. WAPK-RK, nos. 1812 and 1813, Berichte der Landwirtschaftskammer für das Provinz Pommern über die Lage der Landwirtschaft, 1925–1928, 1929–1931.

63. See Dopierała, *Ekonomiczne i Demograficzne Problemy*, 15–16, 26ff., especially 32–33.

64. Regierungspräsident Stettin: Betrifft: Kontractbruch landwirtschaftlicher Arbeiter, 18 October 1925, VL, Rep. 60, no. 2422; Pommersche Landbund Hauptgeschäftsstelle and sämtliche Kreisarbeitgebergruppen, 27 January 1928; Niederschrift über der Sitzung, 19 February 1929, both in BA Potsdam 61 Re 1, Reichslandbund, no. 246.

65. Dopierała, *Ekonomicne i Demograficzne Problemy*, document no. 4, 30–31.

66. Peasants relied upon young single men and women, in addition to family members, for planting and harvesting.

67. This profile is drawn primarily from Hans Weigmann, *Auswirkungen der Siedlung. Baustein zum Siedlungsproblem. V. Teil. Siedlung und sozialer Aufstieg der Landarbeiter* (Berlin: Verlagsbuchhandlung Paul Parey, 1934), 28–44. For a more general discussion of laborer categories, see Jens Flemming, "Die vergessene Klasse: Literatur zur Geschichte der Landarbeiter in Deutschland," *Historische Zeitschrift*, Sonderheft 15 (1986): 392–95, and Manfred Jatzlauk, "Landarbeiter, Bauern und Großgrundbesitzer in der Weimarer Republik," *Zeitschrift für Geschichtswissenschaft* 39, no. 9(1991): 891–92.

68. Änne Klatt, *Familienaufstieg und Siedlung. Eine Untersuchung über den Einfluß der Siedlung auf den Sozialen Aufstieg einzelner Landarbeiterfamilien* (Wupperthal, Elberfeld: J.H. Born, 1933), 17.

69. Ibid.

70. Wilhelm Andreas Henatsch, *Das Problem der ausländischen Wanderarbeiter unter besonderer Berücksichtigung der Zuckerproblem in der Provinz Pommern* (Greifswald: Verlag Ratsbuchhandlung, 1920), 21–38; Bogusław Drewniak, *Robotnicy sezonowi na Pomorzu Zachodnim (1890–1918)* (Poznań: Institut Zachodni, 1959).

71. Weigmann, *Auswirkungen der Siedlung*, 51. The 1930 figure includes Mecklenburg-Strelitz. The number dropped from over thirty-five thousand in 1923 to fewer than fifteen thousand by 1930.

72. Dopierała, *Ekonomiczne i Demograficzne Problemy*, document 2, 8.

73. "Ausländische Arbeiter in Pommern," *General Anzeiger*, no. 299 (28 October 1926). See Herbert, *History of Foreign Laborer*, 123. The Republic permitted the employment of foreigners if an insufficient number of Germans existed to perform the work, and if the employer paid foreigners union-scale wages.

74. Fürstbischofliche Kommissar für Pommern to Oberpräsident Pommern, 10 December 1925, VL, Rep. 60, no. 1486. See also Ruth Weiland, "Das soziale Schick-

sal der deutschen Landwirtschaftlichen Wanderarbeiterfamilien," *Jahrbuch für Na-tionalökonomie und Statistik* 135(1931): 744–78, and Anna Poniatowska, *Polskie wychodźstwo sezonowe na pomorzu Zachodnim 1918–1939* (Poznań: Wydawnictwo Poznańskie, 1971).

75. Prussian Minister of the Interior to all Oberpräsidenten, 2 May 1929, VL Rep. 60, no. 1485. The ministry was particulary watchful during periods of high unemployment.

76. "Gefährdung der diesjährigen Ernte," *Stettiner Abendsblatt*, no. 172 (26 July 1927), found in Rejencja Szczecinska I, Wojewódskie Archiwum Państwowe w Szczecinie (hereinafter cited as WAPS-RS I, followed by folio number), no. 9660; Zuckerfabrik Aktien-Gesellschaft, Demmin to Regierungspräsident Stettin, 8 February 1929, WAPS-RS I, no. 9660.

77. Landwirtschaftskammer Pommern to Reichsarbeitsminister, 1 December 1927, Beschäftigungsverhältnisse im Zuckerrübenbau. Ergebnisse einer Umfrage des Landarbeitsamts Pommern, 19 September 1931, VL Rep. 60, no. 1487.

78. EZA, Konvent Evangelischer Gemeinden aus Pommern, Bestand 46 A, no. 10.

79. Polizeiverwaltung, Cammin to Landrat Cammin, 18 April 1931, no. 11964, reported on the content of a Communist party rally.

80. Weiland, "Soziale Schicksal," 48–67; Poniatowska, *Polskie wychodźstwo sez-onowe*, 112–30.

81. Normann, *Tagebuch aus Pommern*, 102, 130.

82. Fürstbischofliche Kommissar für Pommern to Oberpräsident Pommern, 10 December 1925, VL Rep. 60, no 1486.

83. Poniatowska, *Polskie wychodźstwo sezonowe*,111; Regierungspräsident Stettin, Betrifft: Kontraktbruch Landwirtschaftlicher Arbeiter, 18 October 1825, VL Rep. 60, no. 2422.

84. Redaktions des Gesamtüberblick der polnische Presse, Berlin, 20 and 30 June 1927, WAPS-RS I, no. 9660. The long quotation is taken from the dispatch from 20 June.

85. Monatsbericht. Kreisgruppe Dramburg Arbeitnehmergruppe, May 1925 (dated 3 June 1925), BA Potsdam 61 Re 1, Reichslandbund, no. 248.

86. Krockow, *Reise nach Pommern*, 44; Bismarck, *Aufbruch aus Pommern*, 89; Anlage Köslin, 3 June 1929, WAPK-RK, no. 2231.

87. For a discussion of wage scales in agriculture during the Republic, see Wunderlich, *Farm Labor*, 111–25.

88. This Max Weber clearly saw well before World War I. See Weber, "Entwick-lungstendenzen in der Lage der ostelbischen Landarbeiter" (1894) in Weber, *Gesammelte Aufsätze zur Sozial-und Wirtschaftsgeschichte* (Tübingen: J.C.B. Mohr [Paul Siebeck], 1924), 470–507, especially 477–88. Cf. also Bowman, *Masters and Lords*, 168–69.

89. Wunderlich, *Farm Labor*, 120, 123. The hours in one Pomeranian district, according to Wunderlich, ranged from 2,850 to 2,950 per year.

90. Jatzlauk, "Landarbeiter, Bauern und Großgrundbesitzer," 897–88.

91. Dopierała, *Ekonomiczne i Demograficzne Problemy*, 252.

92. Report on the General Visitation to Stolp-Altstadt, 9–28 May 1932, EZA, Evangelischer Oberkirchenrat collection (hereinafter cited as EOK), Pomerania VI, no. 25. The quotation is found on page 4 of that report.

93. P. Lutschewitz, "Die Arbeit eines pommerschen Dorfpfarrers," *Pommersche Heimatskirche* (August 1955).

94. EZA, Konvent Evangelischer Gemeinden aus Pommern, Bestand 46 A, no. 25.

95. Ibid., no. 162.

96. Weigmann, *Auswirkungen der Siedlung*, 40, doubted the prospects of upward mobility. See also Bismarck, *Aufbruch aus Pommern*, 89; and Jordan, *Unser Dorf*, 65–66, who gives an account of the constant complaining of the estate hand, Emma, who tended the swine and poultry.

97. See Krockow, *Die Reise nach Pommern*, 151–56, for this and other examples that accompany a discussion of the combination of identification and distance that existed between servants and masters.

98. Dönhoff, *Before the Storm*, 52, 55–61; Jordan, *Unser Dorf*, 79; Bismarck, *Aufbruch aus Pommern*, 90.

99. So implies Jordan, *Unser Dorf*, 168.

100. Schwiers, *Das Paradies liegt in Pommern*, 11.

101. Jordan, *Unser Dorf*, 164.

102. For discussions regarding the education of nobles, see Schwiers, *Das Paradies liegt in Pommern*, 18, and Ilse Gräfin von Bredow, *Kartoffeln mit Stippe. Eine Kindheit in der märkischen Heide* (Munich: DTV, 1992), 41–51.

103. EZA, Konvent Evangelischer Gemeinden, Bestand 46 A, no. 225.

104. Marzahn, *Erinnerungen*, 28; Krockow, *Reise nach Pommern*, 41.

105. Dönhoff, *Before the Storm*, 7, 57.

106. See Jordan's descriptions of his family's workers, *Unser Dorf*, 47–93. The coachman occupied the top rung of the social ladder.

107. Report on the General Visitation to Wollin, 20 May to 2 June, 1930, EZA, EOK Pomerania VI, no. 39, 2.

108. EZA, Konvent Evangelischer Gemeinden aus Pommern, Bestand 46 A, no. 145.

109. Ibid., no. 188.

110. Walter Görlitz, "Widerstand gegen den Nationalsozialismus in Pommern," *Baltische Studien* 48 (1961), 65.

111. EZA, Frageboden zum kirchlichen Brauchtum, Sammlung Hist. Ostgebiete, Pommern.

112. Krockow, *Reise nach Pommern*, 132.

113. Bismarck, *Aufbruch aus Pommern*, 91–92.

114. Pastors even mediated disputes over water rights, EZA, Konvent Evangelischer Gemeinden aus Pommern, Bestand 46 A, no. 188.

115. See the excellent collection of essays in *The German Peasantry. Conflict and Community in Rural Society from the Eighteenth to the Twentieth Centuries*, eds. Richard J. Evans and W. R. Lee (New York: St. Martin's Press, 1986) that, among other goals, seeks to restore German peasants as agents of history in contrast to the conceptions of West German historiography in the 1960s and 1970s.

116. See Berdahl, *Politics of the Prussian Nobility*, chapter 2, for an excellent discussion of the meaning of *das ganze Haus*.

117. Jordan, *Unser Dorf*, 185–86.

118. Dönhoff, *Before the Storm*, 17.

119. So observes Jordan, *Unser Dorf*, 186.

120. Krockow, *Reise nach Pommern*, 130.

121. Jordan, *Unser Dorf*, 61. Cf. Walter Rinderle and Bernhard Norling, *The Nazi Impact on a German Village* (Lexington: University of Kentucky Press, 1993), 43.

122. Dönhoff, *Befor the Storm*, 132.

123. The title of Jordan's memoir, *Unser Dorf in Schlesien*, demonstrates the author's determination, conscious or otherwise, to depict the extended network

of human relationships that surrounded the nucleus, his family's modest-sized estate.

124. Scheurig, *Ewald von Kleist-Schmenzin*, 26–41, especially 32.

125. Bismarck, *Aufbruch aus Pommern*, 36.

126. Irmgard von der Lühe, *Elizabeth von Thadden. Ein Schicksal unserer Zeit* (Düsseldorf, Cologne: Eugen Dietrich Verlag, 1966), 46–67.

127. Krockow, *Reise nach Pommern*, 208; See GHdA, Gräfliche Häuser XI (1983), 163–44, for the Krockows' genealogy.

128. Scheurig, *Ewald von Kleist-Schmenzin*, 14–15.

129. "Zwei Erziehungsformen und ihre Auswirkung," *Pommern-Adel* 4, no. 9 (1 December 1928).

130. Jordan, *Unser Dorf*, 180. Krockow, *Stunde der Frauen*, 21–22 reports that at Libussa's wedding Uncle Gerhard, the family's eldest male, toasted Hitler almost as an afterthought.

131. "Die junge Generation des Adels und ihre Verantwortung vor der Geschichte," *Pommern-Adel*, 2, no. 11 (1 February 1927).

132. "Junker und Bürger in Pommern," *Pommern Stimmen* 4, no. 16 (2 May 1927).

133. James N. Retallack, *Notables on the Right. The Conservative Party and Political Mobilization in Germany, 1876–1918* (Boston: Unwin Hyman, 1988), 216.

134. Görlitz, *Die Junker*, 332. According to article 109 of the Weimar Constitution, the noble predicate became part of the name of its bearer and solely an issue of private law. "Familiengeschichte in der Landesabteilung Pommern," *Pommern-Adel* 1, no. 4 (1 July 1925).

135. "Aufstieg oder Niedergang des Adels," *Pommern-Adel* 2, no. 2 (1 May 1926).

136. Report on the *Jungadelfreizeit* on the von Roon estate near Demmin, *Pommern-Adel* 2, no. 7 (1 October 1926). For the strength of anti-Semitism in Pomerania, particularly among the nobility, see Uwe Schröder, "Antisemitismus und Faschismus in Pommern in der Zwischenkriegsperiod," in *Der faschistische Pogrom vom 9./10. November 1938. Zur Geschichte der Juden in Pommern* (Greifswald: Wissenschaftliche Beiträge der Ernst-Moritz-Arndt Universität Greifswald, 1989), 31–32.

137. "Junker," *Pommern-Adel* 3, no. 8 (1 November 1927).

138. Schwiers, *Das Paradies liegt in Pommern*, 38 records her fond memories of the Jew, Wolf, who bought animal hides from the family. Bismarck, *Aufbruch aus Pommern*, 49, lets on that his grandmother on his mother's side came from a wealthy bourgeois Jewish family in Berlin-Wannsee.

139. "Die Wahlarbeit der Landfrau," *Die Gutsfrau*, 8, no. 17 (1 June 1920).

140. *Pommern-Adel* 2, no. 8 (1 November 1926).

141. *Pommern-Adel* 1, no. 11 (1 February 1926).

142. *Elizabeth von Thadden*, 14–15.

143. The last issue of *Die Gutsfrau* appeared in 1923. For a discussion of the Housewives' Association, see Renate Bridenthal, "Organized Rural Women and the Conservative Mobilization of the Countryside in the Weimar Republic," in Jones and Retallack, eds., *Between Reform, Reaction and Resistance*, 375–405.

144. "An die Gutsfrauen," *Heimatklänge*, 9, no. 8 (May 1925).

145. See Bowman, *Masters and Lords*, 162–83. His sensitive discussion of the definitions and applicability of such terms as "patriarchy" and "paternalism" to estate and plantation life does not fully consider the female contribution. Nor does Berdahl, *Politics of the Prussian Nobility*, 44–54, whose exploration of paternalism, though different from Bowman's, excludes the *Gutfrauen* as well.

146. "Als Gutsfrau in Vorpommern," *Die Gutsfrau* 11, no. 7 (January 1923).

147. Bismarck, *Aufbruch aus Pommern*, 61.

148. Krockow, *Reise nach Pommern*, 146.

149. "Wie kann die Frau hilfen, um die wirtschaftliche Einheitsfront zu schaffen?", *Die Gutsfrau* 11, no. 1 (October 1922).

150. "Eine Aufgabe der Landfrauen," *Pommersche Tagespost* 16, no. 187 (7 August, 1926).

151. "Soziale Betätigung für Junge Mädchen. Ein Gespräch," *Heimatklänge* 9, no. 1 (October 1924).

152. Muncy, *The Junker in the Prussian Administration*, 117. For the beginnings of a female role in the Evangelical Church, see Catherine Prelinger, "The Nineteenth-Century Deaconessate in Germany. The Efficacy of a Family Model," in *German Women in the Eighteenth and Nineteenth Centuries. A Social and Literary History*, eds. Ruth-Ellen B. Joeres and Mary Jo Maynes (Bloomington: Indiana University Press, 1986), 215–29. Prelinger points to the increasingly aristocratic composition of the deaconessate.

153. See by contrast the findings of Bonnie G. Smith, *The Ladies of the Leisure Class. The Bourgeoises of Northern France in the Nineteenth Century* (Princeton: Princeton University Press, 1981), 123–61. Men tended to favor a more rational, secular, and bureaucratic form of welfare, while women treated the church and family as the foci of charity.

154. Berdahl, *Politics of the Prussian Nobility*, 56–57.

155. "Kirchliche und staatliche Zuständigkeit hinsichtlich der Gesetzebung über den Kirchenpatronat in Preussen," 18 January 1925, EZA, EOK Generalakten V, no. 75, Bd. 3.

156. Pomeranian Consistory to EOK, 19 April 1933, EZA, EOK Pomerania V, no. 371.

157. Such was the case of Prince von Hohenzollern-Sigmaringen, patron of Manon in the Köslin diocese who presented three candidates for council's consideration, Pomeranian Consistory to EOK 2, March 1920, EZA, EOK Pomerania V, no. 265.

158. EZA, Konvent Evangelischer Gemeinden aus Pommern, Bestand 46 A, no. 10.

159. Krockow, *Reise nach Pommern*, 157; Dönhoff, *Before the Storm*, 18.

160. Wolfgang Schaeffer to LeRoy M. Boelke, 14 June 1962, EZA, EOK Pomerania V, no. 501.

161. Pomeranian Consistory to EOK, 16 July 1929, EZA, EOK Generalakten V, no. 29, Bd. 4.

162. Schwiers, *Das Paradies liegt in Pommern*, 57–58; Report on the General Visitation to Belgard, 25 May to 14 June 1928, EZA, EOK Pomerania VI, no. 5, 7–8, commented that bourgeois estate owners were involved in church affairs, but that as a rule they were not as pious as the nobility.

163. "Adel, Kirche, Vaterland," *Pommern-Adel* 3, no. 12 (1 March 1928).

164. Bismarck, *Aufbruch aus Pommern*, 36; Jordan, *Unser Dorf*, 186. For Jordan's family, church attendance was still considered an obligation despite his family's cool relationship to their pastor.

165. Pomeranian Consistory to EOK, 18 June 1924, EZA, EOK Pomerania V, no. 409; Vorlage des Provinzialkirchenrats. Betreffend Änderung der Grenzen der Kirchenkreis (24 September 1925), in the same file. The merger of Greifswald Stadt and Land was tabled, as was the proposal to divide the parish of Daber because of the Dewitzes' centuries-long patronage, EZA, EOK Pomerania II, 7, I.

166. Pomeranian Consistory to EOK, 22 February 1924, EZA, EOK Pomerania V, no. 342.

167. Pomeranian Consistory to EOK, 27 June 1924, EZA, EOK Pom. V, no. 408.

168. Report of General Visitation to Bütow, 7–28 May 1925, EZA, EOK Pomerania VI, no. 22, 15.

169. Report on General Visitation to Belgard, 25 May to 14 June, 1928, EZA, EOK Pomerania VI, no. 5, 3.

170. Verzeichnis der von Kreissynoden und der theologischen Fakultät zur Provinzialsynode 1920 gewählten Abgeordneten und Stellvertreter; Verzeichnis der zur Provinzialsynode der Kirchenprovinz Pommern gewählten ordentlichen Mitglieder und deren Stellvertreter (1925), EZA, EOK Pomerania II, no. 6, Bd. 3.

171. Herr von Roon on the *Volksbewegung*, Acta betreffend der Ephoren-Konferenz am. 14. und 15. Dezember 1921, Stettin, EZA, EOK Pomerania II,8,II.

172. See Jochen-Christoph Kaiser, *Frauen in der Kirche. Evangelische Frauenverbände im Spannungsfeld von Kirche und Gesellschaft 1890–1945. Quellen und Materialen*, ed. Annette Kuhn (Düsseldorf: Schwann, 1985).

173. *Die Gutsfrau* 8, no. 21 (1 August 1920).

174. Marie von Kleist to Geschäftsstelle, Deutscher Evangelischer Frauenbund, 12 April 1921, Archiv der Deutschen Evangelischen Frauenbund, Hannover (hereinafter cited as DEF), Pommersche Verband 1917–1925.

175. Abschrift, Gräfin von Schwerin to Provincial Association, 29 August 1930; Central Committee to Provincial Association, 30 October 1930, Archiv des Diakonischen Werkes der EKD (Berlin-Dahlem), hereinafter cited as ADW, Central Committee of the Inner Mission; documents concerning the Provincial Association of the Inner Mission in Pomerania.

176. Franklin C. West, *A Crisis of the Weimar Republic. The German Referendum of 20. June 1926* (Philadelphia: The American Philosophical Society, 1985), 143–44.

177. Ulrich Schüren, *Der Volksentscheid zur Fürstenenteignung 1926. Die Vermögensauseinandersetzung mit den depossedierten Landesherren als Problem der deutschen Innenpolitik unter besonderer Berücksichtigung der Verhältnisse in Preußen* (Düsseldorf: Droste Verlag, 1978), 205–14.

178. "Pommern Adel an die Front!," *Pommern Adel* 1, no. 12 (1 March 1926).

179. "Das Siebente Gebot," *Pommersche Tagesblatt* no. 62 (14 March 1926), WAPS-RS I, no. 1820.

180. *Anklamer Zeitung* no. 62 (14 March 1926), WAPS-RS I, no. 1820.

181. *Demminer Tagesblatt* no. 79 (4 April 1926), WAPS-RS I, no. 1820.

182. (10 June 1926), WAPS-RS I, no. 22.

183. Landrat Pyritz to Regierungspräsident Stettin, 23 March 1926, WAPS-RS I, no. 1820; Landrat Randow to Regierungspräsident Stettin, 20 March 1926, WAPS-RS I, no. 1820.

184. "Sabotage des Volksbegehren," *Volksvernunft* (25 March 1926), WAPS-RS I, no. 1820.

185. Court decision of 9 January 1928, WAPS-RS I, no. 22.

186. Landrat Pyritz to Regierungspräsident Stettin, 29 July 1926, WAPS-RS I, no. 1820.

187. Bezirksarbeitersekretariat Stralsund to Landratsamt Bergen, 23 March 1926; Landrat Bergen to Bezirksarbeitersekretariat, 3 April 1926, VL Rep. 65c, no. 77.

188. Landrat Pyritz to Regierungspräsident Stettin, 29 July 1926, WAPS-RS I, no. 1820.

189. Schüren, *Der Volksentscheid zur Fürstenenteignung 1926*, 231–32.

190. West, *Crisis of the Weimar Republic*, 274–83.

191. D. P. Walker, "The German National People's Party: The Conservative Dilemma in the Weimar Republic," *Journal of Contemporary History* 14(1979), 636.

192. Kazuo Ishiguru, *The Remains of the Day* (New York: Knopf, 1989).

193. The influence of Michel Foucault in this regard has been enormous. See especially his *Discipline and Punish. The Birth of the Prison*, trans. Alan Sheridan (New York: Vintage Books, 1979).

Chapter 4. Social Constraints and Political Limitations

1. Rather than employing the term "Protestant," which was considered derogatory in Germany, I prefer to use "Evangelical" unless doing so results in an inappropriate meaning in English. "Evangelical" refers to the Reformation's emphasis on preaching the "Word" (*Evangelium*) found in scripture.

2. For a concise discussion of the Evangelical Church's place in Prussian history, see Rudolf von Thadden, *Fragen an Preußen. Zur Geschichte eines aufgehobenen Staates* (Munich: C. H. Beck, 1981), chapter 6.

3. Karl-Heinz Gehrmann, *Wir Pommern* (Salzburg, Munich: Akademischer Gemeinschaftsverlag, 1951), 27–33.

4. Prussian Consistory to EOK, 5 September 1921: Wintershagen-Stolpmünde (Stolp-Stadt) consisted of four villages and three manorial districts (EZA, EOK Pomerania V, no. 121); Pomeranian Consistory to EOK, 18 June 1924: Behrendorf (Greifswald Land), consisted of twelve manorial districts and sixteen villages (EZA, EOK Pomerania V, no. 356); Pomeranian Consistory to EOK, 8 February 1924: Roggow (Daber) was comprised of one mother and three daughter churches, each consisting of a manorial and a rural commune (EZA, EOK Pomerania V, no. 394).

5. For an analysis of the postrevolutionary attempts to democratize the structure of the Prussian church, efforts that were only partially successful, see Jochen Jacke, *Der Kirchliche Protestantismus nach dem Zusammenbruch des Staatskirchentums 1918* (Hamburg: Hans Christians Verlag, 1976), 151–304. The Old Prussian Union Church embraced the provinces belonging to Prussia before the wars of German unification, including the Rhineland and Westphalia. See Daniel R. Borg, *The Old-Prussian Church and the Weimar Republic. A Study in Political Adjustment* (Hannover and London: University Press of New England, 1984), xii.

6. Paul Troschke, *Evangelische Kirchenstatistik Deutschlands* (Berlin-Charlottenburg: Deutsches Evangelisches Kirchenbundesamt, 1932–33), 6–8.

7. See Marjorie Lamberti, *State, Society, and the Elementary School in Imperial Germany* (New York and Oxford: Oxford University Press, 1989).

8. Pomeranian Consistory to EOK, 13 June 1930, EZA, EOK Pomerania V, no. 12.

9. Kreissynodalvorstand to EOK, 1 August 1933, EZA, EOK Pomerania V, no. 585.

10. Report on General Visitation in Pasewalk, 30 May to 12 June 1928, 3, Handakten des Generalsuperintendenten Kählers, EZA, EOK Pomerania VI; Wehrmann, *Geschichte von Pommern*, 319–20; "Die kirchliche Eingliederung der Siedler und der Siedlungen," Superintendent Land (Rügen), 21 September, 1931, EZA, EOK Generalakten XV, 65, V.

11. Report on the General Visitation to Anklam, 26 May to 14 June 1926, EZA, EOK Pomerania VI, no. 50, 2.

12. Report on the General Visitation to Wollin, 20 May to 2 June 1930, EZA, EOK Pomerania VI, no. 39, 5.

13. Report on General Visitation to Belgard, EZA, EOK Pomerania VI, no. 5, 23.

14. Ev. Pfarramt Cobrieben to Kreissynodalvorstand in Tempelburg, 27 April 1932, EZA, EOK Pomerania V, no. 598.

15. Pomeranian Consistory to EOK, 25 January 1929, addendum to 25 May to 14 June 1928, Report on General Visitation to Belgard, EZA, EOK Pomerania VI, no. 5.

16. *Bote von Pommernstrand. Sontagsblatt der Synode Rügenwalde*, 16, no. 26 (28 June 1925).

17. Tagesbericht des Evangelischen Konsistoriums, 1925, 2, EZA, EOK Pomerania II, 6, III; Niederschrift über die Verhandlung der Superintendentbesprechung, 2 February 1931, EZA, EOK Pomerania II,8,III, 15–16.

18. *Heimatbote. Gemeindeblatt für die evang. Gemeinden der Parochien Tempelburg, Draheim, Heinrichsdorf, Lubow, Pöhlen, Coprieben und Klaushagen mit Neuwuhrow* 7, no. 13 (25 March 1928).

19. *Kirchliches Jahrbuch für das evangelischen Landeskirchen Deutschlands* 61(1934), ed. Hermann Sasse (Gütersloh: Verlag C. Bertelsmann), 123–24.

20. Pomerania ranked third from the bottom in withdrawals from the church. "Schlaglichter auf den neuesten Stand der Gottlosenbewegung," *Gemeindeblatt für das Kirchspiel Großmöllen* 7, no. 3(March 1933).

21. *Kirchliches Jahrbuch*, 80.

22. Report on the General Visitation in Schlawe, 11–27 May 1933, 7–8, EZA, EOK Pomerania VI, no. 11, Report on General Visitation to Schivelbein, 6–22 May 1931, EZA, EOK Pomerania VI, no. 53, 3–4.

23. Pomeranian Consistory to Kirchenkreis Belgard, 25 January 1929, addendum to Report on General Visitation to Belgard, 25 May to 14 June 1928, EZA, EOK Pomerania VI, no. 5.

24. Report on General Visitation to Stolp-Alstadt, 9–28 May 1932, 9, EZA, EOK Pomerania VI, no. 25.

25. "Ein feste Burg ist unser Gott," *Pommersche Tagespost* 21, no. 111(13 May 1931).

26. Pomeranian Consistory to EOK 29 June 1934, EZA, EOK Pomerania V, no. 628.

27. Report on General Visitation to Anklam, 26 May to 14 June, 1926, 6, EZA, EOK Pomerania VI, no. 50.

28. "Bismarck als religiöse Persönlichkeit," *Bote von Pommernstrand* 13, no. 17(23 April 1922).

29. Niederschrift über die Verhandlung der Superintendentenbesprechung am 2. Februar 1931, EZA, EOK Pomerania II,8,III, 14.

30. On the politics of schoolteachers and their status during the Republic, see Rainer Bölling, *Sozialgeschichte der deutschen Lehrer. Ein Überblick von 180 bis zur Gegenwart* (Göttingen: Vandenhoeck and Ruprecht, 1983), 103–35. For a full discussion of the school controversy in Prussia, see Borg, *Old-Prussian Church*, 123–67. See also Geoffrey G. Field, "Religion in the German Volksschule, 1890–1928," *Leo Baeck Institute Yearbook* 25(1980): 41–77, regarding the importance of confessional divisions in Germany and the failure to deconfessionalize education.

31. "Wollt Ihr eine Schule ohne Gott haben?," *Bote von Pommernstrand* 11, no. 3(18 January 1920).

32. Excerpt from the minutes of the meeting of the German Evangelical Church Committee (Deutscher Evangelischer Kirchenausschuss), 24–25 June 1925, EZA, EOK Generalakten XIV,46,I; EZA, EOK Generalakten XIV,9,II, includes a newspaper clipping from 16 July 1919, recording the remarks of the Pomeranian Consistory in answer to the Pyritz Teachers' Association regarding the elimination of sexton

duties; as does a letter from the Pomeranian Consistory to EOK, 4 February 1920, EZA, EOK Generalakten XIV,9,II.

33. "Religionsunterricht und Heimat," *Heimatbote* 7, no. 5(29 January 1928).

34. Pomeranian Consistory to EOK, 15 February 1923, EZA, EOK Generalakten XIV,37,III; Pomeranian Consistory to EOK, 14 March 1925, EZA EOK Generalakten XIV,37,V; Pomeranian Consistory to EOK, 22 April 1927, EOK Generalakten XIV,37,VI; Pomeranian Consistory to EOK, 21 April 1931, EOK Generalakten XIV,37,IX. The above files contain election results.

35. Pomeranian Consistory to EOK, 24 December 1921, EZA, EOK Generalakten XIV,37,III.

36. *Der Reichsbote* 29 January 1920, found in EZA, EOK Generalakten XIV,37,IX; *Hinterpommern* 13 December 1928, found in EZA, EOK Generalakten XIV,37,IX.

37. Pomeranian Consistory to EOK, 1 December 1928, EZA, EOK Generalakten XIV,37, VIII.

38. *Kirchliches Amtsblatt des Evangelischen Konsistoriums der Provinz Pommern* 51, no. 19(9 December 1919). "Lower" duties included opening and closing the church and janitorial services, while the "higher" responsibilities consisted of assisting with communion, playing the organ, and leading schoolchildren in song at burials.

39. "Die Zahl der Volksschulen in Pommern," *Pommersche Tagespost* 19, no. 168(20 July 1929).

40. Minister für Wissenschaft, Kunst and Volksbildung to EOK, 3 January 1930, EZA, EOK Generalakten XIV,9,II.

41. Pomeranian Consistory to EOK, 1 March 1931, EZA, EOK Pomerania V, no. 366.

42. Pomeranian Consistory to EOK, 28 August 1930, EZA, EOK Generalakten XIV,9,II.

43. Report of General Visitation to Schivelbein, 6 to 22 May, 1931, 2; EZA, EOK Pomerania VI, no. 53.

44. Pomeranian Consistory to EOK, 12 November 1926, EZA, EOK Generakten XIV,37,VI.

45. Sonderaufstellung über das Verpachteten (land und forstwirtschaftlich genutzten) kirchlichen Grundbesitz im Ostgebiet (einschl. der *ganzen* Provinz Sachsen) nach den Stand von Ende Dezember 1932, EZA, EOK Generalakten XV,65,VI.

46. Pomeranian Consistory to EOK, 9 January 1926, EZA, EOK Pomerania V, no. 472.

47. Pomeranian Consistory to EOK, 1 February 1926, EZA, EOK Pomerania V, no. 461.

48. Borg, *Old-Prussian Church*, 119.

49. See ibid., 116–22, for a summary of church finances; attachment to letter from EOK to Ministerium für Wissenschaft, Kunst und Volksbildung, 13 October 1930, EZA, EOK Pomerania V, no. 565. The church tax amounted to 1 mark for a *Landarbeiter* family, 6 marks for the schoolteacher, 47. 50 for each of the two *Rittergutsbesitzer*, and 8 marks for peasant families with over 150 morgen (approximately 38 ha.) of land.

50. Gemeindekirchenrat Juchow to Pomeranian Consistory, 12 January 1925, EZA, EOK Pomerania V, no. 238.

51. EZA, Konvent Evangelischer Gemeinden aus Pommern, Bestand 46 A, no. 102.

52. Pomeranian Consistory to EOK, 7 September 1923, EZA, EOK Pomerania V, no. 362.

53. Pomeranian Consistory to EOK, 26 March 1925, EZA, EOK Pomerania V, no. 423.

54. Pomeranian Consistory to EOK, 7 July 1926, EZA, EOK Pomerania V, no. 178.

55. Pomeranian Consistory to EOK, 11 November 1922, EZA, EOK Pomerania V, no. 356.

56. Pomeranian Consistory to EOK, 20 October 1933, EZA, EOK Pomerania V, no. 71.

57. EZA, Konvent Evangelischer Gemeinden aus Pommern, Bestand 46 A, no. 12. EZA, Konvent Evangelischer Gemeinden. Of 226 pastors yielding adequate biographical information (such as personal written recollections, newspapers, and obituaries), 152 (67 percent) were born in Pomerania or returned as young children because of their parents' strong family ties. An additional 19 came from German-speaking communities in Poland or Russia. Ninety-eight pastors in this sampling reported their fathers' occupations, a figure that included 46 pastors' sons, 14 teachers' sons, 10 peasants' sons, and 7 the offspring of officials.

58. Ibid., no. 145.

59. Ibid., no. 186.

60. Ibid., no. 225.

61. Borg, *Old-Prussian Church*, 118; Pomeranian Consistory to EOK, 1 February 1934, EZA, EOK Pomerania V, no. 235 notes that Roloshagen in Grimmen diocese contained a manse with fifteen rooms. Most contained eight or thereabouts.

62. Christian Graf von Krockow, "Gutshaus und Pfarrhaus," in *Das evangelische Pfarrhaus. Eine Kultur-und Sozialgeschichte*, ed. Martin Greiffenhagen (Stuttgart: Kreuz Verlag, 1984), 225.

63. Niederschrift über die Verhandlung der Superintendentenbesprechung, 29 September 1930, EZA, EOK Pomerania II,8,II, 1–5.

64. Borg, *Old-Prussian Church*, 1–28.

65. Consult J. R. C. Wright, *"Above Parties." The Political Attitudes of the German Protestant Church Leadership* (Oxford: Oxford University Press, 1974).

66. Niederschrift des Ephoralkonvents Pommern Ost am 1.u. 2. November 1928, EZA, EOK Pomerania II,8,II, 1.

67. Response of Pastor Ettling, 31 January 1930 to Minister für Wissenschaft, Kunst und Volksbildung, EZA, EOK Pomerania V, no. 453.

68. For discussions as to the meaning of the *Volkskirche*, see David J. Diephouse, *Pastors and Pluralism in Württemberg 1918–1933* (Princeton: Princeton University Press, 1987), 12–22, and Borg, *Old Prussian Church*, 2.

69. "Von der Sendung der Kirche, Zeugnisse vom ersten pommerschen evangelischen Kirchentag" (Stettin: Verlag des Pommerschen Evangelischen Pressverbandes, 1932), 1–2.

70. Niederschrift über die Verhandlungen der Superintendentenbesprechung, 29 September 1930, EZA, EOK Pomerania II,8,II, 8–11.

71. Niederschrift des Ephoralkonvents Pommern-Ost, 1–2 November 1928, EZA, EOK Pomerania II,8,II, 4.

72. Niederschrift über die Verhandlungen der Superintendentenbesprechung, 29 September 1930, EZA, EOK Pomerania II,8,II, 8–11.

73. Eberhard Bethge, *Dietrich Bonhoeffer. Man of Vision. Man of Courage*, trans. Eric Mosbacher, et al. (New York and Evanston: Harper & Row, 1970), 358; Scheurig, *Ewald von Kleist-Schmenzin*, 46.

74. Krockow, *Reise nach Pommern*, 157.

75. Rittergutsbesitzer von Enckewort-Sassenburg and Thomas Beweringen to Pomeranian Consistory, May 8, 1923, EZA, EOK Pomerania V, no. 373.

76. Krockow, *Reise nach Pommern*, 163–64.

77. Report on General Visitation to Schivelbein, 6–22 May 1931, EZA, EOK Pomerania VI, no. 53, 13.

78. Report on General Visitation to Bütow, 7–28 May 1925, EZA, EOK Pomerania VI, no. 22, 11–12.

79. Graf Flemming-Schnatow to Pomeranian Consistory, 6 January 1926, EZA, EOK Pomerania V, no. 466.

80. Complaint from Oberstudienrat Dr. Brunner, 30 December 1925, Pomeranian Consistory to EOK, February 1926; EZA, EOK Pomerania V, no. 379.

81. Pomeranian Consistory to EOK, 16 July 1929; EZA, EOK Generalakten V, no. 29, Bd. 4.

82. A. Bidder to EOK, 21 January 1933, EZA, EOK Pomerania V, no. 524. Bidder wanted to become the pastor of Woldisch-Tychow (Kreis Belgard) and won the backing of the patron, von Borries. Kleist helped him to obtain his citizenship.

83. Pomeranian Consistory to EOK, 9 October 1928, EZA, EOK Pomerania V, no. 167.

84. Pomeranian Consistory to EOK, 19 February 1926, EZA, EOK Pomerania V, no. 55.

85. Report on General Visitation to Stolp-Altstadt, EZA, EOK Pomerania VI, no. 25, 16–17.

86. Pomeranian Consistory to EOK, 29 December 1926 and 6 June 1928, EZA, EOK Pomerania V, no. 503.

87. EZA, EOK Pomerania V, no. 470. Virtually the entire folder is devoted to this controversy of 1926, and it includes the minutes of a meeting between the pastor, the patrons, and the superintendent that were then forwarded to EOK, March 22, 1926.

88. Fricke et al., *Lexikon zur Parteiengeschichte*, Bd. I(1983), 14–29.

89. Soziales Programm der Gesamtverbandes der Evangelischen Arbeiter-Verein Deutschlands, Erfurt, 18 May 1921; ADW, Akten des Central-Ausschusses für Innere Mission betr. Gesamtverband der Ev. Arbeitervereine Deutschlands, no. 404, BIII, 7,I.

90. EAV-Arbeit von Halle bis Erfurt, Bericht 1925–27, EOK Generalakten XII, no. 171, I, doc. 111, 5.

91. Report on General Visitation to Belgard, 25 May to June 14 1928, EOK Pomerania VI, no. 5, 3–4.

92. Report on General Visitation to Bütow, 7–28 May 1925, EZA, EOK Pomerania VI, no. 22, 3.

93. Niederschrift über die Superintendentenbesprechung in Belgard, 4–5 November 1926, EZA, EOK Pomerania II,8,II.

94. Das E.A.V. Werk von 1929–1931, EZA, EOK Generalakten XII, 171, III, doc. no. 162.

95. See Becker, *Handlungsspielräume der Agrarpolitik*, 107–14, for a discussion of the Reich Settlement Law of 1923, and Schmidt and Blohm, *Die Landwirtschaft von Ostpreussen und Pommern*, 38–47.

96. Aufgaben evangelischer Arbeit in der ländlichen Siedlung. Denkschrift des Evangelischen Siedlungsdienst (Undated, ca. 1930), EZA, EOK Generalakten XV,65,I, 16.

97. *Bote von Pommernstrand*, 23, no. 6(6 Februrary 1932).

98. Protokoll der erweiterten Arbeitsausschussens des Ev. Siedlungsdienst, 14 October 1931, Berlin-Charlottenburg, EOK Generalakten XV,65,IV, 8–9.

99. Comment of Hermann Schultz, Niederschrift über die Verhandlung der Superintendentenbesprechung, 2 February 1931, EOK Pomerania II,8,II, 26–35.

100. ESD to Superintendent Lauenburg, 12 March 1931, ADW, Bestand der Evangelischen Siedlungsdienst, AIV, 91, D13.

101. Verhandlungsniederschrift der 4. Beiratssitzung des Evangelischen Siedlungsdienst, 16 April 1931, EZA, EOK Generalakten XV, no. 65, IV.

102. Report of Superintendent of Pasewalk to Pomeranian Consistory, 30 July 1931, ADW, Bestand der Evangelischer Siedlungsdienst, AIII,67,C9.

103. Superintendent Pasewalk to Pomeranian Consistory, 24 April 1930, ADW, Bestand der Evangelischen Siedlungsdienst AIV,91,D13.

104. Pomeranian Consistory to EOK, 18 August 1933, EOK Generalakten XV,65,V.

105. "An das deutsche evangelische Volk," *Heimatklänge*, 9, no. 1(October 1924).

106. "Gutsbesitzer M. und G.," *Bote von Pommernstrand* 15, no. 14(6 April 1924).

107. Ernst Helmreich, *The German Churches under Hitler. Background, Struggle, Epilogue* (Detroit: Wayne State University Press, 1979), 89–94.

108. German-Austrian Mission. Histories of the Various Branches of the Mission from the Date of Their Organization to January 1, 1934, Archive, Historical Department, Church of Jesus Christ of Latter Day Saints (hereinafter cited as LDS), Salt Lake City, Utah. Latter Day Saints missions spread through Pomerania during the Weimar period with chapters established in Demmin (1924), Stargard (1918), Stolp (1930), Belgard (1930), and Kolberg (1926). Stettin, the oldest mission, was founded in 1894.

109. Frieda K. Pahnke, interview by Richard L. Jensen, Salt Lake City, Utah, 1980, typescript, pp. 9–10. LDS, Oral History Program. Pahnke's father had been deeply religious to begin with when he met with Mormon missionaries and was drawn to the Book of Mormon.

110. Protokoll des Ephoralkonvents Ostsprengel Stolp, 3–4 November 1925, EZA, EOK Pomerania II,8,II, 1–2.

111. Pomeranian Consistory to EOK, 6 February 1932, EZA, EOK Pomerania V, no. 302.

112. *Evangelisches Gemeindeblatt Rützow-Alt u. Neu Querzin* 5, no. 4(July 1925).

113. Pomeranian Consistory to EOK, 28 March 1925, EZA, EOK Generalakten XII, no. 161.

114. J. Alden and Amelia W. Bowers Oral History, interview by Gordon Irving. Salt Lake City, Utah, 1974, p. 15, LDS, Oral History Program; Mission President Otto Budge to "All District Presidents of the German Austrian Mission," LDS, German-Austrian Mission, President's Records, p. 35. See Lawrence Foster, *Religion and Sexuality. The Shakers, the Mormons and the Oneida Community* (Urbana and Chicago: University of Illinois Press, 1984), chapters 4 and 5 for an excellent discussion of the Latter Day Saints' beginnings. "Restoration" refers to the Mormon millenial expectation of a return to the faith and practices of early Christianity after the destruction of the old order, essentially the arrival of the kingdom of God on earth.

115. A letter from the Westphalian Consistory to EOK, 23 May 1919, EZA, EOK Generalakten XII,3,IV, remarked on the low social status of the New Apostles.

116. Address of L. H. Christian to Fall Council of Seventh Day Adventists, Milwaukee Auditorium, 13 October 1923, p. 7, Box 58 Secretariat general Files, no. 21,

Archives of the General Conference of the Seventh Day Adventist Church, Washington, D.C. (hereinafter cited as SDA).

117. L. R. Conradi to General Conference, Washington, D.C., 26 September 1921, SDA, Secretariat General Files, Box 47, no. 21.

118. Protokoll des Ephoralkonvents Ostsprengel Stolp, 3–4 November 1925, EZA, EOK Pomerania II,8,II, 3.

119. *Ev. Gemeindeblatt Kolberg St. Georg* 1, no. 4(April 1920); J. Alden and Amelia W. Bowers Oral History, p. 16, LDS Oral History Program. The Bowers noted that they had to talk with the women in order to get through to the men.

120. J. Alden and Amelia W. Bowers Oral History, pp. 8–9, LDS Oral History Program.

121. Robert Richards Burton Oral History, interview by William G. Hartley, Provo, Utah, 1973, typescript, p. 19, LDS Oral History Program.

122. Circular letter of Otto Budge, 22 August, 1933, LDS, German-Austrian Mission, President's Records, no. 23 1/2.

123. W. K. Ising to E. Kotz, 5 June 1927, SDA, Secretariat General files (no. 21), Box 74; Guy Dail to T. E. Bowen, 14 March 1934, SDA, Secretariat General Files (no. 21), (Asst. Secretary), Box 20.

124. Emma Stank Krisch Oral History, interview by Hazel M. Thomson, 1975, typescript, p. 4, LDS, Oral History Program, reports of her father's conversion after a vision; Hugo Fritz Diederich, Family History, ca. 1951, LDS, Oral History Program, notes that his mother wanted answers about life after death when her husband died; Johanna Liedtke Hermann, Reminiscenses 1943, LDS, Manuscript Histories of the Church, saw a vision of Jesus during World War I, and subsequently believed that Lutheranism contradicted the Bible; Fritz Paul Nestripke, Notebook, p. 55, LDS, Manuscript Histories of the Church, heard a voice while he was at the front as a soldier during World War I urging him to be baptized.

125. Polizeidirektor to Königlichen Kreishauptmannschaft, 25 April 1918, Kreishauptmannschaft to Kultus und öffentlichen Unterrichts, 4 June 1918, Acta die Gesellschaft der Mormonen betr. 1894–1933, Kultusministerium Dresden, LDS (cited in LDS catalogue as "Germany. Ministry of Religion"). See Gilbert Scharffe, *Mormonism in Germany. A History of the Church of Jesus Christ of Latter-Day Saints in Germany between 1840 and 1970* (Salt Lake City: Deseret Book Co., 1970), 66–78.

126. Address of L. H. Christian to SDA Fall Council, Milwaukee, 13 October 1923, pp. 5, 7 (quotation found on p. 5), SDA, Secretariat Files, no. 21, Box 58.

127. Address of L. H. Christian to Seventh Day Adventist Church Fall Council, Milwaukee Auditorium, 13 October 1923, p. 7, SDA Secretariat General Files, no. 21, Box 58.

128. Protokoll des Ephoralkonvents Ostsprengel Stolp, 3–4 November 1925, EZA, EOK Pomerania II,8,II, 2.

129. *Quarterly Review of the European Division of the General Conference of Seventh-Day Adventists. Statistical Report of Conferences and Mission Fields for the Fourth Quarter 1925*, vol. 11, no. 4, 2; Protokoll des Ephoralkonvents Ostsprengel Stolp, 3–4 November, 1925, EZA, EOK Pomerania II,8,II, 5, noted that the sects prospered in parishes that were too large.

130. Harold L. Welch (missionary from 1928–31) commended German Austrian Mission President Edward P. Kimball for obtaining more appropriate meeting places that would get the faithful out of beer and dance halls, LDS, Missionaries of the German-Austrian Mission, 1925–1937.

131. George Friedrich Wilhelm Kuehne, History of the George Friedrich Wilhelm Kuehne Family, p. 3, LDS Oral History Program.

132. Guy Dail to W. A. Spicer, 10 January 1929, SDA Presidential Files 11, Box 9.

133. Pomeranian Consistory to EOK, 13 April, 1920, EZA, EOK Generalakten XII,3,IV.

134. Greiffenhagen, ed. *Das evangelische Pfarrhaus*, introduction, 7–9.

135. Jean Wundlerlich Oral History, interview by James B. Allen. Orem, Utah, 1974, typescript, pp. 5–6, LDS, Oral History Program, recalls the anti-Mormon stereotypes that he confronted.

136. L. R. Conradi, Request for Prayer in Behalf of our Persecuted Believers in Soviet Russia (sometime in 1926), SDA, Presidential Files 11, Box 3; M. E. Kern to G. W. Schubert, 23 September 1935, SDA, Presidential Files, 11, Box 94.

137. Roy Anson Welker Oral History, interview by Richard L. Jensen, Star, Idaho, 1973, typescript, pp. 24, 58, 80–81, LDS, Oral History Program, commented that Hitler was helpful to the Mormons because he believed that motherhood was a great principle. Moreover, Welker maintained that the Führer's endorsement of a day of fasting in which the savings would go to the poor came partly through the influence of the Mormons. When asked of his overall impression of Hitler, Welker concluded that the Führer was willful and erratic and evidenced a lack of wisdom, but he showed the Latter Day Saints a great deal of consideration; Frederick Gassner Oral History, interview by Justus Ernst, 1985, typescript, pp. 8–10, LDS, Oral History Program, pp. 8–10: Erich Bernhardt (also in attendance for this interview) reports that in addition to his brother, other Mormon members sided with the Nazis, although the congregation itself was divided.

138. Frederick Gassner Oral History, pp. 8–9, LDS, Oral History Program. According to Erich Bernhardt in attendance for this interview, church members believed that "Hitler would do the work of the Lord. So that the Jews would go to Palestine because they were forced to it economically."

139. Christine Elizabeth King, *The Nazi State and the New Religions: Five Case Studies in Non-Conformity* (New York and Toronto: The Edwin Mellen Press, 1982), 121–45.

140. Hermann Kapler, President, Deutscher Evangelischer Kirchenausschuss to EOK, 20 March 1925, EZA, EOK Generalakten XII, no. 161.

141. Robert Richards Burton Oral History, p. 30, LDS, Oral History Program.

142. Frederick Gassner Oral History, pp. 7–8, LDS, Oral History Program.

143. Herbert Morris Butterfield Oral History, interview exerpts, Riverton, Utah, 1985, typescript, p. 3, LDS, Oral History Program.

144. LDS, Kolberg 1926–1930, General Minutes.

145. "Falsche Propheten," *Bote von Pommernstrand* 16, no. 10(8 March 1925); "Die 'ernsten Bibelforscher' und das Judentum," *Bote von Pommernstrand* 16, no. 11(15 March 1925); Pomeranian Consistory to EOK, 22 January 1924, EZA, EOK Generalakten XII, no. 161.

146. Tätigkeit des Evangelischen Konsistoriums, 1925, EZA, EOK Pomerania II,6,III, 11.

147. Pomeranian Consistory to EOK, 19 September 1930, EZA, EOK Pomerania V, no. 571.

148. Superintendent's letter (Bütow) enclosed in consistorial report, 29 June 1925; Pomeranian Consistory to EOK, 31 July 1925, EZA, EOK Generalakten XII, 47, Adh. A; Vordringen des katholizismus in der Grenzgebieten, report of 5 November 1927, EOK Generalakten XII, 47 Adh. A.

149. Niederschrift über die Verhandlung der Ephoren-Konferenz, 14–15 December 1921, EZA, EOK Pomerania II,8,II, 4–5.

150. Pomeranian Consistory to EOK, 18 June 1924, EOK Pomerania V, no. 524.

151. Vordringen des katholizismus in der Grenzgebieten, report of 5 November 1927, EZA, EOK Generalakten XII, 47, Adh. A, item h.

152. See Diephouse, *Pastors and Pluralism in Württemberg*, chapter 5, and Borg, *Old Prussian Church*, chapter 5.

153. *Bote von Pommernstrand* 15, no. 37(14 September 1924).

154. "Erziehung zur Ehrfurcht," *Gemeindeblatt für das Kirchspiel Großmöllen* 7, no. 5(May 1933).

155. See Cornelie Usborne, *The Politics of the Body in Weimar Germany. Women's Reproductive Rights and Duties* (Ann Arbor: University of Michigan Press, 1992), especially 69–101.

156. "Kinder," *Heimatklänge* 9, no. 6(March 1925).

157. "Ein bedeutsames soziales Hilfswerk der pommerschen Frauenhilfe," *Bote von Pommernstrand* 22, no. 19(10 May 1931).

158. "Die Frau in der Gemeinde," *Bote von Pommernstrand* 16, no. 39(27 September 1925).

159. "25 Jähriges Bestehen der Evangelischen Frauenhilfe in Pommern," *Heimatklänge* 9, no. 1(October 1924).

160. *Bote von Pommernstrand* 12, no. 18(1 May 1921); 116–19; Polizei Präsident Stettin to Regierungspräsident 21 October 1928, WAPS RS I, no. 12142. Report on the Preussenbund's commemoration of the seventieth birthday of the dead empress who the League believed had been betrayed by revolution.

161. Marie von Kleist to Konsistorialrat Meyer, 5 February 1927, DEF, Pommerscher Verband, August 1926 to March 1931, contains the complaint that collection money went mainly to the Ladies Aid; Marie von Kleist to Paula Müller-Otfried, 12 April 1930, same file.

162. "Dorfkirchentag in Eventin," *Bote von Pommernstrand* 22, no. 44(1 November 1931).

163. "Aus der Welt und Zeit," *Bote von Pommernstrand* 23, no. 43(23 October 1932).

164. *Ev. Gemeindeblatt Kolberg St. George* 3, no. 7(July 1922).

165. "Die deutsche Familie," *Bote von Pommernstrand* 14, no. 48(2 December 1923).

166. *Bote von Pommernstrand* 20, no. 7(10 February 1929).

167. "Ehe Reform," *Heimatklänge* 13, no. 1(April 1930).

168. See Usborne, *Politics of the Body*, 156–201 on abortion. As she points out, the law of 1926 (p. 174) was the most lenient in Europe, thus angering conservative circles, although the legislation fell short of the left's demands.

169. "Die drohende Vermännlichung der Frau," *Heimatbote. Gemeindeblatt für die evang. Gemeinden der Parochien Tempelburg, Draheim, Heinrichsdorf, Lubow, Pöhlen, Coprieben und Klaushagen mit Neuwuhrow* 8, no. 13(24 March 1929).

170. "Schutz der Unborenen!," *Heimatbote* 8, no. 30(21 July 1929).

171. "Aus Welt und Zeit," *Bote von Pommernstrand* 19, no. 28(8 July 1928). The church, however, usually did not oppose contraception if it was used to eliminate social diseases and further the cause of eugenics. See Usborne, *Politics of the Body*, 102–55.

172. "Eine Mutter," *Bote von Pommernstrand* 18, no. 19(8 May 1927).

173. "Wie es in der Welt aussieht," *Bote von Pommernstrand* 14, no. 26(1 July 1923).

174. Usborne, *Politics of the Body*, especially 71, 207.

175. For a work that underscores the revolutionary impact of subverting "natural" gender roles, see Judith Butler, *Gender Trouble. Feminism and the Subversion of Identity* (New York and London: Routledge, 1990).

176. "Endlose Ehescheidungen," *Heimatbote* 6, no. 23(5 June 1927); "Bolshevismus und Familie," *Heimatbote* 7, no. 27(1 July 1928).

177. *Bote von Pommernstrand* 16, no. 43(25 October 1925).

178. "Die ländliche Friedhof," *Bote von Pommernstrand* 22, no. 47(22 November 1931).

Chapter 5. Pomeranian Estate Owners

1. For discussions regarding agriculture's poststabilization predicament, see Abraham, *Collapse of the Weimar Republic*, 42–105, 171–219; Deiter Gessner, *Agrarverbände in der Weimarer Republik. Wirtschaftliche und soziale Voraussetzungen agrarkonservativer Politik vor 1933* (Düsseldorf: Droste Verlag, 1976), 13–65; Harold James, *The German Slump. Politics and Economics 1924–1936* (Oxford: Clarendon Press, 1986), 246–82; and Becker, *Handlungsspielräume der Agrarpolitik*, 210–49, especially 233–49. Despite agriculture's declining contribution to Reich income taxes after 1925 because of the low assessment of the value of its property, agriculture assumed a much higher tax burden overall when compared to the prewar period. Although the boon of inflation to farmers can be exaggerated, there is little doubt that the postinflation period was far worse. See Jonathan Osmond, *Rural Protest in the Weimar Republic. The Free Peasantry in the Rhineland and Bavaria* (New York: St. Martin's Press, 1993), 90–93.

2. Becker, *Handlungsspielräume der Agrarpolitik*, 189–99.

3. Ibid., especially 311–57.

4. A. J. Nichols, *Weimar and the Rise of Hitler*, 3rd ed. (New York: St. Martin's Press, 1991), 127.

5. Hans-Peter Ullmann, *Interessenverbände in Deutschland* (Frankfurt am Main: Suhrkamp, 1988), 151–53.

6. GHdA, Adelige Häuser A, XVIII (1985), 379–87. Rohr's family stemmed from ancient Bavarian nobility, some of whose members migrated eastward. Rohr died in 1970 after having served as an FDP representative to the Westphalian Landtag.

7. The legislation provided benefits for a minimum of twenty-six weeks. Employer and employee contributions funded the program, which the labor exchanges implemented. See Richard Evan's introduction, "The Experience of Unemployment in the Weimar Republic," in his and Dick Geary's edited volume of essays, *The German Unemployed. Experiences and Consequences of Mass Unemployment from the Weimar Republic to the Third Reich* (New York: St. Martin's Press, 1987), 5–6.

8. "Der Sinn der Landvolkbewegung," *Deutsches Adelsblatt. Zeitschrift für die Aufgeben der christliche Adels*, 46, no. 20 (11 July 1928).

9. Dopierała, *Ekonomiczne i Demograficzne Problemy*, document no. 14; Bericht der Landwirtschaftskammer für das Provinz Pommern über die Lage der Landwirtschaft, July 1927, WAPK-RK, no. 1812; Niederschrift. Betriebswirtschaftlichen Ausschuss, 26 June 1931 (Landwirtschaftskammer Pommern), GStA Merseburg, Rep. 87B, Ministerium für Landwirtschaft, Domänen und Forsten, no. 13429.

10. According to the Chamber of Agriculture, banks were making life difficult. Anlage, Bericht der Landwirtschaftskammer für das Provinz Pommern, December 1927, WAPK-RK, no. 1812.

11. WAPK-RK, nos. 1812 and 1813 carry Chamber of Agriculture reports from 1925 through 1931; Dopierała, *Ekonomiczne i Demograficzne Problemy*, document no. 19.

12. Bericht der Landwirtschaftskammer für das Provinz Pommern, July 1927, WAPK-RK no. 1812.

13. Anlage, Bericht der Landwirtschaftskammer für das Provinz Pommern, December 1927, WAPK-RK, no. 1812.

14. Pommerscher Landbund Kreisgruppe Franzburg to Pr. Landwirtschaftsminister, 4 June 1927, GStA Merseburg, Rep. 87B, Ministerium für Landwirtschaft, Domänen und Forsten, no. 20609.

15. Bericht der Landwirtschaftskammer für das Provinz Pommern, March 1928, WAPK-RK, no. 1812.

16. Landrat Stolp to Regierungspräsident Köslin, 6 March 1928 (report for 1926–27), WAPK-RK, no. 3407.

17. Dopierała, *Ekonomiczne i Demograficzne Problemy*, doc. no. 14, 82. Landeshauptleuten der Provinzen Ostpreussen, Grenzmark-Posen-Westpreussen, Pommern, Brandenburg, Niederschlesien und Oberschlesien, "Denkschrift. Die Not der preussischen Ostprovinzen," (1930), 16.

18. Schmidt and Blohm, *Landwirtschaft von Ostpreußen und Pommern*, 50–52.

19. Bericht der Landwirtschaftskammer für das Provinz Pommern, March 1930, WAPK-RK, no. 1813.

20. "Denkschrift. Die Not der preussischen Ostprovinzen," 16ff.

21. Bericht der Landwirtschaftskammer für das Provinz Pommern, November 1931, WAPK-RK, no. 1813.

22. For the impact of such an ill-fated agenda on Brüning in particular, see Gerhard Schulz, *Von Brüning zu Hitler. Der Wandel des politischen Systems in Deutschland 1930–1933* (Berlin, New York: Walter de Gruyter, 1992), 804–18, Heinrich August Winkler, *Weimar 1918–1933. Die Geschichte der ersten deutschen Demokratie* (Munich: Verlag, C. H. Beck, 1993), 467–76; Mommsen, *Die verspielete Freiheit*, 436–42.

23. Marie von Kleist to DEF Geschäftsstelle, 13 December 1930, DEF Hannover, Pommerscher Verband, 1926–1930.

24. "Heimat Chronik 1929," *Unser Pommernland* 15, no. 1 (January 1930).

25. "31. Hauptversammlung des Vereins der Industriellen Pommerns," *Pommersche Tagespost*, 20, no. 85 (10 April 1930).

26. Bericht der Landwirtschaftskammer für das Provinz Pommern, November 1930, WAPK-RK, no. 1813. See also Schmidt and Blohm, *Die Landwirtschaft von Ostpreußen und Pommern*. 53–54.

27. "Noch einmal: Retten den Osten," *Pommersche Tagespost* 20, no. 84 (9 April 1930).

28. Richard Blanke, *Orphans of Versailles. The Germans in Western Poland 1918–1939* (Lexington: The University Press of Kentucky, 1993), 127.

29. See the telling argument of Nichols, *Weimar and the Rise of Hitler*, 157, against Knut Borchardt's now famous thesis regarding the unavailability of options except deflation open to Brüning. Estate owners were exempt from the sort of retrenchment that Brüning had to pursue.

30. Mommsen, *Die verspielte Freiheit*, 383. For discussions of *Osthilfe*, see Becker, *Handlungsspielräume der Agrarpolitik*, 265, James, *German Slump*, 266–76; Karol Fiedor, "The Character of State Assistance to the German Eastern Provinces in the Years 1919–1933," *Polish Western Studies* 7, no. 2(1971): 309–26; Bruno Buchta, *Die*

Junker und die Weimarer Republik. Charakter und Bedeutung der Osthilfe in den Jahren 1928–1933 (Berlin: VEB Deutscher Verlag der Wissenschaften, 1929); Gessner, *Agrardepression und Präsidialregierung*, 103ff; and especially Schulz, *Von Brüning zu Hitler*, 62–73, 209–23, 532–36, 591–99, and 800–11.

31. Zu Punkt 9 der Tagesordnung der 45. Vollversammlung, 12 February 1932. Betrifft: Geschäftsbericht der Landwirtschaftskammer Pommern für das Kalendarjahr 1931, GStA Merseburg, Rep. 87B, Ministerium für Landwirtschaft, Domänen und Forsten, no. 13430.

32. The first was Gottfried Reinhold von Treviranus, succeeded by Hans von Schlange-Schöningen, both of them stalwarts of the DNVP.

33. Schmidt and Blohm, *Die Landwirtschaft von Ostpreußen und Pommern*, 56; Schulz, *Von Brüning zu Hitler*, 213–14, 533–36. Details as to the implementation of *Osthilfe* are found in an enclosure with a letter from the Pomeranian Consistory to EOK, 27 March 1931, EOK Generalakten XVI,65,III. The *Landstelle* consisted of an advisory council (*Beirat*) whose members included the provincial governor; the director of the provincial finance office; and representatives of the Chamber of Agriculture, industry, the various trade associations, and credit institutes, as well as a few agricultural laborers.

34. Anlage 8, Sicherung gegen Pachtausfälle im Osthilfe-Notgebiet, Auszug aus der Niederschrift der Finanzreferenten der deutschen evangelischen Landeskirchen, 20–21 October 1932, EZA, EOK Generalakten XVI,65,Bd. 1, Beiheft.

35. Niederschrift. 46 Vollversammlung der Landwirtschaftskammer Pommern, 16 March 1933, GStA Merseburg, Rep. 87B, Ministerium für Landwirtschaft, Domänen und Forsten, no. 13431.

36. Bemerkungen zur Zusammenstellung über Mitgliederbestand und angeschlossene Fläche (Stand vom 1 Juni 1931), BA Potsdam 61, Re 1, Reichslandbund, no. 236a.

37. Buchta, *Junker*, 110.

38. Viktoria Gräfin von Bismarck to Gräfin Freifrau von Nordenflycht, 18 March 1932, VL Rep. 38d, Karlsburg, no. 131.

39. "Ohne Rentabilität keine Osthilfe!", *Pommersche Tagespost*, vol. 21, no. 50 (28 February 1931). In fact, Brüning refused such extremes as a general cancellation of debts and an outright ban on compulsory auctions, despite the overall generosity of *Osthilfe*. See Dieter Gessner, "The Dilemma of German Agriculture during the Weimar Republic," in *Social Change and Political Development in Weimar Germany*, eds. Richard J. Bessel and E. J. Feuchtwanger (London and Totowa, N.J.: Barnes and Noble, 1981), 143.

40. Although Brüning refused to go as far as estate owners demanded, his government did succeed in reducing or eliminating taxes for hard-pressed *Gutsbesitzer*, simplifying the procedures for obtaining assistance, setting moratoriums on interest payments, granting greater protection against foreclosure, as well as squeezing the Prussian government out of the process. See Schulz, *Von Brüning zu Hitler*, esp. 591ff.

41. Abraham, *Collapse of the Weimar Republic*, 86–87.

42. "Machtvolle Landbundkundgebung," *Pommersche Tagespost* 22, no. 28 (3 February 1932).

43. Niederschrift, 46.Vollversammlung der Landwirtschaftskammer Pommern, 16 March 1933, GStA Merseburg 87B, Ministerium für Landwirtschaft, Domänen und Forsten, no. 13431.

44. "Machtvolle Landbundkundgebung," *Pommersche Tagespost* 22, no. 28 (3 February 1932).

45. "Das landwirtschaftliche Genossenschaft in Pommern," *Pommersche Tagespost* 21, no. 140 (18 June 1931).

46. Orlow, *Weimar Prussia, 1925–1933. The Illusion of Strength* (Pittsburgh: University of Pittsburgh Press, 1991), 94–95.

47. Landrat Cammin to Regierungspräsident Stettin, 20 April 1928, WAPS-RS I, no. 1835.

48. WAPK-RK, no. 3025, re: dissolution in Dramburg; WAPS-RS I, nos. 2270 and following contain correspondence having to do with the impact of the dissolution in Pomerania.

49. Georg Wussow to Regierungspräsident Köslin, 22 March 1928, WAPK-RK, no. 3025.

50. "Damit ernten wir kein Brot," *Pommersche Tagespost* 19, no. 161 (12 July 1929).

51. Czarnik, *Stosunki politiczne*, 54–55.

52. On the CNBLP as well as Hugenberg, see *Lexikon zur Parteiengeschichte*, Bd. 2(1984), 506–12; Larry Eugene Jones, "Crisis and Realignment: Agrarian Splinter Parties in the Late Weimar Republic, 1928–33," in *Peasants and Lords in Modern Germany. Recent Studies in Agricultural History*, ed. Robert G. Moeller (Boston, London, Sydney: Allen and Unwin, 1986), 198–232; Attila Chanady, "The Disintegration of the German National People's Party 1924–1939," *Journal of Modern History* 39, no. 1(1967): 65–91.

53. See Donna Karsch, *German Social Democracy and the Rise of Nazism* (Chapel Hill and London: University of North Carolina Press, 1993), 38–62. Unlike Karsch who focuses on the Müller cabinet, however, I am concentrating on parallel developments below.

54. "Gautagung der Landarbeiterverband (Gaue Mecklenburg und Pommern)," 43, no. 50 (1 March 1927); "Imposante Kundgebung der organisierten Landarbeiter des Kreises Randow," 43, no. 94 (23 April 1927).

55. Pommersche Landbund an sämliche Kreisgruppen, 24 December 1928, BA Potsdam, 61 Re 1, Reichslandbund, no. 250.

56. Abschrift. Arbeitgebergruppe des Pommerschen Landbunds to Vorsitzender der Kreisarbeitnehmergruppen des Pomm. Landbunds, 15 April 1929, signed by Flemming; Abschrift; Pommersche Landbund Hauptgeschäftsstelle, 3 December 1928, signed by von Oertzen; President, Landwirtschaftskammer Pommern to Landwirtschaftsminister, 12 July 1930. All of these are found in GStA Merseburg, Rep. 87B, Ministerium für Landwirtschaft, Domänen und Forsten, no. 330. The quotations are drawn from von Oertzen's statement.

57. For discussions of the *Landvolkbewegung*, see Rudolf Heberle, *From Democracy to Nazism* (Baton Rouge: Louisiana State University Press, 1945); Timothy Alan Tipton, *Nazism, Neo-Nazism and the Peasantry* (Bloomington and London: Indiana University Press, 1975); and Gerhard Stoltenberg, *Politische Strömungen im Schleswig-Holsteinischen Landvolk 1918–1933* (Düsseldorf: Droste Verlag, 1962), 107–15.

58. Prussian Minister of the Interior to Oberpräsidenten und Regierungspräsidenten, 5 June 1928, WAPS RS-I, no. 12135.

59. Regierungspräsident Köslin to Minister of Interior, 9 March 1928, WAPK-RK, no. 3407.

60. Landrat Pyritz to Regierungspräsident Stettin, 5 March 1928, WAPS-RS I, no. 12135.

61. Landrat Greifenberg to Regierungspräsident Stettin, 6 March 1928 noted that

3,000 to 3,500 persons attended the demonstration in his county; Landrat Greifenhagen to Regierungspräsident Stettin, 5 March 1928, reported a rally of 5,000
farmers. Both documents in WAPS-RS I, no. 12135.

62. Polizeipräsident Stettin to Regierungspräsident Stettin, 17 July 1929 and 27
August 1929, WAPS-RS I, no. 12135.

63. *Pommersche Tagespost* no. 164 (16 July 1929), found in GStA Merseburg, Rep.
77, Ministerium des Innern, Tit. 4043, no. 201.

64. Abschrift, Regierungspräsident Stettin to Oberpräsident Pommern, 11 May
1930 (includes report of rallies of September 1929); GStA Merseburg, Rep. 77, Ministerium des Innern, Tit. 4043, no. 201.

65. Regierungspräsident Köslin to Minister für Landwirtschaft, 8 June 1928,
WAPK-RK, no. 3407. The contrast between Pomerania's peasantry and that in the
south and west is noteworthy. See Osmond, *Rural Protest in the Weimar Republic.*

66. My summary of the Landrat reports, August 1929, WAPS-RS I, no. 12135.

67. Landrat Anklam to Regierungspräsident Stettin, 8 March 1928; WAPS RS-I,
no. 12135.

68. Regierungspräsident Köslin to Prussian Minister of Interior, 9 March 1931,
WAPK-RK, no. 3407.

69. Landrat Stolp to Regierungspräsident Köslin, 6 March 1928, WAPK-RK, no.
3407; Landrat Kolberg to Regierungspräsident Köslin, 6 March 1928 and 19 March
1928, Regierungspräsident Köslin to Landwirtschaftsminister, 8 June 1928, WAPK-
RK, no. 3407. The last two letters deal with a Dr. Wolfsgramm, a lawyer from
Kolberg who was ejected from the *Landbund*, but could not win support from the
peasants to broaden the *Bauernverein*.

70. Regierungspräsident Köslin to Minister des Innern, 9 March 1928, WAPK-RK,
no. 3407.

71. Schulz, *Von Brüning zu Hitler*, 209, 218.

72. Dopierała, *Ekonomiczne i Demograficzne Problemy*, document no. 4, 30.

73. Landrat Bütow to Regierungspräsident Köslin, 5 March 1928; WAPK-RK,
no. 3407.

74. Landrat Bublitz to Regierungspräsident Köslin, 5 March 1928; WAPK-RK,
no. 3407.

75. Regierungspräsident Stettin to Oberpräsident, 30 August 1929, WAPS-RS I,
no. 12134; Landrat Bütow to Regierungspräsident Köslin, 5 March 1928, Landrat
Kolberg to Regierungspräsident Köslin, 6 March 1928, Landrat Lauenburg to
Regierungspräsident Köslin, 8 March 1928, WAPK-RK, no. 3407.

76. Landrat Naugard to Regierungspräsident Stettin, 3 March 1928, WAPS-RS I,
no. 12135.

77. Landrat Cammin to Regierungspräsident Stettin, 5 March 1928; WAPS-RS I,
no. 12135.

78. "Zehn Jahre Pommersche Landbund," *General Anzeiger* no. 19 (19 January
1929), in WAPS-RS I, no. 12134. On Gerecke, see Jones, "Crisis and Realignment,"
208–9.

79. "Die Bauernfahne in Pommern," *Die Diktatur*, no. 10 (7 March 1931), found
in WAPS-RS I, no. 12134.

80. Prussian Minister of the Interior to Minister für Landwirtschaft, Domänen
und Forsten, 21 August 1931, GStA Merseburg Rep. 77, Ministerium des Innern,
Tit. 404, no. 201.

81. Abschrift, Minister of Interior, 31 March 1930, GStA Merseburg Rep. 77,
Ministerium des Innern, Tit. 4043, no. 201; Landrat Rügen to Regierungspräsident

Stralsund, 17 March 1930, VL, Rep. 65c, no. 981; Landrat Rügen to Regierungspräsident Stralsund, 18 March 1930, same file.

82. Landrat Rügen to Regierungspräsident Stralsund, 18 March 1930, VL, Rep. 65c, no. 981; Landrat Ückermünde to Regierungspräsident Stettin, 23 December 1930, WAPS-RS I, no. 12134.

83. Abschrift der Generalstaatsanwalt to Prussian Minister of Justice, 30 November 1931, GStA Merseburg, Rep. 77, Ministerium des Innern, Tit. 4043, no. 201.

84. *Grimmer Kreis-Zeitung*, no. 29 (11 December 1930), found in WAPS-RS I, no. 11974.

85. Abschrift, Landwirtschaftskammer für die Provinz Pommern, 16 January 1933, GStA Merseburg, Rep. 77, Ministerium des Innern, Tit. 4043, no. 201.

86. Landrat Cammin to Regierungspräsident Stettin, 26 August 1929, WAPS-RS I, no. 12135.

87. WAPS-RS I, no. 12135; WAPK-RK, no. 3410. These folders include a survey conducted in August 1929.

88. Landrat Greifswald to Regierungspräsident Stettin, 9 December 1930, WAPS-RS I, no. 11974.

89. Regierungspräsident Stettin to Prussian Minister of Interior, 9 March 1931; Prussian Minister of Interior to Minister für Landwirtschaft, Domänen und Forsten, 21 August 1931; GStA Merseburg, Rep. 77, Ministerium des Innern, Tit. 4043, no. 201.

90. Prussian Minister of the Interior to Ober and Regierungspräsidenten, 21 November 1930; Prussian Minister of the Interior to same, 4 January 1931; Prezydent Policji w Szczecinie, WAPS, no. 31.

91. Sabine Höner, *Der Nationalsozialistische Zugriff auf Preussen. Preussischer Staat und Nationalsozialistische Machteroberungsstrategie 1928–1934* (Bochum: Studienverlag Dr. N. Brockmeyer, 1984), 14–23. My discussion of the Nazi party's origins in Pomerania is drawn from Czarnik, *Stosunki polityczne*, 279–310; and Bogdan Drewniak, *Początki Ruchu Hitlerowskiego na Pomorzu Zachodnim 1923–1934* (Poznań Wydawnictwo Poznański, 1962), 17–23.

92. See Johnpeter Horst Grill, "The Nazi Party's Rural Propaganda before 1928," *Central European History* 15, no. 2 (1982): 149–85; Mommsen, *Die verspielte Freiheit*, 321–60; and Horst Gies, "The NSDAP and Agrarian Organizations in the Final Phase of the Weimar Republic," in *Nazism and the Third Reich*, ed. Henry A. Turner Jr. (New York: Quadrangle Books, 1972), 45–88.

93. WAPS-RS I, no. 11978. Lippmann wanted the party to remained dissolved.

94. Consult John E. Farquharson, *Plow and Swastika. The NSDAP and Agriculture in Germany 1928–45* (London and Beverly Hills: Sage Publications, 1976), 13–34, and Gustavo Corni, *Hitler and the Peasants. Agrarian Policy of the Third Reich, 1930–1939*, trans. David Kerr (New York, Oxford; Munich: Berg, 1990), 18–38.

95. Bessel, *Political Violence*, 23.

96. See Thomas Childers, *The Nazi Voter. The Social Foundations of Fascism in Germany, 1919–1933* (Chapel Hill and London: University of North Carolina Press, 1983), 129–38; John A. Leopold, *Alfred Hugenberg. The Radical Nationalist Campaign against the Weimar Republic* (New Haven and London: Yale University Press, 1977), 55–83.

97. Jones, "Crisis and Realignment," 207–8.

98. Holzbach, *Das 'System Hugenberg'*, 237–8; Dieter Gessner, "'Grüne Front' oder 'Harzburger Front.' Der Reichslandbund in der letzten Phase der Weimarer Republik—Zwischen Wirtschaftlicher Interessenpolitik und Nationalistischen Revisionsanspruch," *Vierteljahrshefte für Zeitgeschichte* 29(1981), 113. Gessner points out that Hugenberg's support came primarily from the east.

99. Czarnik, *Stosunki politiczne*, 109–11.

100. Chanady, "Disintegration," 83.

101. VL Rep. 65c, no. 82 contains rejections of the Young Plan initiative; Landrat Anklam to Regierungspräsident Stettin, 28 September 1929, WAPS-RS I, no. 1821.

102. Wolfgang Runge, *Politik und Beamtentum in Parteienstaat. Die Demokratisierung Preußen zwischen 1918 und 1933* (Stuttgart: Ernst Klett Verlag, 1965), 150. Runge notes that the District president of Stettin, Halpern, a member of the DDP, threatened to punish 11 magistrates who refused to endorse Lippmann's appeal.

103. Landrat Anklam to Regierungspräsident Stettin, 28 September 1929, WAPS-RS I, no. 1821 (notes the signatures of several members of the Schwerin family and an advertisement appearing in the *Anklamer Zeitung*); Abschrift, Landeskriminalpolizei, 24 October 1929, WAPS-RS I, no. 1821. Among others, Wedel-Fürstensee, Rohr, Zitzewitz-Gross Gansen, and Wedel-Cremzow attacked Lippman for censuring officials who opposed the Young Plan.

104. "Inzwischen den Wahlen," *Pommern Stimmen* 6, no. 27 (7 December 1929).

105. WAPS-RS I, nos. 12007, 12008, 12010, 12011, 12012, 12018, 12019, 12020, 12021, 12023, 12024, 12025, and 12026 contain the reports on the positions of the various newspapers.

106. Flemming, "Konservatismus als 'nationalrevolutionäre Bewegung.' Konservative Kritik an der Deutschnationalen Volkspartei 1918–1933," in *Deutscher Konservatismus*, eds. Dirk Stegmann et al., 295–331.

107. Scheurig, *Ewald von Kleist-Schmenzin*, 65, 85.

108. Übersicht der Beamten pp. des Kreises Grimmen die sich in die Liste des Volksbegehren eintragen haben to Regierungspräsident Stralsund, undated; VL Rep. 65c, no. 82; "Warum Volksbegehren?," VL Rep. 65c, no. 83.

109. WAPS-RS I, no. 1821. This is one of the themes arising in the leaflets against the Young Plan.

110. "Soll die Ausverkauft der deutschen Wirtschaft so weitergehen?," *Pommersche Tagespost* 19, no. 201 (28 August 1929).

111. "Unser Kampf," *Pommersche Tagespost* 19, no. 223 (22 September 1929).

112. *Stargarder Zeitung*, no. 246 (19 October 1929), found in WAPS-RS I, no. 1821.

113. Landrat Rügen. Betrifft Erfahrungen mit das Vorschriften für die Durchführung des Volksbegehren "Freiheitsgesetz," 15 November 1929, VL Rep. 65c, no. 82 (no lobbying); Landrat Naugard to Regierungspräsident Stettin, 15 May 1928, WAPS-RS I, no. 1835. The county magistrate of Naugard, however, had previously decided to maintain the manorial district Kniephof (one of the estates in the Bismarck family) as the election district because of its distance from the nearest commune, 5 kilometers. To safeguard the fairness of elections, he designated the inspector's house as the locale, as opposed to a wing in the manor house itself.

114. An das Oberpräsidium der Provinz Pommern from Landesausschuss Pommern für das deutsche Volksbegehren 14 October 1929, VL Rep. 65c, no. 82.

115. Landrat Landkreis Greifswald to Regierungspräsident Stralsund, 14 November 1929; Landrat Rügen to Regierungspräsident Stralsund, 6 November 1929; VL Rep. 65c, no. 83.

116. Landrat Franzburg-Barth to Regierungspräsident Stralsund, 14 November 1929, VL Rep. 65c, no. 82.

117. Regierungspräsident Stralsund to Prussian Minister of the Interior, 18 November 1929, VL Rep. 65c, no. 83.

118. An den Herrn Abstimmungsleiter für das Volksbegehren-Freiheitsgesetz für den Stimmkreis 6 Pommern Herrn Oberregierungsrat Dr. Honig-Stettin, November 1929; VL Rep. 65c, no. 82; Landrat Landkreis Greifswald to Regierungspräsident Stralsund, 14 November 1929, VL Rep. 65C, no. 83.

119. Abschrift; Der Abstimmungsleiter für das Volksbegehren "Freiheitsgesetz," 4 November 1929, VL Rep. 65c, no. 83.

120. An den Herrn Abstimmungsleiter für das Volksbegehren-Freiheitsgesetz für den Stimmkreis 6 Pommern Herrn Oberregierungsrat Dr. Honig-Stettin, November 1929; VL Rep. 65c, no. 82.

121. Landrat Rügen to Regierungspräsident Stralsund, 6 December 1929; VL, Rep. 65c, no. 82.

122. Landrat Landkreis Greifswald to Regierungspräsident Stralsund, 23 December 1929; Landrat Grimmen to Regierungspräsident Stralsund, 13 January 1929; Regierungspräsident Stralsund to Prussian Minister of the Interior, 23 January 1930; VL, Rep. 65c, no. 83.

123. It is worth restating this argument in light of the appearance of Otmar Jung's article, "Plebiszitärer Durchbruch 1929? Zur Bedeutung von Volksbegehren und Volksentstscheid gegen des Youngplan für die NSDAP," *Geschichte und Gesellschaft* 15(1989), 489–51. Consistent with recent scholarship that stresses the Nazis' anti-elitism and independence, this piece significantly downplays the role of the Young Plan to the Nazis' eventual success.

124. Polizei Präsident Stettin to Regierungspräsident Stettin, October 1929, WAPS-RS I, no. 1821; Regierungspräsident Köslin to Oberpräsident Pommern, 31 August 1929, WAPK-RK, no. 3410.

125. Landrat Franzburg-Barth to Regierungspräsident Stralsund, 6 September 1929; VL Rep. 65c, no. 1009.

126. Abschrift. Landeskriminalpolizeistelle, 19 October 1929; VL Rep. 65c, no. 82.

127. Mommsen, *Die verspielte Freiheit*, 322–42.

128. Regierungspräsident Köslin to Prussian Minister of the Interior, 3 July 1929, GStA Merseburg Rep. 77, Ministerium des Innern, Tit. 4043, no. 296.

129. Ibid.

130. Regierungspräsident Köslin to Oberpräsident Pommern, 31 August 1929, WAPK-RK, no. 3410.

131. Wolfgang Schlichter, "Die Artamanenbewegung-eine Frühform des Arbeitsdienst und Kaderzelle des Faschismus auf dem Lande," *Zeitschrift für Geschichtswissenschaft* XVIII, no. 1(1970), 66–75, esp. p. 68.

132. Prussian Minister of the Interior to Ober and Regierungspräsidenten, 10 December 1926, WAPS-RS I, no. 12121.

133. Polizeipräsident Stettin to Regierungspräsident Stettin, 15 November 1929, WAPS-RS I, no. 12121.

134. Ibid.

135. Landrat Franzburg-Barth to Regierungspräsident Stralsund, 6 September 1929, VL Rep. 65C, no. 1009.

136. Landrat Anklam to Regierungspräsident Stettin, 14 September 1929, WAPS-RS I, no. 12121.

137. Zusammenstellung über die Mitgliederbewegung des Pomm. Landbundes. Vergleich zwischen 1.7.1924, 1.7.1925 und 1.7.1926, Mitgliederbewegung vom 1.7.1930 bis 1.7.1931, BA Potsdam 61, Re 1, Reichslandbund, nos. 234 and 236a. Cf. Osmond, *Rural Protest in the Weimar Republic*, especially 138–40, who argues

that the Nazis capitalized on the weakening of peasant organizations in the Rhineland and Bavaria, in turn the result of declining membership revenues.

Chapter 6: Fluid Boundaries

1. "Wahlerfolge des Nationalsozialistischen Deutschen Arbeiterpartei in Preußen
bei den Landtagswahlen am 20. May 1928 und den Provinziallandtagswahlen am
17. November 1929", GStA Merseburg, Ministerium des Innern, Rep. 77, Tit. 4043,
no. 283. Verzeichnis der Mitglieder der 59. Provinziallandtages von Pommern 1930
(Wahl vom 17 November 1929), VL Rep. 60, no. 477.

2. Pommersche Landbund to Zitzewitz-Groß Gansen, 15 November 1929, BA
Potsdam 61, Re 1, Reichslandbund, no. 252.

3. An die Kreisgruppe Regenswalde, 18 November 1929, BA Potsdam, 61 Re 1,
Reichslandbund, no. 252.

4. Pommersche Landbund (von Oertzen) to Zitzewitz-Gross Ganzen, 15 November 1929; *Der Nachbar* (Pasewalk) 6, no. 30 (24 November 1929); "Pommern!"
(DNVP campaign flyer), all found in BA Potsdam 61, Re 1, Reichslandbund, no.
252.

5. Falter, *Hitlers Wähler*, 110. Every third DNVP vote from 1928 went to the
Nazis in 1930; Gustavo Corni, *Hitler and the Peasants. Agrarian Policy of the Third
Reich, 1930–1939*, trans. David Kerr (New York, Oxford, Munich: Berg, 1990),
24–25.

6. *General-Anzeiger. Stettin und die Provinz Pommern*, 82, no. 256 (15 September
1930).

7. Landrat Cammin to Regierungspräsident Stettin, 21 June 1930, WAPS-RS I,
no. 12183.

8. Landrat Labes to Regierungspräsident Stettin, 11 November 1930, WAPS-RS
I, no. 1841.

9. Landrat Anklam to Regierungspräsident Stettin, 11 November 1930, WAPS-
RS I, no. 1841.

10. Landrat Demmin to Regierungspräsident Stettin, 5 November 1930, Landrat
Anklam to Regierungspräsident Stettin, 11 November 1930, WAPS-RS I, no. 1841.

11. Gliederung der NSDAP in Pommern in Bereiche der Regierungsbezirke Stettin und Stralsund, autumn 1930, VL, Rep. 65c, no. 978.

12. Chanady, "Disintegration," 85–86; Landrat Anklam to Regierungspräsident
Stettin, 11 November 1930, Landrat Saatzig to Regierungspräsident Stettin, 7 November 1930, WAPS-RS I, no. 1841.

13. Landrat Anklam to Regierungspräsident Stettin, 11 November 1930.

14. Landrat Cammin to Regierungspräsident Stettin, 1 November 1930, WAPS-
RS I, no. 1841.

15. Bismarck, *Aufbruch aus Pommern*, 91–92.

16. Landrat Swinemünde (Usedom-Wollin) to Regierungspräsident Stettin, 4 November 1930, WAPS-RS I, no. 1841.

17. See the review article by William W. Hagen, "The German Peasantry in the
Nineteenth and Early Twentieth Century: Market Integration, Populist Politics,
Votes for Hitler," *Peasant Studies* 14, no. 4 (1987): 287.

18. Landrat Saatzig to Regierungspräsident Stettin, 7 November 1930, WAPS-RS
I, no. 1841.

19. Polizei Präsident Stettin to Oberpräsident Pommern, 30 October 1930,
WAPS-RS I, no. 12158; *Neues Pommersche Tagesblatt*, 192 (24 August 1930), WAPS-

RS I, no. 12194; Abschrift Landjägeramt Misdroy, 25 August 1930, WAPS RS-I, no. 12200; Landrat Ückermünde to Regierungspraäsident Stettin, 25 June 1930, WAPS-RS I, no. 11993; Polizei Präsident Stettin to Oberpräsident Pommern, 6 January 1931, WAPS-RS I, no. 11995. See also Czarnik, *Stosunki polityczne*, 279–311.

20. Landrat Ückermünde to Regierungspräsident Stettin, 23 October 1930, WAPS-RS I, no. 1841.

21. Landrat Swinemünde (Usedom-Wollin) to Regierungspräsident Stettin, 4 November 1930, WAPS-RS I, no. 1840.

22. Landrat Naugard to Regierungspräsident Stettin, 29 October 1930, WAPS-RS I, no. 1840.

23. Landrat Anklam to Regierungspräsident Stettin, 11 November 1930, WAPS-RS I, no. 1841.

24. *Stargard Zeitung*, no. 110 (12 May 1930), found in WAPS-RS I, no. 11992.

25. Corni, *Nazism and the Peasants*, 18.

26. Polizei Präsident Stettin to Regierungspräsident Stettin, 4 April 1930, WAPS-RS I, no. 12195; "Versammlungsberichte," *Die Parole*, no. 2, 1 June, 1930.

27. Landrat Rügen to Regierungspräsident Stralsund, 6 September 1929; VL Rep. 65c, no. 1001.

28. "Die Stahlhelm, die Nationalsozialismus," *Pommersche Tagespost*, 20, no. 126 (31 May 1930).

29. Polizei Präsident Stettin to Oberpräsident Pommern, 25 July 1930, 4 August 1930, WAPS-RS I, no. 12146.

30. "Die Stahlhelm, die Nationalsozialismus," *Pommersche Tagespost*, 20, no. 126 (31 May 1930).

31. Orlow, *The Illusion of Strength*, 189–90.

32. Ibid., 122; Abschrift, Regierungspräsident Stralsund, Die Welt am Abend, 21 March 1930; VL, Rep. 65c, no. 1001.

33. "Nationalsozialismus und Landwirtschaft. Parteiamtliche Kundgebung über die Stellung der NSDAP zum Landvolk und Landwirtschaft," reprint from the *Völkischer Beobachter*, 7 March 1930, WAPK, Landratsamt Bütow, no. 11.

34. *Pommern Stimmen* 7, no. 18 (12 September 1930).

35. "Lügen, Lügen und abermals Lügen!," *Swinemünde Zeitung*, 11 September 1930, "National-Sozialistische Versammlung," *Demminer Tagesblatt*, 7 September 1930, found in WAPS-RS I, no. 1840.

36. Bericht über eine NSDAP Versammlung; Grimmen, 23 May 1930, found in VL Rep. 65c, no. 977.

37. "Nationalsozialismus und Eigentum," *General Anzeiger* 82, no. 245 (4 September 1930).

38. Polizei Präsident Stettin, 20 August 1930, WAPS-RS I, no. 12199.

39. *Neues Pommersche Tageblatt*, no. 192 (24 August 1930), found in WAPS-RS I, no. 12194.

40. Landrat Landkreis Greifswald to Regierungspräsident Stralsund, 10 February 1930, VL, Rep. 65c, no. 974.

41. For a recent piece that traces Hugenberg's negotiations with the Nazis, see Larry E. Jones, "'The Greatest Stupidity of My Life': Alfred Hugenberg and the Formation of the Hitler Cabinet, January 1933," *Journal of Contemporary History* 27(1992): 63–87.

42. "Die Ewig gestrigen," *Die Parole*, no. 11 (1 March 1931).

43. "Aus dem Rathaus," *Die Parole*, no. 6 (1 October 1930).

44. Pommersche Landbund Kreisgruppe Rügen. Nachtrag zum Vierteljahrsbe-

richt, 17 July 1931, BA Potsdam, 61, Re 1, Reichslandbund, no. 236a; *Pommersche Landbund Kreisgruppe Rügen an die Hauptgeschäftsstelle der Pommerschen Landbundes*, 28 May 1931, BA Potsdam, 61, Re 1, Reichslandbund, no. 253.

45. Polizei Präsident Stettin to Oberpräsident Pommern, 29 November 1930, WAPS-RS I, no. 12146; Joachim Copius, "Zur Rolle pommersche Junker und Großgrundbesitzer bei der Vorbereitung der faschistischen Diktatur und der imperialistischen Aggressionspolitik (Ein Beitrag zur Auseinandersetzung mit der Junkerapologetik des westdeutschen Publizisten Walter Görlitz)," *Wissenschaftliche Zeitschrift der Ernst-Moritz-Arndt-Universität Greifswald* 20 (1971): 113–16.

46. See Walker, "German Nationalist People's Party," 632, and Leopold, *Alfred Hugenberg*, 84; "Erklärung," 2 February 1932, BA Potsdam 61 Re 1, Reichslandbund, no. 239. Kleist-Schmenzin, among others, remained wedded to the concept of rule by aristocracy.

47. Orlow, *Illusion of Strength*, 204–5; Jones, "Crisis and Realignment," 219.

48. *Greifenhagen Kreiszeitung*, no. 59 (11 March 1931), found in WAPS-RS I, no. 1814.

49. Landrat Anklam to Regierungspräsident Stettin, 6 February 1931, WAPS-RS I, no. 12182.

50. "Vorwärts im Kampf für Heimat und Scholle!," *Pommersche Tagespost*, 21, no. 74 (28 March 1931).

51. "Das Front Marschiert," *Pommersche Tagespost*, 21, no. 85 (12 April 1931).

52. "Der Kampf für Preußens Freiheit," *Pommersche Tagespost*, 21, no. 91 (19 April 1931).

53. Ibid.

54. Polizei-Direktion Stadtkreis Greifswald, 16 July 1931, VL Rep. 65c, no. 977.

55. "Landvolk und Nationale Revolution," *Pommersche Tagespost*, 21, no. 64 (17 March 1931).

56. "Der Landbund ist zur Stelle," *Pommersche Tagespost*, 21, no. 79 (2 April 1931).

57. Orlow, *Illusion of Strength*, 204–5.

58. *Volksbote*, no. 96 (25 April 1931), found in WAPS-RS I, no. 1814.

59. Landrat Rügen to Regierungspräsident Stralsund, 5 May 1931; VL, Rep. 65c, no. 1009.

60. Regierungspräsident Stettin to Min. of Interior, 15 June 1931, reporting results of letters to him contained in WAPS-RS I, no. 1814.

61. Regierungspräsident Stettin to Prussian Minister of Interior, 15 June 1931, WAPS-RS I, no. 1814; Landrat Rügen to Regierungspräsident Stralsund, 17 June 1931, VL Rep. 65c, no. 1009.

62. "Vermerk," Regierungspräsident Stettin, 18 April 1931, WAPS-RS I, no. 1814.

63. *Pommersche Tagespost*, no. 222 (22 September 1931), found in WAPS-RS I, no. 12158.

64. "Sünden der Landwirtschaftskammer," *Die Diktatur*, no. 61 (21 October 1931), WAPS-RS I, no. 12182.

65. Ibid.

66. Bericht Bütow, Landbund Kreisgruppe Bütow, 25 September 1931, WAPK, Landratsamt Bütow, no. 23. For a discussion of the chamber elections and their impact on the National Rural League, see Gies, "NSDAP and Agrarian Organizations," 66–69.

67. See Chanady, "Disintegration," 89, who assigns Flemming to a group of estate owners who objected to the Hugenberg course.

68. Flemming to von Wedel-Kannenberg, 26 November 1931, BA Potsdam 61, Re 1, Reichslandbund, no. 241.

69. Flemming to Rohr, 29 January 1932; Rohr to Flemming, 31 January 1932; Oertzen to Rittergutspächter Schimmelpfenning-Drosedow, 17 February 1932, BA Potsdam 61, Re 1, Reichslandbund, no. 241; "Landwirtpolitik," *Pommersche Tagespost* 22, no. 13 (13 February 1932). For the results of Chamber of Agriculture elections elsewhere in Prussia, see Corni, *Hitler and the Peasants*, 30.

70. "Erklärung," 2 February 1932, BA Potsdam 61 Re, 1, Reichslandbund, no. 239.

71. "Diplomatie oder Revolution? Osthilfe und seine Landvolkführung," *Die Diktatur* 3, no. 75 (9 December 1931); "Bauernfang," Flugblatt (undated), BA Potsdam 61, Re 1, Reichslandbund, no. 239.

72. "Bauernfang," circular (undated), BA Potsdam 61, Re 1, Reichslandbund, no. 239.

73. "Die Bauernschaft für Adolf Hitler," *Der Pommersche Beobachter*, no. 48 (18 June 1932), WAPS-RS I, no. 12183.

74. Cf. Falter, "The Two Hindenburg Elections of 1925 and 1932."

75. Jones "'Greatest Stupidity,'" 66–68.

76. Orlow, *Illusion of Strength*, 157.

77. *General-Anzeiger*, 84, no. 74 (March 14, 1932); 84, no. 101 (11 April 1932).

78. *General-Anzeiger*, 84, no. 116 (26 April 1932); Orlow, *Illusion of Strength*, 159.

79. Orlow, *Illusion of Strength*, 158. Among the east Elbian districts of East Prussia, Frankfurt/Oder, Pomerania, Breslau, Liegnitz, Oppeln, and Magdeburg, Hitler's percentage of the vote was highest (52.6 percent) in Pomerania.

80. "Entscheidungsjahr 1932 mit Hugenberg," *Pommersche Tagespost*, 22, no. 9 (12 January 1932).

81. "Pommersche Wahl-Erkenntnis. Zurück zur Staatspolitik," no. 129, 16 March 1932, VL, Rep. 65c, no. 89.

82. Bessel, *Political Violence and the Rise of Nazism*, 58–59.

83. Polizei Präsident Stettin to Oberpräsident Pommern, 18 January 1932, WAPS-RS I, no. 12146.

84. Bessel, *Political Violence and the Rise of Nazism*, 72; Czarnik, *Stosunki polityczne*, 216–18.

85. Polizei Präsident Stettin to Oberpräsident, 3 March 1932, WAPS-RS I, no. 12146.

86. Polizei Präsident Stettin to Oberpräsident Pommern, 8 March 1932, WAPS-RS I, no. 12146.

87. "Streikbrecher und Stahlhelm," *Pommersche Zeitung*, 1 (17 July 1932).

88. See Abraham, *Collapse of the Weimar Republic*, 98, for Papen's agrarian program.

89. *General Anzeiger* 84, no. 212 (1 August 1932). The Nazis obtained 450,151 votes as opposed to the DNVP's 175,421. In the previous Reichstag election, the DNVP pulled 242,720 votes as opposed to the Nazis' 237,080.

90. Abschrift, Regierung Stettin, 29 September 1932, WAPS-RS I, no. 12197.

91. "Nationalsozialisten-Verfolgen in Naugard," *Pommersche Zeitung* 1 (26 July 1932).

92. Abschrift, Landrat Bütow, DNVP rally held 24 October 1932, WAPK, Landratsamt Bütow, no. 23.

93. "Nationalsozialismus-Eine Gefahr," in Scheurig, *Ewald von Kleist-Schmenzin*, 255–64. See also Jens Flemming, "Konservatismus als 'nationalrevolutionäre Beweg-

ung.' Konservative Kritik an der Deutschnationalen Volkspartei 1918–1933," in *Deutscher Konservatismus im 19. und 20. Jahrhundert*, eds. Dirk Stegmann, Bernd-Jürgen Wendt, and Peter-Christian Witt (Bonn: Verlag Neue Gesellschaft, 1983), 295–331, especially 323 ff.

94. "Die Deutschnationalen am Pranger," *Pommersche Zeitung* 1 (4 July 1932).

95. "Stettin voran!," *Die Parole*, no. 25 (1 May 1932).

96. "Deutschnationale Dolchstoß-politik," *Die Parole*, no. 30 (1 October 1932).

97. For more on this theme, see Bessel, *Political Violence and the Rise of Nazism*, especially 75–96.

98. "Die Schulung," *Die Parole*, no. 25 (1 May 1932).

99. Abschrift, Regierungspräsident Stettin, 30 January 1931, WAPS-RS I, no. 12195.

100. "Die Schulung," *Die Parole* no. 27 (1 July 1932).

101. See Oded Heilbronner, "Where Did Nazi Anti-Semitism Disappear to? Anti-Semitic Propaganda and Ideology of the Nazi Party, 1929–1933: A Historiographic Study," *Yad Vashem Studies* 21 (Jerusalem, 1991): 263–86.

102. Abschrift, Landrat Bütow, 25 March 1931 and 12 February 1932, WAPK, Landratsamt Bütow, no. 23.

103. Abschrift, Polizei Präsident Stettin, 19 October 1931, WAPS-RS I, no. 12195.

104. Amtsvorsteher Züllchow to Landrat Randow, 27 May 1932, WAPS-RS I, no. 12190.

105. "Nationalsozialismus und Landarbeiterschaft," *Der Pommersche Landarbeiter* 1, no. 1 (15 January 1932), BA Potsdam 61, Re 1, Reichslandbund, no. 239.

106. "Die Schulung," *Die Parole*, no. 26 (1 June 1932).

107. Amtsvorsteher Züllchow to Landrat Randow, 16 November 1931, WAPS-RS I, no. 12190.

108. "Die Schulung," *Die Parole* no. 32 (1 December 1932).

109. The most important work on the relationship between the Third Reich and the German working class remains Tim Mason's *Sozialpolitik im Dritten Reich. Arbeiterklasse und Volksgemeinsschaft*, 2nd ed. (Opladen: Westdeutscher Verlag, 1978). Although Mason argues that the Nazi regime was constantly sensitive to evidence of working-class dissatisfaction, a reaction that contributed greatly to the regime's aggressive expansionism, there is no denying that one of the pillars of Nazi rule was the brutal suppression of independent working-class organizations.

110. "Sehr rar ist das Kapital/und bei der Landwirtschaft zumal./Doch wahre Freunde sind nicht da,/Nur Nathan, der Geldverleiher ist nah./Mit listigsmitleidsvoller Miene/naht er sich dem gedrückten Mann/und bietet ihm zum Jahrestermine/ Eine Summe Geldes freundlich an./Ja, Ihr armen deutschen Bauern/Seid wahrhaftig zu bedauern!," *Die Posaune*, no. 9 (October 1931), found in WAPS-RS I, no. 12191.

111. Kriminal und Grenzkommissariat Bütow to Regierungspräsident Köslin, 12 March 1931, WAPK, Landratsamt Bütow, no. 23.

112. Werner Daitz, "Osthilfe, wie es sein soll," *Pommersche Zeitung* 1 (8 July 1932); "Wie ist der Landwirtschaft zu helfen?", *Pommersche Zeitung*, 1 (19 August 1932); Graf von der Goltz, "Wer hilft der Osthilfe,?" *Pommersche Zeitung* 1 (22 July 1932).

113. Schröder, "Antisemitismus und Faschismus in Pommern," 33–34.

114. "An die deutschen Landarbeiter," *Pommersche Zeitung*, 1 (30 August 1932).

115. Kriminal und Grenzkommissariat to Regierungspräsident Köslin, 19 May 1931, WAPK, Landratsamt Bütow, no. 23.

116. "Das Volk soll entscheiden," *Die Parole*, no. 16 (1 August 1931).

117. "Hin zu Pflug und Schwert," *Pommersche Tagespost*, 22, no. 61 (12 March 1932).

118. "Hin zu Pflug und Schwert!", *Pommersche Tagespost* 22, no. 61 (12 March 1932).

119. "Deutschnationaler Vorstoβ," *Pommersche Tagespost* 22, no. 43 (20 February 1932).

120. "Hin zu Pflug und Schwert!", *Pommersche Tagespost* 22, no. 61 (12 March 1932).

121. "Aufstieg und Niedergang des Adels, II, Das Ziel," *Pommern-Adel* 2, no. 2 (1 May 1926). For the racism and anti-Semitism of the nobility in general, especially younger nobles, see G. H. Kleine, "Adelsgenossenschaft und Nationalsozialismus," *Vierteljahrshefte für Zeitgeschichte* 26(1978): 100–43.

122. *Die Parole*, no. 1 (1 May 1930).

123. "Die Schulung," *Die Parole*, no. 29 (1 September 1932).

124. "Nationalsozialismus und Religion," *Die Posaune*, no. 9 (October 1931), WAPS-RS I, no. 12191.

125. Abschrift, Landrat Bütow, 16 February 1932, WAPK, Landratsamt Bütow, no. 23.

126. "Nationalsozialismus und Religion," *Die Posaune*, no. 9 (October 1931), WAPS-RS I, no. 12191.

127. "Pfaffentum," *Die Posaune* no. 18 (25 January 1932), WAPS-RS I, no. 12191.

128. "Die Parteien haben das Wort," *General-Anzeiger* 84, no. 62 (2 March 1932). For an argument that stresses the nobility's fear of the Nazis' Catholicism, see Brian Peterson, "Regional Elites and the Rise of National Socialism, 1920–33," in *Radical Perspectives on the Rise of Fascism in Germany, 1919–1945*, eds. Michael N. Dobkowski and Isidor Walliman (New York: Monthly Review Press, 1989), 172–93, especially 177.

129. Polizeiverwaltung Anklam, 6 March 1931, WAPS-RS I, no. 12182.

130. "Hakenkreuz oder Sovietstern?", *Die Posaune*, no. 18 (25 January 1932), WAPS-RS I, no. 12191.

131. "Kundgebung der NSDAP," *General-Anzeiger* 83, no. 334 (2 December 1931); Landrat Grimmen to Regierungspräsident Stettin, 5 November 1932, WAPS-RS I, no. 12187.

132. The doings of the SA are the dominant concern in correspondence between the district president of Stralsund and the county magistrates, VL, Rep. 65c, no. 88. The *Volksbote* column, no. 174 (27 July 1932), is contained therein.

133. Scheurig, *Ewald von Kleist-Schmenzin*, 116, 130.

134. Report on Ephoralkonvent in Köslin, 1–2 October 1924, EZA, EOK Pomerania II,8,II, 15–23.

135. "Aus der Welt und Zeit," *Bote von Pommernstrand,* 21, no. 39 (28 September 1930).

136. Pomeranian Consistory to EOK, 1 November 1933, EZA, EOK Pomerania V, no. 562; Pomeranian Consistory to EOK, 15 March 1928, EZA, EOK Pomerania V, no. 539; Gemeindekirchenrat Völzkow-Kussenow to EOK, 5 April 1930, EZA, EOK Pomerania V, no. 489.

137. Regierungspräsident Stettin to Minister des Innern, 14 February 1933, regarding Kirchenkreis Saatzig; GStA Merseburg, Rep. 77, Ministerium des Innern Tit. 546e.

138. Pomeranian Consistory to EOK, 8 July 1932, EZA, EOK Generalakten XVI,65,II, Beiheft.

139. Referat des Konsistorialrats Dr. Hünemörder auf der Finanzbesprechung, 20–21 October 1932, EZA, EOK Generalakten XVI, 65,I, Beiheft.

140. Silesian Consistory to EOK, 21 January 1933, EZA, EOK Generalakten XVI,65,I, Beiheft.

141. Auszug aus der Niederschrift der Finanzreferenten der deutschen evangelichen Landeskirchen am 20./21. Oktober 1932, EZA, EOK Generalakten XVI,65,I, Beiheft.

142. Pomeranian Consistory to EOK, 18 May 1933, EZA, EOK Generalakten XVI,65,I, Beiheft.

143. Auszug der Protokoll über die Sonderbesprechung mit den Herren Konsistorialpräsidenten am 11. Nov. 1932 im Rahmen der Besprechung im EOK mit den Herren Generalsuperintendenten und Konsistorialpräsidenten vom 10–11 Nov. 1932, EZA, EOK Generalakten, XVI,65,I, Beiheft.

144. Oberpräsident Pommern to Regierungspräsident Stettin, 30 October 1930, WAPS-RS I, no. 12146; *Pommersche Tagesblatt*, no. 222 (22 September 1931), found in WAPS-RS I, no. 12146.

145. Leitsätze für die politische Betätigung der Geistlichen, 20 May 1920, EZA, EOK Generalakten VI,2,II, document no. 55. For an excellent discussion of the German Evangelical Church's susceptibility to both conservatism and Nazism, see Kurt Nowak, *Evangelische Kirche und Weimarer Republik. Zum politischen Weg des deutschen Protestantismus zwischen 1918 und 1932* (Göttingen: Vandenhoeck and Ruprecht, 1981), especially 205 to conclusion.

146. "Heraus zur Kirchenwahl am 8. Januar 1933," *Die Parole*, no. 32 (1 December 1932); "Zu den Kirchenwahl in Spätherbst," *Pommersche Zeitung* 1, no. 30 (August 1932).

147. Niederschrift über die Superintendentenbesprechung am 19. und 20. September 1932, EZA, EOK Pomerania II, 8, Bd. 3.

148. Pomeranian Consistory to EOK, 6 June 1930, nos. 111–23, EZA, EOK Generalakten VI,16,II.

149. Kriminal und Grenzkommissariat to Regierungspräsident Köslin, 8 September 1930, WAPK, Landratsamt Bütow, no. 23.

150. Pomeranian Consistory to EOK, 15 July 1931, nos. 383–386, EZA, EOK Generalakten VI, 2, II.

151. Pomeranian Consistory to EOK, 21 February 1931, nos. 143–44, EZA, EOK Generalakten VI,2,II.

152. *Volksbote*, no. 288 (10 December 1931), *Naugarder Zeitung*, no. 293 (15 December 1931), both in WAPS-RS I, no. 12188.

153. *Evangelisches Gemeindeblatt für die Kirchengemeinden Anklams* 2, no. 2 (1 January 1933).

154. Marie von Kleist to DEF Vorstand, 29 November 1932, DEF, Pommerscher Verband, 1931–1935.

155. "Schlaglichter auf den neuesten Stand der Gottlosenbewegung," *Gemeindeblatt für das Kirchspiel Großmöllen* 7, no. 3 (March 1933).

156. EZA, Konvent Evangelischer Gemeinden aus Pommern, Bestand 46 A, no. 225.

157. "Schlaglichter auf den neuesten Stand der Gottlosenbewegung," *Gemeindeblatt für die Kirchspiel Grossmöllen*, 7, no. 3 (March 1933).

158. "Aus Welt und Zeit," *Bote von Pommernstrand*, 23, no. 7 (12 February 1933).

159. EZA, Konvent Evangelischer Gemeinde aus Pommern, Bestand 46 A, no. 225.

160. *Anklamer Zeitung*, no. 240 (13 October 1931), found in WAPS-RS I, no. 12182.

Epilogue. Pyrrhic Victory

1. Jones, "'The Greatest Stupidity of My Life,'" 63.

2. Ibid., 74.

3. Hans Mommsen, *Die verspielte Freiheit*, 546; Jones, "The Limits of Collaboration. Edgar Jung, Herbert von Bose and the Origins of the Conservative Resistence to Hitler 1933–34," in *Between Reform, Reaction and Resistance*, 468, sees the fragmentation among elites as crucial to the rise of the Nazis as the dissolution of the liberal parties or the division of the left, in some ways building on the main argument of David Abraham, *The Collapse of the Weimar Republic*, especially 271–318. An essential source for the final years of Weimar is the diary of Reinhold Quaatz, one of Hugenberg's closest political associates, *Die Deutschnationalen und die Zerstörung der Weimarer Republik. Aus dem Tagebuch von Reinhold Quaatz 1928–1933*, eds. Hermann Weiβ and Paul Hoser (Munich: R. Oldenburg Verlag, 1989). See also Larry Jones's explication of the diary, "Die Tage vor Hitlers Machtübernahme. Aufzeichnungen des Deutschnationalen Reinhold Quaatz," *Vierteljahrshefte für Zeitgeschichte* 4(1989): 759–74.

4. In addition to Abraham, *The Collapse of the Weimar Republic*, see Michael Geyer's analysis of the Reichswehr, "Professionals and Junkers: German Rearmament and Politics in the Weimar Republic," in *Social Change and Political Development in Weimar Germany*, eds. Richard J. Bessel and E.J. Feuchtwanger (London and Totowa, N.J.: Barnes and Noble, 1981), 77–133.

5. For a recent account of the "Panzerkreuzer affair," when the Müller cabinet's decision to build new cruisers triggered bitter divisions within the SPD, see Harsch, *German Social Democracy and the Rise of Nazism*, 46–51.

6. See the trenchant remarks of Hans-Erich Volkmann, "Deutsche Agrareliten auf Revisions-und Expansionskurs," in *Die deutschen Eliten und der Weg in den Zweiten Weltkrieg*, eds. Martin Broszat and Klaus Schwabe (Munich: C. H. Beck Verlag, 1989), 345–48.

7. Jones, "'The Greatest Stupidity of My Life,'" 71; Winkler, *Weimar*, 564.

8. For the scandal surrounding Hindenburg's estate, see Mommsen, *Die verspielte Freiheit*, 512; Winkler, *Weimar*, 578–92; and Schulz, *Von Brüning zu Hitler*, 1047–48.

9. Gessner, "'Grüne Front' oder 'Harzburger Front,'" 113. For the weakness of the CNBLP, the party-political embodiment of moderate conservatism, east of the Elbe, see Jones, "Crisis and Realignment," 214–15.

10. For a discussion of SA violence against the left in the Prussian east generally after the seizure of power, see Bessel, *Political Violence and the Rise of Nazism*, 119–46. For Pomerania, consult Drewniak, *Potzątki Ruchu Hitlerowskiego*, 110ff; Thévoz, Branig, and Loewenthal-Hensel, *Pommern 1934/35*, 29–30; and Schröder, "Antisemitismus und Faschismus in Pommern," 34.

11. For discussions of the ambivalent relations between conservatives and Nazis, see my "Consent and Dissent. The Confessing Church and Conservative Opposition to National Socialism," *Journal of Modern History* 53(1987): 53–87, and Jeremy Noakes, "German Conservatives and the Third Reich: An Ambiguous Relationship,"

in *Fascists and Conservatives*, 71–97.

12. Carsten, *Geschichte der Preußischen Junker*, 189, argues that the Junkers ceased to play their traditional political and social roles during the Third Reich, a point I believe needs to be qualified considerably.

13. Corni, *Hitler and the Peasants*, 120; Carsten, *Geschichte der preußischen Junker*, 164–65. For the purge of the civil service, see Caplan, *Government without Administration*, 141–49. The noble presence was most evident in the diplomatic corps. See Hans-Jürgen Doscher, *Das Auswärtige Amt im Dritten Reich* (Berlin: Siedler, 1987).

14. For the Nazis, privation during World War I brought about a weakening of the home front, and thus a leftist revolution, a dilemma that the party would avoid through a combination of brutal repression and aggressive expansionism to wrest from the occupied territories what the home front could not produce itself. See Tim Mason, *Sozialpolitik im Dritten Reich*, 15–42.

15. On the disgruntlement of the peasantry, see Ian Kershaw, *Popular Opinion and Political Dissent in the Third Reich* (Oxford: Clarendon Press, 1983), 33–65.

16. Corni, *Hitler and the Peasants*, 143–55; John Farquharson, *The Plough and the Swastika. The NSDAP and Agriculture in Germany 1928–45* (London and Beverly Hills: Sage Publications, 1976); Kleine, "Adelsgenossenschaft und Nationalsozialismus," 132.

17. See J. A. Perkins, "Nazi Autarchic Aspirations and the Beet-Sugar Industry, 1933–39," *European History Quarterly* 20, no. 4(1990): 497–518, especially 514. Labor shortages greatly increased the burden on rural women, according to Clifford R. Lovin, "Farm Women in the Third Reich," *Agricultural History* 60(1986): 105–23.

18. Corni, *Hitler and the Peasants*, 39–65, 92. Rohr survived in office until the following September when, following a conflict over government intervention in the cereals market, Darré engineered Rohr's resignation.

19. Ibid., 133–34.

20. Schmidt and Blohm, *Die Landwirtschaft von Ostpreußen und Pommern*, 86.

21. See Corni, *Hitler and the Peasants*, 97, who points to the resentment of small dairy farmers because the centralizing and stocking policies of the Reich Food Estate favored big dairy farmers and processing plants.

22. For the agrarian dynamics of Nazi expansionism, see especially ibid., 184–219, 245–68, and Volkmann, "Deutsche Agrareliten," 360–88.

23. "Pommerns Landbund Gleichgeschaltet," *Pommersche Zeitung* 2, (10 July 1933): "Der neue Pommersche Landbund," *Pommersche Zeitung* 2(16 July 1933). The standard essay on the *Gleichschaltung* of the National Rural League is Horst Gies, "NSDAP and Agrarian Organizations."

24. On the bitterness of Pomeranian conservatives toward the sellout of the Stahlhelm, see Bessel, *Political Violence and the Rise of Nazism*, 120. By 1942, Gauleiter Schwede-Coburg who replaced Karpenstein had replaced all conservative and noble county magistrates, according to Manfred Schultz-Plotius, "Ein Überblick über die Tätigkeit der Provinzialverwaltung von Pommern in den Jahren 1933 bis 1945," *Baltische Studien* 49(1962/63): 66–99.

25. Schröder, "Antisemitismus und Faschismus in Pommern in der Zwischenkriegsperiode," 35, and "Zur faschistischen Kriegsvorbereitung im Regierungsbezirk Stettin 1935 bis 1939," Diss. Greifswald, 1985.

26. "Heraus zur Kirchenwahl am 8. Januar 1933!," *Die Parole*, no. 33(1 January 1933).

27. "Die Pommersche Provinzialsynode," *Pommersche Zeitung* 2(31 August 1933). For full descriptions of the *Kirchenkampf* in Pomerania, see Kurt Meier, *Der Evangelische Kirchenkampf* (Halle, Göttingen: Vandenhoeck and Ruprecht, 1976), vol. 1, *Der Kampf um die "Reichskirche,"* 293–97; vol. 2, *Gescheiterte Neuordnungsversuche im Zeichen staatlicher "Rechtshilfe,"* 199–204, as well as Thévoz, Branig, and Loewenthal-Hensel, *Pommern 1934/35*, 112–55. According to Meier, vol. I., 294, Thom, then only thirty-five years old, came from East Prussia.

28. The literature on the conflicts generated by the Reich church is enormous. The standard church histories include J. S. Conway, *The Nazi Persecution of the Churches* (London: Weidenfeld and Nicolson, 1968); Ernst Helmreich, *The German Churches under Hitler*; Meier, *Der Evangelische Kirchenkampf*, 3 vols., and Klaus Scholder, *Die Kirchen und das Dritte Reich*, vol. 1, *Vorgeschichte und Zeit der Illusionen 1918–1934.* (Berlin and Vienna: Ullstein, 1977); vol. 2 *Das Jahr der Ernüchterung 1934. Barmen und Rom* (Berlin and Vienna: Ullstein, 1985). For a discussion of the oppositional Confessing Church as an example of the response of conservative elites to the Third Reich, see my *Confessing Church, Conservative Elites and the Nazi State*.

29. See Kershaw, *Popular Opinion and Political Dissent*, 156–223, 331–57.

30. Specialized works on the Barmen Synod include Rolf Ahlers, *The Barmen Theological Declaration of 1934. The Archeology of a Confessional Text* (Lewiston and Queenston: The Edwin Mellen Press, 1986); and Arthur C. Cochrane, *The Church's Confession under Hitler* (Philadelphia: The Westminister Press, 1962).

31. Meier, *Der Evangelische Kirchenkampf*, vol. I, 296.

32. Petition of four local church leaders in the Schlawe diocese to Bishop Thom, 4 April 1934, EZA, EOK Pomerania V/55–7/16776 Beiheft.

33. Pomeranian Consistory to EOK, 30 October 1933, EZA, EOK Pomerania V, no. 537; Scheurig, *Ewald von Kleist-Schmenzin*, 134, 143.

34. For these and similar illustrations of the role of patrons during the Third Reich, see Eberhard Bethge, *Dietrich Bonhoeffer. Man of Vision. Man of Courage*, trans. Eric Mosbacher et al. (New York and Evanston: Harper & Row, 1970), 357–59; Victoria Barnett, *For the Soul of the People. Protestant Resistance against Hitler* (New York and Oxford: Oxford University Press, 1992), 11, 37, 56, 82; von Jordan, *Unser Dorf*, 190–91; and Bismarck, *Aufbruch aus Pommern*, 64.

35. The "Church Movement of German Christians" (*Kirchenbewegung Deutsche Christen*) originated in Thuringia. Unlike more moderate German Christians who claimed to preserve the distinction between God's revelation and the course of German history, the Thuringians collapsed it. The radicals also wanted to create a single national church, as opposed to the Evangelical Reich Church, as a means of overcoming confessional differences. For the various factions of the German Christian Movement, see Kurt Meier, *Die Deutschen Christen: Das Bild einer Bewegung im Kirchenkampf des Dritten Reiches* (Göttingen: Vandenhoeck and Ruprecht, 1964), and James A. Zabel, *Nazism and the Pastors. A Study of the Ideas of Three Deutsche Christen Groups* (Missoula, Mont.: Scholars Press, 1976).

36. Helmreich, *The German Churches*, 149–50.

37. EZA, Konvent Evangelischer Gemeinden aus Pommern, Bestand 46A, no. 225. This former German Christian superintendent insisted on the guilt of both sides; the German Christians for putting too much trust in the party, the Confessing Church, particularly its most militant members, for dispensing with brotherhood in their dealings with the German Christians. Most German Christians, according to the superintendent, ended up in the neutralist "Wittenberg League."

38. Abschrift, Report on Pastor Damrow, 24 March 1935, WAPS-RS I, no. 12110.

39. Pomeranian Consistory to Reich and Prussian Land Bishop Müller, 22 March 1934, EZA, EOK Pomerania V, no. 615.

40. Landrat Franzburg-Barth to Regierungspräsident Stettin, 18 March 1935, WAPS-RS I, no. 12110.

41. Bericht über Spannungen zwischen Partei und evangelischer Bevölkerung, hervorgerufen durch absichtliche und systematische Eingriffe der Ortsgruppe der NSDAP in das Leben der Kirchengemeinden Tempelburg in Pommern," undated, EZA, EOK Pomerania V, 11–7/16919.

42. See again Kershaw, *Popular Opinion and Political Dissent*, 156–223, 331–57, as well as the relevant chapters in the same author's *The Hitler Myth. Image and Reality in the Third Reich* (Oxford: Clarendon Press, 1987).

43. Denkschrift über die Auswirkungen von Angriffen auf Kirche und Christentum und systematischen Eingriffen in das kirchliche Leben seitens der Ortsgruppe der NSDAP in Tempelburg in Pommern, 30 April 1939, EZA, EOK Pomerania V, 11–7/16919. As the ambiguity of this protest shows, the Evangelical attitude toward Nazi racial policy in the broadest sense, including that of the Confessing Church, was anything but categorically oppositional. See especially Wolfgang Gerlach, *Als die Zeugen Schweigen. Bekennende Kirche und die Juden* (Berlin: Institut Kirche und Judentum, 1987); and Jochen-Christoph Kaiser, *Sozialer Protestantismus im 20. Jahrundert. Beiträge zur Geschichte der Inneren Mission 1914–1945* (Munich: Oldenbourg, 1989), 227 to conclusion.

44. Jordan, *Unser Dorf*, 190, notes how such concerns were mitigated by the common syndrome, "if only the Führer knew."

45. Jürgen von Ramin, "Kampf dem Bolshevismus," *Deutsches Adelsblatt* 51, no. 12 (18 March 1933); Carl Friedrich von Behr-Pinnow, "Zur Rassenfrage," *Deutsches Adelsblatt* 51, no. 36(2 September 1933). For the affinity between landless nobles, in particular, and the Third Reich, see Kleine, "Adelsgenossenschaft und Nationalsozialismus."

46. Johnpeter Horst Grill, "Nobles in the SS: Old Wine in New Bottles?," unpublished paper given at the Southern Historical Conference, 1990, 11. My thanks to the author for sharing his work with me.

47. Bessel, *Political Violence and the Rise of Nazism*, 133. Schröder, "Antisemitismus und Faschismus in Pommern," 35.

48. The leading historian of the resistance is Peter Hoffmann. See especially his *The History of the German Resistance 1933–1945* (Cambridge, Mass.: MIT Press, 1979), and *German Resistance to Hitler* (Cambridge, Mass. and London: Harvard University Press, 1988).

49. The best essay on the future programs on the resistance still belongs to Hans Mommsen, "The Social Views and Constitutional Plans of the Resistance," in *The German Resistance*, ed. Hermann Graml (London: E. T. Batsford, 1970). For Moltke and the Kreisau Circle, see Freya von Moltke, Michael Balfour, and Julian Frisby, *Helmut James von Moltke 1907–1945. Anwalt der Zukunft* (Stuttgart: Deutsche Verlags-Anstalt, 1972), and Helmut James von Moltke, *Letters to Freya. 1939–1945*, trans. Beate Ruhm von Oppen (New York; Alfred A. Knopf, 1990).

50. The resistance is frequently mentioned in Junker memoirs. See Bismarck, *Aufbruch aus Pommern*, 152–61; Dönhoff, *Before the Storm*, 95–97; Jordan, *Unser Dorf*, 190. For a discussion of the nobility's involvement in the resistance, see Carsten, *Geschichte der preußischen Junker*, 184–89.

51. Scheurig, *Ewald von Kleist-Schmenzin*, 189; Thévoz, Branig, Loewenthal-

Hensel, *Pommern 1934/35*, 73. As Krockow in *Reise nach Pommern*, 219–20, acknowledges, active conspirators against the regime from the ranks of the Pomeranian nobility were few.

52. The most comprehensive study of the efforts of the German resistance to seek support from the Allies is that of Klemens von Klemperer, *German Resistance against Hitler. The Search for Allies Abroad. 1938–1945* (Oxford: Clarendon Press, 1992).

Bibliography

Archival Materials

Achiv des Diakonischen Werkes der EKD (ADW), Berlin-Dahlem

Akten des Central-Ausschusses für die innere Mission
  Bestand der Evangelischer Siedlungsdienst
  Gesamtverband der Ev. Arbeitervereine Deutschlands
  Provinzialvereins I.M. in den Provinz Pommern

Archive, General Conference of the Seventh Day Adventist Church (SDA), Washington, D.C.

Presidential Files
Secretariat (Assistant Secretary)
Secretariat General Files

Archives, Historical Department, The Church of Jesus Christ of Latter Day Saints (LDS), Salt Lake City, Utah

Correspondence, Diaries, Family Histories, Notebooks and Personal Papers: Ballard, Rulon Joseph; Diederich, Hugo Fritz; Hermann, Johanna Liedtke; Klopfer, W. Herbert; Kuehne, George Friedrich Wilhelm; Naegelin, Alfred Paul; Nestripke, Fritz Paul; Schulz, Alfred Paul Richard; Sloan, Robert Charles; Valentine, Hyrum Washington; Welker, Roy Anson
Interviews, Oral History Project: Bowers, J. Alden and Amelia W.; Burton, Robert Richards; Butterfield, Herbert Morris; Gassner, Frederick; Krisch, Emma Stank; Pahnke, Frieda K.; Walker, Roy Anson; Wunderlich, Jean
Local Records
  German-Austrian Mission, Histories of the various branches of the mission from the date of organization to January 1, 1934
  German-Austrian Mission, President's Records, 1930–34
  Church Records and Minute Books of Local Church Units, Stettin, Stettin-Centrum, Stettin-West, Stettin-North, Stettin-South, Kolberg, Belgard, Demmin, Stargard, Stolp
  Missionaries of the German-Austrian Mission, 1925–37

Bundesarchiv (BA), Abteilung Potsdam

Reichsarbeitsministerium
Reichslandbund

Deutscher Evangelischer Frauenbund (DEF), Hannover

Anteilnahme der Frau am Staatsleben
Korrespondenz mit verschiedenen Parteien
Ostdeutscher Verband 1912–28
Politische Stellung des Bundes
Pommerscher Verband 1917–26, 1931–35
Verhandlung mit anderen Vereinen nach der Generalversammlung

Evangelisches Zentralarchiv (EZA), Berlin

(Records of the Supreme Church Council [*Evangelischer Oberkirchenrat*] of the Old-Prussian Union Church):
Generalakten
> VI. Teilnahme von Geistlichen an Veranstaltungen politischer Vereine, Organizationen
> XII, 3, IV. Ein Sekte des sogennanten Neuapostolischen
> XII, 14, IV. Baptisten
> XII, 47, Adh. A. Katholizismus
> XII, 76, Beih. A, I, II, III. Volksmissionsarbeit
> XII, 130. Die Mormonen
> XII, 161. "Ernste Bibelforscher" und Wachtum-Bibel und Traktat-Gesellschaft
> XII, 171, I, III. Die Evangelischen Arbeitervereine
> XIV, 1, XXVI. Das Verhältnis der evangelischen Kirche zur Schule
> XIV, 9, II, III. Die Vokation und Verpflichtung der Schullehrer
> XIV, 37, I, IV–VI, VIII–IX, XI. Die Beibehaltung des evangelischen Religionsunterricht in der Schule
> XIV, 49, I. Der Lehrplan für den Religions-Unterricht in der Schule
> XIV, 46, I–II. Vorbildung der Volksschullehrer
> XV, 65, I–II, IV–VI. Siedlungswesen (Bodenreform)
> XVI, 65, I–III; XVI, 65, I, Beiheift. Die Reichshilfe für kulturelle und wirtschaftliche Zwecke

Konvent Evangelischer Gemeinden aus Pommern, Bestand 46 A
Sammlung hist. Ostgebiete, Pommern. Frageboden zum kirchlichen Brauchtum
Rep. Pommern
> I. Konsistorium
> II. Generalsuperintendenten, Superintendenten
> III. Provinzialsynode, Kreissynode
> V. Parochial-und Patronats-Verhältnisse
> VI. Kirchen-Visitation
> XII. Vereine

Geheimies Staatsarchiv preußischer Kulturbesitz (GStA), Abteilung Merseburg

Rep. 77 Preußisches Minsterium des Innern
Rep. 87B Preußisches Ministerium für Landwirtschaft, Domänen und Forsten
Rep. 151 IC Preußisches Finanzministerium
Rep. 169D Preußischer Landtag

Vorpommersches Landesarchiv (VL), Greifswald

Rep. 60 Oberpräsident von Pommern
Rep. 65c Regierung Stralsund
Rep. 38d Karlsburg (Bismarck-Bohlen)

Wojewódskie Archiwum Państwowe, Koszalin (WAPK)

Rejencja Koszalinska (Regierung Köslin)
Landratsamt Bütow/Bytów, 1919–1944r.

Wojewódskie Archiwum Państwowe, Szczecin (WAPS)

Prezydent Policji w Szczecinie/Polizei Präsident, Stettin
Rejencja Szczecinska/Regierung Stettin I

Published Sources

Primary Sources

Newspapers and Periodicals

Bote von Pommernstrand. Sontagsblatt der Synode Rügenwalde
Deutsches Adelsblatt. Zeitschrift der Deutschen Adelsgenossenschaft für die Aufgaben des christlichen Adels
Evangelische Frauenzeitung
Evangelisches Gemeindeblatt für die Kirchengemeinden Anklams
Ev. Gemeindeblatt Kolberg St. Georg
Evangelisches Gemeindeblatt Rützow-Alt u. Neu Querzin
Gemeindeblatt für den Kirchenkreis Bublitz
Gemeindeblatt für das Kirchspiel Großmöllen
General-Anzeiger für Stettin und die Provinz Pommern
Die Gutsfrau. Halbmonatsschrift für die gebildeten Frauen auf dem Lande
Heimatbote. Gemeindeblatt für die evang. Gemeinden der Parochien Tempelburg, Draheim, Heinrichsdorf, Lubow, Pöhlen, Coprieben und Klaushagen mit Neuwuhrow
Heimatklänge. Kirchliches Monatsblatt für die Synode Greifswald-Land
Kirchliches Amtsblatt des Evangelischen Konsistoriums der Provinze Pommern
Die Parole
Pommern-Adel. Nachrichtenblatt für die Mitglieder der Landesabteilung Pommern der Deutschen Adelsgenossenschaft
Pommern Stimmen
Pommersche Tagespost
Pommersche Zeitung
Unser Pommernland. Monatsschrift für das Kulturleben der Heimat
Volks-Bote

Memoirs

Bismarck, Klaus von. *Aufbruch aus Pommern. Erinnerungen und Perspektiven.* Munich and Zurich: Piper, 1993.
Braun, Otto. *Von Weimar zu Hitler*, 2nd ed. New York: Europa Verlag, 1940.

Bredow, Ilse Gräfin von. *Kartoffel mit Stippe. Eine Kindheit in der märkischen Heide.* Munich: DTV, 1992.

Dönhoff, Marion, Countess. *Before the Storm. Memories of My Youth in Old Prussia,* trans. Jean Steinberg. New York: Alfred A. Knopf, 1990.

Gehrmann, Karl-Heinz. *Wir Pommern.* Salzburg and Munich: Akademischer Gemeinschaftsverlag, 1951.

Jordan, Gerhard von. *Unser Dorf in Schlesien.* Berlin: Wolf Jobst Siedler Verlag, 1987.

Krockow, Christian Graf von. *Die Reise nach Pommern. Bericht aus einem verschwiegenen Land.* Stuttgart: Deutsche Verlags-Anstalt, 1985.

――――. *Die Stunde der Frauen. Bericht aus Pommern 1944 bis 1947. Nach der Erzählung von Libussa Fritz-Krockow.* Stuttgart: Deutsche Verlags-Anstalt, 1988.

Lehndorff, Hans Graf von. *Menschen, Pferde, weites Land. Kindheits-und Jugenderinnerungen.* Munich: Biederstein Verlag, 1980.

Noffke, Arthur. *Unvergessenes Pommern. Erzählungen aus Pommern.* Leer/Ostfriesland: Verlag Gerhard Rautenberg, 1976.

Normann, Käthe von. *Eine Tagebuch aus Pommern 1945/46.* Munich: Deutsche Taschenbuch Verlag, 1962.

Schwiers, Liselotte. *Das Paradies liegt in Pommern.* Munich: Droemer Knaur, 1989.

Zitzewitz-Muttrin, Friedrich Karl von. *Baustein aus dem Osten. Pommersche Persönlichkeiten im Dienste Ihres Landes und der Geschichte ihrer Zeit.* Leer: Verlag Gerhard Rautenberg, 1967.

Statistical and Documentary Material

Białecki, Tadeusz, Mazurkiewicz, Magdalena, and Muszyński, Adam. *Podziały Administracyjne Pomorza Zachodniego w latach 1800–1977.* Szczecin: Wydawnictwo Intitut Zachodnio-Pomorskiego, 1970.

Conrad, Johannes. *Agrarstatistische Untersuchungen. IV. Der Großgrundbesitz in Pommern. Jahrbücher für Nationalökonomie und Statistik,* III Folge, X Bd. Jena, 1895: 706–39.

Deutsches Adelsarchiv. *Genealogisches Handbuch des Adels.* 94 vols. to date. Limburg an der Lahn: C. A. Stark Verlag, 1951–.

Dopierała, Bogdan. *Ekonomiczne i Demograficzne Problemy Pormorza zachodniego w świetle Niemieckich materiałów źródłowych z lat 1926–1932.* Poznań: Institut Zachodni, 1959.

Finkelstein, H. W. Graf Finck von. *Die Entwicklung der Landwirtschaft in Preussen und Deutschland 1800–1930.* Würzburg: Holzner Verlag, 1960.

Golling, Martin. *Der Pflanzenbau in Pommern. Grundlagen, Entwicklung und Bedeutung.* Giessen: Wilhelm Schmitz Verlag, 1963.

Granzow, Klaus. *Pommern. Ein Bildband der Heimat mit 159 Fotografien.* Frankfurt: Verlag Weidlich, 1975.

Häbich, Theodor. *Deutsche Latifundien Ein Beitrag zur Berichtung unser Vorstellung von der bestehenden Verteilung des ländlichen Grundeigentums.* Königsberg: Gräfe and Unser, 1930.

Henatsch, Wilhelm Andreas. *Das Problem der ausländischen Wanderarbeiter unter besonderer Berücksichtigung der Zuckerproblem in der Provinz Pommern.* Greifswald: Verlag Ratsbuchhandlung, 1920.

Heß, Klaus. *Junker und bürgerliche Großgrundbesitzer im Kaiserreich. Landwirtschaftlicher Großbetrieb, Großgrundbesitz und Familien-fideikommiß in Preußen (1867/71–1914)* Stuttgart: Franz Steiner Verlag, 1990.

Holder-Egger, Kurt. *Der Gartenbau in Pommern.* Giessen: Wilhelm Schmitz Verlag, 1963.

Hübner, Hans, and Kathe, Heinz. *Lage und Kampf der Landarbeiter im Ostelbischen Preußen (Vom Anfang des 19. Jahrhunderts bis zur Novemberrevolution 1918/19),* 2 vols. Vaduz/Liechtenstein: Topos Verlag, 1977.

Jatzlauk, Manfred. "Agrarstatistische Untersuchungen über die Entwicklung der land-wirtschaftliche Großbetriebe in Deutschland zwischen den beiden Weltkriegen." *Wissenschaftliche Zeitschrift der Wilhelm Pieck Universität Rostock* 7/8 (1989): 36–42.

Landeshauptleuten der Provinzen Ostpreußen, Grenzemark Posen-Westpreußen, Pommern, Brandenburg, Niederschlesien und Oberschlesien. "Denkschrift. Die Not der preußischen Ostprovinzen." 1930.

Müller, Karl. *Die Frauenarbeit in der Landwirtschaft.* M. Gladbach: Volksvereinver-lag, 1913.

Murawski, Erich, and Stein, Erwin. *Pommern. Das Grenzland am Meer.* Berlin-Friedenau: Deutscher Kommunal Verlag, 1931.

Niekammer's Landwirtschaftliche Güter-Adreßbücher. Bd. 1 *Pommern. Güter-Adreßbuch der Provinz Pommern.* Leipzig: Reichenbach'sche Verlagsbuchhandlung, 1914. *Landwirtschaftliches Adreßbuch der Rittergüter und Güter der Provinz Pommern.* Leipzig: Reichenbach'sche Verlagsbuchhandlung, 1921.

Quarterly Review of the European Division of the General Conference of Seventh-Day Adventists. Statistical Report of Conferences and Mission Fields for the Fourth Quarter 1925, 11, no. 4.

Rohr, Hans Olof. *Bodentreuer Adel. Eine Statistik mit Zwei Landkarten.* Berlin: Verlag von Georg Stilke, 1936.

Sasse, Hermann, ed. *Kirchliche Jahrbuch für die evangelischen Landeskirchen Deutsch-lands,* vol. 61. Gütersloh: Verlag C. Bertelsmann, 1934.

Schmidt, Hermann, and Blohm, Georg. *Die Landwirtschaft von Ostpreußen und Pom-mern 1914/18–1939.* Marburg/Lahn: Johann-Gottfried-Herder-Institut, 1978.

Thévoz, Robert, Branig, Hans, and Loewenthal-Hensel, Cécile. *Pommern 1934/35 im Spiegel von Gestapo-Lageberichten und Sachakten,* 2 vols. Cologne and Berlin: G. Grote'sche Verlagsbuchhandlung, 1974.

Treichel, Walter. *Ostland Pommern. Streiflichter aus Wirtschaft, Kultur und Politik.* Berlin: Verlag der Nahe Osten, 1935.

Troschke, Paul. *Evangelische Kirchenstatistik Deutschlands.* Berlin-Charlottenburg: Deutsches Evangelisches Kirchenbundesamt, 1932–33.

Wegner, Marie. *Die Lage der Landarbeiterinnen.* Leipzig: Felix Dietrich, 1905.

Weigmann, Hans. *Auswirkungen der Siedlung. Baustein zum Siedlungsproblem.* V. Teil, *Siedlung und sozialer Aufstieg der Landarbeiter.* Berlin: Verlagsbuchhandlung Paul Parey, 1934.

Weiß, Hermann, and Hoser, Paul, eds. *Die Deutschnationalen und die Zerstörung der Weimarer Republik. Aus dem Tagebuch von Reinhold Quaatz 1928–1933.* Munich: R. Oldenbourg Verlag, 1989.

Weiland, Ruth. "Das soziale Schicksal der deutschen landwirtschaftlichen Wander-sarbeiterfamilien." *Jahrbuch für Nationalökonomie und Statistik.* Dritte Folge. 80 (1931): 744–78.

Secondary Sources

Abraham, David. *The Collapse of the Weimar Republic. Political Economy and Crisis,* 2nd ed. New York: Holmes and Meier, 1986.

Allen, William Sheridan. *The Nazi Seizure of Power. The Experience of a Single German Town*, rev. ed. New York: Franklin Watts, 1985.

Anderson, Margaret Lavinia. "Voter, Junker, *Landrat*, Priest: The Old Authorities and the New Franchise in Imperial Germany." *American Historical Review* 98, no. 5 (1993): 1448–74.

Applegate, Celia. *A Nation of Provincials. The German Idea of Heimat*. Berkeley and Los Angeles: University of California Press, 1990.

Augustine, Dolores L. "Arriving in the Upper Class. The Wealthy Business Elite of Wilhelmine Germany." In *The German Bourgeoisie. Essays on the Social History of the German Middle Class from the Late Eighteenth to the Early Twentieth Century*, eds. David Blackbourn and Richard J. Evans. London and New York: Routledge, 1991, 46–86.

———. "Very Wealthy Businessmen in Imperial Germany." *Journal of Social History* 22 (1988): 299–321.

Baranowski, Shelley. *The Confessing Church, Conservative Elites and the Nazi State*. Lewiston and Queenston: The Edwin Mellen Press, 1986.

———. "Continuity and Contingency: Agrarian Elites, Conservative Institutitons and East Elbia in Modern German History." *Social History* 12, no. 3 (1987): 285–308.

———. "Convergence on the Right. Agrarian Elite Radicalism and Nazi Populism in Pomerania, 1928–33." In *Between Reform, Reaction, and Resistance. Studies in the History of German Conservatism from 1789 to 1945*, eds. Larry Eugene Jones and James N. Retallack. Providence and Oxford: Berg, 1993, 407–32.

———. "The Sanctity of Rural Life: Protestantism, Agrarian Politics, and Nazism in Pomerania during the Weimar Republic." *German History* 9, no. 1(1991): 1–22.

Barkin, Kenneth. *The Controversy over German Industrialization, 1890–1902*. Chicago and London: University of Chicago Press, 1970.

Barnett, Victoria. *For the Soul of the People. Protestant Resistance against Hitler*. New York and Oxford: Oxford University Press, 1992.

Becker, Heinrich. *Handlungsspielräume der Agrarpolitik in der weimarer Republik 1923–1929*. Stuttgart: Franz Steiner Verlag, 1990.

Behrens, C.B.A. *Society, Government and the Enlightenment. The Experiences of Eighteenth-Century France and Prussia*. New York: Harper & Row, 1985.

Berdahl, Robert. *The Politics of the Prussian Nobility. The Development of a Conservative Ideology 1770–1848*. Princeton: Princeton University Press, 1988.

Bergmann, Klaus. *Agrarromantik und Großstadtfeindschaft*. Meisenheim/Glan: Verlag Anton Hain, 1970.

Bessel, Richard. "Eastern Germany as a Structural Problem in the Weimar Republic." *Social History* 3, no. 2(1978): 199–218.

———. "The Formation and Dissolution of a German National Electorate: From Kaiserreich to Third Reich." In *Elections, Mass Politics, and Social Change in Modern Germany*, eds. Larry Eugene Jones and James N. Retallack. Cambridge: Cambridge University Press, 1992, 399–418.

———. *Germany after the First World War*. Oxford: Clarendon Press, 1993.

———. *Political Violence and the Rise of Nazism. The Storm Troopers in Eastern Germany 1925–1934*. New Haven and London: Yale University Press, 1984.

———. "Why Did the Weimar Republic Collapse?" In *Weimar: Why Did German Democracy Fail?*, ed. Ian Kershaw. New York: St. Martin's Press, 1990, 120–52.

Bethge, Eberhard. *Dietrich Bonhoeffer. Man of Vision. Man of Courage*, trans. Eric Mosbacher et al. New York and Evanston: Harper & Row, 1970.

Bigler, Robert M. *The Politics of German Protestantism. The Rise of the Protestant Church Elite in Prussia, 1815–1848.* Berkeley and Los Angeles: University of California Press, 1972.

Blackbourn, David. "Between Resignation and Volatility. The German Petite Bourgeoisie in the Nineteenth Century." In *Shopkeepers and Master Artisans in Nineteenth-Century Europe,* eds. Geoffrey Crossick and Heinz-Gerhard Haupt. London and New York: Methuen, 1984, 35–61.

———. "Peasants and Politics in Germany, 1871–1914." *European History Quarterly* 14(1984): 47–75.

———, and Eley, Geoff. *The Peculiarities of German History: Bourgeois Society and Politics in Wilhelmine Germany.* Oxford: Oxford University Press, 1984.

Bölling, Rainer. *Sozialgeschichte der deutschen Lehrer. Ein Überblick von 1800 bis zur Gegenwart.* Göttingen: Vandenhoeck and Ruprecht, 1983.

Borchardt, Knut. *Wachstum, Krisen, Handlungsspielräume der Wirtschaftspolitik. Studien zur Wirtschaftsgeschichte des 19. und 20. Jahrhunderts.* Göttingen: Vandenhoeck and Ruprecht, 1982.

Borg, Daniel R. *The Old-Prussian Church and the Weimar Republic. A Study in Political Adjustment, 1917–1927.* Hanover and London: University Press of New England, 1984.

Bowman, Shearer Davis. *Masters and Lords. Mid-19th Century U.S. Planters and Prussian Junkers.* New York and Oxford: Oxford University Press, 1993.

Broszat, Martin. *Hitler and the Collapse of Weimar Germany,* trans. Volker Berghahn. Leamington Spa and New York: Berg Publishers, 1987.

Brunner, Reinhold. "Landadliger Alltag und primäre Sozialisation in Ostelbien am Ende des 19. Jahrhunderts." *Zeitschrift für Geschichtswissenshaft* 39, no. 10(1991): 995–1011.

Buchsteiner, Ilona. "Großgrundbesitz in Pommern zwischen 1871 und 1914. Soziale und ökonomische Veränderungen als Ausdruck der Integration des Adels in die bürgerliche Gesellschaft." *Zeitschrift für Geschichtswissenschaft* 37(1989): 329–36.

Buchta, Bruno. *Die Junker und die Weimarer Republik. Charakter und Bedeutung der Osthilfe in den Jahren 1928–1933.* Berlin: VEB Deutscher Verlag der Wissenschaften, 1959.

Butler, Judith. *Gender Trouble. Feminism and the Subversion of Identity.* New York and London: Routledge, 1990.

Cannadine, David. *The Decline and Fall of the British Aristocracy.* New Haven and London: Yale University Press, 1990.

Caplan, Jane. *Government without Administration. State and Civil Service in Weimar and Nazi Germany.* Oxford: Clarendon Press, 1988.

Cardoza, Anthony. *Agrarian Elites and Italian Fascism. The Province of Bologna 1901–1926.* Princeton: Princeton University Press, 1982.

———. "The Long Good-Bye: The Landed Aristocracy in North-Western Italy, 1880–1930." *European History Quarterly* 23, no. 3(1993): 323–58.

Carsten, Francis L. *Geschichte der preußischen Junker.* Frankfurt am Main: Suhrkamp, 1988.

———. *The Origins of Prussia.* Oxford: Clarendon Press, 1954.

Castellan, Georges. "Zur sozialen Bilanz der Prosperität 1924–1929." In *Industrielles System und politische Entwicklung in der Weimarer Republik,* eds. Hans Mommsen, Dietmar Petzina, and Bernd Weisbrod. Düsseldorf: Droste Verlag, 1971, 104–11.

Chanady, Attila. "The Disintegration of the German National People's Party 1924–1939." *Journal of Modern History* 39, no. 1(1967): 65–91.

Childers, Thomas. *The Nazi Voter. The Social Foundations of Fascism in Germany, 1919–1933*. Chapel Hill and London: University of North Carolina Press, 1983.

———. "The Social Language of Politics in Germany: The Sociology of Political Discourse in the Weimar Republic." *American Historical Review* 95, no. 2(1990): 331–58.

Clark, Christopher. "The Politics of Revival. Pietists, Aristocrats, and the State Church in Early Nineteenth-Century Prussia." In *Between Reform, Reaction, and Resistance. Essays in the History of German Conservatism*, eds. Larry Eugene Jones and James N. Retallack. Providence and Oxford: Berg Publishers 1993, 31–60.

Conway, John S. *The Nazi Persecution of the Churches, 1933–1945*. London: Weidenfeld and Nicolson, 1968.

Copius, Joachim. "Zur Rolle pommersche Junker und Großgrundbesitzer bei der Vorbereitung der faschistischen Diktatur und der imperialistischen Aggressionspolitik (Ein Beitrag zur Auseinandersetzung mit der Junkerapologetik des westdeutschen Publizisten Walter Görlitz)." *Wissenschaftliche Zeitschrift der Ernst-Moritz-Arndt-Universität Greifswald* 20(1971): 113–16.

Corni, Gustavo. *Hitler and the Peasants. Agrarian Policy of the Third Reich*, trans. David Kerr. New York, Oxford, Munich: Berg Publishers, 1990.

Czarnik, Andrzej. *Stosunki polityczne na Pomorzu Zachodnim w okręsie republiki weimarskiej 1919–1933*. Poznań: Wydawnictwo Poznańskie, 1983.

Diephouse, David J. *Pastors and Pluralism in Württemberg 1918–1933*. Princeton: Princeton University Press, 1987.

Drewniak, Bogusław. *Początki Ruchu Hitlerowskiego na Pomorzu Zachodnim 1923–1934*. Poznań: Wydawnictwo Poznańskie, 1962.

———. *Robotnicy sezonowi na Pomorzu Zachodnim (1890–1918)*. Poznań: Institut Zachodni, 1959.

Eggert, Oskar. *Geschichte Pommerns*. Glückstadt/Elbe: Buchdruckerei Gerhard Rautenberg, 1961.

Eley, Geoff. "Conservatives and Radical Nationalists in Germany: The Production of Fascist Potentials, 1912–28." In *Fascists and Conservatives. The Radical Right and the Establishment in Twentieth-Century Europe*, ed. Martin Blinkhorn. London: Unwin Hyman, 1990, 50–70.

———. "German History and the Contradictions of Modernity." In *Society, Culture and Politics in Germany 1870–1939. New Approaches*, ed. Geoff Eley. Ann Arbor: University of Michigan Press, forthcoming.

———. *Reshaping the German Right. Radical Nationalism and Political Change after Bismarck*. New Haven and London: Yale University Press, 1980.

Engelberg, Ernst. *Bismarck. Urpreuße und Reichsgründer*. Berlin: Siedler Verlag, 1985.

Evans, Richard J., and Lee, W. R. *The German Peasantry. Conflict and Community in Rural Society from the Eighteenth to the Twentieth Centuries*. New York: St. Martin's Press, 1986.

Falter, Jürgen. *Hitlers Wähler*. Munich: C. H. Beck, 1991.

———. "The Two Hindenburg Elections of 1925 and 1932: A Total Reversal of Voter Coalitions." *Central European History* 23, nos. 2/3(1990): 225–41.

———, and Kater, Michael. "Wähler und Mitglieder der NSDAP. Neue Forschungsergebnisse zur Soziographie des Nationalsozialismus 1925–1933." *Geschichte und Gesellschaft* 19(1993): 155–77.

Farquharson, John. *Plow and Swastika. The NSDAP and Agriculture in Germany 1928–45*. London and Beverly Hills: Sage Publications, 1976.

Fiedor, Karol. "The Character of State Assistance to the German Eastern Provinces in the Years 1919–1933." *Polish Western Studies* 7, no. 2(1971): 309–26.

Field, Geoffrey. "Religion in the German Volksschule, 1890–1928." *Leo Baeck Institute Yearbook* 25(1980): 41–77.

Flemming, Jens. "Die Bewaffnung des 'Landvolks.' Ländliche Schutzwehren und agrarischer Konservatismus in der Anfangsphase der Weimarer Republik." *Militärgeschichtliche Mitteilungen* 2(1979): 7–29.

———. "Großagrarische Interessen und Landarbeiterbewegung. Überlegungen zur Arbeiterpolitik des Bundes der Landwirte und des Reichslandbundes in der Anfangsphase der Weimarer Republik." In *Industrielles System und politische Entwicklung in der weimarer Republik*, eds. Hans Mommsen, Dietmar Petzina, and Bernd Weisbrod. Düsseldorf: Droste Verlag, 1974, 745–78.

———. "Konservatismus als 'nationalrevolutionäre Bewegung.' Konservative Kritik an der Deutschnationalen Volkspartei." In *Deutscher Konservatismus am 19. und 20. Jahrhundert. Festschrift für Fritz Fischer zum 75. Geburtstag und 50. Doktorjubiläum*, eds. Dirk Stegmann, Bernd-Jürgen Wendt, and Peter-Christian Witt. Bonn: Verlag Neue Gesellschaft, 1983, 295–331.

———. "Landarbeiter zwischen Gewerkschaften und 'Werksgemeinschaft.'" *Archiv für Sozialgeschichte* 14 (1974): 351–418.

———. *Landwirtschaftliche Interessen und Demokratie. Ländliche Gesellschaft, Agrarverbände und Staat 1890–1925.* Bonn: Verlag Neue Gesellschaft, 1978.

———. "Die vergessene Klasse: Literatur zur Geschichte der Landarbeiter in Deutschland." *Historische Zeitschrift.* Sonderheft 15 (1986): 389–418.

Fontane, Theodor. *Effi Briest*, trans. Douglas Parmée. Middlesex: Penguin Books, 1967.

Foster, Lawrence. *Religion and Sexuality. The Shakers, the Mormons and the Oneida Community.* Urbana and Chicago: University of Illinois Press, 1984.

Foucault, Michel. *Discipline and Punish. The Birth of the Prison*, trans. Alan Sheridan. New York: Vintage Books, 1979.

Fricke, Dieter, et al. *Lexikon zur Parteiengeschichte. Die bürgerliche und kleinbürgerliche Parteien in Deutschland (1789–1945)*, vols. 1–3. Cologne: Paul Rugenstein, 1985.

Fritsche, Peter. *Rehearsals for Fascism. Populism and Political Mobilization in Weimar Germany.* New York and Oxford: Oxford University Press, 1990.

Gall, Lothar. *Bismarck. The White Revolutionary*, vol. 1, trans. J. A. Underwood. London, Boston, Sydney: Allen and Unwin, 1986.

Gerschenkron, Alexander. *Bread and Democracy in Germany*, rev. ed. Ithaca and London: Cornell University Press, 1989.

Gessner, Dieter. *Agrardepression und Präsidialregierung in Deutschland 1930 bis 1933. Probleme des Agrarprotektionismus am Ende der Weimarer Republik.* Düsseldorf: Droste Verlag, 1977.

———. *Agrarverbände in der Weimarer Republik. Wirtschaftliche und soziale Voraussetzung en Voraussetzungen agrarkonservativer Politik vor 1933.* Düsseldorf: Droste Verlag, 1976.

———. "The Dilemma of German Agriculture during the Weimar Republic." In *Social Change and Political Development in Weimar Germany*, eds. Richard J. Bessel and E. J. Feuchtwanger. London and Totowa, N.J.: Barnes and Noble, 1981, 134–54.

———. "'Grüne Front' oder 'Harzburger Front.' Der Reichslandbund in der letzten Phase der Weimarer Republik—Zwischen Wirtschaftlicher Interessenpolitik und Nationalistischen Revisionsanspruch." *Vierteljahrshefte für Zeitgeschichte* 29(1981): 110–23.

Geyer, Michael. "Professionals and Junkers: German Rearmament and Politics in the Weimar Republik." In *Social Change and Political Development in Weimar Ger-*

many, eds. Richard J. Bessel and E. J. Feuchtwanger. London and Totowa, N.J.: Barnes and Noble, 1981, 77–133.

————, and Jarausch, Konrad. "The Future of the German Past. Transatlantic Reflections for the 1990s." *Central European History* 22, nos. 3/4(1989): 229–59.

Gibson, Ralph, and Blinkhorn, Martin. *Landownership and Power in Modern Europe*. London: HarperCollins Academic, 1991.

Gies, Horst. "The NSDAP and Agrarian Organizations in the Final Phase of the Weimar Republic." *Nazism and the Third Reich*, ed. Henry Ashby Turner Jr. New York: Quadrangle Books, 1972, 45–88.

Gilbert, Ursula Susanna. *Hellmuth von Gerlach (1866–1935). Stationen eines deutschen Liberalen vom Kaiserreich zum 'Dritten Reich'*. Frankfurt am Main, Bern, New York: Peter Lang, 1984.

Görlitz, Walter. *Die Junker. Adel und Bauer im deutschen Osten; geschichtliche Bilanz von 7. Jahrhunderten*. Glucksburg: Ostsee, C. A. Starke, 1956.

————. "Widerstand gegen den Nationalsozialismus in Pommern." *Baltische Studien* 48(1961): 63–74.

Grill, Johnpeter Horst. *The Nazi Movement in Baden 1920–1945*. Chapel Hill: University of North Carolina Press, 1983.

————. "The Nazi Party's Rural Propaganda before 1928." *Central European History* 15, no. 2(1982): 149–85.

————. "Nobles in the SS: Old Wine in New Bottles?" Paper given at Southern Historical Association Annual Meeting, 1990.

Groh, John E. *Nineteenth Century German Protestantism. The Church as Social Model*. Washington, D.C.: University Press of America, 1982.

Hagen, William. "The German Peasantry in the Nineteenth and Early Twentieth Century: Market Integration, Populist Politics, Votes for Hitler." *Peasant Studies* 14, no. 4(1987): 273–91.

————. "How Mighty the Junkers? Peasant Rents and Seigneurial Profits in Sixteenth-Century Brandenburg." *Past and Present* 108(1985): 80–116.

————. "The Junkers' Faithless Servants: Peasant Insubordination and the Breakdown of Serfdom in Brandenburg-Prussia." In *The German Peasantry. Conflict and Community in Rural Society from the Eighteenth to the Twentieth Centuries*, eds. Richard J. Evans and W. R. Lee. New York: St. Martin's Press, 1986, 71–101.

————. "Seventeenth-Century Crisis in Brandenburg: The Thirty Years' War, the Destabilization of Serfdom, and the Rise of Absolutism." *American Historical Review* 94, no. 2(1989), 302–335.

————. "Working for the Junker: The Standard of Living of Manorial Laborers in Brandenburg, 1584–1610." *Journal of Modern History* 58, no. 1(1986): 143–58.

Haines, Michael R. "Agriculture and Development in Prussian Upper Silesia, 1846–1913." *Journal of Economic History* 42(1982): 355–84.

Hamilton, Richard. *Who Voted for Hitler?* Princeton: Princeton University Press, 1982.

Harnisch, Hartmut. *Kapitalistisch Agrarreform und Industrielle Revolution. Agrarhistorische Untersuchungen über das ostelbische Preußen zwischen Spätfeudalismus und bürgerlichdemokratischer Revolution von 1848/49 unter besonderer Berücksichtigung der Provinz Brandenburg*. Weimar: Hermann Böhlaus Verlag, 1984.

Harsch, Donna. *German Social Democracy and the Rise of Nazism*. Chapel Hill and London: University of North Carolina Press, 1993.

Heberle, Rudolf. *From Democracy to Nazism*. Baton Rouge: Louisiana State University Press, 1945.

Heilbronner, Oded. "Where Did Nazi Anti-Semitism Disappear to? Anti-Semitic Propaganda and Ideology of the Nazi Party, 1929–1933: A Historiographic Study." *Yad Vashem Studies* 21(1991): 263–86.

Helmreich, Ernst. *The German Churches under Hitler. Background, Struggle, Epilogue* Detroit: Wayne State University Press, 1979.

Herbert, Ulrich. *A History of Foreign Labor in Germany, 1880–1980. Seasonal Workers/Forced Laborers/Guest Workers*, trans. William Templer. Ann Arbor: University of Michigan Press, 1990.

Hoffmann, Peter. *German Resistance to Hitler*. Cambridge, Mass., and London: Harvard University Press, 1988.

———. *The History of the German Resistance 1933–1945*. Cambridge, Mass.: MIT Press, 1979.

Holmes, Kim R. "The Forsaken Pact: Agrarian Conservatism and National Socialism in Germany." *Journal of Contemporary History* 17(1982): 671–88.

Holzbach, Heidrun. *Das 'System Hugenberg.' Die Organisation bürgerlicher Sammlungspolitik vor dem Aufstieg der NSDAP*. Stuttgart: Oldenbourg, 1981.

Höner, Sabine. *Der Nationalsozialistische Zugriff auf Preußen. Preussischer Staat and Nationalsozialistische Machteroberungstrategie 1928–1934*. Bochum: Studienverlag Dr. N. Brockmeyer, 1984.

Hühne, Werner. *A Man to Be Reckoned With: The Story of Reinhold von Thadden-Trieglaff*. London: SCM Press, 1962.

Hussain, Athar, and Tribe, Keith. *Marxism and the Agrarian Question*, vol. 1 *German Social Democracy and the Peasantry 1899–1907*. Atlantic Highlands, N.J.: Humanities Press, 1981.

Ishiguro, Kazuo. *The Remains of the Day*. New York: Alfred A. Knopf, 1989.

Jacke, Jochen. *Der Kirchliche Protestantismus nach dem Zusammenbruch des Staatskirchentums 1918*. Hamburg: Hans Christian Verlag, 1976.

James, Harold. *The German Slump. Politics and Economics 1924–1936*. Oxford: Clarendon Press, 1986.

Jatzlauk, Manfred. "Landarbeiter, Bauern und Großgrundbesitzer in der Weimarer Republik." *Zeitschrift für Geschichtswissenschaft* 39, no. 9(1991): 888–905.

Jones, Larry Eugene. "Crisis and Realignment: Agrarian Splinter Parties in the Late Weimar Republic, 1928–33." In *Peasants and Lords in Modern Germany. Recent Studies in Agricultural History*, ed. Robert G. Moeller. Boston: Allen and Unwin, 1986, 198–232.

———. *German Liberalism and the Dissolution of the Weimar Party System 1918–1933*. Chapel Hill and London: University of North Carolina Press, 1988.

———. "'The Greatest Stupidity of My Life': Alfred Hugenberg and the Formation of the Hitler Cabinet, January 1933." *Journal of Contemporary History* 27(1992): 63–87.

———. "Die Tage vor Hitlers Machtübernahme. Aufzeichnungen des Deutschnationalen Reinhold Quaatz." *Vierteljahrshefte für Zeitgeschichte* 4(1989): 759–74.

———, and Jarausch, Konrad. *In Search of a Liberal Germany. Studies in the History of German Liberalism from 1789 to the Present*. New York, Oxford, Munich: Berg Publishers, 1990.

Jung, Otmar. "Plebiszitärer Durchbruch 1919? Zur Bedeutung von Volksbegehren und Volksentscheid gegen des Youngplan für die NSDAP." *Geschichte und Gesellschaft* 15(1989): 489–510.

Kaak, Heinrich. *Die Gutswirtschaft. Theoriegeschichtliche Untersuchungen zum Agrarwesen im ostelbischen Raum*. Berlin and New York: Walter de Gruyter, 1991.

Kaiser, Jochen-Christoph. *Frauen in der Kirche. Evangelische Frauenverbände im Spannungsfeld von Kirche und Gesellschaft 1890–1945. Quellen und Materialen*, ed. Annette Kuhn. Düsseldorf: Schwann, 1985.

Kaschuba, Wolfgang, and Lipp, Carola. *Dörfliche Überleben. Zur Geschichte materieller und sozialer Reproduktion ländlicher Gesellschaft im 19, und frühen 20. Jahrhundert.* Tübinger: Tübinger Vereinigung für Volkskunde, 1982.

Kater, Michael H. *The Nazi Party. A Social Profile of Members and Leaders, 1919–1945.* Cambridge, Mass.: Harvard University Press, 1983.

Kershaw, Ian. *The 'Hitler Myth.' Image and Reality in the Third Reich.* Oxford: Clarendon Press, 1987.

———. *Popular Opinion and Political Dissent in the Third Reich. Bavaria 1933–1945.* Oxford: Clarendon Press, 1983.

———, ed. *Weimar: Why Did German Democracy Fail?* New York: St. Martin's Press, 1990.

King, Christine. *The Nazi State and the New Religions: Five Case Studies in Non-Conformity.* New York and Toronto: The Edwin Mellen Press, 1982.

Klatt, Änne. *Familienaufstieg und Siedlung. Eine Untersuchung über den Einfluß der Siedlung auf den Sozialen Aufstieg einzelner Landarbeiterfamilien.* Wupperthal, Elberfeld: J. H. Born, 1933.

Kleine, Georg H. "Adelsgenossenschaft und Nationalsozialismus." *Vierteljahrshefte für Zeitgeschichte* 26(1978): 100–43.

Klemperer, Klemens von. *German Resistance against Hitler. The Search for Allies Abroad, 1938–1945.* Oxford: Clarendon Press, 1992.

Kluge, Ulrich. *Die deutsche Revolution 1918/1919. Staat, Politik und Gesellschaft zwischen Weltkrieg und Kapp-Putsch.* Frankfurt am Main: Suhrkamp, 1984.

Koch, H. W. *A History of Prussia.* London and New York: Longman, 1978.

Kocka, Jürgen, ed. *Bürgertum im 19. Jahrhundert. Deutschland im europäischen Vergleich*, 2 vols. Munich: DTV, 1988.

Kohler, Eric D. "Revolutionary Pomerania, 1919–20. A Study in Majority Socialist Agricultural Policy and Civil-Military Relations." *Central European History* 9(1976): 250–93.

Koshar, Rudy. *Social Life, Local Politics and Nazism. Marburg 1880–1935.* Chapel Hill and London: University of North Carolina Press, 1986.

Krockow, Christian Graf von. "Gutshaus und Pfarrhaus." In *Das evangelische Pfarrhaus. Eine Kultur-und Sozialgeschichte*, ed. Martin Greiffenhagen. Stuttgart: Kreuz Verlag, 1984.

Lamberti, Marjorie. *State, Society and the Elementary School in Imperial Germany.* New York and Oxford: Oxford University Press, 1989.

Lehmann, Hartmut. "Pietism and Nationalism: The Relationship between Protestant Revivalism and National Renewal in Nineteenth-Century Germany." *Church History* 51(1982): 39–53.

Leopold, John A. *Alfred Hugenberg. The Radical Nationalist Campaign against the Weimar Republic.* New Haven and London: Yale University Press, 1977.

Lieven, Dominic. *The Aristocracy in Europe, 1815–1914.* New York: Columbia University Press, 1992.

Lovin, Clifford. "Farm Women in the Third Reich." *Agricultural History* 60(1986): 105–23.

Lüdtke, Alf. *Police and State in Prussia, 1815–1850*, trans. Pete Burgess. Cambridge and New York: Cambridge University Press, 1989.

Lühe, Irmgard von der. *Elizabeth von Thadden. Ein Schicksal unserer Zeit.* Düsseldorf and Cologne: Eugen Dietrich Verlag, 1966.

Machtan, Lothar, and Milles, Dietrich. *Die Klassensymbiose von Junkertum und Bourgeoisie. Zum Verhältnis von gesellschaftlicher und politischer Herrschaft in Preußen-Deutschland 1850–1878/79*. Frankfurt am Main: Verlag Ullstein, 1980.

Mann, Thomas. *Buddenbrooks*, trans H. T. Porter. New York: Vintage Books, 1961. (Originally published in 1901.)

Manstein, Peter. *Die Mitglieder und Wähler der NSDAP 1919–1933. Untersuchungen zu ihrer schichtmäßigen Zusammensetzung*. Frankfurt am Main, Bern, New York, Paris: Peter Lang, 1988.

Mason, Tim. *Sozialpolitik im Dritten Reich. Arbeiterklasse und Volksgemeinschaft*, 2nd Opladen: Westdeutscher Verlag, 1978.

Mayer, Arno J. *Politics and the Diplomacy of Peace-Making 1918–1919*. New York: Alfred A. Knopf, 1967.

Meier, Kurt. *Die Deutschen Christen: Das Bild einer Bewegung im Kirchenkampf des Dritten Reiches*. Göttingen: Vandenhoeck and Ruprecht, 1964.

———. *Der Evangelische Kirchenkampf*, 3 vols. Göttingen: Vandenhoeck and Ruprecht, 1977–84.

Moeller, Robert G. "Dimensions of Social Conflict in the Countryside." *Central European History* 14(1981): 142–68.

———. *German Peasants and Agrarian Politics 1914–1924. The Rhineland and Westphalia*. Chapel Hill and London: University of North Carolina Press, 1986.

———. *Peasants and Lords in Modern Germany. Recent Studies in Agricultural History*. Boston, London, Sydney: Allen and Unwin, 1986.

Möller, Horst. *Parliamentarismus in Preußen 1919–1932*. Dösseldorf: Droste Verlag, 1985.

Mommsen, Hans. "The Social Views and Constitutional Plans of the Resistance." In *The German Resistance*, ed. Hermann Graml. London: E. T. Batsford, 1970.

———. *Die verspielte Freiheit. Der Weg von der Republik von Weimar in den Untergang 1918 bis 1933*. Berlin: Propyläen Verlag, 1989.

Moore, Barrington. *The Social Origins of Dictatorship and Democracy*. Boston: Beacon Press, 1966.

Mosse, Werner. "Adel und Bürgertum im Europa des 19. Jahrhundert. Eine vergleichende Betrachtung." In *Bürgertum im 19. Jahrhundert. Deutschland im europäischen Vergleich*, ed. Jürgen Kocka. Munich: DTV, 1988, 276–314.

Mühlberger, Detlev. *Hitler's Followers. Studies in the Sociology of the Nazi Movement*. London and New York: Routledge, 1991.

Muncy, Lysbeth. *The Junker in the Prussian Administration under William II, 1888–1914*. Providence: Brown University Press, 1944.

———. "The Prussian *Landräte* in the Last Years of the Monarchy: A Case Study of Pomerania and the Rhineland in 1890–1918." *Central European History* 6(1973): 299–338.

Nichols, A. J. *Weimar and the Rise of Hitler*, 3rd ed. New York: St. Martin's Press, 1991.

Noakes, Jeremy. "German Conservatives and the Third Reich: An Ambiguous Relationship." In *Fascists and Conservatives. The Radical Right and the Establishment in Twentieth-Century Europe*, ed. Martin Blinkhorn. London: Unwin Hyman, 1990, 71–97.

———. *The Nazi Party in Lower Saxony 1921–1933*. London: Oxford University Press, 1971.

Nowak, Kurt. *Evangelische Kirche und Weimarer Republik. Zum politischen Weg des deutschen Protestantismus zwischen 1918 und 1932*. Göttingen: Vandenhoeck and Ruprecht, 1981.

Orlow, Dietrich. *Weimar Prussia 1918–1925. The Unlikely Rock of Democracy*. Pittsburgh: University of Pittsburgh Press, 1986.

———. *Weimar Prussia 1925–1933. The Illusion of Strength*. Pittsburgh: University of Pittsburgh Press, 1991.

Osmond, Jonathan. *Rural Protest in the Weimar Republic. The Free Peasantry in the Rhineland and Bavaria*. New York: St. Martin's Press, 1993.

Patch, William L., Jr. *Christian Trade Unions in the Weimar Republic, 1918–1933. The Failure of "Corporate Pluralism."* New Haven and London: Yale University Press, 1985.

Pedlow, Gregory. *The Survival of the Hessian Nobility 1770–1870*. Princeton: Princeton University Press, 1988.

Perkins, J. A. "The Agricultural Revolution in Germany, 1815–1914." *Journal of European Economic History* 10(1981): 71–118.

———. "Dualism in German Agrarian Historiography." *Comparative Studies in Society and History* 28(1986): 287–306.

———. "The German Agricultural Worker, 1815–1914." *Journal of Peasants Studies* 11(1984): 3–27.

———. "Nazi Autarchic Aspirations and the Beet-Sugar Industry, 1933–39." *European History Quarterly* 20, no. 4(1990): 497–518.

Peterson, Brian. "Regional Perspectives on the Rise of National Socialism, 1919–33." In *Radical Perspectives on the Rise of Fascism in Germany, 1919–1945*, eds. Michael N. Dobkowski and Isidor Walliman. New York: Monthly Review Press, 1989, 172–93.

Peukert, Detlev J. K. *Der Weimarer Republik: Krisenjahre der Klassischen Moderne*. Frankfurt am Main: Suhrkamp, 1987.

Pflanze, Otto. *Bismarck and the Development of Germany*, vol. 1. *The Period of Unification, 1815–1871*. Princeton: Princeton University Press, 1990.

Plaul, Hainer. *Landarbeiterleben im 19. Jahrhundert. Eine volkskundliche Untersuchung über Veränderungen in der Lebensweise der einheimischen Landarbeiterschaft in den Dörfern der Magdeburger Börde unter Bedingungen der Herausbildung und Konsolidierung des Kapitalismus in der Landwirtschaft. Tendenzen und Treibkräfte*. Berlin: Akademie der Wissenschaft der DDR Zentralinstitut für Geschichte. Veröffentlichung zur Volkskunde und Kulturgeschichte, Band 65, 1979.

Poniatowska, Anna. *Polskie wychodźstwo sezonowe na pomorzu Zachodnim 1918–1939*. Poznań: Wydawnictwo Poznańskie, 1971.

Powis, Jonathan. *Aristocracy*. New York: Basil Blackwell, 1984.

Prelinger, Catherine. "The Nineteenth-Century Deaconessate in Germany. The Efficacy of a Family Model." In *German Women in the Eighteenth and Nineteenth Centuries. A Social and Literary History*, eds. Ruth-Ellen B. Joeres and Mary Jo Maynes. Bloomington: Indiana University Press, 1986, 215–29.

Puhle, Hans-Jürgen. *Agrarische Interessenpolitik und Preußischer Konservatismus im Wilhelminischen Reich (1893–1914). Ein Beitrag zur Analyse des Nationalismus in Deutschland am Beispiel des Bundes der Landwirte und der Deutsch-Konservative Partei*. Hannover: Verlag für Literatur und Zeitgeschehen, 1966.

Raupach, Hans. "Der interregionale Wohlfahrtsausgleich als Problem der Politik des Deutschen Reiches." In *Die Staats-und Wirtschaftskrise des Deutschen Reiches 1919/33*, ed. Hans Raupach, Dietmar Keese, Wilhelm Treue, Ursula Hallbruch, Rudolf Vierhaus, and Werner Conze. Stuttgart: Ernst Klett Verlag, 1967, 13–34.

Reif, Heinz. *Westfälischer Adel 1770–1860. Vom Herrschaftsstand zur regionalen Elite*. Göttingen: Vandenhoeck and Ruprecht, 1979.

Retallack, James N. *Notables of the Right. The Conservative Party and Political Mobilization in Germany 1876–1918*. Boston: Unwin Hyman, 1988.

Rosenberg, Hans. "Die Pseudodemokratisierung der Rittergutsbesitzerklasse." In *Machteliten und Wirtschaftskonjunkturen: Studien zur neueren deutschen Sozial-und Wirtschaftsgeschichte*, ed. Hans Rosenberg. Göttingen: Vandenhoeck and Ruprecht, 1978, 83–101.

Runge, Wolfgang. *Politik und Beamtentum im Parteienstaat. Die Demokratisierung Preußen zwischen 1918 und 1933*. Stuttgart: Ernst Klett Verlag, 1965.

Saul, Klaus. "Der Kampf um das Landproletariat. Sozialistische Landagitation, Großgrundbesitz und preussischer Staatsverwaltung 1890 bis 1903." *Archiv für Sozialgeschichte* 15(1975): 166–208.

———. "Um die konservative Struktur Ostelbiens: Agrarische Interessen, Staatsverwaltung und ländliche Arbeitsnot. Zur Konservativen Landarbeiterpolitik im Preußen-Deutschland 1889–1914." In *Deutscher Konservatismus im 19. und 20. Jahrhundert. Festschrift für Fritz Fischer zum 75. Geburtstag und 50. Doktorjubilaum*, eds. Dirk Stegmann, Bernd-Jürgen Wendt, and Peter-Christian Witt. Bonn: Verlag Neue Gesellschaft, 1983, 129–98.

Scharffe, Gilbert. *Mormonism in Germany. A History of the Church of Jesus Christ of Latter-Day Saints in Germany between 1840 and 1970*. Salt Lake City: Deseret Book Co., 1970.

Scheurig, Bodo. *Ewald von Kleist-Schmenzin. Ein Konservativer gegen Hitler*. Oldenburg and Hamburg: Gerhard Stalling Verlag, 1968.

Schieder, Wolfgang. "Die NSDAP vor 1933. Profil einer faschistischen Partei." *Geschichte und Gesellschaft* 19, no. 2(1993): 141–54.

Schissler, Hanna. "Die Junker. Zur Sozialgeschichtlichen und historischen Bedeutung der agrarische Elite in Preußen." In *Preußen in Ruckblick*, eds. H.-J. Puhle and H. -U. Wehler. *Geschichte und Gesellschaft*. Sonderheft 6. Göttingen: Vandenhoeck and Ruprecht, 1980, 89–122.

———. *Preußische Agrargesellschaft im Wandel: Wirtschaftliche, gesellschaftliche und politische Transformationsprozesse von 1763 bis 1847*. Göttingen: Vandenhoeck and Ruprecht, 1978.

Schlichter, Wolfgang. "Die Artamanenbewegung—eine Frühform des Arbeitsdienst und Kaderzelle des Faschismus auf dem Lande." *Zeitschrift für Geschichtswissenschaft* 18, no. 1(1970): 66–75.

Scholder, Klaus. *Die Kirchen und das Dritte Reich*, vol. 1, *Vorgeschichte und Zeit der Illusionen 1918–1934*. Berlin and Vienna: Ullstein, 1977; vol. 2, *Das Jahr der Ernüchterung 1934*. Berlin and Vienna: Ullstein, 1985.

Schröder, Uwe. "Antisemitismus und Faschismus in Pommern in der Zwischenkriegsperiod." In *Der faschistische Pogrom vom 9./10. November 1938. Zur Geschichte der Juden in Pommern*. Greifswald: Wissenschaftliche Beiträge der Ernst-Moritz-Arndt Universität Greifswald, 1989, 31–41.

———. "Zur faschistischen Kriegsvorbereitung im Regierungsbezirk Stettin 1935 bis 1939." Diss. Greifswald, 1985.

Schulz, Gerhard. *Von Brüning zu Hitler. Der Wandel des politischen Systems in Deutschland 1930–1933*. Berlin and New York: Walter de Gruyter, 1992.

Schultz-Plotius, Manfred. "Ein Überblick über die Tätigkeit der Provinzialverwaltung von Pommern in den Jahren 1933 bis 1945." *Baltische Studien* 49 (1962/63): 66–99.

Schumacher, Martin. *Land und Politik. Eine Untersuchung über politische Parteien und agrarische Interessen 1914–1923*. Düsseldorf: Droste Verlag, 1978.

Schüren, Ulrich. *Der Volksentscheid zur Fürstenenteignung 1926. Die Vermögens-auseinandersetzung mit den depossedierten Landesherren als Problem der deutschen Innenpolitik unter besonderer Berücksichtigung der Verhältnisse in Preußen.* Düsseldorf: Droste Verlag, 1978.

Schwabe, Klaus, ed. *Die preußischen Oberpräsidenten 1815–1945.* Boppard am Rhein: Harald Boldt Verlag, 1985.

Smith, Bonnie G. *Ladies of the Leisure Class. The Bourgeoises of Northern France in the Nineteenth Century.* Princeton: Princeton University Press, 1981.

Snowden, Frank M. *The Fascist Revolution in Tuscany 1919–1922.* Cambridge: Cambridge University Press, 1989.

Stachura, Peter. "National Socialism and the German Proletariat, 1925–1935. Old Myths and New Perspectives." *Historical Journal* 36, no. 3(1993): 701–18.

Stolberg-Wernigrode, Otto Graf zu. *Die unentscheidene Generation. Deutschlands Konservative Führungsschichten am Vorabend des Ersten Weltkrieges.* Munich and Vienna: R. Oldenbourg Verlag, 1968.

Stoltenberg, Gerhard. *Politische Strömungen im Schleswig-Holsteinischen Landvolk 1918–1933.* Düsseldorf: Droste, 1962.

Stupperich, Andrei. *Volksgemeinschaft oder Arbeitersolidarität. Studien zur Arbeitnehmerpolitik in Deutschnationalen Volkspartei (1918–1933).* Göttingen and Zürich: Muster-Schmidt Verlag, 1982.

Suval, Stanley. *Electoral Politics in Wilhelmine Germany.* Chapel Hill and London: University of North Carolina Press, 1985.

Thadden, Rudolf von. *Fragen an Preußen. Zur Geschichte eines aufgehobenen Staates.* Munich: C. H. Beck, 1981.

Tipton, Frank B., Jr. "Farm Labor and Power Politics: Germany, 1850–1914." *Journal of Economic History* 34(1974): 951–79.

———. *Regional Variations in the Economic Development of Germany during the Nineteenth Century.* Middletown, Conn.: Wesleyan University Press, 1976.

Tipton, Timothy Alan. *Nazism, Neo-Nazism and the Peasantry.* Bloomington and London: Indiana University Press, 1975.

Treskow, Rüdiger von. "Adel in Preußen: Anpassung und Kontinuität einer Familie 1800–1918." *Geschichte und Gesellschaft* 17, no. 3(1991): 34–69.

Turner, Henry Ashby, Jr. *German Big Business and the Rise of Hitler.* New York and Oxford: Oxford University Press, 1985.

Turner, Victor. *Drama, Fields, and Metaphores. Symbolic Action in Human Society.* Ithaca and London: Cornell University Press, 1974.

———. *The Ritual Process. Structure and Anti-Structure.* Ithaca: Cornell University Press, 1969.

Ullmann, Hans-Peter. *Interessenverbände in Deutschland.* Frankfurt am Main: Suhrkamp, 1988.

Usborne, Cornelie. *The Politics of the Body in Weimar Germany. Women's Reproductive Rights and Duties.* Ann Arbor: University of Michigan Press, 1992.

Vascik, George. "Agrarian Conservatism in Wilhelmine Germany: Diederich Hahn and the Agrarian League." *Between Reform, Reaction, and Resistance. Studies in the History of German Conservatism from 1789 to 1945*, eds. Larry Eugene Jones and James N. Retallack. Providence and Oxford: Berg Publishers, 1993: 229–60.

Volkmann, Hans-Erich. "Deutsche Agrareliten auf Revisions und Expansionskurs." In *Die deutschen Eliten und der Weg in den Zweiten Weltkrieg*, eds. Martin Broszat and Klaus Schwabe. Munich: C. H. Beck Verlag, 1989, 334–88.

Walker, D. P. "The German National People's Party: The Conservative Dilemma in the Weimar Republic." *Journal of Contemporary History* 14(1979): 627–47.

Webb, Steven B. "Agricultural Protection in Wilhelmian Germany: Forging an Empire with Pork and Rye." *Journal of Economic History* 42, no. 2(1982): 309–26.

Weber, Max. "Entwicklungstendenzen in der Lage der Ostelbischen Landarbeiter" (1894). In *Gesammelte Aufsätze zur Sozial-und Wirtschaftsgeschichte.* Tübingen: J. C. B. Mohr (Paul Siebeck), 1924, 470–507.

Wehler, Hans-Ulrich. *Deutsche Gesellschaftsgeschichte.* vol. 1, *Vom Feudalismus des Alten Reiches bis zur Defensive Modernisierung der Reformära 1700–1815;* vol. 2, *Von der Reformära bis zur industriellen und politischen 'Deutschen Doppelrevolution' 1815–1848/49.* Munich: C. H. Beck Verlag, 1987.

———. *Das Deutsche Kaiserreich 1871–1918.* Göttingen: Vandenhoeck and Ruprecht, 1973.

West, Franklin C. *A Crisis of the Weimar Republic. The German Referendum of 20 June 1926.* Philadelphia: The American Philosophical Society, 1985.

Winkler, Heinrich-August. *Von der Revolution zur Stabilisierung. Arbeiter und Arbeiterbewegung in der weimarer Republik 1918 bis 1924.* Berlin/Bonn: JHW Dietz Nachf., 1984.

———. *Der Schein der Normalität. Arbeiter und Arbeiterbewegung in der Weimarer Republik.* Berlin/Bonn: JHW Dietz Nachf., 1985.

———. *Weimar 1918–1933. Die Geschichte der ersten deutschen Demokratie.* Munich: C. H. Beck, 1993.

Wright, J. R. C. *'Above Parties,' The Political Attitudes of the German Protestant Church Leadership.* Oxford: Oxford University Press, 1974.

Wunderlich, Frieda. *Farm Labor in Germany 1810–1945. Its Historical Development within the Framework of Agricultural and Social Policy.* Princeton: Princeton University Press, 1961.

Zabel, James A. *Nazism and the Pastors. A Study of the Ideas of Three Deutsche Christen Groups.* Missoula, Mont.: Scholars' Press, 1976.

Zimmer, Detlev. "Soziale Lebensläufe und individuelle politische Biographien. Das Beispiel der Familie von Helldorf (Haus St. Ulrich)." *Zeitschrift für Geschichtswissenschaft* 40, no. 9(1992): 834–52.

Zofka, Zdenek. *Die Ausbreitung des Nationalsozialismus auf dem Lande. Eine regionale Fallstudie zur politischen Einstellung der Landbevölkerung in der Zeit des Aufstiegs und der Machtergreifung der NSDAP 1928–1936.* Munich: Kommissionsbuchhandlung R. Wolfe, 1979.

Index